E. SYLVIA PANKHURST
Portrait of a Radical

Sylvia Pankhurst in 1915

E. SYLVIA PANKHURST

Portrait of a Radical

Patricia W. Romero

YALE UNIVERSITY PRESS
New Haven and London 1990

Designed by Ann Grindrod

Set in 11/12 pt Baskerville by Boldface Typesetters, London EC1 and printed in Great Britain at The Bath Press, Avon.

Library of Congress Cataloging-in-Publication Data

Romero, Patricia W.
    E. Sylvia Pankhurst: portrait of a radical

    Bibliography: p.
    Includes index.
    1. Pankhurst, E. Sylvia (Estelle Sylvia), 1882–1960.
    2. Women social reformers—Great Britain—Biography.
    3. Feminists—Great Britain—Biography.   4. Radicals—
    Geat Britain—Biography.   I. Title.
    HQ1595.P34C87   1986   305.4′2′0924   [B]   86–7796
    ISBN 0–300–03691–4 (cloth)
    ISBN 0–300–04482–8 (paper)

For Jeff in gratitude and for Richard L. Coe.
For Christine Sadler Coe in memoriam

Contents

Illustrations

(The illustration on page 276 is reproduced by kind permission of
Dr Richard Pankhurst. The publishers regret the omission of this
acknowledgement in the first edition.)

Preface

Sylvia is probably the best known of the Pankhurst women involved in the suffrage movement before the First World War. Her mother founded the Women's Social and Political Union (WSPU) in 1903, and her sister Christabel later became its formal leader. But Sylvia wrote *The Suffragette* and later *The Suffragette Movement* and *The Home Front*. All three works are autobiographical, and the first two have a fundamental place in the literature of the movement, if only because they have some qualities of a source, and are not merely secondary authorities. Until recently the accepted view of the movement and of Sylvia closely matched Sylvia's own. This biography will suggest another interpretation of Sylvia Pankhurst in relation to her times— one that is, on occasion, less favourable than her account of herself. This book is not a history of the suffrage movement: Sylvia's life is much broader than that crusade, and she exaggerated her own role in it.

I first came upon Sylvia on a visit to Addis Ababa, Ethiopia. As a feminist, my imagination was caught by this English woman who loyally served the Ethiopian monarchy from the first days of the Italian invasion until her death in Ethiopia in December 1960. On a visit to Trinity Cathedral, I was struck by her impressive tomb. She was the only foreigner buried in an area reserved for the patriots of the Italian war. Her son, Richard, was then living in the country. With his support, I decided to prepare a small monograph on Sylvia's Ethiopian service.

The scope of the project began to grow. I found that to understand Sylvia Pankhurst the Pan-Africanist, I also had to understand Sylvia Pankhurst the monarchist—and beyond that Sylvia the anti-Fascist of the early 1930s, the communist of the early 1920s, and the suffragette and socialist of the 1910s. Sylvia is also remembered as a feminist, but she was in many ways an opportunist in her early years. As she grew older, feminism became an issue of some importance to her, but the major causes of her life were the non-feminist ones.

The search for Sylvia led back to Britain and to British social history. It also led to research in Amsterdam, Romania, Italy and Ethiopia, and to personal interviews with many of the people who had known her at diverse phases of her career. As the search progressed, my view began to change. I discovered a career that was more significant than I had suspected. I discovered a much more complex woman: a person who was in some respects less admirable than the one I had expected to find.

Her career was that of a multi-sided radical publicist who served so many causes that, in the end, her life was synonymous with much of English social protest during the half-century after 1910. In this case the label 'radical' should not be misunderstood. Sylvia had little in common with the English radical tradition of the nineteenth century. Her form of radicalism was less precise, but it involved uncompromising insistence on the most thorough and extreme version of whatever cause she espoused. In her communist period, she stood to the left of Lenin; in her monarchist period, she supported King Zog of Albania as well as Haile Sellassie.[1]

Sylvia Pankhurst's personality was that of a charismatic leader. She was a complex individual who made enemies easily, yet inspired lasting respect and devotion among her followers. The early part of her life revealed an inconsistent quality. She joined a cause, fought hard, then switched to another even before the first battle had been won, as though the cause were all—or nothing. She would rather accept nothing and fight for another all than compromise. The anti-Fascist campaign of the early 1930s, however, brought some consistency. Sylvia was one of the earliest in Britain to speak out against Fascism. Her activities as an anti-Fascist led her to Ethiopia at a time when most others, if they were aware of Fascism at all, turned to events in Spain. The love affair with Ethiopia, brought her ultimately to spend her last days among a people welcoming and grateful for her many efforts on their behalf.

Sylvia Pankhurst was self-centred, opinionated, immature, obsessive, highly strung, and single-minded in whatever cause she made her own. She was not subtle—radicals rarely are—and these characteristics often denied her the support she wanted. The Foreign Office and Special Branch—anti-feminist to the core—kept detailed files on much of her life in England, but they rarely took her seriously. Female followers in her many campaigns regarded her as a heroine, and so did some men. But one thing about Sylvia stands out in all of her campaigns: no one ever remained neutral about her.

Sylvia was a self-appointed leader, sometimes self-serving, yet never self-indulgent. She invested all her considerable energy in her causes, often tilting with the proverbial windmills in the process. If there were no real enemy, she created one. Where the enemy was genuine, as in the case of Italy's attack on Ethiopia, her efforts as publicist matched the protagonists' combat on the battlefield.

She was in contact and correspondence with some of the most

---

[1] The spelling of Ethiopian names comes from Edward Ullendorff (ed)., *The Autobiography of Emperor Haile Sellassie I: 'My Life and Ethiopia's Progress 1892–1937* (London, 1976).

important personalities of her day, including George Bernard Shaw, who admired her, and the Emperor Haile Sellassie I, who respected her. Although only on the fringes of international crusades for suffrage and peace, she was known to and at times esteemed by their leaders. If she was a failure—measured by the successes of those with whom she identified—she was a magnificent failure in the extent of her sacrifice for others and for her altruism in the cause of mankind. Above all, Sylvia was a great personality. She fought. She cared. She was a Pankhurst. Like her mother, Emmeline, and her sisters, Christabel and Adela, Sylvia was always out in front and sometimes even bent on head-on collision with her family and colleagues. Among these strong women, Sylvia did not always hold her own during her lifetime, but history may judge her the most effective Pankhurst of them all.

There are many people to whom I owe so much during the long years of researching and writing this book. Although my editor, Robert Baldock, did not enter the picture until the book was far along the road to completion, I want especially to thank him for his faith in me and, indirectly, in Sylvia's story. He will hold a special place in my heart in the years to come. Miss M. W. H. Schreuder, archivist of Sylvia's papers at the International Instituut voor Sociale Geschiedenis, has been most cooperative and helpful during my several trips to Amsterdam. While I am grateful to her, I am distressed at the Instituut rules which prohibit extensive quotation from documents deposited there. I wish to thank the staff members from the inter-library loan office at the Johns Hopkins University Library: they were always pleasant and extremely helpful. In addition I owe a debt of gratitude to David Henige, the University of Wisconsin Library; Terry McCarthy and the late Henry Fry of the Labour History Museum in London; the London School of Economics; the British Museum; Tower Hamlets library; Marx House; the Suffragette Fellowship; the Public Records Office, London; the Humanities Research Centre, the University of Texas; the Manuscript Collection, Library of Congress; the National Library of Australia; Hans Panofosky and Northwestern University Library; the Roosevelt Library, Hyde Park; and especially Gordon Phillips, archivist at *The Times*.

Among the many people who aided me with personal memories of Sylvia, Richard Pankhurst gave me early leads to those in England and Ethiopia who knew his mother during her various crusades. He also read and criticized the first edition of this book. I thank him for pointing out some typographical errors and some errors in fact. I am extremely grateful to Sylvia's friends and colleagues who gave me their time and shared their memories. Some died before this manuscript was completed and, among them, I came to know and care for Princess Rosalie Viazemsky as a personal and loving friend: I hope she understood how grateful I was. Before she died she read a draft of the first chapter and was excited about renewing her acquaintance with Sylvia through the biography. Mrs Ivy Tims was most generous and helpful, as were Lord Amulree, Annie Barnes, and Francis Beaufort-Palmer. I will remember them as very special people. Edward Ullendorff graciously permitted me an interview in London. Vinigi Grottanelli and Musa Galaal shared their memories with me while they were in Baltimore for an African Studies Association meeting in 1978. Musa is no longer here to receive my thanks. Arthur Dudden surprised me, when we were together at a meeting in Bryn Mawr, with an account of his visit to West Dene. Dr A. Petrescu, in Romania, shared his childhood memories of the Pankhurst family visit to his own family in 1934, and provided me with copies of correspondence between his father and Sylvia in the years that followed.

In the summer of 1973, I interviewed T. R. Mackonnen in Nairobi— my first foray into Sylvia's Ethiopian years.

In Ethiopia I talked with Emmanuel Abraham, Afä Wärq Tekle, Mary Tedasse, and others who had known Sylvia during her years of dedication to that African kingdom. All revealed affection for her and through their memories I came to understand her Ethiopian years in ways that would not have been possible through archival sources. Jill Craigie (Mrs Michael Foot) was especially generous with her time and suggestions. I would never have mastered even the rudiments of the British parliamentary system had it not been for her considerable input and I am much in her debt. John C. Spencer provided invaluable help with the Ethiopian chapters and Kenneth Morgan read and commented on several chapters in a much earlier draft.

Others who did not know Sylvia but were helpful in tracing papers and archival material deserve special mention and thanks. Dan H. Laurence, bibliographer of George Bernard Shaw, has been most generous in supplying me with Shavian comments to or on Sylvia. I am grateful to Professor Roberto Viverelli who kindly supplied me with materials from Italian Secret Police Reports, and to Professor Eduardo Saccone for translating them. Thanks, too, to Frank Dane who sent me materials from his mother, Else Frankels' archive. I owe a special debt to the late James Klugman for his help on Sylvia's communist period, and to John Higham and George Brooks who provided references to works I would otherwise have missed.

Among many friends who read and commented on the manuscript at various stages I would like especially to mention the late Laurence Lafore, whose untimely death prevented me from thanking him in person. In addition, I am grateful to David and Eileen Spring, Jacqueline Wehmueller, Dorothy Helly, Keith Irving and Christine Sadler Coe— all of whom rendered considerable criticisms and invaluable suggestions. Mity and Mark Gann, as well as Deha Owen, have been supportive friends over the years. They know Sylvia almost as well as I do. My son, Jeffrey Romero, typed the entire manuscript on to the word processor and I have shown him my gratitude for that yeoman effort in the dedication.

Finally, although I have already thanked Richard Pankhurst elsewhere in this Preface, for this paperback edition I must add a few words pertaining to the reception of the book by Richard and his wife, Rita. It is understandable that the next generation of Parkhursts should feel pained at some of the revelations in this life of Sylvia. While my heart goes out to them and my sympathies are with them, as Sylvia Pankhurst's biographer I am compelled by the rules of scholarship to stand by my findings.

Baltimore, Maryland
1989

PART 1
The Women's Movement

1
The early years

Sylvia,
    You are the queerest idiot genius of this age—the most
ungovernable, self-interested, blindly and deadly wilful little
rapscallion-condottiera that ever imposed itself on the infra-red
end of the revolutionary spectrum as a leader.
    —George Bernard Shaw to Sylvia, 12 September 1929

In the last decades of the Ethiopian empire, his Imperial Majesty
Haile Sellassie planned Trinity Cathedral in Addis Ababa as a shrine
dedicated to his achievements and to those of his immediate family, as
well as to members of the Ethiopian nobility who had died in the
defence of their country against Italian aggression in the 1930s. He
buried his empress within the cathedral, alongside the burial place of
his favourite son and the site he planned for his own tomb. In front of
the cathedral, among the graves of the noble patriots involved in the
war against Fascism, was one anomaly. This was a marble monument
in the form of an open book, a monument more central, impressive
and larger than those to the memory of Ethiopian patriots who had
died in the war. Yet this tomb commemorated a foreigner, and on its
open pages lay the inscription:

Estelle Sylvia Pankhurst
Manchester, England
1882
Addis Ababa
November, 1960

The monument was no more anomalous than Sylvia Pankhurst's life. As
the European invasions of Africa were about to accelerate into the compe-
titive annexation that marked the European 'scramble for Africa' in the
last two decades of the nineteenth century, Sylvia's life began. It ended in
the great year of African decolonization, when one African nation after
another moved to independence. In some respects the events of 1960 were
a triumph for Haile Sellassie, by then a symbol of African resistance and
pan-African liberation movements. Sylvia Pankhurst had devoted herself to the emperor's cause since 1935, publishing first the *New Times and
Ethiopia News*, and then the *Ethiopia Observer*, in Addis Ababa.

But Sylvia Pankhurst was already more than fifty years old when she took up the Ethiopian cause. Behind her lay a string of other careers, any one of which would have sufficed for an ordinary lifetime. Having begun the twentieth century as an art student of promise and achievement, she moved into the early feminist movement, becoming one of its most aggressive suffragettes. Then, during the First World War, she moved on to an equally militant pacifism and slid from the middle-class radicalism of her family background to the radicalism of the British far left. (The British Radicals, mostly members of the Liberal Party in the late nineteenth and early twentieth centuries, were active reformists, and not extremists, as implied by Sylvia's own involvement with the British far left in later years.) By the beginning of the war her political base was East London, and she was already publishing the *Woman's Dreadnought* (later *Workers' Dreadnought*), one of the early mouthpieces of the British communist movement. In 1920 she went to Leningrad for the second session of the Third International. Though expelled from the communist movement soon afterwards, for the next fifteen years she actively supported a kaleidoscopic array of radical causes—from free love to environmental protection, from birth control to European anti-Fascism. It may seem incongruous that a woman stigmatized by Lenin as a 'left-wing' communist should end her life as a supporter of a feudal monarch. Yet Sylvia's life had an internal consistency. It left a more significant mark on the fabric of her time than her maverick course might indicate.

Sylvia's lineage in itself was enough to set her on an eccentric course.[1] Her grandfather, Henry Francis Pankhurst, was born in Cheshire. The son of a conservative Anglican schoolmaster, in his adult years he became a Liberal and a Baptist, and settled in Manchester as an auctioneer and valuer of antiques and fine art. His son, Richard Marsden Pankhurst, was educated at Manchester Grammar School and at Owens College, at that time not itself a degree-awarding institution. As a result, his BA, LLB, and finally the unusual distinction of an earned LLD in 1863, were granted by London University. He continued his legal studies at Lincoln's Inn, where he was called to the Bar in 1867, but returned to practise on the Lancashire circuit, where he retained the title of Dr Pankhurst, as he was known throughout his life.

Richard Pankhurst's career, however, was frequently interrupted by activities arising out of a strong interest in radical Liberal politics, which led him one further step on the leftward course begun by his father. His heroes were Ernest Jones, the Chartist democrat, and John Stuart Mill. His own inclinations took him into the movement for working men's education, manhood suffrage, and then women's suffrage; later he moved enthusiastically into socialism, agnosticism, republicanism and anti-imperialism. Though he remained loosely associated with the Liberal Party—an extremist among the radicals—and later with the Independent Labour Party (ILP), and though he stood for local government office several times, he was always unsuccessful at the polls, largely because of his advanced views. The political causes Sylvia's father espoused in his generation were, in short, just as radical as those she pursued in her own. Sylvia broke emotionally and politically from her mother, but not from the memory of her father's political activism.

Emmeline Goulden Pankhurst, twenty years her husband's junior, was born into comfortable middle-class circumstances. Her father, Robert Goulden, had progressed from office-boy to co-owner of a textile factory in northern England, and had married the daughter of a Manx farmer. Even with a family of ten children to support, he was a fairly prosperous man. He too had a predisposition toward reform, perhaps as a result of his humble background. He supported the causes of anti-slavery and adult suffrage; he opposed the acquisition of empire, and flirted briefly with pacifism. Though not particularly active in these movements, the Gouldens occasionally attended Lancashire meetings to hear speakers representing various causes.

Emmeline was the second of the Goulden children, and the eldest daughter; as her father's favourite she, and not the eldest son, was chosen to study abroad. She spent some years in France where she specialized in French literature at the École Normale Supérieure. While there she became acquainted with Noémie, daughter of the Marquis de Rochefort, an egalitarian French nobleman who refused to use his title. This acquaintance with republicanism re-enforced the liberal ideas already rooted in her background.

Richard Pankhurst's rich and variegated career in political agitation belies his family background—or as much as we know of it—which was markedly more rigid and middle-class than that of Emmeline. Richard was the youngest of four children; the eldest, John, married a woman his parents disapproved of and emigrated to America. Of the other children, one died; and one sister married an actor—an unfortunate choice from the parents' point of view—and was banished from the family home. It therefore fell to Richard to care for his elderly parents, and he delayed marriage until after his father's death, in 1878, when he was already thirty-nine years old—not an untypical age for a professional man of his time.

While living with his parents, Richard Pankhurst had been active in several reforms, including the passage of the Married Women's Property Act. Before 1870 a married woman in England had no voice in the way her property was managed; nor could she draw on her income without the consent of her husband. By 1879, when Richard and Emmeline were engaged to be married, Pankhurst was so deeply immersed in campaigning for the passage of a comprehensive Married

Richard Pankhurst

Emmeline Pankhurst, 1927

Women's Property Act that Emmeline suggested they live together outside the bonds of matrimony until the Act was passed. But Pankhurst's radicalism was tempered by his own middle-class background and that autumn the two were married.

The sober Richard and the charming Emmeline produced five children. Christabel, known to history for her role as a suffragette, was born in 1880. Sylvia followed two years later, then Adela, who is remembered in Australia, where she made her home, for her radicalism in the service of various causes. The two Pankhurst sons died in their youth. In all Sylvia's published work, references to her childhood are coloured by what she believed was her mother's favouritism for Christabel. Emmeline did indeed give much of her attention to her eldest daughter, especially during the heyday of the suffrage movement, but we have only Sylvia's view on her attitudes toward her children when they were young. Sylvia wrote, in *The Suffragette Movement*:[2]

> In 1880 Emmeline's first child was born. She was eager to be a mother, and threw herself with characteristic energy into the labours of maternity. Subsequent children . . . were handed over to a nurse, but this first darling was her own charge. . . . In May 1882, came a second child, myself. Mrs Pankhurst called her Estelle, the doctor added Sylvia. . . . the girls had been named from the heroines of Coleridge and Shakespeare. . . .

Early on she chose to be called Sylvia. The first son and third child, Frank, was born in 1884, after their parents had successfully seen the Married Women's Property Bill passed; when Adela was born, in 1885, their father was standing for parliament.

The children grew up amidst the turmoil of political campaigns, along with crusades which included all the major radical issues of the day. Dr Pankhurst, joined by his wife, opposed oppression wherever he found it; he was an early proponent of Indian independence and welcomed the birth of socialism as a means to conquer all Britain's ills, foreign and domestic. And he was a republican, an unpopular cause even among radicals.[3] When, fifty years later, Sylvia embarked on her own self-appointed mission to save Ethiopia for its emperor, she saw nothing contradictory between her ideals and those of her father. Both father and daughter came unerringly to the aid of the underdog.

The Pankhurst family was almost constantly on the move. Sylvia was born in Old Trafford, a suburb of Manchester. Soon, and primarily for financial reasons, the family moved to the home of Emmeline's parents at Seedley Cottage, Pendleton, on the outskirts of Salford, where Frank was born. It was a large household: in addition to various aunts and uncles, the two grandparents, Emmeline and Richard Pankhurst and their three children, there were servants and the childrens' nanny. The preponderance of adults brought benefits, with the children gaining individual attention. Christabel and Sylvia were enthusiastic actors at this time. They created a little theatre—perhaps as a result of their grandfather's interest in amateur theatricals—and members of the household made costumes for them to dress up in when they performed. Theatre was popular in the cotton towns of the north, as were musical evenings, held either in the home or, more substantially, at the Free Trade Hall, Manchester. The girls seem to have had an early introduction to public speaking before audiences and were encouraged to act by members of their extended family.

Dr Pankhurst's perennial involvement in politics and his radical obsessions soon caused a decline in the Goulden business. The Pankhursts, with Adela on the way, moved again. This time they crossed the Irwell river to Manchester proper and settled in Green Hayes, on Daisy Bank Road. The open countryside and the dark pollution that characterised Manchester in the late nineteenth century provided quite a contrast for the family. Finances remained tight; servants and the nurse added to the cost of a growing family. Financial difficulties followed Dr Pankhurst's concentration on his causes, which included the poor, non-paying clients, and trade unions.

Emmeline had always assumed that her father planned to settle a sum of money on her after her marriage.[5] Goulden had supported his daughter and her growing family for two years. Now, faced with the prospect of having to settle equal amounts on all five of his daughters, he declined. What followed presents the first glimpse of those qualities of steel which later characterize Emmeline in the suffrage movement: she showed her father no mercy, and severed all connection with both parents until after her father's death, when she re-established communication with her mother.

Another setback came in 1885, when Pankhurst stood for Parliament. During the campaign his religious views came under scrutiny. Although privately an agnostic, he was accused of atheism. It was common, according to the radical Jacob Bright, a supporter of Pankhurst, that 'when it was difficult to find anything in a man's character to attack', to label him an atheist.[6] This question mark over his religious views, as well as his known republicanism (and call for the abolition of the House of Lords), brought his defeat.

Neither Christabel nor Sylvia had any religious education so had no understanding of what it meant to be an atheist. Dr Pankhurst patiently explained how, when once a Baptist Sunday school teacher, he had first come into contact with the poor, most of whom had been uneducated. Sympathy for them grew into a broader sympathy for the working class, and hence a conversion to socialism: he would correct the wrongs of the world by working for social change with all the energy and evangelical fervour of an earlier religious experience. Although the Pankhurst children were forbidden to receive religious instruction at school, Sylvia recalled sitting in class pretending to study her extra assignment in history, but listening in awe to the rest of the class being treated to excerpts from the Bible. She acted out her interest in religion by painting Biblical scenes. Christabel went further still, and, with the emotional drive so common in her family, devoted the last years of her life to a millennial Christian sect which believed in an imminent second coming of Christ.[7]

After the defeat at Rotherhithe, the family moved again—this time to London where they settled near Hampstead. In a move that was bold for its time, Mrs Pankhurst opened a business. Middle class women were just beginning to step out on their own, most into the teaching profession or the civil service. It was rare indeed for a woman to open and run her own shop and the Doctor's support of his wife was not lost on his daughters. Emmeline's shop, Emerson and Company, featured examples of socialist art such as William Morris wallpapers, colourful milking-stools, and other types of bric-a-brac emerging from the Arts and Crafts movement. Although Emerson and Co. reflected the utopian socialist trends with which the Pankhursts were involved, it made no money. Part of the problem may have been Emmeline's neglect of the store in favour of frequent commuting back and forth to Manchester with her husband. During his mother's absence Frank fell ill. When diphtheria was diagnosed, the girls were whisked away and their parents rushed home from Manchester. He died in September 1888, a little over four years of age. Sylvia seems to have taken his death especially hard, recalling that time in her life as a period when she 'longed to die'.[8]

With Dr Pankhurst busy commuting between home and work, his extra-curricular activities were necessarily limited—sufficiently, perhaps, to restore his image in Manchester. The family bought and redecorated a fashionable house in Russell Square, and instead of closing down Emerson and Co., Emmeline moved the business closer to town—where it continued losing money. The Russell Square house provided the children with access to a wider world. The British Museum was close by and they went there often.[9] Lacking the audience provided in the Goulden home, the girls replaced theatre productions with a newspaper called 'Home News'. A wide assortment of people came to call in Russell Square: Russian revolutionaries came to discuss the conditions of life under Tzarist rule, giving Sylvia her first touch of pity for a people she would later idealize. Women suffragists from America also called.

Friends of the Pankhursts among the radical, socialist and emerging labour movement, like Tom Mann and Annie Besant, frequently visited the home. The children were invited to be present when guests were there, an unconventional practice for Victorian England but a rather ordinary one in the Pankhursts' circle. Dr Pankhurst encouraged his daughters to take an active interest in events that concerned him, and the children had an early introduction to politics. Sylvia attended her first public meeting when she was eight. Her parents took her to hear H. M. Hyndman at a local meeting of the Social Democratic Federation (SDF), the most radical socialist organization in England.

Hyndman came to Marxism earlier than most British socialists, having read Marx's works in French before their English translation. An economic theorist of some repute, he was also the product of inherited wealth and could indulge himself in organizing a Marxist circle without suffering the economic strictures which dogged Dr Pankhurst. Although we do not know if Pankhurst read Marx, the Social Democratic Federation was the kind of organization which appealed to him. By the 1890s the SDF was reduced to a few left-wingers, and had to find meeting rooms wherever it could. On the night Sylvia described, they met above a stable, with bucolic odours wafting up from below: Emmeline whisked her family from the stable as soon as Hyndman finished his talk. (The discovery of a flea on her sleeve meant that middle-class fears outweighed socialist enthusiasm.[10])

Emerson and Co. continued to lose money. The first Christmas in Russell Square was an unhappy one for Sylvia. Instead of a longed-for violin, she received empty boxes. Nearly forty years later she recalled that incident with bitterness, directed toward her mother. Later she got a violin, but never learned to play it, and again she blamed her mother for being too busy to find a teacher.[11] In these years the children discovered books. They listened to the works of Jules Verne, Alexander Dumas and Charles Dickens. Dickens made an especially profound impression on Sylvia, who recalled tears running down her cheeks when she heard, for instance, of the misfortunes of Oliver Twist and his little band of orphans.[12]

The Pankhurst home was on the north-east side of the Square where the Russell Hotel now stands. Living there meant playing in the narrow terrace garden behind the house or in the square across the street. Emmeline was opposed to formal schooling, insisting that the children be taught at home. When funds were available, a tutor was engaged; otherwise the girls were predominantly self-taught. The enterprise was none too successful for, if Sylvia's memories are accurate, Emmeline discouraged them with 'criticisms too devastating for the effort to survive'.[13] Emmeline's sister, Mary, had by then come to live with them and told stories or read them her poetry. Aunt Mary was also something of an artist and Sylvia frequently turned to her for encouragement with her sketches. Dr Pankhurst admired his daughter's work, and he, too, encouraged her artistic skills. When she was still a small child, she would come to him with recently completed drawings. Sometimes he lifted her on to his lap, studied her sketches, and told her a story. He never let the opportunity pass, however, without reminding Sylvia of her duty to serve other people.

Sylvia was more than a little jealous of Christabel's outgoing nature that drew applause in and out of the family circle. With a tinge of bitterness combined with a frank falsification of her own feelings, Sylvia remembered Christabel as 'our mother's favourite; we all knew it, and I, for one, never resented the fact. . . . It was a joy to me to walk beside her, half a step in arrear. . . . she was tenacious of her position as the eldest and favourite, but she exercised it on the whole without offence.'[14] In contrast, Sylvia tended to be shy and reserved. Whether or not her father realized her need for love and affection or merely gave it on occasion is not known. But his warmth and encouragement was appreciated by Sylvia in a way that Emmeline's was not.

A domestic pattern of sorts existed between the many moves during these years. As was the custom in middle class circles, the family gathered around the piano on Sunday afternoons, and while their mother played, the children entertained their father with familiar melodies. Sylvia found that on these occasions singing helped to relieve some of the pent-up emotions that seemed 'at times close to torture'.[15] Family get-togethers were limited to this one day of the week when neither parent was caught up in work or politics. Although they had their nanny, and later a tutor, and although the two older girls were almost always together, Sylvia continued to feel neglected. She was a shy, neurotic, somewhat mousy child who often gave way to feelings of martyrdom. She took herself very seriously, and she was difficult. She was, however, creative and imaginative.

The sorrow surrounding Frank's death was somewhat lessened by the birth of another son, Harry. After his birth, the Pankhursts decided the move to London had been a mistake. They had also run into problems in renewing the lease on their house because of a clause which Dr Pankhurst had overlooked. London legal business had not come his way; Emerson and Co. steadily drained their limited income; the big house on Russell Square was difficult to maintain; and the staff had again been augmented by a nurse for Harry. In addition, the Doctor's health had become a problem, making the long journey to Manchester a drain both physically and financially.

Their next move took the family to a watering-place at Southport, where they hoped Dr Pankhurst's health would improve. Sylvia remembered Southport as the place where she had frequent contact with her mother: there were no servants and Mrs Pankhurst assumed the role of housewife in their small home. But 'this dull little town proved by no means congenial to Mrs Pankhurst, to whom social interest and excitement were the very breath of life'.[16] Emmeline was soon 'so languid . . . she felt herself unable to take a short stroll down Lord Street to see the shops'.[17] It was during this brief sojourn in

Southport that the girls had their first experience of education outside the home. Sylvia loved school. Her first and only report there showed her second in a class of nine. (Christabel was ninth in her class of fourteen.) Sylvia was regarded as 'a most promising pupil'[18] which was creditable for a girl of ten entering school for the first time. But, much to the sorrow of the children, the family moved again before they could enter a second term.

This time they went to Disley, in Chester, another rural setting sixteen miles from Manchester. Emmeline, probably recalling her youth, took to rural life with abandon, although she did not have responsibilities for her children since the staff and Aunt Mary were back. Sylvia was happy in this setting, taking their small fox terrier when she went off alone to sketch from nature. But sadness came too at Disley, with domestic troubles. Aunt Mary had married after leaving Russell Square but the marriage had turned out unhappy. Women, of course, were bound to their husbands and divorce was almost out of the question. Another aunt, her father's sister who had been banished from home, came to stay with them for a time too; her ne'er-do-well husband had mistreated her. But, after a brief stay, and despite encouragement from the family to leave him, she returned to her husband and died soon afterwards.

The picture of marriage provided by Sylvia's own parents, however, could not have been viewed as anything but positive. Dr Pankhurst regarded himself a lucky man. He adored his beautiful, outgoing wife and revelled in his children. Emmeline, absorbed in her husband's reforms, was enraptured with the man who indulged her every whim, though she was not always thoughtful in return.[20] She was not a woman who could submerge herself and her own interests in marriage. Her expectations were to receive; her husband's desire was to give, even when he had nothing concrete on which to base such desire. The children were raised in highly individualistic style for Victorian England. So long as the children had the security of their father's presence and Emmeline received his support, they could all exist in a world of radical politics, apart from their middle-class surroundings, but together as a happy unit. Mrs Pankhurst believed in disciplining her children, and made them eat what was placed before them without complaint.[21] The Doctor punished his children by delivering long lectures.

After a few months on the farm Dr Pankhurst's health improved and the family moved again. Now it was back to the sooty skies of Manchester—a poor substitute for the open blue of the country. Manchester at this time was the fourth largest city in England and the heart of the Lancashire industrial region, where the mechanization of the textile industry had set in train the industrial revolution more than a century earlier. In 1830 the first railway was built between Manchester and Liverpool, its major outlet to the sea some 32 miles away. Gradually a ring of industrial towns had grown up in the region, while the old working-class districts in Manchester had become some of the most depressing slums in the industrial world. The dominance of textiles gave way to new plants for heavy industry and chemicals, and the slum population swelled, drawn by plentiful jobs but with low wages and miserable housing. Manchester's river, the Irwell, and its tributaries were polluted with mill refuse. Coal-burning power-plants and chemical factories spewed grime into the sky, whence it settled gradually on to streets and homes. Middle-class families like the Pankhursts lived in more salubrious neighbourhoods within the mill towns, but the districts with spacious homes like theirs were surrounded by rat-infested slums, and the contrast could have hardly been lost on a family already aware of its social responsibilities.

The older children were again enrolled in school after tuition with a governess at Disley. They attended the Manchester High School for Girls, where both Sylvia and Christabel excelled. Sylvia's social experiences at school, however, were not positive. Dr Pankhurst had continued his prohibition against religious instruction and Sylvia was teased by classmates because she was again forced to study other subjects while they read the Bible. Already the victim of so many moves and of such eccentric parents, she made few, if any, friends in these crucial teenage years and never had a lively out-of-school life. Instead she relied on her family, continued her drawing, and became involved—perhaps excessively so—with the causes and concerns of her parents.

The Pankhurst home at 4 Buckingham Crescent stood in a wooded area of the city, with large old houses surrounded by trees and beautiful gardens. None of the Pankhurst family attempted any serious gardening (the notion that activism and gardening did not mix remained with Sylvia throughout her life); but Sylvia and her siblings roamed freely through the spacious grounds. Sometimes the children played together; more often Sylvia wandered off alone, sketching whatever captured her interest.

In Manchester, where Dr Pankhurst's reputation as a city solicitor as well as perennial reformer was well known, his daughters bore the brunt of his peculiarities. He was, however, admired by many people in the city: those who saw him as their champion, and those with whom he shared his ideals. Robert Blatchford, editor of the radical weekly journal, the *Clarion*, belonged to the latter category. Blatchford came to socialism from a life of extreme poverty. Through hard work and good connections he, with several friends, founded the socialist paper and formed clubs that promoted outdoor activities, among them the *Clarion* cyclist club, which the Pankhursts joined. As members of the club, the family toured the countryside. Sylvia's memories of summer 1897 include a secondhand, homemade bicycle that was too small for her and had her puffing in an effort to keep up with her more athletic sister, 'a veritable torture' which turned her 'crimson' as Christabel prodded her on. Christabel had a proper bike.[23]

As a follower of William Morris, Blatchford drew heavily on utopian socialism rather than the austere Marxian socialism of Hyndman and the Social Democratic Federation. Blatchford appealed to many in the late nineteenth century—he was reputed to have converted more people to socialism than any other of his generation—by removing the rigid discipline of ideology and doctrine and preaching a socialism of happiness and togetherness.

Emmeline's hopes for and interest in Christabel had long been recognized if not accepted by the other children. She had watched Christabel turn into a charming and beautiful young girl. Sylvia, probably the more talented of the two, was studious, pale and withdrawn. Adela was variously considered as a pet or a problem, depending on her behaviour. Harry was still a baby. When Christabel received special favours, Sylvia tended to resent them in silence, with anger building slowly inside her. The Pankhursts gave Christabel dancing lessons while Sylvia's violin sat on the shelf. Christabel seemed to enjoy what Sylvia no doubt regarded as the frivolity of dance, at least until grammar school, when she concluded that people would think her 'brains were in her feet'.[24] Then she determined to be more studious.

Nowhere in Sylvia's memories of her girlhood does she reveal how she thought her parents saw her. Nor is there a serious view of Adela in either Sylvia's work or in Emmeline's ghost-written autobiography. Christabel, in an edited version of her life, told how Adela once entertained thoughts of being a teacher, but this was merely a passing reference to her younger sister. Adela had her own memories. She attributed the erratic education the girls received to their father, while Sylvia blamed their mother for keeping them from school. Adela wrote that Christabel was 'twelve years old before she understood subtraction but that was a deficiency in the way our father had educated her and Sylvia. I went to school when I was six and stayed until I was nearly sixteen and only left to let Christabel go to university and Sylvia to stay abroad after her art scholarship was exhausted.'[25]

Although Harry never became actively involved with his parents' crusades—as did the girls—he developed a passing interest in women's suffrage. The Pankhursts had been active in the movement in London and Manchester, and in 1889 were among the founding members of the Women's Franchise League.[26] Harry had grown up with suffrage as with no other cause. When he was in the sixth form of Manchester Grammar School he debated the issue with classmates, opposing a motion against granting the vote to women. On this occasion, a former classmate recalled, 'he spoke with fair fluency and much earnestness but he lacked somewhat . . . in logical clearness'.[27] Harry was small, thin and sickly as a little boy, and never had the opportunity to engage in the more robust play that might have helped him develop emotionally as well as physically. He, too, was a loner. Surrounded by older sisters, missing the parents who were often away or otherwise busy, Harry did not fit well within the family, nor did he make friends. His early schooling was under the guidance of an elderly man who ran a small school that catered for pupils of all ages, of whom Harry was the youngest. He spent his after-school hours dolefully watching other children at play or finding workmen in the area with whom he could strike up a conversation.

If Harry was a fragile boy, his parents did not think it important that he learn to play the rough games of his classmates. The servants provided some warmth and affection, as they did in other Victorian families. Only when the Pankhurst children had to deal with the cruel, outside world of their childhood and adolescence did they face a hostile environment. On the other hand, they had the opportunity to meet some of the most interesting people of the day, including the artist-poet and socialist, William Morris, and John Burns, the working-class politicians. Burns came frequently to the Pankhursts' 'at homes' in London. He was unique to their circle, having worked from the age of ten, and moved into politics after a stint with the temperance and trade union movements. Burns was fiery and emotional in his dedication to socialism, but was perceived by middle-class English radicals like the Pankhursts as an unspoiled original whose working-class roots made him all the more attractive.

The Fabian Society was an altogether different left-wing movement. Founded by a group of intellectuals interested in incremental reform, it included George Bernard Shaw, Beatrice and Sidney Webb, and, for a time, H. G. Wells. Later they were joined by the Labour theorist G. D. H. Cole and his wife, Margaret, both of whom felt sympathy for Sylvia when she was later rejected by her mother and Christabel.[28] The Pankhursts joined the Fabians after they reached London, but they were never close to the leadership and direction of the movement, and its general stance on most issues was too moderate to inspire them. The Fabians favoured gradual reform, but they also saw themselves as an élite who knew better than working-class leaders like John Burns the direction that the country should take and how it should change.[29]

Always a maverick politically, Dr Pankhurst found his ideological haven in the Independent Labour Party (ILP). Formed in 1893 with James Keir Hardie as its leader, the Party represented a cross-section of former Liberals, working men, and those with socialist and radical leanings. The Pankhursts met Hardie first at the International Labour Conference in London in 1888. The next year they renewed the acquaintance in Paris at the International Socialist Congress. Hardie, a Scot, was, like John Burns, of working-class origin. He, too, came to trade unionism out of involvement with the temperance movement—a good school in public oratory. He was first business agent for a miners' union; then he founded the Ayrshire Miners' Union in 1886, became secretary of the Scottish Miners' Federation, and in 1888 was the first secretary of the Scottish Labour Party. It was this move that brought him to national prominence and into contact with the Pankhursts.

Hardie's move into Parliamentary politics began with the foundation of the Independent Labour Party (ILP). About a dozen men of working-class origins already held seats in Parliament, and the Liberals had offered Hardie a safe constituency if he would join them. But he turned it down as the middle-class embrace that had bought off, as he saw it, so many of the working-class candidates who had tried to work within the Liberal Party. The ILP was his alternative.

Although the solidly middle-class Richard Pankhurst and the working-class Hardie were socially far-removed, they were kindred spirits in their mutual goal to uplift the masses through parliamentary reform. Pankhurst seemed to find more comfort in association with people like Hardie than with people from his own class. He never joined the élite gentlemen's clubs, nor did he form friendships with other barristers in London or Manchester. He remained on the fringes of his profession. In 1894 Pankhurst joined the ILP, beginning his political activities during a by-election that year when Frank Smith, a close friend of Hardie's, stood for Parliament. Smith was a Christian Socialist with a Salvation Army background, and shared with Hardie a belief in spiritualism—not the sort of person Pankhurst would normally have supported, were it not for the Party. Smith was defeated at the polls, but his campaign set the tone for the general election in 1895. By that time Richard Pankhurst had become a member of the National Administrative Council for the ILP and was one of the 28 candidates in the election, not one of whom was elected. Keir Hardie lost in West Ham, and Pankhurst failed to win Gorton.

Pankhurst made his campaign in Gorton something of a family affair. Emmeline went to Gorton almost daily with Christabel and Sylvia to provide youthful support. Wherever they went, people spoke of their father kindly, raising their hopes for success at the polls. On the eve of the election Emmeline took Sylvia through the dark streets to the public houses, where she implored men 'with glistening eyes and thirsty lips' to come and vote.[30] Whatever their promises of the night before, morning sobriety did not produce the desired results. Pankhurst took defeat in his stride, but Sylvia was so overcome with grief that she cried throughout his speech of thanks to his supporters. Perhaps Sylvia's tears were prophetic: this was the last election in which her father would stand.

Emmeline Pankhurst was the only member of the family to win an election that year—as ILP candidate for the Chorlton Board of Poor Law Guardians in her Manchester District.[31] Here we see a pattern

developing in which the younger Pankhurst women would begin viewing their mother as a political role-model. In 1894 women were beginning to seek office in local government elections: it was mother, not
father, who proved successful at the polls.

At the Board of Guardians Emmeline was placed in an administrative position; responsible for the budget and overall running of the local
institution. Appalled by conditions she found during an inspection of
the Chorlton workhouses, Emmeline agitated among the other Guardians for improved facilities, greater comfort for the aged, improved
quality of food; and especially segregation of children so that they
could be spared the diseases and misfortunes suffered by the older
people. She was a strong advocate of new and more suitable housing,
which she thought should be designed on a village pattern and set in a
rural area so as to create a better environment for the children. These
were utopian goals, but before her term of office expired some of her
projects were completed.

Home life for the Pankhursts in Manchester differed little from the
pattern established in Russell Square. The children enjoyed the steady
stream of visitors, including socialists from the Continent. The old
Marquis de Rochefort (still refusing to use his title) came, followed by
his daughter, Noémie Dufaux, who lived in Geneva. Wilhelm Liebknecht, the German socialist, came to their home as an old man,
bringing Karl Marx's daughter, Eleanor. Sylvia probably hardly knew
the much older Eleanor, but the two women proved to have much in
common. Each devoted herself to highly individualistic crusades, and
each, too, abandoned artistic careers for lives of tireless activism.[32]

The children, according to Christabel, had a very happy family life:
'Those were the best of all years. If politics and movements did mean
forgoing some things that other people's children had, these children
had not our Father and Mother, our interesting life.'[33] Sylvia concurred. Christabel's memories were not unlike those of Sylvia. Dr
Pankhurst 'sparkled' and his 'courtesy in the home was complete . . . '
Pankhurst, however, had no sense of humour, and outside the home,
he was incapable of warmth or laughter. His family was important to
him, and Emmeline 'was queen'.[34] The sisters had at this time different views about their mother. Christabel wrote warmly of her in later
life; Sylvia's views, distorted by time perhaps, were shallow and hostile.[35] In fact, Emmeline was a free-spirited but, in many ways, devoted
mother. She left her children to their nurses and governesses just as
did most other mothers of her class and her time. But she favoured her
eldest daughter, and was oblivious to the slights and hurts which
Sylvia began to store up.

As for Richard Pankhurst, we have seen how his radical views
affected his relations with his wife's family and his professional career.
A reporter later writing Pankhurst's obituary in the *Manchester*

Guardian, characterized him as a man who took his role of citizen seriously. He was 'an occasional contributor' to the paper as a columnist, but was more frequently in print with his letters to the editor. Among his last campaigns was that for free speech in Manchester parks. His wife joined him and was arrested for breaking the prohibition against free speech in one of the parks. 'In the pursuit of what he deemed the public good he was indifferent to considerations of personal interest. Uncompromising in his opinions, he never entertained ill-will towards his opponents. Indeed his disposition was always kindly and genial.'[36] The Lord Mayor of Manchester, who did not share Pankhurst's political views, nevertheless described him as 'a man of sterling honesty, of great uprightness and perfect sincerity'.[37] He was reputed to have enormous enthusiasm which he threw into all his work. Sylvia inherited his enthusiasm and need for causes, Christabel his eloquence. Another view came from Helen Moyes, former suffragette and experienced journalist. Moyes recalled that: 'Men I knew who knew Doctor Pankhurst and knew all about him said he was a "difficult person" and "rather arrogant" and "dogmatic" and he was rather likely to "antagonize rather than win people".'[38] This description fits his daughters in their own campaigns, and seems a more accurate picture of the man than the eulogies after his death.

What is lost to the record is how Pankhurst was viewed by the working class and the poor—the people to whom he became a self-chosen apostle and whose causes he championed at the material expense of his own family. Whether it was Pankhurst's abrasive personality or, as Sylvia suggests, his ties with Keir Hardie that alienated people, the family again fell on hard times as he increased his involvement in the ILP. The City of Manchester took its business elsewhere for a time as did others. Like all new political parties, the ILP was composed of fringe elements which advertised Pankhurst's radicalism by association: businessmen hesitated to have their interests represented by a man wearing the socialist banner. The long, tense miners' strike of 1898 in South Wales found Pankhurst in the forefront of support for the strikers. At the height of the dispute, Pankhurst took to the public platform arguing for government ownership of the mines. This stand did little to endear him to the Manchester business establishment.

Pankhurst's political defeats, with the tensions created by his support for the miners, losses in business and diminishing income exacerbated the ulcer that had plagued him intermittently for years. But he kept the pain to himself and embarked on a crusade to improve housing for the poor. Sylvia accompanied her father to the slums of Ancoats, Gorton and Hulme, and watched him speak from his soapbox platform, his 'high squeaky voice'[39] calling on the people to demand better housing from local officials. Years later, Sylvia would take her own soapbox to the East End of London and make a similar plea to the people. Her lessons in public speaking and her commitment to the underprivileged found their roots in the dingy streets of Manchester, where her father's voice 'stirred [her] as perhaps he stirred no auditor'.[40]

One of Dr Pankhurst's struggles on the return to Manchester had been his advocacy of a ship canal from Manchester to the sea. This particular crusade was based on rational considerations of the city's needs, not on radical support for less well-accepted projects among the bourgeois fathers of Manchester. The 35½-mile canal with five locks was finally built at a cost of over £15 million. For the late nineteenth century the costs were great, but in May 1895, Manchester finally had its outlet to the sea, and ships could sail straight to the point of manufacture to pick up and unload goods. The anti-monarchist Pankhurst's moment of triumph came when he gave the opening address at a ceremony attended by Queen Victoria. Later, he and his family were passengers on the maiden voyage of a barge down the canal. Sylvia remembered her father's joy as he experienced one of his few victories. His speech, which prophetically called attention to the dangers of pollution, was widely reported in England and on the Continent.

Pankhurst was a prolific writer and frequently in demand as a speaker at socialist meetings. Like many utopian socialists, he was interested in education, believing that good education would produce good citizens; and from them would evolve a better society.[41] When he took on a project, he bombarded the press with letters to the editor, and wrote to friends high and low to enlist them in his cause. In so doing, he was educating his middle daughter, who learned and later followed his pattern. Sylvia never recognized that her father's model was not the best one for political success.

By spring 1897, Pankhurst's health had become a matter for anxiety. His ulcer was causing constant pain, but surgery for ulcers was unknown and he gained little relief from medication. Emmeline decided that rural life would provide a cure, so the family moved to a country house in Cheshire while he commuted to Manchester. The summer passed peacefully and Pankhurst seemed to recover. After the return to Manchester, his professional life had picked up when restored to his position as a solicitor for the Manchester Corporation. He chose to withdraw from all outside activities other than his continuing interest in women's suffrage. He acted as legal counsel for the suffrage group while handling city legal business. With his return to full-time employment, Emmeline decided she could keep a long-standing promise to Noémie Dufaux. They had agreed that each would exchange daughters for one year—meaning, of course, that Christabel would be exchanged with the Dufaux daughter. In the summer of 1898, Emmeline arranged to take Christabel to Geneva, where the Dufaux were living; she would return in the Autumn with their daughter. The remaining Pankhurst children stayed at home with their father.

Sylvia had begun art lessons the previous winter with an artist neighbour, Elias Bancroft. She was happy to be left behind and ecstatic over the creative opportunity to work under Bancroft, who was well known and regarded in Manchester. The younger children were supervised by the servants. Dr Pankhurst was lonely for his wife, from whom he had never been long separated. Soon after her departure he wrote, 'When you return we will have a new honeymoon and reconsecrate each to the other in the unity of the heart.'[42] But there was to be no second honeymoon. In September, as Emmeline was planning to leave Geneva with the Dufaux daughter, a telegram arrived, advising her to return immediately. Believing she had been summoned to the bedside of frail Harry, Emmeline quickly departed alone for Manchester. Once across the English Channel, and in a railway carriage full of strangers, Emmeline saw the announcement of her husband's death on the back page of the *Manchester Guardian*.

Sylvia had grown closer to her father during her mother's absence. When time allowed, she accompanied him home from his office, as she did on the Saturday he was stricken. The two walked home arm-in-arm, and met for lunch. Pankhurst was too ill to eat, and excused himself on the pretext that he was tired. Soon afterwards, Sylvia went to his room and found him slumped in a chair. She summoned servants and a doctor. For the next three days and nights she kept vigil at his bedside, taking little rest. The strain of nursing him was too much for an emotional sixteen-year-old. Early on Tuesday morning she arrived at her father's bedside and found her younger brother and sister, with the servants, standing by his bed. He was sinking fast. One servant took the younger children away, and the cook remained with Sylvia until the end.

On her father's death, Sylvia became hysterical. She seemed to blame herself: 'From the depths tears were rising . . . I rushed away into the blazing sunshine in the garden. All went dark. I fell on the grass and knew no more. . . . Rage and grief contended within. Reproaches died unuttered.'[43] The whole family had been dependent on Pankhurst for emotional support; each of the children relied on him for affection and encouragement. For Sylvia, who unrealistically hero-worshipped her father, the loss at such an impressionable age merely increased her idolatry, leaving a permanent emotional scar from which she never fully recovered.[44]

Emmeline's brother, Herbert, arrived to help deal with the tragedy, and in their mourning the family was surrounded by friends. During the funeral procession, 'thousands of people' lined the streets 'to pay final homage' as the bier passed.[45] The working class, the poor and trade unionists turned out in force to honour their dead champion.

The attention in death after so many had scorned him in life gave comfort to his family. For a brief moment in their lives, Sylvia and her mother were close. Christabel had remained in Geneva, and Emmeline turned to her second daughter as they consoled each other in their grief.

2
Radical Artist and Radical Love

Be careful to eschew all vagueness. It is better to be caught out
in going wrong when you have had a definite purpose, than to
shuffle and slue so that people can't blame you because you
don't know what you are at. Hold fast to distinct form in art.
Don't think too much of style, but set yourself to get out of you
what you think beautiful, and express it . . .
—William Morris, from J. W. Mackail, *The Life of William
Morris* (London, 1899)

Richard Pankhurst's death left the family without its central figure and
with little income. He had invested in obscure stocks, on some of which he
lost heavily, and, after his death—as throughout his life—there was little
cash in hand. The family behaved strangely in relation to money. Mrs
Pankhurst, raised in the same reforming tradition as her husband,
always had access to money while she lived in her father's home, and
continued to spend more freely than her husband's resources allowed,
even though she shared his sympathy with the nonconformist, dissent-
ing ideology that cared little for material acquisition. Sylvia, for the
most part, inherited her mother's free-spending approach, and also
her father's lack of concern for personal gain.

Robert Blatchford, who had moved the *Clarion* to London, believed
the family was impoverished and offered to launch a fund in his newspaper. It was Blatchford's habit to organize in nearly every issue fund
drives for those comrades who had 'sacrificed for the cause'.[1] Mrs
Pankhurst declined his offer: she asked instead that a hall for working
men be built in her husband's name. What happened, however, was
that a number of admirers and recipients of favours from Dr Pankhurst wrote to the *Manchester Guardian* asking that a fund be established to aid the widow and her children. The *Manchester Guardian*
ran several notices of appeal for the fund, and no doubt other efforts
were made to elicit donations from supporters. Even his opponents
recognized that Pankhurst's public commitments had prevented him
from making money and that, in consequence, his family were near
destitution.[2] The resulting fund was eventually designated for the
benefit of the Pankhurst children, or in 'such manner as the Executive
committee appointed saw fit to benefit the family'.[3] There was no
mention of using it to build a hall.

To alleviate the family's financial plight Mrs Pankhurst herself decided to sell the family home and move to a smaller house. She also sold some paintings to meet her husband's debts. A trust of about £1000 was established, some of which may have come from the fund. But by 1902 Mrs Pankhurst was no longer allowed to draw on the capital because, in the time-honoured tradition, the male trustees wished to save the balance of £200 for Harry's education.[4]

Mrs Pankhurst, whose elected position on the Board of Guardians was unsalaried, was forced to resign and take paid employment—a political sinecure as part-time Registrar of Births and Deaths. She did not however abandon ILP politics and, in 1900, was elected to the Manchester School Board.[5] In a ghost-written account of her life in this period, Mrs Pankhurst concentrated on her problems with the school system without mentioning her home life or her children. She may have remembered these years mainly as a struggle to survive, and for the emptiness she felt after the 'irreparable loss' of her husband. Even in reduced circumstances, the family retained their old servant. But Mrs Pankhurst suffered from migraine headaches and attempted more than she could accomplish—'it was a home of distressful atmosphere'.[6] Herbert Goulden did what he could to help his sister and her children with their move, and saw them settled in new quarters. Adela remained at the Manchester School for Girls, Harry at Mr Lupton's school. Sylvia, whose drawings had received some critical notice from friends, won a scholarship to study design at the Manchester School of Art.[7]

Sylvia's health was not much better than her mother's in the wake of her father's death. She suffered from severe headaches and neuralgia, which may have been partly psychosomatic, since she continued to blame herself for her father's death, and much of the time she was emotionally depressed.[8] As a consequence of her illness and absence from school, Sylvia dropped out of the second year of her scholarship. Instead, she attended part-time—with her mother paying the small fee —and worked in the new Emerson's store her mother had opened in Manchester to make extra money.

In her third year of art school—her second on a scholarship—Sylvia's spirits lifted. She studied with Walter Crane, a socialist artist disciple of William Morris, and director of the School of Design, and with Henry Cadness, Crane's deputy. Crane became, for a brief time, a father substitute: she was devoted to him. Cadness was soon impressed with her talent and encouraged her to pursue design as a career. During her first year at the School he chose Sylvia to design a page for an illuminated address being prepared for King Edward VII, who was coming to Manchester to open the Wentworth School of Design as a new part of Owens College. Sylvia was less than excited about the recipient of her work but was pleased to be asked to participate.[10] After she

Sylvia Pankhurst as artist, 1904–5

completed her work on the design, she took to the streets with other socialists and distributed anti-royalist propaganda.[11]

From childhood, Sylvia enjoyed going off by herself and drawing whatever caught her eye. She had sought and received special attention from her father through her art. In fact, one of her earliest drawings had been a portrait from memory of her dead brother, Frank. She believed her drawing failed to capture Frank's likeness as perfectly as it might have done, but recalled her father 'encouraged me kindly, saying he could see Frank in my drawing very clearly'.[12] At the Institute she continued her work in portraiture, but found her primary interest where encouragement was greatest—in design.[13]

Sylvia's parents were familiar with the work of the pre-Raphaelite artists and poets, and especially admired the socialist artist, William Morris. As a child, Sylvia had met Morris when he visited the family's London home. From her writings, published and unpublished, and from her work in design, it is clear that he represented her artistic inspiration. She was influenced by Cadness and Walter Crane, but, in romantic fantasy, she saw herself as an artist who would brighten the world of the poor with the richness of her designs. At one point her declared goal was to decorate the halls of the working people, where she could design and hang bright banners to bring some inner light to their lives.[14]

Morris himself had been influenced by the pre-Raphaelites, who responded to industrialization with a retreat to medieval artistic styles. He was a member of the Arts and Crafts Movement, and one of the artists Emmeline had featured at Emerson and Co. Crane had studied with Morris and brought both the pre-Raphaelite and Arts and Crafts techniques with him to Manchester. The pre-Raphaelites used trees, birds, flowers, and heavy bold lines as outlines to convey warmth; Morris went a step further in the Movement, believing it was not possible to 'disassociate art from morality, politics, and religion.'[15] In her idealistic youth, Sylvia pictured herself in this same tradition. Her pictures of trees, flowers and bushes were made of the flat design elements common to the period, and are seen in illustrations from publications such as *The Pageant*, issued by Shannon and Rickells.

In her final year at the Institute, Sylvia's record was impressive. She won a national silver medal for mosaic design, a Primrose medal, and the highest honour then available at the Manchester School, the Procter Travelling Scholarship, which enabled her to go abroad for an extended period of independent study. Because of her interest in design and mosaics, she chose to visit Venice to study the Byzantine influence in mosaic art in particular. Her original itinerary also included Florence, but in the end she spent the entire trip in Venice.

Meanwhile, Christabel had returned home, having remained in Geneva for a year after her father's death. According to Sylvia, Mrs Pankhurst had decided to open the Manchester branch of Emerson's for Christabel to run; but Christabel was not interested in the speciality store and paid little attention to the business. While Sylvia may have worked there as often as time allowed, her jealousy of Christabel became a serious family issue. Christabel may have been spoiled and neglected the business, but she had an increasing role in her mother's affections, filling the gap left by her husband's death. From the time of Christabel's return to Manchester to Mrs Pankhurst's death many years later, the eldest daughter led, advised and at times controlled her mother to such an extent that the three younger children often felt ignored.

The Boer war began as Christabel returned from the Continent, and it too contributed to the unhappiness of the Pankhursts. The ILP opposed the war, and so did the Pankhursts. The war, however, was generally popular in Manchester, and the children were exposed to a variety of public pressures. Frail Harry was physically attacked leaving school and had to be helped home by the headmaster. At the Manchester School for Girls Adela was hit in the face by a book thrown by a teacher.[16] Sylvia followed the radical views of Walter Crane in an article she wrote for a school magazine so closely that a fellow student threatened to put a brick through her window if the offending article were not withdrawn. Emmeline resigned her membership of the Fabian Society because the Webbs supported the war.[17]

But this harrassment by the conventional world was not new: whatever their own views, those of their radical father were well enough known in Manchester to earn the children jeers and a certain isolation from their peer group. And their mother's unconventional ideas about raising children did not help: Harry needed glasses for his schoolwork, but Emmeline was opposed and refused them. Adela was forced to leave school at sixteen to help support the family because Christabel and Sylvia were otherwise occupied. Like Sylvia, Adela resented their mother's favouritism towards Christabel. When Christabel went to Owens College to study law in order to follow in their father's footsteps, Adela wrote, 'She was not interested in law and even disliked it but she had a remarkable memory and could learn anything out of a book even without understanding its principles.'[18]

In spite of the tensions between Mrs Pankhurst and her children, she decided to accompany Sylvia to the Continent, first to stay with the Dufaux family in Geneva, then on to Venice. Similarly, Sylvia, whose memoirs were written in strongly emotional terms, later described her first trip to the Continent as pleasurable. With her mother to herself, enchanted by the landscape and away from Christabel's influence, she travelled in relaxed mood across France to Switzerland. In Geneva, Sylvia found Dufaux to be an artist who appreciated her sketches, and, even in the 1930s, after much bitterness had passed between mother and daughter, the visit brought back warm memories. She wrote pathetically in *The Suffragette Movement* that, in those brief days together, 'we were so happy'.

Basking in M. Dufaux's praise Sylvia set off for Venice with her mother, and Mme Dufaux; they arrived 'in the brief violet twilight'. Sylvia's recollection of her first impressions of the city brings to mind a picture she might have painted: 'Venice first seen in the soft irridescent gold of the shining sun: a wondrous city... Venice in the mournful loveliness of pale marble palaces, rising in the velvet darkness of the night.'[19] In 1902, as for centuries, Italy was still the centre of a flourishing textile industry. Now, three decades after national unification, it had an advanced network of rail communication between the major cities. But it remained a poor country: the bulk of its population consisted of peasants eking out a subsistence on small parcels of land. Socialism was on the increase in 1902, but not on the scale found in the more industrial areas of England, France or Germany. Where socialism was preached it was mainly the intelligentsia who listened. Italy was a centre of artistic culture, not mass political foment.

And this is what Sylvia too found the most appealing. Venice for her was a living historical art collection. Palaces, churches, decorated bridges across canals, reflected many styles of architecture and recalled Venice's former importance as a centre of trade. Venetian mosaics portrayed the confluence of East and West from the Byzantine occupation of the city in the tenth century. When construction began on St Mark's in 1050, merchants travelling to the East were required by law to return with objects for the cathedral. Thus it became a continuing reflection of Byzantine art and architecture with gold inlaid mosaics covering much of its interior. St Mark's was shaped in the form of a cross, with a small dome on each of the four arms and a large dome in the centre, surrounded with oriental gems, glittering colours streaming down from the tall ceiling. It was on this ancient monument to the Venetian past that Sylvia chose to concentrate her study of mosaics. She sketched too: children fascinated her, and she frequently drew them on her early morning outings.[20] One early incident involved children: told by Mme Dufaux, whose knowledge of Italian was limited, that 'avanti' meant 'go away' and was to be used in case of threatened assault Sylvia used it while sketching to discourage inquisitive children. It only made them press closer.

She soon learned another Italian word, 'brutta' (plain-looking) which she applied as much to her unstylish dress as to her looks.[21] Sylvia's lack of interest in clothes or her own appearance remained throughout her life. She lacked Christabel's natural beauty and, like her mother, she made no effort to improve on nature with cosmetics. Nor did she have her mother's handsome charm. She was of average height—five feet four inches—slender, with thick sandy hair, and heavy-lidded but expressive blue eyes—attractive in an indeterminate way. Her eyes often reflected warmth and compassion, and her smile lent a certain lilt to and broadened an otherwise elongated face.

The canals of Venice, narrow with little bridges, fascinated Sylvia. She produced a beautiful oil painting of one of the smaller canals, and spent many mornings sketching in bright colours the fruit-stalls found all over the city. She rose at five in the morning, went to the streets to paint until eight, then returned home for breakfast. After eating, she changed her painting materials and went to St Mark's, where she copied the mosaics; to San Giorgio degli Schiavani 'to copy the Carpaccio's'; or some other church to copy designs. In the afternoon she went to the Rialto to capture its moving crowds, or to paint people working in the stalls. Sometimes she would try to paint Venetian scenes in the moonlight from her balcony, until, she said, her hands shook.[22] Though her memoirs tended to overstatement, Sylvia worked hard in Venice and what remain of her paintings bring her visit to life.

As winter came, Sylvia enrolled in the Accademia delle Belle Arti, on the Grand Canal. Studying landscapes but briefly, she was surprised to receive a certificate in that discipline upon her arrival back in Manchester. She also tried to attend a life-drawing class, but the instructor dispatched her to another room without a model: all the other students and models were male. Undaunted, Sylvia quietly returned the next day and was allowed to stay. But she did not reveal her improving command of Italian, and listened with interest to what was said, including references to herself as the 'quiet one'.[23]

Sylvia became lonely after the departure of her mother, in spite of the heavy work schedule. But soon she became friendly with her landlady, the widowed Countess Sophie Bertelli Algarotti. Madame Sophie had many friends, but no intimate relatives living near by. She grew fond of Sylvia and the relationship deepened into a kind of adoptive motherhood. When the time came for Sylvia to leave Venice, Madame Sophie begged her to stay on. Florence by that time was no longer possible, nor of particular interest to Sylvia. The Venetian interlude had not been without private incident, however. A friend of Madame Sophie's, an old count, tried to seduce Sylvia.[24] (In later life she believed that that incident spoiled her memories of Venice and of Madame Sophie. But she did briefly return to Venice in 1906, in the company of Emmeline Pethick-Lawrence).

The trip home brought yet another aggressive encounter. This time the conductor on her train to Paris tried to kiss her. On reaching Paris, she went immediately to Thomas Cook to report the unsettling incident.[27] Sylvia had had so little contact with men, other than those in her immediate family and her teachers, that she lacked the sophistication of other women her age travelling alone: she remained a psychological (as well as physical) virgin.

Departure was prompted by a summons from Manchester advising that Sylvia was needed to help at home while Christabel continued with her education. Madame Sophie countered with an offer of a permanent home and financial help for the further development of her talent. Although the temptation was great, Sylvia returned home.[25] She may not however have returned immediately for Adela, in later life, wrote resentfully that she had to go to work because Sylvia had overstayed her leave on the scholarship and Christabel had begun university.[26] Emmeline had rented rooms above Emerson's for an art studio and, during spare moments from work in the shop—which were many—Sylvia painted. She sold several of her Venice works to raise money, some of which went to the family because the store was still mortgaged. Christabel's studies were not so restricting as to prevent her from attending political meetings and developing new friends among a young, activist group of feminists. Although Emmeline was still a registrar of vital statistics, and was also involved with the School Board, stimulated by Christabel, she returned to politics and to the suffrage movement which was by then growing in popularity in northern England.[28] Sylvia was alone much of the time, except for evenings with Harry and Adela, and even then she did domestic chores like knitting and darning.[29] To compound the slight Sylvia felt after abandoning her studies in Venice for the sake of the family— or more precisely for the sake of Christabel—her mother helped

Christabel make her own trip to Venice so that she could see, according to Sylvia, 'what I had seen'.[30]

Meanwhile, the construction of Pankhurst Hall had begun in Manchester. The committee in charge asked Sylvia to design the interior. Nothing could have pleased her more; her love for her father and respect for his memory remained for the rest of her life. She set to work, with a team of assistants for the heavier tasks.[31] The principal theme was to be the lives of working people, symbols depicting the virtues of purity, beauty, and love—and all in the pre-Raphaelite style. In case the symbols were not enough, each was captioned, and at the entrance to the hall she inscribed:

'AS THIS HALL BEARS THE NAME OF A PIONEER WHOSE LIFE WAS GIVEN FOR AN IDEAL AND FOR THE FUTURE, EMBLEMS OF THE FUTURE AND THE IDEAL HAVE BEEN CHOSEN WITH WHICH TO DECORATE IT.'[32]

Walter Crane opened the newly-decorated hall, and Sylvia gave her first public lecture, explaining the meaning of the decorations. She was so nervous that she forgot to take off her gloves.[33]

After the excitement of the opening, Sylvia grew bored at Emerson's and in her tiny studio. With her mother's consent she entered a national competition for a scholarship at the Royal College of Art in London. When the results were announced in 1904, Sylvia, despite her failure in geometry, headed the list. With a two-year scholarship and a £50 living allowance, she made her way to London. Finding tiny quarters off Fulham Road, in Chelsea, she was horribly lonely yet happy at the opportunity to continue her studies. Harry was not far away, and the two met at weekends. She made a few friends at the College. One, a young man of advanced political views, kept in touch with her until old age and even later contributed some of his original work to be sold for the benefit of one of her charities.[34] But most of the 'first year students in my day suffered intense depression . . . we were made to suffer an abject feeling of incompetence.'[35] One of the immediate problems was the recent and unpopular curriculum change which called for a full six months' architectural training during the day, and allowed for life drawing only in brief sessions in the evening. Since Sylvia was weak in mathematics, architectural study had no appeal. In what may have been a self-defeating move, Sylvia confronted the principal, and requested that the policy be changed. In so doing she incurred the enmity of the principal, and the rules went unchanged.[36]

A further problem which confronted her, and which may also have worked to her disadvantage, was that of discrimination against women at the College. In theory, competition for scholarships was open to all, but in fact only one a year was awarded to a woman. Employment for art graduates was difficult to find; for women more so. As a result,

(*left*) Sylvia Pankhurst *c.* 1906:
Suffragette and Artist

(*below*) Keir Hardie, with note to
Sylvia *c.* 1905–6

Sylvia's scholarship was not extended at the end of her two years. By that time, too, she had begun her involvement in the suffrage movement in London, and those activities weighed against her. In the summer of 1906 she experienced another blow when she was denied admission to a class in stained-glass work.[37]

Although it was common for small groups of students to share rooms to save money, Sylvia chose to live alone. She paid ten shillings a week for her lodgings and helped the family finances by designing textiles at school during the week and selling her designs on Saturdays. She said she sent most of the money to her mother and family, but Emerson's was in fact one of her paying customers.[38] As a loner, Sylvia held back from companionship, perhaps from shyness. As a child she had no close friends beyond the family, nor in young adulthood did she seem to want them. She developed no schoolgirl crushes on boys her age at the College. Indeed, she regarded anything other than total dedication to art a frivolity.

It was to Keir Hardie, her parents' old friend from the Independent Labour Party, to whom she turned for companionship and solace and in whom she found a soul mate. Her memories of Hardie reached back to her thirteenth year, when he had visited the Pankhurst home in Manchester. Her father was standing as an ILP candidate for Gorton, and Hardie came to discuss strategy with him. Sylvia, advised of his coming, rushed home from school to find him 'in the big armchair, a sturdy figure in rough brown homespun jacket, with a majestic head, the brow massive, the gold-brown eyes deep set. . . . The strength of a rock, the ruggedness of a Scot moorland, the sheltering kindness of an oak, the gentleness of a St Bernard dog.'[39]

After Dr Pankhurst died, Hardie remained close to the family and visited them in Manchester whenever he could. When Christabel took up politics, Emmeline renewed her interest in the ILP. Gossip in Labour circles even suggested that Hardie and Emmeline were having an affair.[40] Between the Gorton candidacy of 1895 and 1904, when Sylvia reached London, Hardie had welded together a party which presaged the Trades Union Congress and led to the establishment of a Labour Representation Committee (LRP) in Parliament, direct ancestor of the Labour Party formed to fight the general election in 1906.

It was partly the formation of this party that led Mrs Pankhurst to organize the Women's Social and Political Union (WSPU) in Manchester. The very hall which Sylvia decorated in memory of her father excluded women as members, a discovery Sylvia made when working there. This exclusion was seen as the last straw by the Pankhursts. As a first step, Mrs Pankhurst, Christabel and others decided to form a women's auxiliary to the LRP to agitate for women's rights. This group, each member of which had an ILP background, first met at the Pankhurst home in Nelson Street in the autumn of 1903. Mrs

Pankhurst kept the organization separate and distinct from both the LRP and the other suffrage societies.[41]

Keir Hardie, admirer of John Stuart Mill and Dr Pankhurst, was one of the most ardent supporters of the call for 'votes for women'; he supported Emmeline from the first. But it was a sensitive issue for the radical left. The Chartist movement of the nineteenth century included women's suffrage in the original Charter of Rights and Liberties in 1838, but later dropped it for fear that it would compromise the other claims of working men. The ILP had then revived the issue as part of its demand for universal suffrage, lumping together the cause of men who were still disenfranchised with that of all women. The suffragists' claim, taken up by Emmeline, 'Suffrage for women on the same terms as it is, or may be granted, to men', paralleled the ILP's stand until repeated failures to extend the suffrage resulted in total frustration and forced the women into specific action.

Hardie's early childhood had been one of tragic deprivation. Born in 1856, the illegitimate son of a poor Scots serving girl, Mary Keir, he began life as an outcast.[42] When he was three, his mother married David Hardie, from whom he took his last name. The marriage was plagued with problems from the beginning; the senior Hardie was a hard-drinking, often unemployed seaman, who tormented his wife for her illegitimate child. Mary had no option but to stay, bearing him more children, accepting his drunkenness, and living in poverty. At the age of eight, James Keir Hardie went to work in the mines; at twenty-three he moved briefly into business, before turning to a career of journalism, followed by union activity. His marriage brought unhappiness: first, his mother turned him out of the house for marrying Lillie, the daughter of a pub-owner[43]; then later, as Hardie's life led him into a wider world Lillie stayed in Old Cumnock to raise their three children.

Hardie attended night school while working in the mines during the day, and read widely to increase his vocabulary and enlarge his perspectives beyond the tiny Scottish community. During his life he founded four newspapers, wrote several books and pamphlets, and contributed a weekly column, first for *The Labour Leader*, which he edited and partially owned, and later for the Merthyr *Pioneer*, which he founded.

Raised as an agnostic by his parents, Hardie first encountered religion through the temperance movement. He joined the Evangelical Union when he was twenty-two. In 1881 he left organized religion and, like the Pankhursts, converted to socialism. In the words of a recent biographer, Kenneth O. Morgan, Hardie's dream of a future, socialistic society was 'romantic, utopian, suprarational. It was the product of a poet as much as a political outlook.'[44] It was therefore a more adequate substitute for religious belief than a more 'scientific' socialism could ever be. Hardie believed that every socialist should preach and follow the 'sermon on the Mount.' In a pamphlet of 1907, *From Serfdom to Socialism*, he outlined his concept of socialism, which 'was fundamentally ethical, a vision of justice and equality born of a new society'.[45] This view was in keeping with other strains of British socialism of the day, including those of Richard Pankhurst and Robert Blatchford of the *Clarion* (although Hardie thought Blatchford's view of socialism was frivolous). This was the gospel by which Sylvia grew up and the basis for the utopia she searched for in so many different campaigns in her life.

Hardie and his lifelong friend, Frank Smith, who also had deserted nonconformist religion, maintained links with the world beyond through their shared belief in spiritualism, reincarnation and extrasensory perception. Hardie and Smith consulted horoscopes, believed in palmistry, and attended seances, each promising to communicate with the other when either died.[46] Yet this side of Hardie was known only to his intimates. For the masses he drew on the Old and New Testament. He was a romantic orator who used the Bible for familiar themes to bind his audience closer to him and to his political views, which themselves owed much to popular religion. He would ask his audience whom they would serve: 'Labour or socialism?' Or, in full voice, he would call them to 'Come out from the House of Bondage . . . and give glory to your Creator by support to the Labour Party.' Hardie employed Robert Burns, too, as a means of reaching the common man.

A contemporary, Frederick Rogers, saw Hardie as an 'idealist rather than the politician.' Rogers worked in the labour movement during the early years of the party and knew Hardie well, admiring his 'selfless devotion to an ideal'. 'It is this steady integrity of purpose, combined perhaps with a touch of old-fashioned Scotch mysticism, which gives him his hold on the working classes.' Finally, he 'taught in politics an old truth: that men must believe before they can be saved'.[47]

Morgan describes Hardie as an 'eccentric', a 'bohemian' who 'entered the labour movement as much for private reasons as from an identity with the proletariat'.[48] This same statement might well describe Sylvia Pankhurst. And they shared many other characteristics. Both were uncomfortable in large political movements, preferring to attach themselves to small groups; even then, they were often schismatic. Both leaned toward helping the downtrodden, and both were sensitive to the misery in the lives of the poor. Hardie was an opponent of empire. Through columns in his papers and in his other writings, he called for an end to the British colonial system. Above all, like Sylvia, he was a pacifist. And he remained devoted to his mother throughout his life much as Sylvia remained devoted to her father.

The good and simple woman Hardie married, however, endured many of the injustices he sought to eradicate in his stand for women's rights. He was away from home much of the time and never earned enough to support his wife and children in accordance with his rising social position. But he lived frugally and spent little on himself—the same nonconformist trends were here as with the Pankhursts—to the exclusion of his family.

In 1895, Hardie lost his seat in Parliament. Instead of returning home, he travelled, lectured and worked for the Independent Labour Party. It was during this time that he made his first trip to the United States, arriving in the midst of a series of labour struggles. Among other areas of strife between business and labour was the Pullman strike of 1894, which had landed socialist Eugene V. Debs in jail. Before leaving America, Hardie visited Debs in jail, where their discussion revealed an even grimmer picture of American labour conditions. After his return to England, it was four more years before Hardie re-entered Parliament. In 1900, he was returned for Merthyr Tydfil, again as an ILP candidate. Merthyr was located near the Black Mountains, in the heart of the mining district, and it was here that Hardie could identify with the problems of his constituents. At first he was uncomfortable with the song-loving, hard-drinking Welshmen, but he joined the Welsh Party and supported them on issues of regional importance.

In 1904, when Sylvia returned to London, Hardie was forty-seven years old; she was twenty-two. The deprivations of his youth and early adulthood had aged him. He was a small man, with craggy features, and a warm, generous face surrounded by a mane of white hair. His eyes were brown, sensitive and electric. He had always been responsive to women, and was known to have engaged in several light flirtations with girls in the labour movement. One affair, with Annie Hines, may have been more than flirtatious.[48] But, it was Sylvia who enflamed his passions, releasing an emotional flow that his wife, Lillie, seems never to have unleashed. Living alone as he did when Parliament was in session, and travelling for much of the recess, he was seldom at home. He liked and needed the company of people; more than anything, he needed the love and adoration of a woman. To Sylvia, Hardie was in part a substitute for her dead father and in part a political hero. He offered the emotional security of an older man who was patient and encouraging as she adapted to life in London, but he was also on hand to soothe her worries and often to smooth her path in her working life.

At Hardie's flat in Nevills Court she found the kind of people she had met when her father was alive: 'Socialists . . . Russian exiles, writers, musicians, dreamers of dreams'.[49] Nostalgia soon gave way to deep love between Hardie and Sylvia. Theirs was not the love of fairy tales, when all ends happily in marriage. Hardie had no intention of leaving his wife and children for another woman. Sylvia's emotional instability, a product of her early childhood, and her self-dramatization, which deepened in the insecure aspects of their love affair, were not in themselves appealing to Hardie; but the by-product, her dependence on him and the outflow of emotion, were the sustenance he needed and was not finding in his marriage.

The Labour leader spent as much time with Sylvia as his schedule and hers would allow. He left no written record of their time together. Hers are found in both *The Suffragette Movement* and in *The Home Front*, written more than twenty years after their affair had ended, and apt to reflect romantic fantasy as much as fact; yet with the few remaining letters between them, we can reconstruct something of the relationship.

Sylvia visited Hardie often at Nevill's Court. He came to her flat when she lived near Kensington Gardens. They seem not always to have been discreet about being seen together, but Sylvia was known to other members of the Labour leader's group as a Pankhurst, and therefore as a family friend—at least in the early days of their relationship. She came to his office in Parliament, and together they would walk in St James's Park. On one occasion Hardie, doubtless without irony, took Sylvia with other members of the ILP executive committee to see *Romeo and Juliet*. Frank Smith was among the group, and Sylvia was surprised at the end of the evening, to hear him inquire as to the author of the play.[50]

The two spent much time together walking in parks. No doubt this reflected the lack of means for other entertainment, as well as a common interest in nature. Sylvia remembered that 'at rare intervals during the following years, I went with Keir Hardie, or with him and others, for a day in the country. . . . At such times he was merry, and liked to talk of pleasant, childish remembrances'. When he was ill and staying at Richmond, Sylvia visited him at his hotel 'many times' where, she wrote, they sat on the terrace or walked in Richmond Park.[51]

Sylvia was a demanding figure in Hardie's life at this time. Her love for him was of the same intensity that later characterized her involvements in her causes—all or nothing. He, on the other hand, had many commitments which included a great deal of travel. He tried to keep in touch, writing her notes and postcards from places he visited. On one occasion, after Sylvia had complained to him of her loneliness, he wrote, 'I hope that your depression has lifted and that you are busy with your pen and sketchpad'. On another trip he sent her a postcard, mentioning an art gallery he had visited in Copenhagen. He was trying to identify himself with her interests in his absence, and merely signed the card 'Keir'.[52] Sometimes he ended his notes 'affectionately'; at others, merely initialling the letter 'K'. She tore the signatures from her letters to him, which survived. From the few remaining notes Hardie wrote to Sylvia we know he called her 'little sweetheart'. In one, he looked forward to 'smoothing the pathway of my little sweetheart. May it be ever so', no doubt referring to a meeting he had arranged between them. On another occasion he wrote to his 'Little Sweetheart' that he could not meet her in the park because he had declined to go to Hyde Park for a meeting 'on the plea of another engagement'. 'That', he said, 'closes the park against me for lunch. For other reasons which I can explain when we meet, I want you to come here. . . . Come down Holborn and down Chancery Lane—That is the best way for you. . . .' Was he trying to hide this particular meeting with her? Or, was he concerned about a young woman alone on the streets after dark?

Supporting his wife and family in Scotland, and maintaining his love affair with Sylvia, Hardie shared his secret only with Frank Smith, who sometimes accompanied them on their country outings.[53] In the evenings, when alone in his flat, Hardie would light a fire, produce 'bread, butter, and Scotch scones, the main staples of his diet, and tea. . . . After a simple meal, he would light his pipe and seat himself for a chat, a brief one; for work' always claimed his time. Sometimes, if he was not too busy he would read aloud to her, with only candles to illuminate the room. The stillness around them was broken by the soft sound of his voice, reading from Robert Burns:

> As Fair art thou, my bonnie lass
>   so deep in luve am I:
> And I will luve thee still, my dear,
>   Till a' the seas gang dry:
> Till a' th seas gang dry, my dar,
>   And the rocks met wi' the sun;
> I will love thee still, my dar,
>   While the sands o' life shall run.
>   (A Red, Red Rose)

On other evenings, Hardie would prepare a quiet supper and afterwards, while he worked on parliamentary or Labour Party business, Sylvia would sit and sketch, capturing his face in portraits, two of which survive. One, in oils, conveys Sylvia's strong feeling for the man. It stresses his wisdom with strong lines outlining his face and hair; she portrayed his kindness through soft facial expression and an almost twinkling quality about his eyes. This picture, in the National Portrait Gallery, London, represents Sylvia's love transferred to the canvas. The second portrait was done in chalk, a medium commonly used by her. It seems to have been drawn hastily and with less precision, showing a heavier, wrinkled Hardie, a man weighed down with worry, holding the pipe for which he was widely recognized.[54]

Compared with her portraits of working women, the portraits of Hardie show vivacity and offer a much clearer definition of facial features. While many of her women's features are drawn in proportion the face conveys nothing of the personality. Almost all the portraits were done in watercolour or chalk. The weaknesses may be attributed to several factors. Sylvia knew the women only slightly, if at all.

Furthermore, they were not supposed to represent real people, but symbols—abstract female members of an abstract working class. She wanted to show the futility of their lives, expressed in emptiness of expression.[55] Perhaps too she was simply unable to capture human personality in its full complexity when dealing with ordinary people. In her own self-portrait, which she drew for Hardie in chalk, she portrayed herself as pretty, poised and youthful.

Sylvia's relationship with Keir Hardie seems almost certainly to have been physical. In one letter written while in prison, Sylvia longed to 'feel your dear length pressing on me until my breath comes short'.[56] In another letter she referred to their kisses. The affair changed her from an innocent woman-child to a sexually aware and probably sexually active adult. Sylvia had no earlier experience with sex, and probably knew very little about it. Hardie, too, may have been ignorant of sex for pleasure except in the early years of his marriage; and he may have been inhibited because of his illegitimate birth. There were then crude mechanical devices for birth control, and the age-old practice of *coitus interruptus* was widely practised by working-class men.

The love affair began soon after Sylvia moved to London, and continued into 1912. After that, either because of outside pressures or because of Hardie's declining health, the intensity diminished, though they remained good and close friends. On the back of one envelope among the collection of his notes to Sylvia, was the word 'Advent'. It was written about 1912 when she was organizing the suffrage movement from Bow in London's East End. There is now no way of interpreting what beginning she was referring to. Was it the beginning of the end of their love affair? Or, is there some possibility that she was pregnant with Hardie's child? If she was, she must have miscarried during her frenzied bouts of militancy and imprisonment. Sylvia did not believe in abortion.

As her second year at the Royal College of Art drew to a close, Sylvia was thrown on her own resources. Henry Cadness, hearing of her misfortune, wrote to her not to 'lose heart because you have not gained another scholarship . . . your opportunity will come by striving'. One of the few friends she made at the College also wrote expressing regret at Sylvia's failure and offering encouragement.[57] But it was Keir Hardie who came to the rescue when the term ended and Sylvia had found no employment. She was by this time caught up in her mother's affairs in London and had little time for her art, but her income ceased when the scholarship ended, and she had no money. Hardie suggested that she sell some of her sketches to the *Pall Mall Gazette* along with an article based on her recent prison experiences as a suffragette.* In

---

* *See* Chapter 3, p.45.

1907 she agreed with the paper to write an article for payment of £10 and embarked on a new career, following in Hardie's footsteps. Henceforth, when times were hard Sylvia put pen to paper, writing articles, drawing sketches and, later, producing books to sustain her independent lifestyle.

3
The March of the Women

> ...at her side stood her three daughters...Christabel stood at
> her front rather than her side. It always seemed to me that
> Christabel was the darling of her heart and to save her from risk
> she was always ready to expose herself to any suffering.
> —Henry Nevison, *Fire of Life* (London, 1935), 252.

The history of the women's suffrage movement has been interpreted
by many. Sylvia was among the first to chronicle the early years of her
mother's movement in *The Suffragette*, published in 1911, at the height
of the militant movement.[1] The origins of the Women's Social and
Political Union are complex and have little direct bearing on the life of
Sylvia Pankhurst. The familiar litany of names begins with Mary
Wollstonecraft, who, in 1792, published her *Vindication of the Rights of
Woman*—a plea for equality between the sexes. The philosopher John
Stuart Mill took up the cause of women's rights in Parliament in 1867.
Two years later he published his feminist tract, *On the Subjection of
Women*. In the late nineteenth century, Lydia Becker organized the
Manchester Suffrage Society, and edited the *Women's Suffrage Journal*
until her untimely death by suicide in 1890. Richard Pankhurst was a
friend and supporter of Becker's and it was through his involvement
with the Manchester Society that Mrs Pankhurst joined the campaign.
Becker, however, believed in quiet dedication and did not seek publicity in the manner that came to characterize the Pankhurst women.

Mrs Millicent Fawcett followed more closely in the footsteps of
Lydia Becker, and before the first decade of the twentieth century,
Fawcett had brought together and founded a number of small societies
all over England, and placed them under the overall umbrella of the
National Union of Women's Suffrage Societies (NUWSS). There were
female trade unionists like Esther Roper and Eva Gore-Booth, whose
North of England Society first attracted Christabel to the movement.[2]
And, in Manchester, the elderly Elizabeth Wolstenholme-Elmy, who
had worked with Dr Pankhurst, elected to bring her prestige to Mrs
Pankhurst's organization in the early days of the WSPU.

The suffrage movement in England experienced the personal conflict, power struggle and general divisiveness that mark any organized
movement. Even within the Pankhurst camp, accounts vary as to who

did what and why in the early days of the movement. Put succinctly, Dr Pankhurst's interest in the Manchester Suffrage Society engaged Emmeline, after her marriage, for a brief period: both became involved with the ILP and several other radical causes. After Richard died, Emmeline confined her own interests to the ILP, her work as Registrar of Births and Deaths and, after 1900, to her elected position on the Manchester School Board. Christabel, a law student in Manchester, became friendly with Eva Gore-Booth and Esther Roper. After limited involvement with, and interest in, their society, Christabel joined her mother's WSPU which had been founded in October 1903.

There were several reasons given for founding yet another suffrage society in the Manchester area. Sylvia thought that her mother was jealous of Christabel's friendship with Gore-Booth and Roper and in her loneliness formed the WSPU to bring Christabel back home.[3] Mrs Pankhurst claimed that she formed the WSPU as a special-interest group to spur the Labour Party to support votes for women when its own goal was universal suffrage. George Dangerfield, in *The Strange Death of Liberal England*, perhaps best described Mrs Pankhurst's motives when he wrote that she would never stand behind the lines when she could stand in front. Martin Pugh, drawing on the work of Liddington and Norris, went beyond Dangerfield in perceiving that Mrs Pankhurst and Christabel were not able effectively to lead the large component of mostly women textile workers, who comprised the membership of the North of England Society. After a year or so in competition for members with the North of England Society they 'went in pursuit of the drawing rooms of London, thereby depriving themselves of a real mass movement'.[4] It is unlikely that Mrs Pankhurst founded the WSPU with the intention of moving to London, but she lost no time in returning to the capital when the opportunity presented itself.

A few months after founding the WSPU, and while operating out of their home in Manchester, Emmeline and Christabel called on Bruce Glasier, a founder member of the ILP and then its chairman. Glasier —a Scot of middle-class background—was no advocate of votes for women. He reported their visit in his diary—a misogynist view, but nevertheless one that reveals the strains between mother and daughter and some of the ILP leadership from the beginning.[5]

> . . . a weary ordeal of chatter about women's suffrage from 10:00 p.m. to 1:30 a.m.—Mrs. and Christabel Pankhurst belabouring me as chairman of the party for its neglect of the question. At last get roused and speak with something like scorn of their miserable individual sexism, virtually tell them that the ILP will not stir a finger more than it has done for all women suffragists in creation. Really the pair are not seeking democratic freedom, but self importance. . . . Christabel paints her eyebrows grossly and looks selfish, lazy and willful. They want to be ladies, not workers and lack the humility of real heroism.

Suffragette leaders: from left to right, Lady Constance Lytton, Annie Kenny, Mrs. Pethick-Lawrence, Christabel Pankhurst, Sylvia Pankhurst and Vera Holme, the first professional woman chauffeur in Britain, who drove Mrs. Pankhurst.

Suffragette leaders of the WSPU

While her mother and sister were busy with their organizational activities on behalf of votes for women, Sylvia was continuing her art studies and her affair with Keir Hardie in London. In the summer of 1904, Sylvia returned to Manchester and found that the WSPU had already recruited a few organizers—Annie Kenney, a Lancashire working-class woman and a devotee of Christabel, and Teresa Billington, an Irish woman whose independent spirit brought her into the WSPU and later took her out of it in a split over democratic principles. Mrs Flora Drummond, a middle-aged rough-and-ready woman, later known as 'General Drummond' because of her leadership qualities, was also aiding the WSPU in its recruitment drive when Sylvia arrived. Drummond, Kenney, Billington, Mrs Pankhurst and Christabel had formed a tightly-linked group. Kenney, however, continued working in a mill at Oldham until Mrs Pankhurst sent her to London in 1906, where she became a full-time organizer for the WSPU. Because Sylvia, too, was anxious to join them, she was granted a few speaking assignments. These were less than sensational, joining as she did on the platform 'a negro preacher' on one side and 'a long-haired medicine vendor' on the other.[6]

Sylvia's involvement with the WSPU was brief: in the autumn she returned to London, while Mrs Pankhurst was still tied two nights a week to her part-time job in Manchester. Christabel, continuing her law studies, worked with the WSPU as time allowed—hers was never a grassroots involvement with any organization. In 1905, at a Liberal Party meeting, though, Christabel and Annie Kenney decided to confront the politicians present on votes for women by sending a note to the chairman demanding a statement. When, at the end of the meeting, the chair ignored the note and would not recognize the women—while at the same time answering questions put forward by men—Kenney jumped on her seat and shouted her question. Stewards rushed forward and in the ensuing fracas both women were arrested, but not before Christabel deliberately sealed her fate by spitting in the face of one of the policemen, thus committing the first of a series of acts of civil disobedience for which the WSPU would become notorious in the years to come.[7] When Christabel was sentenced, Sylvia noted scornfully that 'Mrs Pankhurst, to whom her firstborn had ever been the dearest of her children, proudly and openly proclaimed her eldest daughter to be her leader'.[8]

In London, Sylvia was establishing herself in socialist circles. When she first took up her place at the Royal College she joined the Fulham branch of the ILP, and she seems to have enjoyed cordial relations with other members. Most of her activities were confined to her classes at the College, but after she settled in, she invited a few women students to her rooms on Saturday afternoons where they painted and took turns posing as models for each other.[9] The WSPU and suffrage activities were far from her mind until her mother decided to launch her movement in London.

Mrs Pankhurst made repeated trips to Parliament, lobbying for the vote and, in the process, interrupting Sylvia's quiet life by rushing in and out of her tiny flat on Park Walk. Sylvia occasionally accompanied her mother to Parliament, thereby gradually slipping into WSPU activities and neglecting her work at the College. Mrs Pankhurst was followed by Annie Kenney and Teresa Billington, who also stayed with Sylvia when they were in town. Seeing herself on the sidelines except where accommodation was concerned, Sylvia responded by founding the first London branch of the WSPU. The original membership consisted of Annie Kenney (now an organizer in London), Sylvia as honorary secretary, an aunt and her landlady. And when Mrs Pankhurst chose to direct her own energies toward mobilizing London, she asked Sylvia to book a hall from which she could formally launch the WSPU on a large scale.

With Keir Hardie's help, Sylvia hired the large Caxton Hall but Mrs Pankhurst was far from pleased when she found that her daughter had selected an auditorium which, because of its size, might prove an embarrassment rather than the moment of triumph which she had anticipated. Again, Hardie came to the rescue. He had earlier introduced Sylvia to George Lansbury, a budding politician in London's East End. Now Hardie and Sylvia turned to Lansbury for help in filling the hall mostly with poor women from Bow and Bromley who attended more for the refreshments than the political message. At this time too, Hardie introduced Sylvia to the Irish playwright, George Bernard Shaw with whom she began a long correspondence.[10]

On one of Mrs Pankhurst's early visits to London, Hardie introduced her to the wealthy socialists Emmeline and Frederick Pethick-Lawrence. While Annie Kenney was commuting between Manchester and London, Emmeline Pankhurst persuaded Mrs Pethick-Lawrence to take over the finances of the growing London branch of the WSPU, and until Mrs Pankhurst and Christabel arrived, Emmeline Pethick-Lawrence worked closely with Sylvia and Annie Kenney to build a solid organizational base for the movement. At her first meeting with Sylvia, Mrs Pethick-Lawrence saw her as a young woman whose 'face had the roundness and the smoothness of a child. In contrast to her childish face was the outer hardness of her character... she had a strong will, trained to endure.'[11]

Sylvia continued nominally in charge of the London WSPU office until, for reasons unexplained, she resigned her honorary secretaryship —despite her mother's instructions that she should stay on until the headquarters moved from Manchester to London. When Christabel graduated in the spring of 1906, with first-class honours, she immediately joined her mother in the move. Soon after the elder sister arrived in the city, she put an end to the use of East End women as demonstrators, an act that Sylvia deeply resented: Christabel believed that

Parliament would be more impressed with a 'feminine Bourgeoisie' than a 'feminine proletariat'.[12] Thus began the breach between Emmeline and Christabel on one side, and Sylvia on the other. Sylvia remained loyal to her father's socialist principles which she now saw embodied in Keir Hardie. Hardie, in turn, had little to do with the drawing-rooms of the middle classes to which Mrs Pankhurst and Christabel found themselves increasingly drawn.

In spite of Sylvia's feeling about the shift away from working-class women, she did not immediately break with the WSPU—she took part in demonstrations, designed posters and banners and occasionally drew illustrations for *Votes for Women*, the official organ of the WSPU founded by the Pethick-Lawrences. Furthermore, in this period, Sylvia travelled round England, subsidised probably by the Pethick-Lawrences, visiting factories, mills and rural areas where women were employed. Her findings, together with her illustrations, were published in *Votes for Women*.[13]

Emmeline Pethick-Lawrence had chosen the WSPU colours of green (for hope), white (for purity), and purple (for dignity). Dresses were specifically designed, in these colours, with matching sashes or ties as accessories. In keeping with the quasi-military tone of the movement, badges were designed to be awarded for particular acts of valour. One, designed by Sylvia, was 'a miniature portcullis, bearing the broad arrow in purple, white, and green' which the ladies wore on their bosom when in full attire.[14] When she resigned from the secretaryship of the London Branch, Sylvia felt that she was literally squeezed out of her rooms in Park Walk. She had, by that time, lost her scholarship and was virtually penniless. She claimed not to have received a salary from the WSPU, but she must at least have had travel expenses. In any event, she found new rooms on the Embankment and fell into what appears to have been a deep depression. She describes herself as 'racked with pain' at the time; but Keir Hardie turned up, helped her unpack, and took her out to dinner, thus restoring her rapidly to good spirits.[15]

Christabel remained at the centre of her mother's universe and became increasingly popular—in Sylvia's words, 'idolized by hundreds, perhaps thousands'. And although Sylvia later claimed they never quarrelled,[16] elsewhere she wrote with a tinge of bitterness that, 'I detested her incipient toryism. . . . [but] I admired her, and took pleasure in her, as I had done since we were children together in Russell Square'.[17] In fact, from childhood Sylvia had consistently resented the achievements of her sister. But outwardly, at least, the Pankhursts appeared united. The latent trouble was rooted in their parents' favouritism. Neither Sylvia nor Adela had the temperament readily to accept second place and act as a mere supporter, although Adela was only briefly in the movement, as a paid organizer. Both retained their socialist convictions and, perhaps as a form of rebellion, acted on them in ways that annoyed Emmeline and Christabel in their search for political identity.

Sylvia's first experience as a militant suffragette (as opposed to the non-militant suffragists) came in the autumn of 1906. Some WSPU women on trial had been summarily sentenced without what Sylvia regarded as a proper hearing. She went before the trial judge to protest. The court was crowded and the judge was occupied with another case. He ordered her out of the courtroom. Sylvia then attempted to speak to passers-by outside the court, somehow believing this would alter the situation of women already sentenced. Although Sylvia had lost her voice and could not speak, she was nevertheless arrested for using abusive language and for obstruction and sentenced to fourteen days in the third division of the women's prison, the section reserved for common criminals.[18] This experience seems to have triggered her total conversion to the cause.

In prison, and perhaps for the first time, Sylvia came into contact with women from a very different social background. Between 1905 and 1914, 34,915 women were imprisoned in England and Wales: some were foreign, some very young—girls pregnant and destitute, or nursing mothers. There were old women, recidivists who would return repeatedly throughout their lives, drunks; the mentally retarded; and finally the inevitable large contingent of prostitutes. As the militant suffrage movement gained momentum, numbers of middle-class women swelled the prison population and became a hidden part of the statistics of the British prison system.

At the time Sylvia was arrested there were no female inspectors to monitor arrangements in women's prisons but two years later, in 1908, Dr Mary L. Gordon was appointed an inspector for much of the period that Sylvia was in and out of prison. According to Dr Gordon, the women she encountered were 'injured, either by paralysis of initiative, or distortion of point of view, by false envisagement of their individual problems, by perversion of attitude, or by emotional conflicts and mental illness'.[19] She referred to the suffragettes and their complaints about prison life in contrast to those made by their fellow prisoners. Prison work, according to Gordon, was not drudgery or hard labour, at least to women who normally worked on the outside. Some worked in the laundries, others in the kitchens; some scrubbed floors, or shovelled coal into the furnaces. There were lighter tasks, too, such as polishing furniture or dusting. For middle-class women like Sylvia, Christabel and their mother, accustomed all their lives to servants, even light tasks may have appeared demeaning, if not arduous. Prison food seemed to them unfit to eat. For the poor it was nourishing—studies revealed that many gained weight during their prison sentence. Gordon wrote: 'In so far as the coarse food and clothing is a punishment

(*left*) WSPU poster designed by Sylvia Pankhurst

(*below*) Sylvia Pankhurst coming out of Holloway Prison after early imprisonment

to the well-brought-up prisoner, it perhaps equalized things a little' between them and the less privileged prisoners with whom they had to live.[20]

Sylvia's education began in the Black Maria which took her and her fellow prisoners to Holloway prison. 'Some of the women in the van were shrieking words I had never heard before,' she recalled; but they were words she would surely hear over and over again in the years to come.

Once at Holloway, they passed through the rites of prison reception. They bared their breasts for a brief and perfunctory examination by a male physician (British prisons then had no women doctors). At a later stage, they handed over their clothes to the prison authorities. Perhaps the most uncomfortable moment for the middle-class women of the WSPU was the bath ordeal. It was a 'miserable place with piles of dirty clothing heaped on the floor. . . . The baths were indescribably dirty', and Sylvia shuddered at stepping into water 'clouded with scum of previous occupants'.[21]

After the bath, each woman selected a prison outfit from the piles of 'dark, chocolate-coloured serge' on the floor and pulled shoes from a rack. Sylvia, unlike her mother and sister, had never been concerned with her appearance. Beyond a genuine horror at the baths, she reported much of the rest as a sociological experience. Next, Sylvia entered the third division alone, where creature comforts like meals sent in from the outside were not allowed, while her sister suffragettes went off as a group to the second. Her greatest discomfort was the unfamiliar conditions and unknown rules. The mattresses and pillows were filled with 'some kind of shrub' and seemed 'hard and comfortless as stone'. The cell contained a single sheet and blanket, inadequate for warmth. Prison routine was frightening—a matron banging on the door demanding her 'pint' (mug) to serve a meal of oatmeal gruel and water. Sylvia, as 'No. 12', slipped into anonymity along with so many others.[22] After breakfast came chapel, when the prisoners lined up in rows to hear the chaplain lecture them on the plight of sinners.

Sylvia differed from her mother and sister in her reaction to prison life. They were intent on the cause, and their memoirs say little about the experiences of prisoners—indeed, Christabel was only imprisoned three times in her career as 'prime minister' of the movement. The queenly Mrs Pankhurst, who was sent to Holloway almost as often as her second daughter, once mentioned hearing a wrongly accused woman in childbirth, but Sylvia thought that most of the human tragedy passed her mother by. She placed emphasis on the uniform she was forced to wear, while Sylvia recorded her impressions of the 'shrunken forms of frail old grannies', their 'withered faces', or the 'tense, white looks and burning eyes of younger women'.[23]

In the third division, Sylvia could have no visitors. Her days were routine but empty. She cried at her loneliness and sorrow for her fellow prisoners. The only book in her cell in the first days was the Bible, and its print was too small to read. The total experience, 'the haste, the lack of privacy, the character of the food, the want of exercise, the solitary confinement . . . told their tales on most prisoners, producing digestive and other disorders'.[24] Gordon's prolonged study reveals, however, that this was not the case with the majority of prisoners.

After a week Sylvia was moved to the first division and treated as a political prisoner. Here books, better food and companionship were available. Keir Hardie sent her books and a note of reassurance. Hardie (along with a peer in the House of Lords) registered parliamentary complaints about the treatment of the prisoners. Long after Mrs Pankhurst and Christabel had turned against Hardie and attacked him, and despite criticism from his own party of his commitment to votes for women, his belief in the movement and his love for Sylvia kept him in the forefront of the agitation for their cause.

While Sylvia was in prison she wrote poems to Hardie. A few survive, undated, but were clearly written before her most militant phase and after she reached the first division, where she sometimes had sketch-pad and pen. On the pain of separation she wrote 'how surely I looked away from you'; and she longed for his caress, and to feel 'your kisses on my mouth'.[25] To be locked away from the world of activity was an ordeal for Sylvia, as it was for the many women protesters who were to follow in the pre-war years. Her love for Hardie and his failing health increased the burden. It took courage for him to get in touch with her directly in Holloway, and he was grateful that she could turn her loneliness into love poems for him to read on her release. For her, their love was a source of strength in confinement:[26]

> When grey days come I do not mourn the sun,
> Dear face so fond to me
> Dear sturdy neck that my arms love to twine
> Curls that are white before their time
> Dear healing hands, dear breast
> To which I cling and sob my sorrows

Despite her yearning for Hardie, Sylvia's first act on her release from Holloway was to hasten to the press to publicize her experience. It had been WSPU custom to play down prison conditions and focus attention on the movement itself. Independent as always, Sylvia broke with her sister's policy and talked with journalists about prison conditions. 'I found the Press eager for news from Holloway; I gave dozens of interviews and distributed my sketches for publication. Probably even Christabel would now feel content that there was no danger of losing the Votes for Women trail in a quagmire of prison reform.'[27]

This first formal breach with Christabel's policy served notice that Sylvia had to be kept at arm's length if the goals of the WSPU were to take precedence over her own.

Fenner Brockway (later Lord Brockway) recalled all three Pankhursts when they were working together in the WSPU. Sylvia, he thought, 'might have been the daughter or the wife of any working-class person . . . there was a little bit of the artist about her. . . . Her clothing just flung about her.' Christabel had a slim figure, was well dressed and 'attractive but cold'. She could 'move an audience but . . . not by human emotion as much as calling them to battle'. Sylvia, conversely, acted and spoke from the heart. Brockway once found her speech 'almost inspired . . . not logically prepared but with emotion on the reason why women should have the vote'. As for Mrs Pankhurst, he remembered her voice was 'like music . . . it would throb like an organ'. Her lectures were 'reasoned but also filled with some emotion and passion'.[28] Sylvia blended her mother's passion with still more emotion, leaving logic to Christabel.

Helen Fraser, a journalist and WSPU member who knew all of the Pankhurst women in London, gives another insight. She described Mrs Pankhurst as 'nice looking, dressed well in good taste' and 'a very good speaker, not superb, but extremely good'. She remembered Christabel for her taste in clothes (fashionable and expensive) and as a 'complete little autocrat' with a 'one-track mind'. Mrs Pankhurst 'would never have been a militant suffragist on her own, if she made the decision': she idolized Christabel. And Fraser quoted Stella Cobden-Sanderson, daughter of Richard Cobden, the nineteenth-century free-trader: 'Mrs Pankhurst would walk over the dead bodies of all her children except Christabel and say, "just look what I have done for the cause".'[29] But, Fraser added, one admired Mrs Pankhurst even when disagreeing with her.

In Parliament, votes for women continued to be an issue: Keir Hardie and other members of the ILP unsuccessfully tried the route of a Private Member's Bill—it was talked out.[30] Hardie's interest in the women's suffrage movement brought problems within his own Party, where he insisted on supporting the WSPU in Party speeches and in the *Labour Leader*. Philip Snowden, a friendly ILP member and a supporter of women's suffrage, agreed with Ramsay MacDonald and others that Hardie had led the ILP too far into the feminist movement. Sylvia was the beacon for his commitment but, within the Party, it was generally believed that Hardie was under Emmeline's spell. But there were tensions in the ILP beyond the suffrage issue. Some members associated certain financial irregularities within the ILP with Hardie, and the younger members were jockeying for leadership. Hardie threatened resignation from the leadership. He had in fact planned to hold on for another year only when, in the spring of 1907, he became seriously ill. He suffered probably from nervous exhaustion and may have had a slight stroke. At first a friend, Frank Smith, nursed Hardie in his rooms at Nevill's Court, but later he was moved to a nearby nursing home. Sylvia visited him regularly, but his recovery was slow and eventually he returned to his home in Cumnock for prolonged rest. From St Thomas he wrote to Sylvia: 'I feel as though I had passed through fire and water and a long valley of bitterness . . . I prayed, I longed. I cried . . . to be more stollid [sic] and self-contained. I feel I am now.'[31]

Hardie supporters and sympathizers—though none from the ILP—raised money to send him on a trip around the world to regain his health. If he and Sylvia corresponded during his months abroad, the letters are lost. He may briefly have broken off the relationship with her. Joseph Fels, an American philanthropist, went with him and recalled that he was totally immersed in the places he visited, including South Africa, Australia and India from where he set off a flurry of protest in the British press by his outspoken criticism of British policy, supporting, as he did, Indian independence. On his return he wrote a series of articles on India for the *Labour Leader* and published these as *India: Impressions and Suggestions*.[32]

In Hardie's absence, Sylvia continued her suffrage activities. She spoke at by-elections, supporting the candidate most likely to work for votes for women; she drew illustrations (which were rarely published) and wrote articles for *Votes for Women*. In Christmas 1907, she joined her mother and Christabel for a brief holiday, but the experience was unhappy in part because she received a letter which left her 'unable to control my restless misery in the face of their cheerful chatter'.[33] Sylvia's tendency in autobiographical writing to identify emotionally with a range of past memories suggests that even in the late 1920s, when she wrote *The Suffragette Movement*, the memory of that letter brought to mind the sharpness of the pain she felt at that time. It was probably from Hardie, and must have hinted at separation. His return in March 1908, however, brought him back into her life, and their love affair soon began again.

Another problem entered Sylvia's life when Harry arrived from Scotland, his apprenticeship with a builder having ended abruptly, leaving him penniless and with nowhere to go. His health was frail, and the family decided to send him to secretarial school. Sylvia and Christabel bought him a much needed pair of glasses—against their mother's eccentric opposition—and put him to work for the WSPU in his free time. Now all four Pankhurst children were immersed in their mother's organization—Adela, unhappily so; Sylvia, contributing in her independent way; Christabel, supreme in command; and Harry, dutifully chalking slogans on pavements and, as his father had done before him, standing on a soapbox on street corners, speaking to passers-by.[34]

Harry, however, soon left to train as a professional gardener in a commune founded by Joseph Fels at Mayland in Essex. In 1910, as his mother was about to embark for America, he came down with infantile paralysis. Sylvia later described Harry's illness and her mother's response in venomous terms:[35]

> So ruthless was the inner call to action, that, finding her son thus stricken, she persevered with her intention. It must be added that she would thereby have the opportunity of earning money which might be needed for her boy, but there was never a moment of doubt as to where she should be substituted—on the platform or by the bedside of her son. The movement was paramount. She left us two together, not knowing what might be his fate.

The sisters nursed their younger brother during the several months of worsening illness. In Sylvia's view, he was overworked and maltreated at the Fels Farm and her mother's lack of concern was inevitably responsible for his decline in health.[36] However, she gives another insight into Mrs Pankhurst when Harry died after several months of pain. 'His mother was broken as I had never seen her; huddled together without a care for her appearance, she seemed an old, plain, cheerless woman.'[37] Sylvia wrote a loving tribute in *Votes for Women*, removed her belongings from the Embankment rooms, moved to Linden Gardens, and 'there endeavoured to gather up the broken threads of my life'.[38] Emmeline's brother, Herbert Goulden, again stepped in to help his sister, paying Harry's funeral expenses and buying his cemetery plot.[39]

While Harry was still apprenticed to the Fels Farm, the WSPU was involved in increased militancy—mass demonstrations and repeated, though unsuccessful, deputations to the Prime Minister. Frederick Pethick-Lawrence donated a vast sum for a Hyde Park demonstration to take place in June 1908, a demonstration that was designed to be the largest and most successful to date. The WSPU opened shops all over London featuring the now familiar white, green, and purple and mass-produced banners for decoration. Contingents came from all over Britain, with groups of notable women at the head. A quarter of a million people were expected, but the *Times* reported an actual number that might have been three times that. Sylvia's group from Chelsea, Fulham and Wandsworth was 7000 strong, and she joined nineteen other speakers on the rostrum. Other women of note included Mrs George Bernard Shaw, the second Mrs H. G. Wells, Mrs Thomas Hardy and a delegation from the Fabian Society (although without the Society's leading lady, Beatrice Potter Webb). Among the male supporters were Bernard Shaw, H. G. Wells, Keir Hardie and a journalist, Henry Nevinson.[40] The demonstration showed a new level of acceptance by the audience. Speakers spoke without fear of harassment, though

Miss Sylvia Pankhurst, Mr. Lansbury, and Miss Daisy Lansbury.

Bow Militants

Christabel was heckled by a group of youths. In the past, the suffragettes had often been attacked by young rowdies. Mrs Pankhurst frequently suffered verbal abuse and had once been severely beaten; Sylvia herself had also met vigorous intimidation.[41]

The problem was to find a tactic that would move the government to act. One possibility was to go further in the direction of mammoth demonstrations like that in Hyde Park, and the Pethick-Lawrences continued in that direction. In 1909 they sponsored a gigantic suffrage fair at the Prince's Skating Rink in Kensington. The object was to raise funds and publicize the WSPU, but the sheer size of the event was also meant to put subtle pressure on the government. They asked Sylvia to design decorations for the event, including hangings 150 feet wide by 250 feet long to cover the walls of the huge hall. She in return recruited some of her former fellow students from the nearby Royal College of Art, and they set to work, with Sylvia drawing the basic designs and others completing them in the hall itself.

The design was essentially a decorative frieze on the theme 'They Who Sow in Tears Shall Reap in Joy', and Sylvia later regarded it as the most significant of all her works as an artist, as did many others. Again the designs drew inspiration from the work of Walter Crane and William Morris; Sylvia used Crane's style of lettering in bold, large and straight lines alongside Morris's more ornate style for other design motifs and the flat tree effect that marked some of her earlier designs.[42] It was unfortunate that Asquith, the Prime Minister, stayed away: Sylvia included a dove carrying an olive branch for his sake.

Asquith at the time was more concerned with the issue of Irish Home Rule than with votes for women. Labour, allied to the Liberals and against the Conservatives, were divided on the issue of enfranchisement. The Conservatives were also divided on the issue, but they had been out of power since 1906. Sylvia—looking beyond the women's issue, which was contrary to Christabel's position—supported Irish Home Rule. (On this subject she and Asquith were in agreement although he would have regarded her support as beneath contempt.) Later, in 1914, when she had her own suffrage society, she led a delegation of working-class women to Parliament to lobby in favour of Home Rule as well as votes for women. The group was intercepted by the police, some were dispersed, and Sylvia was arrested.

Until 1908, militancy had been successful in focusing public attention on the women's goals, but it had not convinced Asquith's divided government. After 1908, according to Martin Pugh, 'militancy became a prop of the WSPU as it had to keep momentum going.'[43] By 1909, despite increased militancy, the WSPU and the Pankhursts had fallen from the headlines. In 1910, hopes were raised when a Round Table Conference was held on a Parliamentary Bill which would have given votes to some women under certain conditions. The participants failed to agree and nothing came of the proposals. But the idea that another bill was under discussion was enough to restore confidence among some women that action might be taken that year.

Over 4000 peaceful demonstrations were held between May and November 1910. The suffrage societies, all briefly united, busied themselves organizing demonstrations, marches and meetings. Their aim was to impress upon Members of Parliament that they represented the majority of women in the country and to win the vote from a position of strength.

When Parliament reassembled in November a suffrage amendment was added and passed by a majority of 167. It appeared that after long years of struggle and personal sacrifice the women would get the vote during 1911. At least, that is how it appeared outside Parliament.

One of the major inhibitions denying women the vote was fear of their numbers. Because women outnumbered men in the total population, men in Parliament—of all parties—feared that women would upset traditional voting patterns. Liberals believed they would vote Conservative; Labour feared they would vote Liberal or Conservative; and Conservatives, many of whom were in principle sympathetic, believed the Lords would throw out any Suffrage Bill in any case. Supporters had to compromise on a Bill which limited the franchise to female property owners—a small segment of British women at the time.

But even a limited Bill did not reach the statute book in 1911. In November, Asquith announced that during the coming session, he would introduce an electoral Reform Bill. When asked specifically about votes for women, Asquith replied that his views on the subject were well-known. By ignoring women, and casting his play so as to incorporate competency as a criteria, he infuriated even the most peaceful of the suffragists. Mrs Bernard Shaw, one of the mildest of suffragists, best expressed the furore when she said Asquith's speech filled her with 'an impulse of blind rage . . . the vilest male wretch who can contrive to keep a house of ill-fame shall have the vote, and that the noblest woman in England shall not have one because she is a female'.[44]

The WSPU leadership experienced the same blind rage. Having been double-crossed by Asquith after a long and peaceful truce in which the women were all but assured of the vote, Christabel abandoned all pretence of supporting either government or politicians. Some doubted the wisdom of her new strongly militant tactics, as they had doubted the wisdom of her tactics in the past. In 1908 she had been sentenced to Holloway after unsuccessfully defending herself in the famous Bow Street trial.[45] Charles Hands of the *Daily Mail* knew both Christabel and her father. He doubted Christabel's ability to handle her own case in any event, and recalled Dr Pankhurst's defence of some dockers on strike, which resulted in 'heavier sentences than they would have received' because of his provocation in the courtroom. He feared that Christabel would do the same.[46] Among her followers, however, Christabel was lauded for her brilliant defence; by 1908 Christabel was the acknowledged leader of the WSPU.[47]

With Christabel in prison, Emmeline Pethick-Lawrence invited Sylvia to take over the movement's direction from the Pethick-Lawrences' rooms in Clements Inn. At that stage, in December 1908, the other non-militant suffrage societies invited the WSPU to participate, peacefully, in a meeting with David Lloyd George who was speaking for the government. Sylvia promised to treat Lloyd George fairly, but lacked real control over Christabel's following. The WSPU delegation occupied the front row and, on signal and without Sylvia's knowledge, threw off their coats and appeared in prison dress. A violent brawl ensued, involving the women and Liberal stewards. Sylvia used the incident to obtain favourable press publicity for the movement, but the incident further divided the two sisters.[48] Sylvia had moved too far into the limelight, and Christabel resented her emphasis on violence: 'She told me on her release that too much fuss had been made about the violence; she was ever a stoic in such matters.'[49]

The conflict was partly a personal matter between sisters, but it grew out of large constitutional issues of WSPU organization that originated in 1907 when Teresa Billington, Mrs Charlotte Despard and Edith How Martyn had left the movement, and the WSPU ranks had closed behind them. The issue was one of principle: whether there was to be democratic or autocratic direction over the organization. The Pethick-Lawrences told Mrs Pankhurst to scrap the constitution so that they, and Christabel, could run the organization autocratically from Clements Inn. That might have met with general support, but in fact Mrs Pankhurst was away from London much of the time. The real autocrat was Christabel, and 'dissension in the ranks' came to Mrs Pankhurst's attention. She decided that Teresa Billington should be expelled.[50] Billington and others immediately formed the equally militant Women's Freedom League.

The next split was with the ILP. Christabel and Mrs Pankhurst abandoned their old allies, including Keir Hardie, because, according to an embittered Sylvia, they wanted to swell their ranks with a large non-affiliated group of women and 'to attract the support of wealthy Conservatives opposed to Labour views'.[51] (Actually they wanted the freedom to approach individual MPs on the matter of the vote whatever their party affiliation.)

Sylvia and Adela both opposed scrapping the constitution, but they continued in the ranks until 1911 when Adela left the movement. Sylvia showed her devotion to the cause by undergoing repeated prison terms and the ordeal of forced feeding. Christabel was criticized for remaining relatively unscathed by the rigours of prison and later for running away to Paris to escape the pressure. The argument in her defence was that, like any general, she stayed behind the lines to draw up strategy. Geraldine Lennox, an activist on the WSPU battle-front, wrote that it was the 'wish of all that she should go free, for on her depended everything. . . . she was the balanced, clear-sighted brain of the Movement.'[52] Someone, indeed, had to keep the administration going. Mrs Pankhurst and Christabel were both conscious that the WSPU was *their* organization, so it was natural for them to agree between themselves as to their respective roles. Mrs Pankhurst was fifty at the time of the hunger strikes: it was more dramatic to publicize her ordeal. Sylvia could always be relied on to dramatize the role of the younger generation.

Mrs Pankhurst visited America in 1910, leaving behind her dying son. But the money she raised was sufficient to give the increasingly troublesome Adela her freedom from the WSPU and send her to Australia where she remained for the rest of her life.

American women were then involved in their own struggle for the vote and many of them looked to the British women for guidance as well as support. Emmeline captivated her large American audiences and the American press alike. F. W. Bullard described her in the New York *Herald* as a 'cultivated, quiet and thoughtful matron' whose face was 'framed with hair streaked with grey'. At the lectern he saw her manner change—'It is when the eyes wake into action one begins to see the woman who led the suffragettes all these years.' He found her speaking voice 'disappointing' but with 'good quality' and 'an occasional throb of earnestness'. Her speech, however, was considered brilliant. It was a well-argued, logical statement of women's goals which drew in part from her past experience as a Poor Law Guardian and her concern for destitute women, as well as women of her own class. She linked the actions of British suffragettes to past revolutions. 'It was ungentlemanly, it was rude to cut off the head of Charles I. It was very discourteous to seize the tea in Boston Harbour. And it was very unceremonious of us to interfere with the golf game of Mr. Asquith . . . ' (The suffragettes had attacked Asquith on a golf course earlier, sending the Prime Minister off the course while the women chanted slogans.) With this kind of intellectual discourse, Emmeline was judged as an able woman, at times 'magnetic' in her appeal.[53]

Emmeline set a WSPU record for travel. The fees she received, after expenses, were her own, but a large percentage of the receipts were said to have been donated to the WSPU. No one in the family ever seemed to have enough money; and Mrs Pankhurst was not adept at managing hers.

Both Emmeline Pankhurst and Christabel turned down overtures from publishers to write their accounts of the suffrage movement.

Neither had time, and Sylvia doubted if her mother could sit still long enough to write a book. When Sylvia was contacted, she jumped at the chance. *The Suffragette*, her first book, grew out of her series of articles in *Votes for Women*. It was a dry, generally factual account of the movement up to 1909. The book appeared in England in 1911 just as the militant movement reached increasing pitch after the failure of the second Conciliation Bill. It sold well. An American edition followed almost immediately and was circulated among suffragists there. *The Times* reviewer called it a 'spirited narrative' and *TP's Weekly* found it admirable and descriptive of the movement 'through which women are striving to express constructive social reform'.[54]

Following the success of her book, Sylvia visited America in 1911. Emmeline accompanied her to Southampton, but Sylvia crossed the Atlantic alone, and was entertained on board by the ship's doctor. Light flirtation apparently led the doctor to expect Sylvia's favours. She later recalled to Keir Hardie that 'it was silly of me to let the doctor take me to his cabin . . . and I was quite lucky that the incident wasn't more unpleasant'.[55]

On her arrival in New York, Sylvia learned that the booking agent had organized only two engagements. Her first lecture in New York, however, brought wire-service press coverage, and, as a result, 'telegrams for dates poured in'.[56] The lecture was arranged by Harriet Stanton Blatch, who had been a suffragette in England, and was now one of the leaders in the US. Mrs Pankhurst had left New York only a few weeks before her daughter arrived, and there was some question among the Americans as to how many English women they should invite to speak, especially as the lecture fees drained American suffrage resources. Blatch answered the criticism with proof that British suffragettes were good business: after deducting her own fee, Mrs Pankhurst had raised 1000 dollars in one lecture alone.[57]

Sylvia's first lecture was 'a great success'.[58] Introduced as 'the daughter of the greatest political leader the world has ever known', she gave a well-received talk, and 'her youth and earnestness' (she was then thirty) were impressive. The *New York Times* described her as 'a little rosy-cheeked slip of an English girl' who 'held the attention of a distinguished New York audience . . . for over an hour and a half'.[59] Sylvia recalled the experience as traumatic. Although she had lectured in much of Britain, she was nervous as she approached her first American audience.

That feeling never completely disappeared. At the end of the month, in Kansas City, her appearance was that of 'a pair of big blue eyes looking appealingly from a child face, the soft brown hair parted in the middle and gathered back with a total disregard for prevailing fashion . . . one could not help comparing her with a frightened child' until she started talking, and then 'she caught and held attention whether or no'.[60] In Cincinnati her audience was spellbound.[61]

In all, Sylvia spent three months in the States, travelling the length and breadth of the land. She wrote long letters, sometimes of twenty or more pages, to Keir Hardie, describing the people with whom she stayed, her meetings, and the varieties of the American landscape. She renewed an acquaintanceship with Alice Paul, founder of the American Women's Party, who had been active in the WSPU first in Glasgow, and later in London. Paul, too, had seen the inside of an English prison, having been convicted of rock-throwing during the early days of militancy. Sylvia also had the pleasure of meeting the pioneer American social worker, Jane Addams, at Hull House in Chicago.

She described a professor she met at Bowdoin College in Maine as 'a most unlearned man. He would have made an excellent ploughman'. The people in New Brunswick were 'snobs to say the least of it'. In St John's, New Brunswick, Sylvia first heard rumblings of possible war with Germany. She dutifully wrote to Hardie of the possibility of war, paying scant attention to its implications. She enjoyed meeting Max Eastman and lost her head to the Lewisohn sisters who were working with the poor on New York's East Side. Pittsburgh was full of 'great wealth . . . squalid poverty of new immigrants, the nightmare of industrialism'. Indianapolis, one of her stops *en route* to Chicago, was ugly—'Oh what a tragedy mankind has made of this poor land. I wish I'd never seen this ugly place.'

While in Chicago, Sylvia stayed with her paternal uncle. She found her American cousins unbearable—the 'wife is absolutely empty-headed'; the house was full of 'cheap and hideous things. Sylvia took the wife to dinner at Hull House where she was 'a dead weight' the entire evening.[62]

'Longing for the sight of' Keir Hardie, Sylvia made her way to St Louis where 'sordid' streets and 'pornographic' shops shocked her. But she addressed 600 businessmen after lunch and 'held their attention for an hour'.[63] The precise itinerary of this first trip to America is uncertain. In *The Suffragette Movement*, she combined both the 1911 and 1912 trips into one account, and some cities were visited twice—Chicago, Indianapolis, Milwaukee, Boston and New York, for example.[64]

In Massachusetts she visited the women's reformatory at Framingham. Here she was invited to decorate the chapel, but lack of time and funds to cover her costs forced her eventually to turn down the commission.[65] However dismal her picture of America at the time of her first visit, she wrote in *The Suffragette Movement* (1931) that 'some day I might become an American citizen'.[66] Her private thoughts on emigration at the time were quite different. She was concerned about 'How many thousand of my own country people have left home and kindred to build up a new life in this new world and have found here a grave for their hopes and perhaps their souls.'[67] These are hardly the sentiments of a prospective citizen.

From Boston Sylvia wrote to Hardie of her overwhelming loneliness. She was a stranger to her surroundings, travelling alone, and undergoing the kind of culture shock common to a first visit overseas. She told him she tried not to rebel at separation, acknowledging that 'It's my own making, in a way, this time'. In an apparent attempt to ensure his sympathy she added 'perhaps I ought not to think I have less than I want'. In this letter, too, she turned to extrasensory perception as a way of bringing them together. 'If such a thing as a wireless telegraph can exist surely there isn't anything unreasonable in being able to communicate human thoughts. . . . when people have discovered the full power of thought transference . . . when we can understand . . . we shall just sit back and look at each other . . . and as much as I love my Darling's arms about me, sweet as kisses are, I rather think it would tend to make us less dependent on those kinds of things.'[68] While Hardie had long been interested in the after-life, had attended seances, and was something of a mystic, in this case he preferred the pleasure of physical contact.[69]

Sylvia's return to England was an anti-climax. There was little for her to do and despite her long, lonely letters to Hardie, his presence never really met her needs for outside involvement. After the failure of the second Conciliation Bill, the suffrage movement had become increasingly militant. In 1911 Ethyl Smyth captured the martial spirit of the women with 'March of the Women', which was adopted as the WSPU anthem. Immediately after Asquith announced his intention to introduce a Reform Bill for men only, a Cabinet minister made a provocative speech in which he explained the government's position: 'In the case of the suffrage demand there has not been the kind of sentimental uprising' which accounted for the passage of the Reform Bill of 1832 or later violence in 1867 during the Hyde Park demonstrations.

That speech acted as a lighted match to a fuse. It set in train the first serious attack on private property. Christabel, with the connivance of the Pethick-Lawrences, planned a campaign of window-breaking throughout the West End of London. As a result, Mrs Pankhurst and the Pethick-Lawrences were arrested and charged with conspiracy and Christabel fled to Paris. The Pankhursts then decided to embark on massive destruction of property and virtually took the movement underground for the purpose, advising members to avoid arrest.[70]

Mrs Pankhurst's first reaction to Asquith's treachery had been a telegram to Clements Inn: 'Protest Imperative.'[71] Christabel, before her flight to Paris, sought willing volunteers to renew the militant campaign. Deputations tried unsuccessfully to meet Asquith, and several men and women were arrested when, in frustration at not seeing him, they turned against the police. The campaign of violent militancy was underway. Sylvia, working on a display for the WSPU Christmas Fair, did not join in the violence this time because she did not want to risk another gaol sentence.[72]

Soon after Christmas 1911, again almost in her mother's footsteps, Sylvia embarked on her second trip to America. This time she had trouble with speaking engagements, as the American public had cooled towards British suffragettes with news of increasing violence in England. Eventually, Sylvia's agency organized engagements across the country taking her as far as California, where she 'fell in love' with the 'orange trees, the colours of the mountains backed by their purple clouds' and the warm sunshine. She travelled to New Mexico, which she described to Hardie as 'the strangest most desolate country.... Sometimes at rare intervals, we passed a cluster of sun-dried huts on a little strip of cultivated land—an Indian reservation; sometimes a dark Indian, his figure crouching low, would be seen swiftly running across the sand— the desert, all that civilization had left to them.'[73]

She caused a stir in Nashville, Tennessee, when she spoke at Fisk University, then a segregated black school. She failed to understand, as she wrote to Hardie, and later repeated in *The Suffragette Movement*, that the criticism she received in the white-controlled press was not because she visited Fisk, but because she advocated the vote.[74] In Nashville, she also visited a women's prison and described the wretched condition of a black woman in the act of being locked up. She wrote to Hardie: 'Poor little nigger, poor little woman, her misery, her terror, her cries, as they dug their fingers in her flesh and dragged her mercilessly'.[75]

On this trip, too, she missed Hardie. She waited vainly for his letters which seemed too few. She longed to be in his arms and away from it all.[76] Too often the suffragettes were viewed as man-hating spinsters or unhappily married women who vented their frustrations with their husbands through militancy in the suffrage movement. Sylvia had many weaknesses, but she also had a tender, loving nature which, like many women similarly involved in the franchise struggles, reflected the duality of the times in which they lived.

On her long trip from the West to the Midwest, Sylvia experienced the extreme discomfort of winter cold. Her train from Fargo, North Dakota, to St Paul had no heating—the pipes burst, and she lost her hot water bottle. To Hardie she wrote that 'Some said it was one hundred twenty below zero, others said one hundred forty degrees—no mind, it was cold!' To make matters worse, there had been no suffrage society in North Dakota, so her visit would have been wasted had she not urged them to organize one 'on the spot'; which they did: 'The Votes for Women League of North Dakota.' Despite her freezing train carriage, Sylvia wrote a long descriptive passage detailing the natural beauty she encountered on the long trip east: 'There are great wide plains covered with spotless snow and woods with last year's leaves brown upon them still. The sky is pure andl limpid blue, pale grey, and latest, palest gold with the bright . . . sun sinking lower and lower.'[77]

One of her greatest thrills on her second trip to America was her visit to Milwaukee, where she spent several days in the company of the socialist mayor and his progressive councillors. In letters to Hardie, she extolled the virtues of the mayor, but when he gave a short speech calling for votes for women—which was the purpose of their meeting—Sylvia thought he lacked 'enthusiasm'.[78]

On the whole, her American tours gave her a new maturity. She was moved by the open blue skies she saw in the American West, horrified by the blight of eastern cities. She wrote, in 1911 and 1912, of the dangers to the atmosphere from the massive industrial complexes in Gary and Indianapolis in Indiana, and in Pittsburgh. She spotted the approaching pollution at Lake Michigan. She met and was touched by the tragic conditions affecting Indians and blacks. By the time she returned to England to resume her militant protest for the vote, she had foreseen what Americans themselves would begin to realize some fifty years later.

4

A Radical Organization
of her Own

I have always believed in the simple statement that we are all
members one of another. If you take a woman and torture her
you torture me...
  —George Bernard Shaw, quoted in *Women's Dreadnought*

Sylvia returned to London in March 1912, to find the police had raided
the WSPU offices; the Pethick-Lawrences and Mrs Pankhurst had
been arrested and were awaiting trial; and Christabel was in hiding in
Paris, under the pseudonym Amy Richards. In Sylvia's absence the
government had become more oppressive than ever in its efforts to
stop the violence of the WSPU after the failure of the Conciliation Bill
in November 1911.

Sylvia saw Christabel's absence as her opportunity to head the
movement. Disguising herself as a nurse, she slipped across the Channel to visit her sister and get her sanction. Christabel, however, had
chosen Annie Kenney as her deputy; and furthermore, she advised
Sylvia 'to keep out of harm's way as there was no need of [her] services'.[1] Sylvia was 'not of the same opinion', but there was nothing she
could do. Under Annie Kenney, and at Christabel's direction, the
WSPU continued to attack private and public property.

Thinking she could still find a niche in the WSPU leadership, despite Christabel, Sylvia went to Ireland where there was an active and
militant suffrage society. A kind of frantic energy seemed to come over
her at this time, possibly because her public image depended on her
being seen as one of the WSPU leaders when she had, in fact, been
dropped altogether from her sister's plans.

Sylvia arrived in Dublin, unannounced and unexpected. She later
wrote that she assumed WSPU headquarters had notified the local
WSPU group of her intentions, which were to lead a suffrage group to
the prison where Irish women were being forcibly fed.[2] She approached a
surprised group of suffragettes who were then meeting in Phoenix
Park, and taking the rostrum, she called on them to follow her to the
prison. A mêlée broke out when the police arrived, and Sylvia found
herself in Dublin jail, where an angry local WSPU official reproached

her for jeopardizing the official's work.[3] Someone arranged to release her, but only on the condition that she take the next boat back to England. 'Opposition from those to whom I should naturally look for support' left her no alternative.[4]

Her return to London coincided with yet another and surprising split within the WSPU. Christabel, or Mrs Pankhurst, or both, had decided to dispense with the Pethick-Lawrences because of their opposition to an increasing underground militancy. The Pethick-Lawrences had supported window-breaking and milder action, but as the WSPU women rampaged and violence increased, they became critical. When thousands of pounds' worth of damage resulted from one particularly heavy siege, the Pethick-Lawrences and Mrs Pankhurst refused to pay the fines. All three went to jail. Emmeline Pethick-Lawrence followed the now almost traditional WSPU pattern of going on hunger-strike in Holloway, and was forcibly fed. Frederick, in the men's jail, also refused to eat and was forcibly fed five times.[5] During their imprisonment, however, the several insurance companies involved banded together to seize and auction the Pethick-Lawrences' country home, because it was impossible to sue an organization (in this case, the WSPU), and the insurance companies were forced to make restitution for the damage done by the WSPU militants. In the final analysis, the Pethick-Lawrences, who opposed the increased militancy, were forced to pay its toll by sacrificing their health and through their wallets. But it was not the Pethick-Lawrences who engineered the split with Mrs Pankhurst and Christabel. The breach was unexpected and is hard to explain. Some believed that Mrs Pankhurst was jealous of their close relationship with Christabel and wanted to get her daughter back under her wing. Others, including Sylvia, believed that Christabel was bent on further violence and did not want to involve the Pethick-Lawrences further.[6]

Christabel's earlier divisiveness in Manchester, when she split with Eva Gore-Booth and Esther Roper and the North of England Society to join her mother in the rival WSPU, cannot be ignored. In her single-minded campaign for the vote, biting the hand that fed her was no more offensive than cutting the ties that initiated her into the suffrage movement. In fact, Sylvia, in *The Suffragette Movement*, blamed Christabel for the split,[7] while in the biography of her mother she placed the blame directly on Mrs Pankhurst.[8]

At the time neither Emmeline nor Frederick Pethick-Lawrence was ready to accept the decision without protest. They insisted that Christabel come to England to discuss the matter further. Christabel arrived in disguise, but the conflict was not resolved. The Pethick-Lawrences were only just out of jail and needed rest, so they went to Canada and later visited Christabel on the Continent, hoping she had changed her mind. Instead, they found her adamant. When they found that compromise was out of the question, the Pethick-Lawrences remained in the larger movement by keeping and editing *Votes for Women*, while Mrs Pankhurst and Christabel took complete control of the WSPU. Mrs Pankhurst found new offices at Lincoln's Inn.[9] Sylvia was not involved in any negotiations between the two factions and was shocked at the turn of events. She maintained friendly relations with the Pethick-Lawrences and submitted articles periodically to *Votes for Women*.[10]

Emmeline Pethick-Lawrence came to believe that Mrs Pankhurst and Christabel gradually 'lost all sense of touch' with the outside world during the years 1912–14. She and her husband had advocated autocracy over democracy, but in retrospect they saw that 'all dictatorships carry within themselves the seeds of their own decay'.[11] Mrs Pankhurst's comment on the split was: 'When Divorce has been decreed, it was best for the two parties never to meet.'[12] This too had been her view in her earlier break with her father.

The break with the Pethick-Lawrences came when the WSPU was in its most militant phase. Middle-class women and increasing numbers of working-class women pursued their crusade against the government with vigour. Christabel launched her own paper—*The Suffragette*—from her exile in Paris. Annie Kenney, in disguise, travelled back and forth as messenger between England and France. In the first issue of *The Suffragette* Sylvia's byline appeared over news of her campaign in London's East End.[13] Christabel seemed willing to let Sylvia start a branch of her own among the slum-dwellers, despite the apparent break in relations between the two sisters. In fact, Christabel could do little to control Sylvia's actions from Paris, and knowing she was in the East End away from the centre of activities may have suited Christabel's purpose.

The East End of London had long been a port-of-entry for an unwanted immigrant population. Jewish immigrants escaping from pogroms in Eastern Europe settled in Whitechapel, where they experienced a still hostile, but less overt, anti-Semitism and took employment mostly into the sweated work of tailoring, bookbinding and shoemaking. Italian immigrants moved in, swelling the already crowded tenement houses. The Irish, already a settled community of sorts, made room for the newcomers. Ben Tillett had organized the Irish dock-workers into a union, and from a position of power among the powerless, the Irish practised ethnic exclusion in their union. But no matter what their origin, or trade, the immigrants huddled together in the slums, sharing the common problems of poverty and discrimination.[14]

Soon after Sylvia opened her campaign in the East End, the area became the scene of a major political battle dominated by the WSPU from Lincoln's Inn. Increased militancy brought fewer women to jail because they were under orders to avoid arrest: but for the unlucky numbers captured there were more hunger strikes and increased incidence of forced feeding. Reports of forced feeding were met with increasing horror both by the public and in the Commons. George Lansbury, by this time Member of Parliament for Bow and Poplar, joined Keir Hardie and Philip Snowden in questioning repeatedly the Prime Minister about the practice. Lansbury was temporarily suspended from the House for using the unparliamentary term 'blackguard' in addressing the Prime Minister in the Chamber during debate —a somewhat typical outburst. Bruce Glasier described him at a Labour Party conference around the same time: 'Lansbury's conduct during the discussion on any topic in which he is concerned is always abominable. He interrupts, shouts, squabbles with the chairman and all around him.'[15] Lansbury resigned his seat and announced his intention to run again—this time on the issue of votes for women.

The announcement, in November 1912, brought Mrs Pankhurst and Christabel into his camp. Grace Roe and Annie Kenney returned to the East End to run his campaign. Sylvia was ignored. In the end, the campaign was dominated by the WSPU, and the candidate overshadowed by the issue. The traditional working-class men in Lansbury's constituency, accustomed to wielding authority in their own homes, were not the voters to charge with returning an all-out suffrage candidate. The fact that Lansbury lost the election by 751 votes surprised no one but Lincoln's Inn and Lansbury.[16] Although Christabel heralded his defeat as a 'personal triumph',[17] she immediately lost interest in his political fortunes.

But Sylvia and Lansbury became allies of a sort over the next few years. She frequently consulted him in her attempts to help her East End constituents; and he worked with her organization, as did his wife and daughter (and briefly, his son), especially in their wartime work in the East End. He ran the *Herald* (later the *Daily Herald*) and often published Sylvia's writings. In these years, when she was frequently in trouble with the government, he ran sympathetic stories about her. Sylvia and Lansbury were also united in their stand for adult suffrage —that is, universal suffrage to include disenfranchised men as well as women. Adult suffrage was still a contentious issue. Many of its opponents used the issue as a ruse for not supporting votes for women. The Women's Trade Union League, headed by Margaret Bondfield (a future Minister of Labour) and Mary MacArthur, took refuge in their call for adult suffrage, because 'it was important to keep within the labour movement and avoid alienating other unions'[18]—men in other unions who opposed giving middle-class women the vote (or, in the case of some, *any* women).

Increasing militancy on the part of the WSPU drove more recruits over to the opposition, including men and women from all walks of life. The National League for Opposing Women Suffrage, founded in

1910–11, grew out of an earlier organization started by women in opposition to the vote, and included such well-known men as Conservative Lords Curzon and Cromer; prominent women in the professions; married women; and, as might be expected, members of the royal family. In 1912 another Conciliation Bill was defeated in Parliament. This time, political considerations aside, the blame could be laid squarely at the feet of militant suffragettes, whose massive destruction of property alienated many previous supporters in the House.[19]

In her isolation, Christabel became increasingly radical and unrealistic as to how her orders affected the British public. It was at this time that she also began to display strong anti-male prejudices. After Lansbury's bid, which she saw as useful for the WSPU, she eliminated any joint efforts with men's parties. Subsequently, she published a series of articles in which she linked votes for women with white slavery and venereal disease—both long-standing concerns with socialists quite apart from the franchise issue.

In Christabel's eyes, all the evils which affected women were related to their inability to vote. Men in general, and not only Asquith and the politicians, became her target. The series, later published in book form as the *Great Scourge*, carried long diatribes against venereal disease. Although this was a problem, her facts were questionable—she claimed, for instance, that 75–80 per cent of men were affected with gonorrhoea.[20] (It is unclear whether she meant all men, or just British men.) The Pankhurst tendency toward polemics emerged naturally, but it was not effective in inspiring a larger audience to action. While her motives were pure enough, the slogan 'Votes for Women and Chastity for Men' was unlikely to win any male converts.[21] It did win over some of the clergy.

The split with Lansbury and the decree that men were no longer welcome in the WSPU led to the final break between Christabel and Sylvia. Sylvia continued her drive in the East End in competition with 'General' Florence Drummond and Annie Kenney from Lincoln's Inn. Lansbury occasionally helped her raise funds for her marches to Westminster and used his considerable influence to muster supporters. On one occasion, he obtained money from his long-time friend, the American soap philanthropist, Joseph Fels, to pay for a suffrage parade from Poplar to the House of Commons.[22]

Sylvia also accepted Lansbury's invitation to speak on the same platform in the Albert Hall in support of striking Irish workers, thus openly defying Christabel's rule prohibiting public appearances with men.[23] This act of defiance symbolically broke the tenuous threads which held her East End branches with Lincoln's Inn. It is difficult to unscramble the complications surrounding this last split within the WSPU ranks. Neither Mrs Pankhurst nor Christabel wrote about the controversy. Sylvia's own account is obviously biased. Inertia at

Lincoln's Inn, arising from Christabel's exile and Mrs Pankhurst's repeated imprisonments, probably kept Sylvia nominally within the circle longer than other circumstances would have allowed. Adela claimed that the WSPU militant tactics had driven her out as early as 1911.

Adela's own experiences with Christabel that year have some bearing on Christabel's paranoia. When Adela realized that militancy was out of control, she warned Christabel, but her older sister ignored her advice as she tried to ignore Sylvia: 'I never regarded them [militant tactics] . . . as more than the drum that attracts attention and brings up the crowd to hear the message . . . I knew all too well after 1910 we were rapidly losing ground. I even tried to tell Christabel . . . but unfortunately she took it amiss—was even persuaded I was about to found a counter-organisation with myself as leader.'[24] Adela recognized that Sylvia had 'started a party', and added that Sylvia had invited her back from Australia to join it.[25] If Adela, on the other side of the world, recognized that Sylvia was moving out on her own, it could hardly escape Christabel in Paris. Given each of the Pankhurst's desire for publicity and Sylvia's special need to compete for her mother's attention, her behaviour at this time is more easily understood.

In the summer of 1913, the *Daily Mail* published an article suggesting that the WSPU was suffering financially from loss of membership and disorganization. The *New York Times*, suspecting that Sylvia was partly responsible for the leak, approached her and asked her to name her price for an article discussing the *Daily Mail*'s allegations. Sylvia asked a high fee—$350 (£72.90)—which the *New York Times* agreed to pay. When the article was finished, however, there was no reference to the WSPU. The entire article concerned Sylvia, her living conditions in the East End, and her most recent experience in jail.[26] If Christabel and Mrs Pankhurst also suspected Sylvia's involvement in the leak to the *Daily Mail*, they had far more reason to dismiss her from the WSPU.

Charges of poor administration within the WSPU were so frequent that Mrs Pankhurst had to confront the issue at a public meeting. Ill and only recently out of jail, she nevertheless revealed some interesting figures. At the end of June 1912, the WSPU had £152,000 ($760,000). A year later the balance was £141,000. This was curious, considering that the Pethick-Lawrences lost their country house when the WSPU refused to pay for damage caused by its members. In any event, the result is a double-edged moral issue: either Mrs Pankhurst should have come forward to save her old friends from financial embarrassment on her behalf, or she was withholding the truth about the size of the WSPU treasury.[27]

The first public acknowledgement of the Pankhurst family split came in November 1913. The *Daily Herald* noted Sylvia's presence on the platform with George Lansbury: 'Industrial rebels and suffrage rebels march nearer together'. By appearing with Lansbury in a public forum, Sylvia had broken Christabel's 'golden rule' which forbade suffragettes from being seen in public with men. Christabel reacted to the press report by publishing a quick denial in *The Suffragette* saying that Sylvia was present in Albert Hall in 'her personal capacity' and not 'officially representing the WSPU'. But she also allowed Sylvia to reply on behalf of the East London Federation of the WSPU in a way that made clear that Sylvia formed the policy of that branch, whatever her sister's instructions from Paris.[28]

This was only the tip of the iceberg. Christabel had protested to Sylvia that she, Christabel, had been invited first in any case (though how she—the fugitive in France—could have attended is problematical).[29] After Sylvia's reply in *The Suffragette*, she wrote more harshly, blaming Sylvia for having issued a circular explaining her role at the Albert Hall meeting: 'In a recent letter to me you referred to the fact that we do not ask you to speak at meetings. The reason for this is that it is essential for the public to understand you are working independently of us.' She continued: 'As you have a complete confidence in your own policy and way of doing things, this should suit you perfectly. There is plenty of room for everybody in this world, but conflicting views and divided counsels inside the WSPU there cannot be.'[30]

These two letters with their strongly critical references were the last from Christabel that Sylvia ever kept. She wrote about the split in *The Suffragette Movement* some fifteen years later, but her perspective by this time suffered not only from the anger she had felt at the time but also from the deepening rift in the intervening years. Christabel, on the other hand, still carried news of Sylvia's imprisonments in *The Suffragette* and maintained the surface appearance that there was no discord.

Sylvia took the argument to Annie Kenney and the other WSPU branches in a circular letter. She claimed that the WSPU had not drawn crowds at recent meetings and that this justified her having taken the opportunity to speak at a gathering of 10,000 at the Albert Hall. She went on to say that Annie Kenney and other WSPU members were also willing to speak at large meetings at any time. Kenney immediately wrote a note to all branches disassociating herself from that statement, and Grace Roe appended an official statement from Christabel denying any present or future connection with Sylvia or her East End organization.[31] Sylvia, always quick to overreact, issued her own press release. In fact, the only obvious support she lost was that of the Kensington branch of the WSPU, which had helped her to get started in the East End.[32] Even then, the honorary secretary wrote a personal note to Sylvia regretting the split and indicating her own private support.[33]

Mrs Pankhurst finally entered the argument through Rita Childe

Dorr, her American ghost-writer. Given Sylvia's constant striving to attract her mother's attention, the use of a go-between was tactically inept if it was not intended as a snub.[34] The split in the Pankhurst ranks soon became international news, reaching the *New York Times* just before Christmas 1913. Mrs Pankhurst lost patience when bad publicity threatened problems within her organization, and in an angry letter to Sylvia wrote: 'You are unreasonable, always have been and I fear always will be. I suppose you were made so . . . I am sorry but you just make your own difficulties by an incapacity to look at situations from other people's point of view different from your own. Perhaps in time you will learn the lessons that we all learn from life.'[35] It was quite clear whose side Mrs Pankhurst was on in the quarrel between the sisters, a fact which contributed much to Sylvia's behaviour in the following months.

Once she had entered the controversy, Mrs Pankhurst rubbed salt in Sylvia's wounds by writing from Paris to insist that Sylvia drop the word 'Suffragette' from the title of the East London Federation, claiming the name was the sole prerogative of the WSPU. The label 'Suffragette' had been applied to the WSPU by the *Daily Mail* reporter as a way of distinguishing the militants from their more conservative suffragist sister societies. Emmeline and Christabel submitted to her a list of more acceptable names for Sylvia's East End group; but Sylvia defiantly retained the name.

By February the press had contacted Christabel for her version of the split. She told the *New York Times'* Paris correspondent that Sylvia's band of militancy differed from that of the WSPU; which endangered only property, while Sylvia's endangered lives. The charge was untrue. What Christabel apparently had in mind was news of Sylvia's 'People's Army'. The press had reported in November 1913 that it had already signed up some 700 men and women prepared to 'do damage' when Parliament reassembled.[36] In fact, the People's Army had been recruited to protect East End suffragette meetings after the 'Cat and Mouse Act' was passed in 1913.

It had been nearly universal practice in the WSPU, in Sylvia's East End Suffragette Federation and in the Women's Freedom League for a woman to begin a hunger strike as soon as she was committed to Holloway. The government's response was the 'Cat and Mouse Act', by which the government proposed to abandon forced feeding but instead kept the women in jail until their condition appeared to be weakening due to self-starvation. They were then released on 'licence' to recuperate, but if a woman out on licence spoke in public she was rearrested. The purpose of Sylvia's 'Army' was to form a protective barrier around 'mice' who were breaking the terms of their licence by addressing suffrage meetings. The *Daily Citizen* ridiculed the army as 'athletic Amazons' with 'broomsticks' when it appeared in force to guard Sylvia and her followers.[37] The rhetoric surrounding the army was frequently that of violence, but in fact it was pure bluff and bluster, a publicity device designed by Sylvia.

Sylvia had also been criticized by members of the WSPU for portraying Christabel as a dilettante in Paris. Her second-in-command, Grace Roe, who visited her nearly every week, described her life there as lonely and burdensome, as she tried to run an organization and compile material for the *Suffragette* in exile. But Annie Kenney remembered with pleasure her weekend visits: 'Saturdays in Paris were a joy. We would walk along the river or go to the Bois or visit the gardens.'[38] The *New York Times*' correspondent observed that 'if the papers are to be believed, Christabel has taken a fondness for clothes and turned "into a perfectly charming woman".'[39] She was apparently anxious to end her exile and only stayed on to avoid being imprisoned on her return.[40] There is some truth in both allegations. Christabel was circulating in French political society and her past record did not indicate a penchant for jail. She was quoted as saying that she 'preferred to be seen only on the platform or in the Dock with sword never sheathed'.[41]

As Christabel strengthened her affinity with international politicians and journalists, Sylvia moved towards the working class. G. D. H. Cole thought that the elder Pankhursts treated Sylvia badly because she was first and foremost a socialist and some contemporary press commentary agrees.[42] There may have been a 'kind of inverted snobbism' in her identification with the poor, as Lord Brockway characterized it,[43] and her early reception in the East End was cool. Annie Barnes, one of Sylvia's early East End followers, recalls that Sylvia's neighbours were hostile at first, but when they saw that she was committed to both improving their lives and to winning the vote, 'everyone she knew came to love her'.[44] Sylvia's magnetism soon brought more followers than detractors. Once she settled in, she organized and led demonstrators to Downing Street and to Parliament, and held weekly meetings in Victoria Park off Old Ford Road.

Hers was not the first reform movement situated in the East End. General William Booth had founded his Salvation Army there. Annie Besant had led the 'Match Girls' Strike' in 1889, with support from Mrs Pankhurst during her socialist days. Social workers moved into the slums by day, and out by night. One-third of the population of East London was living in such a state of chronic destitution that the largely volunteer social services could barely scratch the surface of the poverty. Overcrowded tenements, lack of sanitation, often no running water except one tap centrally located for an entire household, were not uncommon to many living there.

In Bow and Bromley Sylvia found conditions differed from those she had described for the mill girls and pit head workers in England's industrial north. Her artist's eye had captured the emptiness in these women's lives, but she was not inclined to sketch women and children of the East End. Even before she moved to Bow, she visited the area from her rooms nearby, walking through streets full of garbage and human waste. She saw the dim, yellow gaslights glowing faintly in the dense fog near the London docks. She saw children standing on street corners in rags. She saw beggars reaching out of dark doorways, while the streets teemed with the stunted slum dwellers, drawn from lack of nourishment and the fatigue of grinding poverty. It was to cure these ills that Sylvia launched her utopian campaign for the vote in East London.

She set up branches in the East End modelled on those of the WSPU elsewhere. From Bow she sent organizers to Stepney, Hackney, Bethnal Green and Poplar. The membership of each branch elected officers. The officers, in turn, met once a week at headquarters, with Sylvia as honorary secretary and Norah Smyth as financial manager. Norah was soon to become treasurer. The total membership does not seem to have been large—by May 1914, Sylvia claimed eight branches in the East End, listing some 60 active members altogether. From the minutes of the ELFS, however, even that small figure seems exaggerated. Bow and Bromley, Sylvia's home base, was the most active, followed by Poplar, where various members of the Lansbury family were listed as supporters. The few followers were loyal, but most of the women in East London were too involved with the stringencies of daily life to afford either the time or the money for outside activities.[45]

Norah Smyth's father had died some years earlier, leaving her financially independent. It was her wealth that got the East London Federation off the ground and kept it running through many difficult moments. Sylvia, like her mother, had no financial sense; she plunged into new programmes, hired organizers and expanded her operation from a shoe-string campaign into a wide area, chiefly at Norah's expense. Sylvia maintained that she supported herself from outside sources during her East London campaign. She once told a visiting reporter that one of her 'principles was that a revolutionary should earn her own living'.[46] And indeed, she would sell some of her art—hastily executed works for the most part—to offset an immediate financial crisis. As a publicist, however, she succumbed to her flair for the dramatic when she described her experience with the East London Federation; for in practice, she was too occupied with public meetings and organizational matters, as well as her frequent jail sentences, to paint many pictures or otherwise earn an independent living. She lived on Norah's income and funds raised by her membership, with occasional donations from West End sympathizers.

With an organization of her own, Sylvia now had a platform from which to express her views, otherwise unavailable to her when she was on the fringes of the WSPU. She could promote her programme from

71

the soapbox, on street corners, in small 'at homes' among her East End constituents; sometimes she spoke in large hired halls. Frequently on Saturday afternoons, when more women were free from work, she spoke at demonstrations sponsored by the East London Federation in Victoria Park, near her headquarters on Old Ford Road. She seems not to have been much in demand in the provinces where her mother and other members of the WSPU travelled often.

It would be valuable to know the basis of Sylvia's beliefs, what motivated her to try to right the world's wrongs, what philosophical principles made her a pacifist as well as a suffragette or carried her through her career from pacifistic socialism to militant defence of a monarchy. For all her writing, however, Sylvia left little theoretical record of that kind. Her public statements were not so much reasoned arguments about why women should have the vote or about any other issue as emotional outbursts, designed to move her audience. Even *The Suffragette Movement*, which gave her a chance to deal with philosophical underpinnings, is a chronicle of events and adventures, many of them her own. She did not deal in depth or in detail with the ideological differences between herself, her mother and Christabel. Most of her public speeches were calls for unspecified action, like the meeting in Victoria Park where she told the crowd that they were 'fighting for free speech . . . but most of all for freedom from poverty and all its shameful consequences which was the lot of many women'.

It was in the East End that Zelie Emerson first became a significant factor in Sylvia's life. It is uncertain how she came to England and into contact with the Pankhursts. She was the daughter of a Michigan banker and industrialist. Her mother had known Andrew Carnegie in Pittsburgh before the family moved to Michigan.[47] In 1903/4 Zelie Passauent Emerson attended the University of Michigan in the College of Literature, Science and Arts. She did not graduate but came to London and joined the WSPU.[48]

Zelie and Sylvia had much in common. Zelie was two years younger; both had lost their fathers early in life—Zelie when she was twelve. Zelie's mother was active in local politics and was something of an eccentric. When young, Zelie had been short and heavy-set with brown hair, a shy manner, and eyes that 'disappeared in wrinkles when she smiled', which was often.[49] She had no sisters of her own and served as a faithful companion and friend of Sylvia from 1912 to 1914 and briefly later, in some ways taking the place of the remote Christabel. She developed what might be called a crush on Sylvia, but we have no way of knowing whether she was a lesbian, latent or active.[50] She died a spinster. There has been speculation that some women who were active in the suffrage movement were, indeed, lesbians. With a movement as widespread and as liberating as the suffrage movement, one would have no problem conjecturing that women (and men) of all sexual preferences were among its supporters.

East London *c.* 1912 (*from left*) Norah Smyth, Sylvia Pankhurst, Zelie Emerson

Norah Smyth, a tall, dark, thin, handsome woman, dressed in the liberated fashion of the period, wearing ties and dressing as much like a man as possible. This affectation in dress reflected the desire for emancipation and was common among the more liberated, especially those, like Norah, who could afford the new style.[51] On the other hand, both Norah and Sylvia came to accept what were for the time very advanced views on matters pertaining to sexual liberation. We know nothing about the complexities of their personal relationship. Norah never married. Sylvia herself was deeply in love with Keir Hardie in these years, and as Dame Ethyl Smyth later characterized her, if it had not been Keir Hardie, it would have been someone else. It appears that after her affair with Hardie ended she submerged herself in one crusade after another, and did not immediately seek a new lover.

Soon after the East London Federation became an independent society, Zelie suggested that it should publish its own newspaper. Sylvia agreed and launched the paper in March 1914, with herself as editor.[52] The paper was destined to be controversial from the start. The controversies began with the printer, who insisted on the right to suppress unverified accounts for fear of libel. Sylvia was remarkably stoic about the first few cuts, but soon found a printer in the East End who printed what she submitted, libel now being Sylvia's problem, not the printer's.[53]

The *Women's Dreadnought* usually comprised two pages, printed like the broadsheet newspapers then in vogue, with columns running down the full length of each page. Headlines did not reflect current affairs but issues dealing with the vote. Pictures and illustrations (usually not by Sylvia) appeared on the front page, and sometimes captioned illustrations inside. The weekly leader or editorial was written by Sylvia. It also carried announcements of suffrage meetings and various news items of concern to women in the East End, along with a growing coverage of international suffrage activities, including a brief note that Russia had extended property rights for women in 1914. While there were occasional references to Mrs Pankhurst and her repeated imprisonments, Sylvia began here her policy of ignoring Christabel which lasted the rest of her life. (She was, of course, mentioned in Sylvia's various writings on the suffrage movement.)

Zelie originally intended to use the paper as a freesheet to help recruit members, but the group soon voted to sell it for a halfpenny an issue.[54] In the beginning sales were low and subscribers almost non-existent. Some who remained in the WSPU subscribed out of an interest in Sylvia's work. As the Federation became better organized, it opened a campaign to sell the paper door-to-door in East London. Members of the branches were assigned the responsibility of canvassing their neighbourhoods, both for sales and for new members. The first edition of the *Dreadnought* announced a weekly print-run of 20,000. By the third issue, 21 May, 1914, total sales were listed as just over 100 copies, and pleas were being made to support the paper. Fund-raising activities included sales of baked goods in local Bow and Bromley shops and, on Friday and Saturday, stalls on the Roman Road which accepted goods baked by the Federation's members. Those women who were most active—mostly older women whose children were no longer a drain on them—took copies of the paper to underground stations, to sell them to passengers as they came and went from the trains. During the processions and demonstrations at which larger numbers of women were present, the paper was freely distributed as propaganda for the Federation as well as for the movement. As with other suffrage organizations, banners, badges, picture postcards and other paraphernalia identifying the East London Federation of Suffragettes were sold at the headquarters. Sylvia's 'Cat and Mouse' licence was raffled, each ticket costing 6d.[55]

One method of appealing for readership was through the columns of the *Dreadnought*. Realizing that her name drew her supporters, Sylvia concentrated on herself. Whenever she was in England, she wrote all the editorials, which often described her latest prison experience. But, knowing her audience was composed largely of the poor, she also wrote case studies of others in similar circumstances she met on her travels. In one article she described the potato pickers she had observed during one of her tours for the WSPU:

Following in the wake of the plough was a long line of women, stooping and bending over the furrows, groping with their hands in the loose soil, and gathering up the potatoes as they came . . . They were poor creatures, clad in vile shapeless rags, sometimes pinned, sometimes tied around them with other rags or bits of string. There were old, old women, with their skin gnarled and white sullen faces . . . every woman's eyes were fiery red . . . the woman's movement calls here as it calls all other women.[56]

Another tactic was to incite the East Enders against the police, whom many saw as their enemy: 'They said that you were roughs and anarchists,' she wrote, and 'that I was an anarchist and ought to have known better than to . . . play on your "evil passions". I said that you would all be ashamed to do their horrible work.'[57]

There is no record of how successful Sylvia's 'self-denial weeks' were, but she frequently asked her poor readership and supporters to deny themselves what meagre rations they had in order to support her paper and the Federation. This custom had been practised by the WSPU and its mostly middle-class supporters, but it was hardly practical in the East End. The fact that Sylvia could and did make such requests presents an interesting comparison between her stated goals to aid the downtrodden and her active interest in sustaining her own organization.

Little is known about the activists among her followers. Mrs Melvina Walker, who for a time wrote a column in the *Dreadnought* was listed merely as a Poplar docker's wife. She, along with Mrs Ives, Mrs Charlotte Drake, and briefly Mrs Payne, appear frequently in the Federation minutes, usually seconding motions made by 'Miss Pankhurst'. Occasionally they are cited as having introduced suggestions of their own.

Mrs Payne who lived close to the headquarters on Old Ford Road, worked with her shoemaker husband, making shoes in their home through outside contracts. It was to Mrs Payne that Sylvia went after one of her arrests when she was free under licence. The Paynes later figured in one of her wartime enterprises, the boot factory. Mrs Walker often spoke at public meetings, including suffrage demonstrations, spending one month in jail after a particular virulent speech at Limehouse Town Hall. Through her husband's work as a docker, Mrs Walker was able to bring the Federation to the notice of other dockers' wives; and, when Sylvia turned to communism after the war, Mrs Walker followed her, joining Sylvia on the pages of the *Dreadnought* in railing against Allied intervention in the Russian–Polish war in 1921. Mrs Payne and most of the older suffrage supporters dropped away when the organization veered to the extreme left.[58]

Mrs Drake gained ascendency in the ELFS, but the Federation was clearly under Sylvia's domination. The minutes indicate it was run on democratic principles under that domination, with suggestions at least coming from the floor, although most action was based on Sylvia's rhetoric.

The enthusiasm of Sylvia's following was as much an outpouring of frustration against the conditions of life in East London as it was a desire for the vote. Instead of staying in their dreary, overcrowded rooms where they spent their few off-work hours, the working-class women of the Federation distributed the *Dreadnought*, chalked pavements to announce future meetings and demonstrations, and generally became involved in activities that took them beyond their own narrow world. Sylvia identified with these women, their problems and their poverty, and, to that extent, she incited them to active rebellion against their lot of ceaseless deprivation. While much that she wrote in books, articles and, in particular, her newspaper, reflected her sense of melodrama and her increasing radicalism, Sylvia had a special charisma that attracted many East Enders, especially women, to her. In her personal relationships and on a one-to-one basis, empathy, sympathy, joy, were offered to those who came to her. Time after time people talked about her many acts of kindness and of her generosity—unheralded by her in print —which marked the woman behind the face of radical propagandist.

The People's Army drew many rebellious souls. Sylvia's, Norah's and Zelie's rhetoric of potential violence against Whitehall stirred the disenfranchised men and women to join the Army, to drill, and to 'arm' themselves more as a way of acting out their anti-authoritarian feelings than a sign of impending civil disobedience. Much of the propaganda for the vote and for the Army was designed to stir the women to an awareness that their lives could change. The traditional underdog, Sylvia reasoned, had to be prodded by whatever means. Her emotionally-charged speeches moved large audiences to respond with enthusiasm. But when the cheering stopped, other mechanisms were needed to keep the masses motivated. In 1914, one not very successful scheme Sylvia conceived was the production of a suffrage play, 'Liberty or Death of a Popular Uprising of the Vote'. By applying the revolutionary theme to the vote, she hoped both to entertain and to educate the audiences at the headquarters on Old Ford Road. But theatre was not a high priority for East Londoners, and her play, set in the East End with cockney characters, failed to draw audiences.[59]

Another of Sylvia's campaigns was the no-rent strike, copied from the Chicago garment workers. The object was not so much to harm the landlords as to awaken them to the cause of votes for women so that they in turn could influence Parliament. Whether landlords would actually have responded as predicted is doubtful, but, in the event, few tenants withheld their rent and the scheme collapsed. The concept, however, remained attractive; after the onset of war, one member wanted the East End to protest by staging a no-rent strike to express their displeasure at a capitalist war.[60]

With the paper circulating in much of the East End, the army drawing attention—much of it ridicule—in the press, and public meetings raising the consciousness of East London, Sylvia decided to tackle the local politicians. By late 1913 she had a considerable following of female and some male supporters. The Lansbury connection was still good and Willie Lansbury was active in her suffrage campaign. But the borough councils in the East End were not among her supporters. Councillor F. Thorne of Poplar accused Sylvia and her middle-class friends of having 'no more sympathy with the people of Bow and Bromley than they have with the people of South Africa'. And, he added, 'the late member from Bow and Bromley [Lansbury] who had put himself at the head of these women, reminded him of Don Quixote seated on an ass riding full tilt at a windmill'.[61]

The immediate problem was to get the use of council-owned halls for suffrage meetings. The borough council prohibited their use by the Federation and other suffrage groups on the grounds that the halls were being used for 'seditious purposes'. In retaliation, Sylvia lined up her followers and they paraded around the private homes of the borough councillors. One outraged councillor announced that he was prepared to turn a water hose on full blast if the women marched on his home.[62] The demonstrations failed in their purpose.

Then Sylvia brought in her Army. The People's Army stormed the Poplar borough council meeting, throwing stink bombs, bags of flour, stones and 'other missiles'. As the flour-covered councillors tried to free themselves of the mess, the women went wild and started pushing the men around. As the mêlée continued, the police were summoned, but they refused to enter the building. The socialist members with whom Sylvia had some rapport stood as a group and tried to repel the advancing women; but other, more timid councillors, including councillor Thorne, retreated. Unfortunately for Sylvia and her group, the attack on the councillors served to enforce the determination among the councillors that the women should not use their halls for suffrage meetings.[63] This was the only major skirmish in which the People's Army ever engaged.

But no matter how militant the East London Federation might be, the WSPU still received more publicity. Sylvia's mother was setting records for imprisonment during 1913. When Sylvia and Zelie were arrested for throwing stones at a bank's window, Mrs Pankhurst quietly paid Sylvia's and Zelie's fine thus securing their release.[64] Another incident, which did result in imprisonment, indicates that, despite her devotion to the cause, Sylvia was not above a certain vanity. She was sitting on a platform with Zelie, who was the first speaker:[65]

Zelie spoke . . . witty and engaging. I sat behind her, half numbed by the cold . . . and wondering how the damp cold would affect my throat, which had been troubling me of late, and whether I should be able to make myself heard when my turn came . . . As she stopped I was suddenly all alert. My voice rang loud and very clear.

After her speech, and with her audience enthused, Sylvia led some of them to an undertaker's shop in Bow. She reached in her pocket, took out a piece of flint, and flung it through the window. She was, of course, arrested, along with Zelie, who threw a stone at the Liberal Club a few seconds later.[66]

Sylvia and Zelie endured the confinement in Holloway in different but equally onerous ways. After refusing to eat for three days, Sylvia was forcibly fed. She tried to fight off the six wardresses and two doctors, but they overwhelmed her and she succumbed to the ordeal which she found degrading and 'shattering [to] one's nerves and one's self control'.[67] Rule 243A allowed them to wear their own clothes; and, according to Sylvia, she hid her art supplies in the folds of her clothing. But the lack of food and water, combined with the strain on her body from retching after each feeding, gradually wore down her strength and she could no longer use the materials. She was not allowed visitors, nor could she see Zelie. The doctors told her to exercise, but she refused to leave her cell without her friends. Days wore on, with always the same routine: doctors and wardresses arrived to force sometimes one, sometimes two, steel gags between her teeth. Someone would seize her and 'thrust a sheet' under her chin. She closed her eyes and set her teeth against the intruder, and then 'a man's hands' forced his way into her mouth with 'a steel instrument' puncturing her gums. This symbolic rape, carried out with superior strength, was always met by a writhing body which resisted for as long as possible the probing tubes until finally, giving way to the inevitable, it allowed the unwanted nourishment to enter.[68] Sylvia, like her mother and many other militants, seemed always to force herself through even more extreme tortures than the movement demanded—not only prison and hunger strikes, but thirst and sleep strikes as well.

Three weeks and three days after Sylvia started on this hunger strike she was finally allowed to see Zelie, who had become emaciated. 'I saw a little figure moving towards me, so changed from her plump rotundity . . . with pinched, wistful face'.[69] Through various forms of deception, Zelie had managed not to eat for fourteen days before she was discovered. Then, she too, had been forcibly fed, though Zelie had been fed through a nasal tube, which the wardresses slipped into her nose and forced down her throat. One suffragette nearly died when the tube went into her lungs by mistake, causing them to fill with liquid and producing pneumonia.

If Sylvia was surprised by Zelie's loss of weight, the sight of her shocked the American, especially her bloodshot eyes with the veins 'ruptured by forcible feeding'[70] which were sunken into a drawn, lifeless face and her gaunt frame which was barely able to support its remaining weight. Zelie, who had attempted suicide at one point, had taken part in some of the prison activities while Sylvia sat in solitude, and had discovered a way to post letters to the outside world, a discovery she promptly shared with Sylvia. Sylvia immediately wrote to her mother, from whom she was still estranged: 'I am fighting . . . I resist all the time. My gums are bleeding.'[71]

Was it to win the vote that Sylvia put herself through such torture? Or were her motivations mixed, including especially at this time, the need to top Christabel in her mother's affections? In Mrs Pankhurst correspondence during this period, she stressed her deep concern for her second daughter. Apparently, that concern was shared with people other than Sylvia, who continued to punish herself ceaselessly.

Sylvia also wrote to Keir Hardie. It appears that Mrs Pankhurst, and almost certainly Christabel, as well as other members of the WSPU close to the family, knew of Sylvia's affair with Keir Hardie.[72] But the relationship was at this time losing its earlier glow. Fenner Brockway believed that Hardie was tiring of Sylvia's repeated forced feedings and subsequent attempts to publicize her hardships. Or perhaps her involvement in the movement at this juncture had closed off that remaining shred of personal life—love for a single individual which was eclipsed by a sort of Messianic complex, and love for the group of fellow sufferers. Sylvia was aware that her sister's newspaper had begun systematic attacks on Hardie, although Mrs Pankhurst claimed to have no knowledge of it at the time. Despite the waning of their love affair, Sylvia deplored the way her mother and sister had turned against the Labour leader. After the WSPU had turned its back on Hardie, Emmeline, on visiting Sylvia at her sickbed, feared meeting him. Relations would have been particularly tense because of Mrs Pankhurst's earlier attachment to Hardie, and the recent attacks on him by Christabel. But, in replying to her mother's questions, Sylvia responded with finality: 'He will not come again.'[73]

Sylvia's letters to her mother seem to have won her a degree of sympathy. We know that Mrs Pankhurst was concerned about Sylvia's nervous problems which had plagued her since her father's death. Sylvia herself wrote that while she was in Holloway she feared that her 'nervous system would be completely deranged'.[74] And, in a letter to a supporter, Mrs Pankhurst wrote sympathetically of her daughter: 'Sylvia is going on well. Nerves quieter and stronger but it will be some time before she recovers . . . Her eyes which were very blood shot are getting better. How could they do it?'[75]

Despite Sylvia's condition, her mother stayed with her for only two or three days, accompanying her to her convalescence, before going on to 'spend the weekend with Christabel in Boulogne'. Yet Sylvia's condition was indeed weak, as described by a WSPU member called to her bed in the nursing home: 'The sight of two great gobs of blood in the thin drawn face moving restlessly from side to side on the pillow, is a memory that even the horrors of war—and I saw many in France in

1914–1915—have had the power to dim. Sylvia suffered much. So did the mother who knelt by her bedside. . . . The other's face was as the face of one being crucified.'[76]

Almost immediately after her recovery, Sylvia broke the provisions of her 'Cat and Mouse' licence and appeared on public platform. She and her mother were both in and out of jail under the Act, and both took pleasure in appearing in disguise and being whisked off by supporters minutes before the police arrived, or being captured and returned to jail. On one occasion, one of Lansbury's daughters was mistaken for Sylvia, was arrested and taken to the police station, only to be released later after the case of mistaken identity was proven. On another occasion, in order to evade the police, Sylvia allowed her cheeks to be rouged (make-up was against her feminist principles), and a pillow stuffed in her skirt gave her the impression of an anonymous pregnant woman. These incidents were rare moments of amusement for Sylvia's followers.[77]

Sylvia made nine visits to Holloway during six months of 1914. Often in the violence which accompanied a police rush for Sylvia, members of her organization were injured trying to protect her. The police carried truncheons and bludgeoned their way into a crowd. Violence soon followed many public meetings which Sylvia addressed (an interesting parallel to the violence which succeeded speeches by pacifists Mahatma Gandhi and Martin Luther King Jr. later in the century). On one occasion, when Sylvia was speaking illegally, a policeman fractured Zelie Emerson's skull.[78] After a few days' rest in London, Zelie was packed off to America, so ending her radical commitment to the British suffrage movement.

Between bouts with the police, time spent in Holloway and administrative tasks at Federation headquarters, Sylvia and Norah sometimes found time for a few days' travel on the Continent. On one occasion they slipped out of England undetected and went to Denmark, where Sylvia rested for a few days. They then went on to Norway where Sylvia had accepted a speaking engagement, but she was too weak from recent fasts in prison, and had to cancel her lecture. As she never missed an opportunity to be in the public eye, she must have been very weak indeed. She did, however, muster the strength to write an article describing her ordeal by forced feeding.[79] In Finland, she met other suffragists. Back in Copenhagen, and stronger, she spoke, much to the delight of an American sympathizer who was present and described the occasion: 'The daily papers could not enough tell their surprise to find this great youth and charm joined with so much eloquence; behind her words, even in the timbre of her voice, one knows the deepness of her conviction which had quite an irresistible effect on the listeners.'[80] The change of scene and rest renewed Sylvia's vitality and she and Norah were able to return to Old Ford Road and her many activities in the ELFS.

Sylvia Pankhurst with Johanne Munter, Copenhagen 1913

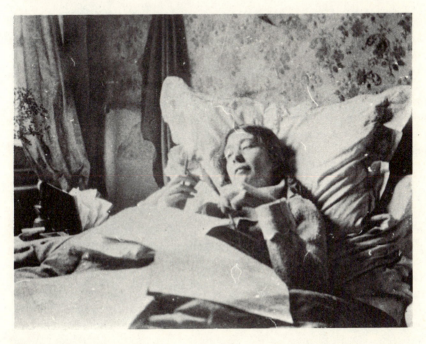

ESP recovering from hunger strike in the East End, July 1913, in the house of Mr and Mrs Payne, 20 Ford Road, Bow

Sylvia's *Dreadnought* articles, published at this time, were often informative, but they were not always accurate. She developed a habit in the *Dreadnought*, which she retained for the rest of her publishing life, of using statistics which suited her purpose, without troubling to verify their accuracy and rarely, if ever, mentioning their source. Although she did not begin her activities in the suffrage movement as a propagandist she gradually assumed that role after she began publishing her own newspaper. She seemed to believe that more was better. By producing figures which were high (or low depending on her need at the time), she felt that she was aiding her cause of the moment and it is in that light that most of Sylvia's inaccuracies must be judged. She was always in too much of a hurry to be calculating and clever in her attacks. She wrote and spoke from emotion, her statements supported by fragmentary pieces of information collected along the way.

At this point she also began a practice of damning the British government which she carried into future crusades. In the matter of the vote, of course, the government was at fault; but, when she travelled abroad, she always found something to praise in preference to the English equivalent. In Copenhagen, she told the American correspondent that it had been her wish 'when I got out of Holloway . . . to get to a country where men are kind to their women, and here I am now'.[81] On a brief trip to Hungary, where she addressed the Hungarian suffrage society, she 'discovered' that the government there was superior to that of Britain in its care of destitute children.

Back home, in March 1914, Sylvia placed her health in a very precarious condition. Again in Holloway she set a record for self-abuse. She went without food, water or sleep until she was so weary and weak that when she was allowed out under licence, she was unable to stand without assistance. She had committed herself, however, to a planned march on Westminster Abbey, the intention of her East End Federation being to seek a 'higher authority than the Government' for help in getting votes for women. She was placed on a stretcher and carried by eight men and women including Henry Nevinson from her East End headquarters to Westminster Abbey. The spectacle of her East End followers looking 'worn with toil and want of food' and walking beside the stretcher bearing the suffragette, 'very white and ill', was such that many onlookers joined in the procession. By the time Sylvia was carried past Charing Cross, about 800 men and women accompanied her. At Westminster Abbey the pilgrimage had grown to about 3000.[82]

The Reverend C. A. Wills, an Anglican priest from the East End, was in the procession. Finding that Westminster Abbey was 'full' and the doors locked, Reverend Wills held a service on the steps. Since the object of attention, however, was Sylvia, Wills called for everyone to listen to her weak call for votes for women. Lying on the stretcher, pale and exhausted from the strain of the journey across town, Sylvia roused herself for only a brief moment: she was heard to say that her crusade for the vote was centred on the need for women to 'get better conditions for themselves' before her voice faltered and an ambulance was summoned to take her back to Old Ford Road.[83]

In April Sylvia was again arrested in violation of her licence. She returned to Holloway, where she once more pushed her body to the limit by refusing food, water and sleep for six days. Her release followed the same pattern, only this time she was carried by stretcher to Victoria Park, where she spoke briefly to her assembled followers without interruption or arrest. In Victoria Park she said the campaign for the vote was nearing victory, and she pledged that she personally would do whatever was necessary to bring Asquith to submission.[84] Her editorials in the *Dreadnought* pursued the same theme. But despite these continued threats and campaigns the government remained unmoved.[85]

Sylvia wrote Asquith an open letter published in the *Dreadnought* stating her intention to return once more to jail where she would give up food, water and sleep, even if released, until such time as the government acquiesced to her demands:

> Do you realize that since I was arrested for a speech to the people who had come in procession from East London to Trafalgar Square, in which I asked them to go to your house in Downing Street, to hoot you for your refusal to give votes to women, I have spoken at dozens of immense public meetings when liable to re-arrest by the police and in each case the general public . . . have rallied around me to a man and a woman, to protect me from the police. . . .
>
> The Suffrage deputations that you have received hitherto have been composed of well-to-do middle and upper-class women. The women down here . . . are keenly desirous of stating their views . . .

Then Sylvia warned Asquith that if he failed to receive her group, she would return to jail and 'I will not merely hunger strike but when I am released I will continue my hunger strike at the door of the Strangers Entrance of the House of Commons and will not take either food or water until you agree to see my deputation.'[86] A picture of Sylvia in the same issue had the caption 'Is She to Die?'. A few days later she was again in jail, but Asquith made no attempt to rescue her. Inside, Sylvia kept her promise; outside, crowds of supporters picketed Holloway, carrying placards with the *Dreadnought* caption. For the moment, much of the drama and attention of the movement focused on Sylvia.

Asquith, who had not responded publicly or privately to Sylvia's threats, was unmoved. In a letter to Venetia Stanley, he wrote:

> Another small complication is that Sylvia Pankhurst, whom McKenna is letting today out of prison—she has been 8 days without food or drink—proposes to continue her 'strike' to the point of suicide, either at her own

home or until I receive a deputation of East End suffragists! I don't want, if I can help, to secure her the martyr's crown, but *que faire?*[87]

In fact, public opinion took Sylvia's side in this instance, not strictly because of her actions, but because of the considerable publicity which had resulted from the forced feeding over the past year. In their first issue of the *New Statesmen*, the Webbs (who were not sympathetic to the suffragette campaign) called for the government to stop the inhuman practice. They wrote that numbers of women, 'including Sylvia Pankhurst, have undergone in prison a course of severe physical punishment to which they have not been sentenced. . . . Everybody knows that the women are going to get the vote' so forced feeding was unnecessary.[88] Later, the Webbs argued convincingly that the Cat and Mouse Act, which allowed women out on licence, and then put them back in prison when they appeared on public platforms, was illegal. What precedent, they asked, was there for returning women to jail without another trial?[89] The well-educated, and mostly left-of-centre readership of the *New Statesmen*, wrote letters to the editor in which they uniformly opposed forced feeding, even though most did not support the militant suffragettes. In protesting against the practice, one reader may also have thrown some light on the increasing violence falsely attributed to the WSPU. An old cannon at Dudley Castle had been fired, and out came a banner proclaiming 'Votes for Women'. The WSPU was immediately held responsible, but further investigation showed it to be a prank of male students at nearby Birmingham University.[90]

A survey of letters to the editor written in 1913 and early 1914 indicates that, if sympathy for an individual woman was offered at all, Mrs Pankhurst seemed to be the main focus of public concern.[91] She had been in and out of prison; she had fasted and been forcibly fed; and she, as leader of the WSPU, dominated whatever headlines there were on this issue. In the public's view, Sylvia took a very back seat to her mother, despite the *Dreadnought* and its almost single concentration on her.

We have no way of knowing what motivated Sylvia to endure the psychological and physical torture to which she subjected herself at this time. It was certainly her intention to force the Prime Minister into action; she may have wanted to compete with her mother for publicity on the larger stage; or, she may have hoped to rekindle her mother's sympathies. The Pankhurst iron will, combined with an emotionally unbalanced and weakened condition, helped her through the strike at Holloway. But the government paid no attention. On her release, she demanded she be carried to the House of Commons, where she lay on the steps and began her vigil.

As *The World* reported it:

It was a strange gathering, one of the strangest that the movement has yet brought together. And, in the middle, lay the frail-looking fighter who meant at any cost to see this thing through. And she saw it through. It took nearly two hours. With her in the car were a nurse and a woman friend; by the door stood (Nevison) with a bowed head, someone from Parliament who was sympathetic would come to bring a message or carry one back for her; a dramatic turn was given . . . when, on receiving the final message that the Speaker would not allow her even the Shelter of St. Stephen's Hall, she was carried to the little door at the side of the main entrance and laid there on the steps. Friends were swept aside by the police, only detectives and MP's were allowed to go close to her, to stare down at the prostrate figure on the stone steps. . . . When the news came that the Prime Minister would see the woman the following Saturday, women and men, West and East, broke into wild cheering . . . [92]

In dealing with Sylvia's dramatic challenge, Asquith could not help but remember that, barely two weeks earlier, the suffragette Emily Wilding Davison had died on Derby Day after throwing herself under the King's horse on the race track. But he acted as he had all along when challenged: he refused to see her, although he did finally agree through an intermediary to see her deputation. Sylvia regarded this as a victory. Indeed, in later years she claimed that in forcing Asquith to receive her East End deputation, she had set him on the path towards granting votes to women.[93] This, of course, was purely fantasy on her part; and nothing ultimately came of his meeting with her group.

Sylvia came to believe later that it was Christabel who prevented the action, and who ultimately deprived women of the vote in 1914. According to her published account, Sylvia met Lloyd George at Downing Street as soon as she was well enough to discuss the issue and after her deputation had met with Asquith. It was through Lansbury's intervention that she met Lloyd George, and Lansbury was present during her interview. Lloyd George, she wrote, agreed to introduce a Private Member's Bill, on the condition that another truce, encompassing all of the organizations, was agreed. In this instance, Sylvia either incorrectly recalled the facts, or changed them to suit her version of events. Lloyd George, as a member of the Cabinet, was not in a position to introduce a Private Members Bill, and therefore could have made no such promise. Christabel, again acording to Sylvia, had decided that after the failure of the earlier Conciliation Bills, nothing other than a government-sponsored bill would succeed. She was later proved correct. At the time, she refused to cooperate.

Upon learning of Christabel's rejection of 'her' plan, Sylvia telegraphed her sister that she was on her way to Paris. Before she could leave, Christabel sent a crisp wire to Norah Smyth: 'Tell your friend not to come.' Mrs Pankhurst further fuelled the situation by announcing her own intention to return to jail and continue fasting.[94]

Now out of the limelight, and with publicity focusing on her mother and the WSPU, Sylvia undertook a series of lectures abroad. First she went to Austria, where she met other suffragists in Vienna.[95] From there, she travelled to Germany for a brief visit before returning undetected to Britain. Although she was forbidden to leave the country under the Cat and Mouse Act, she kept readers of the *Dreadnought* fully informed about her travels.[96]

The years in which British women worked, suffered and dedicated themselves to the vote are full of drama, conviction and commitment. But the Pankhurst family suffered conflict beyond the issues of the movement alone. Emmeline, Christabel and Sylvia were complex women. All three were self-centred. Christabel and her mother could and did share the WSPU because each had an equally leading, publicity-drawing role within it. Sylvia, on the fringes of this movement, as she was in all her crusades, wrote herself into the history of the movement while defaming and, at times discrediting, both her mother and sister.

When, in 1918, some women were granted the vote based on both an age and property qualification (i.e. aged 30 and above with £5-worth of property), Sylvia was involved in another cause and barely noted the event. Christabel and Mrs Pankhurst took no little share of the credit for their pre-war militant campaigns, and, for the later stages, they gave most of the credit to Lloyd George, who favoured votes for women.[97] Asquith wrote in his memoirs that 'the changed conditions brought about by the War' were responsible for the women's triumph.[98] Adela, the most politically astute on this issue, wrote from Australia that credit for the vote should go to Mrs Fawcett and the NUWSS, since 'Mrs. Fawcett knew enough about politics not to turn her organization over to the war'. 'Of one thing I am sure', Adela wrote, 'is that women did not get the vote for supporting the war, because Christabel and my mother threw in their support without making conditions, and in politics those who do so never get the rewards from the politicians.'[99]

Martin Pugh credits Mrs Fawcett and the NUWSS with staying out of militant involvement, and working behind the scenes to recruit male supporters for the vote. But he does not give final credit for the partial victory in 1918 to any one suffrage organization. Furthermore, he discounts women's wartime activity as having any effects on the minds of parliamentarians: 'Ultimately the war's effect was indirect; by creating a coalition [government] it circumvented the party split on franchise; and it harnessed at last the women's clause to a government bill'.[100] This Bill extended the franchise to all men; and once society was levelled by allowing all men the vote, there was nothing to prohibit 8.4 million women over the age of 25 from joining them.

In yet another and more recent interpretation of the suffrage movement in Britain, Leslie Parker Hume concluded that the militant suffragettes assumed a subordinate role in winning votes for women.

Hume agrees with Adela in attributing the victory to Mrs Fawcett and the National Union of Women's Suffrage Societies.[101]

But, for Sylvia, as she looked back in 1930/31 on the suffrage movement, the triumph was in part her own. She had humbled Asquith, and much of her activity in the future found her using the suffrage movement as an example of victory over adversity. 'I was yet in spirit raised about the battle,' she wrote. 'I felt no touch of the small frictions and irritations apt to intrude in ordinary life. Viewing the great movement, working and planning for it, I could say, and still say it, those were tremendous days.'[102]

Vera Brittain thought Sylvia 'marshalled her forces with the remorseless precision of a military dictator. Yet she sought and accepted the martyr's crown of suffering and exacted from her followers no more than she was willing to endure herself.'[103]

PART 2
War and Communism

Losing a Friend and Gaining a Cause

'There is, I feel sure, a very general feeling of relief in the House of Commons and in the Labour Party now that Keir Hardie's body lies mouldering in the grave.'
—George Bernard Shaw, quoted in *Women's Dreadnought*

In the summer of 1914, the approach of a major war raised serious concern in socialist circles throughout Europe. The popular mind had been filled since the Boer War with sentiments of jingoistic nationalism, but the socialist hope had been that worker would not fight worker when the final test came. Keir Hardie warned Sylvia that war on the Continent was inevitable. At the end of July, he returned from an emergency conference of the International Socialist Bureau in Brussels, still loyal to the goals of international socialism but disillusioned and unable to influence his Labour colleagues in a pacifist direction.[1]

Hardie and Sylvia were both concerned with another issue that raised the question of pacifist principles. Protestant leaders in Ulster violently opposed Home Rule for a united Ireland already projected by Act of Parliament. In the spring and summer of 1914, the extra-legal Ulster Volunteers prepared for civil war, and a pacifist solution might have been to bow to Ulster's threats. But Hardie urged the government to stand firm in the cause of a united Ireland, and Sylvia became drawn into Irish affairs. On 4 August when Britain declared war on Germany, Sylvia was in Dublin, this time speaking in favour of Home Rule. As soon as she got word that war had been declared, she crossed the Irish Sea on the first passage available; only to discover that she was travelling with men who were already being posted to Belgium.[2]

In Parliament, meanwhile, the Labour representation shifted rapidly towards support for the war, despite earlier talk about the efficacy of a general strike in the cause of peace. Ramsay MacDonald and Keir Hardie alone opposed the government on the declaration of war. Ramsay MacDonald resigned from the leadership of the Labour Party, which supported the government. His opposition was partly party-political as well as pacifist. MacDonald questioned the entênte with France, whose terms nevertheless tied Britain to the detailed alliance between France and Russia, and Tsarist Russia was currently the enemy of socialism everywhere, not only domestically but also with regard to the threat it posed in terms of future imperialism. Only Hardie, George Lansbury and Philip Snowden among the parliamentary Labour members (and Sylvia on the fringes of the movement) concurred with his opposition to the war. The pacifists staged a late protest on 2 August with a Trafalgar Square demonstration that failed miserably. On MacDonald's resignation the leadership passed to Arthur Henderson, who came to Parliament with strong ties to the Trades Union Congress (TUC). The ILP opposed the war but the Labour Party supported it. In fact, the majority of Labour leaders supported the war, including Ben Tillett, leader of the dock workers and once a friend of Sylvia's.[3]

Sylvia arrived in London after the Trafalgar Square failure to find Hardie dejected and forlorn. She had seen little of him in recent months because of her own suffragette activities. His earlier 'heart-wrung warnings of the great catastrophe' had failed to move her, in spite of her 'deep love and respect for him'.[4] But she now readjusted her goals to fit his and made opposition to the war her new cause.

Not so the rest of the suffragette movement. Christabel from Paris saw the coming of the war as 'nature's vengeance . . . God's vengeance upon a people who held women in subjection'.[5] But she soon moved to support the cause of patriotism. Sylvia viewed the war, rather, as a manifestation of capitalist and imperialist greed, but, instead of resigning herself to 'God's vengeance', she recognized a new opening in the form of jobs for women and linked the advent of the war with a new drive for votes. But she also tried to link the feminist and peace movements, arguing that votes for women was a way to peace now that 'all women's organizations in the world call for peace'.[6] This stand was not adopted, however, by the majority of women's organizations and certainly not by the WSPU; Christabel temporarily ceased publication of *The Suffragette* and left Paris for Lincoln's Inn. Sylvia kept the *Dreadnought* going, propelled her ELFS into anti-war activity, and began to consider the problems the East End would face in wartime.

400 Old Ford Road, surrounded by narrow streets of squalid pubs and mostly tenement housing quickly became, when war was declared, a centre of activity. Some people sorted donated clothing while others cooked dishes which could be distributed to the poor who were caught up in the actuality of England at war. For the moment, at least, no demonstrations were planned in Victoria Park, a stretch of green half a mile down the Mile End Road, which was an otherwise depressing, rundown and uninvitingly gloomy district of London.[7] The East End, subject of numerous sociological studies, housed the class of men who eventually formed the bulk of the British armed forces. Largely unskilled, the majority earned barely enough to support their families in peacetime. War brought shortages, inflation and job dislocation.

Some East Enders joined the army or navy following the declaration of war, leaving behind a deprived group of dependants—elderly mothers and fathers, wives and children. There were no immediate state allowances for these dependants. Governmental administration was in a state of confusion in the war's early stages, and those left without support had to struggle for whatever means were at their disposal or do without and starve. With the Conscription Act of 1916, men who had not volunteered were marched off to the trenches, leaving still more wives and children with inadequate resources, although by 1916 sums contributed by the government had been modestly increased.

Sidney and Beatrice Webb had made a study of conditions in Poplar (the larger district that included Bow and Bromley) where Sylvia worked. In 1914 about 160,000 people lived in the crowded borough, which housed many small factories, countless sweatshops and sweet-making factories, but no heavy industry. Most workers, including many women, were unskilled and unorganized. About 6000 women were employed as tailoresses; a further 1600 made confectionery. In the case of the men, about 4000 were dockworkers and 3000 general labourers. The more skilled were better off and worked outside the borough, principally in the metal trades. Their unions were affiliated to the TUC, which had a growing voice in the Labour Party after Arthur Henderson's rise to leadership. In 1914, however, neither organized labour nor the Labour Party wielded effective influence over the capitalist goals of the Liberal government and the opposition Unionist Party.[8]

After the war broke out, Bow and Bromley were in considerable distress. Confectioners suffered from the spiralling price of sugar. Tailors lost business, although one factory which made uniforms was working overtime.[9] The number of children receiving free school meals in September 1914 was 3800, 1000 more than in the previous year. These figures are based on a study carried out by the Webbs a year earlier, but show the general state of poverty which existed when the war began.

Meanwhile, the Mayor of Poplar set up a Local Representative Committee a few weeks after the declaration of war calling on 60 different organizations—religious groups, special-interest groups, the borough council, women's trade unions and, of course, suffrage societies. Some fifteen members of the committee were women, and Sylvia and two working-class women represented the ELFS. A subcommittee chosen by the head of the Central Committee in Women's Employment in central London was quickly established to deal specifically with the problems of women workers. Sylvia applied for membership, but the governing council directed the secretary to reply that 'membership is limited to societies affiliated with the Labour Party'.[10] It took little reading between the lines to recognize that maverick pacifists like Sylvia were not welcome in Labour circles during the war years.

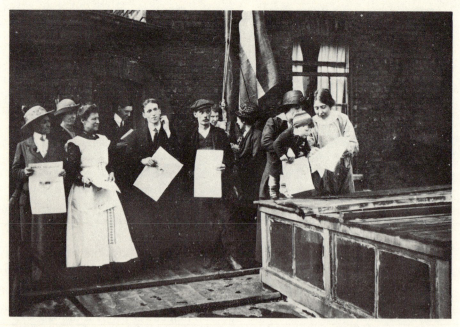

Hoisting the colours at 400 Old Ford Road, Bow, 5 May 1914 (*far right*) Sylvia
Pankhurst with George Lansbury's grandson

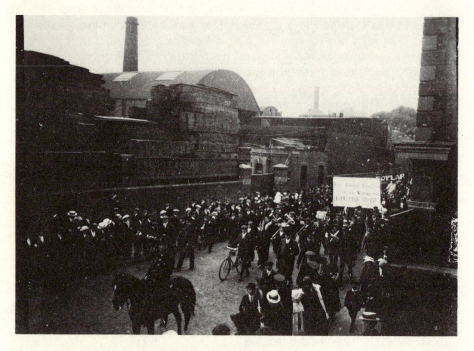

Procession to Victoria Park on Women's Day, 30 May 1915

Sylvia began her own relief organization, leaving the Webbs and the War Emergency Council to deal with bureaucratic red tape, which they did badly, first from inefficiency and later from lack of supplies. Sylvia set off to see the President of the Board of Trade with some of her ELFS following. With shortages immediately noticeable in the first weeks of war and prices rising, Sylvia argued that the government should nationalize food supplies and apply price controls. Stressing the plight of East Londoners, where average wages were low, and where profits were likely to accrue to middlemen, Sylvia followed the pacifist-socialist rhetoric of the ILP. Only in this case, as Cabinet ministers knew from past experience, she had the Pankhurst energy and drive to make a louder protest than her fellow ideologues.

Sylvia campaigned for her constituents in the East End with the tactics of the suffrage movement, bombarding the Cabinet, the Board of Trade, and the press with case studies of extreme hardship.[11] The press sympathized briefly with Sylvia's good intentions. In late October 1914, the *Christian Commonwealth* sent a reporter to cover the myriad activities at 400 Old Ford Road, and published an article comparing the two worlds of East and West London at the onset of war. Finding in the East End that 'people are mainly concerned with what they shall eat and drink and wherewithal they shall be clothed', the reporter crossed town where 'the world seems transformed into one vast drapery establishment and all the food is carefully concealed from sight'. Back in the East End, the reporter settled on 400 Old Ford Road, where 'people are bustling here and there' with 'great activity' all on account of 'Miss Sylvia Pankhurst'.[12]

Realizing that charity or relief was not the answer to long-term problems of health, education and maintenance, Sylvia plunged with her customary vigour into a series of endeavours designed to prevent the young and old alike in her neighbourhood from going without essentials. She described some of the problems which confronted her at Old Ford Road; 'Our offices . . . daily thronged with women and children, penniless, starving, ill from privation, the rent unpaid the landlord threatening eviction.' When women and children were desperate for help, but could not get to Old Ford Road, they turned to Sylvia with appeals by post. One letter printed in the *Dreadnought* conveyed the sense of urgency felt by many: 'I am a poor mother of two sons at war and I am nearly starving. If we ask for help we are told to sell our homes [i.e. furniture].' Faced with the confusion of her constituents and their actual privations, Sylvia began publicizing public works programmes that would alleviate some of their miseries. She called for better housing, more schools, food and garment factories, all to be located in East London.[13] The government did embark on a limited programme to improve housing, but wartime was not the time when urban reforms took priority.

At Christmas, when the war was fully occupying the nation's attention, Sylvia and Norah Smyth set off to Scarborough for a holiday. German submarines had attacked the Yorkshire coastline during recent weeks, leaving their mark on the town and its people. With wounded occupying available space, the two women stayed only long enough to investigate the problems of people Sylvia had known during her youth. They then decided to go to France to see the war at close hand and to visit Mrs Pankhurst, who was then in Paris. Holiday spirit was sadly lacking in Paris. The Germans had been stopped at the Marne in the early autumn, only fifteen miles from Paris, but trench warfare was developing along an increasingly immobile front. The fighting continued close by, and the French wounded were streaming back to hastily converted hospitals.

The Christmas spirit was missing between mother and daughter as well. Mrs Pankhurst had with her Nurse Pine (who had tended numerous suffragettes in years past) and would 'speak of nothing but the war'.[14] If Sylvia expected relations with her mother to be less strained with the arrival of war and the cessation of suffrage militancy, she was mistaken. Mrs Pankhurst had abandoned the ideals of the ILP, including pacifism, and she now moved in broader political circles. Sylvia retained her father's radical socialist-pacifist views, so that each held strongly opposing views. The visit was not a success. Her mother, a 'contemptuous irony in her voice', inquired of her daughter's recent activities. In reply Sylvia mumbled something about the East End and let the matter drop. Her feelings of rejection survived the meeting: 'we were distant from each other as though a thousand leagues had intervened; an aching void in truth; for we were near, so poignantly near in the memory of old efforts and old loves.'[15]

Sylvia and Norah also visited Dr Flora Murray, who had occasionally treated suffragettes in 'her hospital' at the Claridges Hotel. Dr Murray, together with her nursing staff, had volunteered her sevices to the French when the British found no place for her, and was busy treating wounded soldiers. Another acquaintance of Sylvia's, H. D. Harben, was also in Paris. Using his considerable resources as an heir to the Prudential Insurance fortune, Harben was financing another hospital at the Majestic Hotel.[16] Sylvia applauded the Murray–Harben efforts while remaining critical of her mother's support of Britain's entry into the war.

Back in the East End, Norah and Sylvia were reunited with Zelie Emerson, who had returned from America and was once again heading the sales drive for the *Dreadnought*. Zelie had run the paper in their absence and still followed Sylvia with a rare devotion, but she was otherwise uninvolved in the war-related activities at Old Ford Road. The *Dreadnought*, however, was almost entirely given over to the war, dealing with food and clothing shortages in the East End and the relationship between wages and women's work, but with few references to suffrage.[17]

This was a fundamental shift, not only for Sylvia but for the feminist movement as a whole. Before the war, she had followed the lead of the suffrage movement and had given first priority to the vote, although she and other suffragettes had always voiced the need for better wages for working women and for greater opportunities in the professions. From the onset of the war, she altered her priorities, seeing money as the crux of women's problems in a world controlled by male capitalists. She placed equal wages first, with the vote as a supporting measure. Her mother, in support of the government, however, had preceded her in calling for equality in pay—a fact that Sylvia never acknowledged.

Sylvia's personal transition can be traced back to before the war and the move to the East End. At first she was still so involved in the emotional call of the suffrage movement that her pronouncements went unheard, but the coming of war found her secure, financially and emotionally, with her own tightly-knit organization of followers in the East End. In her position as leader of the ELFS, she turned from suffragette to feminist, with an overriding concern for economic problems. As a suffragette she had promoted universal suffrage, although she had remained nominally loyal to the WSPU's single-minded approach of 'Votes for Women'. After the split, Sylvia was not long in lending her support to Lansbury's campaign for *universal* suffrage.[18] Only once did she deviate from that position, and that was when she believed a Bill giving votes to soldiers and sailors, debated in Parliament in 1916, would be detrimental to women still in pursuit of that elusive goal.[19]

In her new feminist-economic approach, Sylvia argued that the men's trade unions should open their ranks to female members and put them in a position to bargain for equal pay. Assessing the wartime need for workers, Sylvia saw from the beginning that women would be drawn into the factories, and she predicted that unless action were taken by women, they would receive less pay than men had in those same jobs. Margaret Bondfield of the TUC, a less conspicuous woman in the suffrage movement, was active in the cause of higher wages. Mary MacArthur, wife of Labour Member of Parliament, W. C. Anderson, and an active member of the War Emergency Workers National Committee, was placed in charge of a committee responsible for finding work for women. Sylvia led a deputation to MacArthur which included Mrs Drake and Mrs Walker, hoping that through her influence, and that of her husband on the larger committee, dependants' allowances might be raised beyond their then current limits. Mrs Drake made an eloquent plea, complete with a budget, which illustrated that the current allowances were insufficient to feed a family of four and still enable them to pay their rent. She spoke of women she knew who were starving in order to feed their children and provide for basic essentials. On their departure, Mrs Drake noted that the East End deputation felt 'bitterly the contrast between the surroundings they had visited and those of the thousands of poor souls that we all know of'.[20]

Sylvia was denied a position on the War Emergency National Committee and a voice in the TUC; she was superseded in the larger sphere of public involvement by MacArthur and Bondfield; but an opportunity to reach the ear of the Inner Councils appeared in the spring of 1915. When the ELFS was invited to send two delegates to the Labour Party's War Emergency Conference Sylvia went and was immediately active, submitting amendments to a series of resolutions already under consideration by the committee. Along with the persistent call for equal pay for equal work, and female membership in the TUC, the ELFS (mostly led by Sylvia) suggested that 'adequate maintenance, which shall in no case be less than the value of one pound a week shall be provided for women in connection with the government training schemes'.[21] Although Sylvia later took credit for initiating these goals, Mary MacArthur and other women in the TUC had earlier advocated the one pound minimum rate and Sylvia probably merely publicly voiced what they were working for behind the scenes.

In the optimistic expectation that the war would soon end, Sylvia looked beyond, to the role of women in the labour market when men returned from the front. Recognizing the need for heads of households with large numbers of dependants to work, Sylvia and the ELFS went beyond other progressives in resolving that 'the government shall make itself responsible for the maintenance of the workers displaced as the result of the war, until suitable work at an adequate wage can be found'.[22] The concept was laudable in its foresight. Unfortunately for Sylvia, the War Emergency Council did not act on her recommendations. While her intentions were sincere, her lack of pragmatism militated against her; the Council turned to other, more reasoned, opinions from women like Bondfield and MacArthur.

In Bow, on a more practical footing, Sylvia and Norah, with volunteers from the ELFS, established a range of new services. They advertised in the *Woman's Dreadnought* for second-hand clothing, especially babies' clothes, distributing it from the Women's Hall on Old Ford Road. Sylvia's friends in the West End were generous in their support, as they were in providing money to buy milk and eggs for hungry babies and small children. During the first year of the war, Sylvia collected moderately large sums from these donors (sometimes as much as £10), while her East End membership scoured their neighbourhoods for extra shillings.

In order to make clothing available, and to provide employment for both men and women, Sylvia opened a garment factory at the Women's

Hall in October 1914. Mr Payne, the shoemaker, too old for war, was brought in to manage a cooperative boot factory. With donations running high, and hopes even higher, wages at the factories were set at Sylvia's goal of one pound per week—higher than the sweated industries under private ownership in the East End and higher still than the workrooms established under government auspices. When it came to setting salaries, Sylvia's notions of what was possible outweighed what was indeed practical. Higher wages called for higher retail prices and the ELFS did not want to price themselves out of the market. Norah Smyth no doubt picked up the difference between cost and price.

In October 1914, Sylvia followed the lead of the Women's Emergency Corps by opening a toy factory at the rear of the Women's Hall, with Norah underwriting the costs of its operation.[23] The first toys were wooden and flat, easily made and quickly marketable. Sylvia drew artistic help for toy design from a former acquaintance at the Royal College of Art. Since the Germans had cornered most of the toy market before the war, especially the production of dolls, no one in Britain was in a position to take over, and no patterns existed. After some experimentation between Sylvia and her artist friend, they produced stuffed dolls, selling the first set to Selfridge's. Sylvia, acting as sales representative, hired a cab and personally delivered the new product. Soon they added 'negro and Japanese babies' from their original patterns. Shares were sold to those who could afford a stake in the toy factory, with Norah, as financier, a major stockholder. When they began to make a profit, they turned the firm into a cooperative. They hired a secretary, R. Hercbegova, from Hungary, who soon rose to manager. In the mid-war years, production was again increased to include 'lambs, bulldogs, monkeys, Little Black Sambos, and even the duo dolls, "Jack and Jill"'.[24] In one of the last acts prior to his death, Walter Crane freely donated to the toy factory prints of his drawings, Labour cartoons and children's books, and suggestions for jigsaw puzzles.

With so much activity flourishing at the Women's Hall, new quarters were needed to house the ever-expanding programmes. Sylvia acquired 438 Old Ford Road, an old public house which she 'scrubbed, cleansed, and renovated' and opened as 'The Mother's Arms', a precurser to modern child-care centres. She hired three nurses to look after the physical needs of the children. Mrs Minnie Lansbury, George Lansbury's wife, directed the centre, with Norah again underwriting at least part of the costs.[25]

Crowding yet another agency into 400 Old Ford Road, Sylvia opened the first of several 'Price Cost Restaurants' on the ground floor of the building. Here, the hungry could buy a meal for the cost of the food and preparation. Jobs were created for cooks. A handwritten menu, no doubt worked out by Sylvia who was chief executive of all

East London Toy Factory, 1915

'Price Cost Restaurant' in the Woman's Hall at 500 Old Ford Road, Bow, opened
August 1917 Sylvia Pankhurst third from left at rear table.

operations, was composed a week at a time and featured such nourishing main courses as stew or steak and kidney pie. The restaurant offered soups as 'starters', served with milk and occasional desserts.[26]

British consumption of sugar at the beginning of the war was enormous. Mrs Payne, who emerged from a primarily housekeeping role to become one of the most active of Sylvia's followers, presented a budget to the Board of Trade during one of the East London deputations, claiming the hardship of being able to buy only five pounds of sugar each week for her family of four. She claimed this was half the ration her family consumed before the war: this figure is too high to be realistic, but it was in keeping with the sometimes propagandistic statements which Sylvia and her followers made in order to draw attention to the hardships which really existed. The 'Price Cost Restaurants' not only provided food for those who had none, but a more balanced diet than the East Enders were accustomed to at home.

Sylvia Pankhurst now became a local employer. Among her many designations, she added yet another role, that of director of education, when she started a Montessori School on the second floor of 'The Mother's Arms'. The school served two groups: young children in the East End (the process of selection was never clear) and the children of ILP members who had gone to jail as conscientious objectors, including the daughter of A. Fenner Brockway, journalist-editor of the *Labour Leader*, who was jailed during the war.[27]

Linking the ideological pursuits of feminism, socialism and pacifism, Sylvia led her crusade from East London to Westminster, where time and again she sought interviews with Cabinet ministers to discuss food shortages, relief for the poor and equal wages; but to each issue she attached her call for peace. The Prime Minister ignored her resolutions as he had ignored her earlier petitions for the vote. The pages of the *Dreadnought* during the war years, especially 1914–16, were filled with Sylvia's editorials and articles discussing the issues of wages, food shortages, relief, and always the call for peace. Busy as she was supervising factories, clothing distribution, restaurants (two more opened in 1914 and 1915), nurseries, and day-care centres, Sylvia found time to organize demonstrations in Victoria Park (aligning votes for women with equal pay), and to travel around England lecturing. At Brighton in November 1914, she spoke on 'War and Victimization of Women'[28] a theme about which she persisted. In her efforts to become a political leader in Bow, she listened to complaints from her constituents, and, in the best political tradition, took such complaints to whatever source seemed likely to offer help. She frequently printed (and edited) in the *Dreadnought* letters from irate or frustrated women,[29] and she herself wrote letters to the editor of the *Manchester Guardian*, which often printed them, and to *The Times*, which did not.

Deriving her livelihood from sporadic attempts to paint and sell, and from Norah's generosity, together with whatever freelance editorial work she could pick up, Sylvia displayed the same tendency she had shown during the suffrage movement: she lived on little (bread and margarine mostly) and trusted that enough would come in to defray expenses. This was the pattern throughout her life, and, fortunately, she almost always had an admirer on hand to bail her out before her capacity to borrow was exhausted. When that did happen, she did as Keir Hardie had advised when she was a penniless art student—she picked up her pen and wrote. There was usually a newspaper willing to pay for the privilege of carrying Miss Sylvia Pankhurst as a by-line, and her activities, though not always as socially acceptable as her current work in the East End, were usually newsworthy. Writing in the illustrated *Sunday Herald* in the summer of 1915, Sylvia informed a broader public of the undertakings in which she and the ELFS were then involved. Finding 'official bodies bound up in red tape', they were forced to set up their own relief work by the urgent need of the people. She described the tiny empire she had built at 400 and 438 Old Ford Road, including her newest enterprise, a jam factory which processed fruit that had been donated.[30] What she failed to mention was that she and Norah had discovered, through her women's network, that one of the jam factories in the East End was adulterating their product with wood chippings for seeds in an otherwise synthetic process, and was selling the 'jam' at inflated prices.[31] Sylvia's protests resulted in getting the factory closed down.

Sylvia also wrote about the many deputations 'which have gone to various government offices requesting high pensions, better wages for women'.[32] Later that summer, she submitted a column to the *Weekly Dispatch*, protesting at the low pay for women in government work and suggesting that women worked for government contractors at 'sweated rates'.[33] Still later, at a paid lecture, Sylvia followed the theme of women and work, but pointed out that middle-class women were moving into paid employment while poor women were left out. Class prejudice existed in war as in peace, and when employers were able to hire well-spoken, semi-educated women, they selected them over those whose needs outweighed their background. While it was 'patriotic' for middle-class women to work, poor women whose husbands had gone to war were the last to receive government help; they frequently failed to understand the process of obtaining a pension and were left standing at the gates, unnoticed by their middle-class counterparts and the employers.[34]

Lloyd George became a particular target of Sylvia's. She bombarded him with notes requesting deputations, and with longer letters demanding better wages for female munitions workers. (Lloyd George was Minister of Munitions and Secretary for War from July to December 1916, before he became Prime Minister in the coalition government.) One of her several demonstrations against the government led her to

Westminster, where she demanded 'a man's wage for a man's job'. This particular demonstration grew out of Lloyd George's promise to her mother that women munitions workers were to be paid the same rate as men; the Minister of Munitions, however, balked at equal wages for women who were not yet trained. Sylvia saw this as an excuse for withholding wages from women, and after the demonstration, she returned home to fire off a lengthy letter charging him with breaking his word. Where her earlier suffrage statements had often been emotional in tone, she was learning to deal seriously with economic issues. To Lloyd George she wrote, 'The government has refused to interfere with the law of supply and demand where the buying and selling of food is concerned . . . in keeping down high prices . . . but by compulsory arbitration and forced labour it nullifies the law of supply and demand where wages are concerned. It is a short-sighted policy to starve the people.'[35] Lloyd George did not reply.

What especially rankled the pacifist was the employment of women in war work, such as munitions. And it rankled her socialist self when women employed in the tedious and skilled job of making hairbrushes for soldiers and sailors were making less money than before the war, yet the government was buying the hairbrushes at the old price or more from the manufacturers.[36] In May 1915, at the annual Woman's Day Demonstration, Sylvia again urged higher wages for women, and again linked wages to the vote.[37] Throughout the war she continued to use the call for the vote as a mechanism for obtaining the goals she and the ELFS were pursuing. While the vote occupied a lower place in her hierarchy of demands, she realized that her public identity depended on her role as a suffragette; she used that notoriety, now and later, to draw attention to her current crusade.

Had Sylvia never written *The Home Front*, concerning her activities in Bow and Bromley during the war, those activities may have come to light in a more sympathetic way. For example, in *The Home Front*, Sylvia omitted the myriad activities, similar to her own in the East End, which were being carried out under the banner of the United Suffragists. A cursory reading of *Votes for Women* at that time indicates that all of her advertised organizations—the Montessori School, 'The Mother's Arms', Self-Denial Week (cutting down on groceries), the 'Price Cost Restaurants'—were being duplicated by other suffrage groups in other parts of London and England. Press cuttings and interviews with those who knew her at the time reveal far more about her service to the community and of her real dedication to the people of Bow.

The Home Front makes much of her role as a political leader serving the abstract many. Her greater contribution was her direct service to the widows, the orphans, the hungry and the disabled. Some she helped from her headquarters in Old Ford Road, others through intervention with government officials to cut through red tape, especially in helping wives of servicemen to obtain their allowance. Often she herself accommodated homeless women until she could find adequate quarters for them. On one occasion, a pregnant orphan girl came to Old Ford Road, having nowhere else to go, and Sylvia took her in.[38] A homeless boy appeared. He stayed so long he almost became part of Sylvia's newly constituted family. Unmarried and unable to give up her love for Keir Hardie, she seemed to need the affection of the women and children around her as much as they needed her energy and drive working on their behalf.

Not all of the clients in the East End were endearing, however, and in one of the rare amusing passages of Sylvia's voluminous writings, she described a crippled, pregnant girl in the East End who, even in childbirth, insisted she was not pregnant but had a tumour. Sylvia managed to call a doctor and assist in the delivery of the 'tumour' after an agonizingly long and painful breech birth. When the soldier responsible reappeared to find himself a father, he quickly departed again, leaving the crippled woman to support the baby alone. Through the Bow network, Sylvia discovered his name and serial number, and wrote to him, 'I hope you will let us arrange a little wedding breakfast for you at the Women's Hall. Please let me have the date of your marriage when it is fixed . . . '. A reluctant groom, 'weak and garrulous, . . . with something keen and ferrety about the nose and eyes . . . ' appeared to toast his bride. Sylvia was not sure in the final moments as to whether she 'had committed a mortal sin in helping to tie those two together permanently. She will get her separation allowance . . . but they will produce more children.' Here she flirts with eugenics, a topical question at the time and one which she must have been familiar with through various tracts, some of which circulated in socialist circles.[39]

During the war, when the government debated making prostitution illegal, Sylvia and the ELFS took up the cause of the prostitutes, petitioning unsuccessfully on their behalf. In early 1915, her organization joined with the United Suffragists in forming 'The League of Rights of Soldiers and Sailors', whose purpose was to 'secure for its members adequate separation allowances and pensions' and to look into all cases of 'neglect and delay' on the part of the government. The WSPU dissident, Mrs Despard, became President of the League, working with Sylvia as a pacifist to secure the measures. One no-rent strike was successfully carried out. A landlord raised his rent by 3d a week but was forced to retract when Sylvia and the ELFS organized the 56 tenants into withholding their rent.[40]

Not all on the 'home front' was as favourable as the *Dreadnought* and Sylvia's memories implied. The ELFS were plagued with disharmony. Membership dropped; problems with paid organizers resulted in constant moves from one location to another; and some members of the executive committee resigned over squabbles with organizers and each other. Sales of the *Dreadnought* slumped in even the most supportive area of Bow during the summer of 1915. In short, Sylvia was caught up in personality conflicts with her membership and organizers, and problems with her paper's sales.[41] A wealthy supporter from the West End resigned as honorary financial secretary, but a dedicated female doctor who treated the needy in the ELFS clinic stepped in.[42] Surviving records do not indicate Sylvia's or the ELFS budgets of these early years; but, from the beginning of the war, Sylvia effectively introduced the concept of deficit spending. Norah Smyth and the financial secretary had to find the salaries of paid organizers and sales agents for the *Dreadnought*, and the *Dreadnought* did not sell well in local shops or with outside agents. While Sylvia reported sales of 1000 copies in April 1916, in Bow alone, Mrs Drake found them 'at a new low in November'.[43]

In the spring of 1915 Sylvia's friend and supporter, Lady Sybil Smith, arranged a display of toys from the toy factory at the country house of the Waldorf Astors, which included a country weekend for Sylvia at the Astor estate, Cliveden, near Maidenhead. When Lady Sybil and Sylvia arrived, they were greeted by servants and shown to their rooms; but not before Nancy Astor (the first woman to take a seat in Parliament) was informed of the death of a friend at the front. Mrs Astor withdrew. Sylvia saw her mourning as 'Regrettable, truly: yet save for the cause, I should have been glad for her absence. Already I began to feel myself a fish out of water . . .'.[44]

The contrast between Maidenhead and Bow was more pronounced at a sumptuous dinner. Her host tried to make conversation with the austere Sylvia by mentioning two letters he had recently received from Christabel. Sylvia preferred to 'talk with him of his efforts to secure clean and pure milk for children'. The next day they visited a hospital for the wounded on the Astor estate, with no attention yet paid to the toys from the East End. Sylvia's patience became strained. When Mrs Astor said she hoped Sylvia 'taught her women to be good', Sylvia answered that goodness was not her mission but she did try to spur them to revolt against their hideous conditions. Only good manners, and perhaps some fascination with eccentricity, saved Sylvia from returning empty-handed. Lady Sybil collected £15 from the guests and Mrs Astor contributed another £5, although Sylvia left early after having spoken her mind to several of the party. At that time she was an inflexible socialist, dedicated to the poor amongst whom she lived and worked. This inflexibility meant that she once again lacked the pragmatism necessary to accomplish her goals and extract from wealthy people like the Astors and their guests the help she needed in carrying out her mission in East London.

Part of her resentment of people like the Astors (and other less wealthy supporters) may have come from memories of her youth. Although her family were middle-class, they were almost always on the brink of poverty. Sylvia did not have the financial cushion of women like Emmeline Pethick-Lawrence, who came from the comfortable middle-class, or Beatrice Webb, who was from a wealthy family. They could and did distance themselves from the poor East-Enders whose cause they too served intermittently. Sylvia's identification with her followers would appear to have been grounded in more than humanitarian goals.

Socialists joined organized Christian religion as a considerable force in the East End. Socialist Sunday schools were prevalent in all districts; here the 'Ten Commandments' of socialism were drilled into the pupils with the same conviction that spurred other children to learn those found in the Old Testament. Parallels between organized religious and socialist teaching were so obvious that it was easy for a nonconformist Christian like George Lansbury or Keir Hardie to embrace the tenets of socialism with no conflict. For instance, the first commandment of socialism (as taught in the Sunday schools) called for the 'love of fellow students as they may become your fellow workers and companions in life'. Another law was 'do not think he who lives in his own country should hate and despise others'.[45] This commandment was in line with other aspects of British socialism ('emotional socialism', as Lenin called it) and it was associated with the pacifist wing of the ILP. But few East Londoners were pacifists; the first call for volunteers was met as eagerly there as elsewhere.

Nor were the people of the East End peaceful among themselves. Pub brawls were common; ethnic and other group rivalries were strong. Jews became a common target as migration caused further overcrowding in the ghettoes. Such respected politicians as George Lansbury played on the irrational fears of the older residents, creating tension that sometimes gave way to violence. After one such incident, Sylvia, writing in the *Dreadnought*, advocated patience with the immigrants until they could assimilate British culture. To speed the process she advocated a school for foreigners, similar to that established in the United States by Charlotte Perkins Gilman.[46] This idea, while laudable, never came about. Sylvia already had too many enterprises going to start yet another school.

The trade most commonly associated with Jews was tailoring. Fear for their own job security incited non-Jews working in the trade to acts of violence; they believed the new immigrants were willing to work for almost nothing, undercutting them in wages, even if they did not take their jobs. Jewish women, 'a vast reservoir of "slave" labour in most trades' represented a threat to their own menfolk as well as the men and women in the non-unionised trades.[47] War brought no change in attitudes. If anything, hostilities increased. In May 1917, the *Dreadnought* carried the headline 'A Pogrom in London'. Sylvia, educating her readers, described Jews in London as 'the people who have no country', and who 'are always most cruelly opposed by tyrannical governments'. She described the cramped conditions of the Jewish community in the East End, a 'teeming human population . . . packed away in any spaces not occupied by the industries from which they live'. And soldiers, Sylvia reminded them—the same people who were so hostile to pacifists— also discriminated against Jews.[48]

Germans too in the East End, long established in homes and shops, suddenly found a hostile climate. Jingoism of the worst sort resulted in physical and material damage to people of German extraction. Crowds stormed bakeries, broke equipment and stole bread. They attacked individual homes, broke windows, and sometimes wounded the occupants. After the *Lusitania* was sunk by German submarines, an especially violent attack was launched against German merchants and members of the German community. In the East End Sylvia counselled tolerance, invoking the concept of the 'fellow man' taught in all Sunday schools. The ugly mood of prejudice continued however, exacerbated by the Zeppelin raids which caused considerable damage in the East End, and violence once more broke out. Sylvia's efforts to get British soldiers to intercede and stop the rioting were fruitless. In dismay, she concluded, 'Alas, poor Patriotism, what foolish cruelties are committed in thy name.'[49]

Ancient hostilities re-emerged on another front as well. Christabel and Mrs Pankhurst had rushed back to support the war effort. On her return from France, one of Christabel's first public acts was to address an audience at the London Opera House, calling on men in the audience to volunteer. Sylvia attended and visited her sister and Mrs Pankhurst backstage. She later recalled the meeting as through a veil.[50] Sylvia was particularly disillusioned with her mother for abandoning her father's pacifist principles, believing it ironic that her mother could have met her father at a peace rally, 'and in later life repudiate two of her daughters [Sylvia and Adela] for their opposition to war'.[51] Sylvia blamed Christabel for this change, but Mrs Pankhurst had formed a lasting passion for the French, and an equally strong hatred for the Germans during her school-days in Paris. Mrs Pankhurst and Christabel once more occupied the limelight, touring England in the patriotic cause. When Mrs Pankhurst publicly repudiated her two daughters,[52] Sylvia continued her attack on the war from the East End, while Adela in Australia published an anti-war book, *Put Up the Sword*.[53]

Yet another of Sylvia's old relationships was severed in the early months of the war. Zelie Emerson wrote to Sylvia, asking why she was no longer called upon to speak. She admitted belonging to both the ELFS and the WSPU and wondered whether that might be the reason for the coolness. They had worked together in the suffrage movement, then in the East End where Zelie had worked on the *Dreadnought*. Zelie may have become critical of the movement in some way, perhaps of Sylvia's pacifism, although she was to work at Hull House after she returned permanently to America. At that time, however, Zelie clearly wanted to re-establish their old friendship. She wrote: 'I am still a "self-righteous little prig" but I would like to know what else I am, too...'. She continued, 'nothing can ever alter my feeling toward you'; and when the war was over, 'I may be of service to you and the cause for that is after all the only thing that matters.' A poem 'To Sylvia Pankhurst' was enclosed:[54]

> You did not understand, & in your eyes
> I saw a vague surprise,
> As if my voice came from some distant Sphere
> Too far for you to hear;
> Alas! in other days it was not so
> Those days of long ago.
>
> II
> Time was when all my being was thrown wide
> All veils were drawn aside
> That you might enter anywhere at will.
> Now all is hushed and still
> Save for a sound recurring more & more
> The shutting of a door.

Remaining 'as ever yours, Zelie Emerson', she dropped out of the movement in Britain, carrying with her a lock of Sylvia's hair.[55]

It was in September 1915 that Sylvia suffered the greatest emotional loss since her father's death. Standing on the platform at a Trafalgar Square anti-war demonstration, Sylvia heard the newsboys calling, 'Death of Keir Hardie'.[56] Their early passion had cooled in the last three or four years as Sylvia's many commitments in the East End replaced the days of walks and talks in the country and quiet visits to Nevills Court. Perhaps she no longer needed the reassurance Hardie's fatherly presence had offered in the old days when she had no niche of her own. He in turn was preoccupied with his opposition to government proposals, such as the expulsion of Italian anarchists. (Ironically, a man in this category would later succeed him in Sylvia's attentions.) He was burdened by Irish and labour problems, and his activities in connection with the International Socialist Bureau had drained him.

With the declaration of war, Hardie's strong emotions flowed unchecked. He was too tired to do more than fear the burden of an unwanted, indeed a despised, war. Hardie disliked Ramsay Mac-Donald intensely, but he supported him on the war issue along with Philip Snowden, pointing out that MacDonald, not the Labour Party, would suffer from the public's reaction.[57] Snowden, who worked closely with Hardie during the last days, called him a 'prophet and seer', and believed that the war had taken his life as much as if he had been killed in action. Hardie himself believed he was 'inspired with a mission'.[58] When his mission failed, he felt unable to go on.

Beatrice Webb noted Hardie's death in her diary. She had written earlier that he was 'vain and egotistical', 'used up', 'with no real faith left in the Labour Movement as a revolutionary force'.[59] But on his death she felt less qualified to describe him. 'When I came across him in 1912–1914 he had become the picturesque prophet of the Labour Movement . . . a disheartened prophet . . . unlike other leaders he had kept himself unpolluted by personal ambition or desire.' She found him without 'vim' at the end: 'when it became clear to his sincere but limited mind that Labour leaders in Parliament were no different from aristocrats . . . in carrying out revolutionary programmes, he gave up'. It was, she concluded, the war which 'finished him and his devoted followers declared with some justification that he died with a broken heart.'[60]

Early in the war, Hardie had suffered a stroke. He had been admitted to a nursing home in 1915, but, by late May, it was clear that he was no better. He dictated a letter to Frank Smith for Sylvia to let her know he was coming to Nevills Court to clear out his possessions and put his affairs in order. He reminded Sylvia that he still had her letters from America and from elsewhere, some of which he thought publishable. The note advised her: 'you could use your discretion as to which are most worthy of being kept . . . I have not *now* the capacity for dealing with such a matter.' He also had at Nevills Court 'two products of your genius there, one hangs over the fireplace . . . '; that one, 'I have so closely associated with you that I should not like to part with it . . . '.[61]

Sylvia visited her former lover at the time he appointed. It was a moment of sadness with the veil of permanent separation so heavily upon them that neither could handle the situation well. Hardie was ill and tired. Had he not known her so well, he might have expected more from Sylvia than her rejection of his offer of books or some keepsake. When in a childish moment she told him that she did not 'want to be given anything' Sylvia was putting her own feelings first, even before those of the man who had coached her, had been a stoic presence on whom she could depend, and was, in the end, the only true love of her life. Hardie, on her departure, spoke the words that Sylvia might have uttered; telling her that she 'had been very brave'.[62]

In late June, again from the nursing home, Hardie wrote, 'In about a week I expect to be gone from here, with no more mind control than when I came.' Signing his note with 'love', he passed from her life and went home to Cumnock where he was nursed during the final months of his life by the wife he had scarcely known or appreciated in those last years. Sylvia had 'no direct word of him'.[63] Frank Smith, as Hardie's closest confidant, wrote to Sylvia soon after his death: 'I know how deeply and sincerely he loved you in his mind and heart.'[64]

There is no questioning Sylvia's grief, possibly tinged with guilt at her neglect. She had to face his absence, and with a finality that had not been apparent when he left the nursing home for Cumnock. She hid from friends and followers and spent the day after his death writing a tribute to him for the *Dreadnought*. Sylvia was able to display a maturity which was lacking when she went to see him for the last time at Nevills Court. The obituary is the finest example of her love. Rather than speaking of her own loss (which she did with mawkish sentiment in the *Suffragette Movement*, and in an even more dramatized version in *The Home Front*) she wrote a highly personal account in which she spoke of him as 'The truest of friends . . . to those in trouble than any human being I have even known'.[65]

His death could not have been totally unexpected to her; his exile in Cumnock indicated that whatever fragments of their affair still remained existed only in memory. Yet she wrote in *The Home Front* as if his death was a complete surprise: 'Fervently the mind is sought to transform what might have been to what was, nay is, is, is . . . bringing the dead to life, renewing again the dear old comradeship, making it dearer yet and more complete.'[66]

Sylvia Pankhurst's portrait of Keir Hardie (National Portrait Gallery)

She devoted the entire 16 October issue of the *Dreadnought* to Hardie. George Bernard Shaw contributed a touching statement.[67]

> There is, I feel sure, a very generous feeling of relief in the House of Commons and in the Labour Party now that Keir Hardie's body lies mouldering in the grave. I wish I could revive their dread of him by adding that his soul goes marching on; but I do not feel so sure about that: he seems for the moment to have taken it with him. . . . I really do not see what Hardie could do but die. . . .

Earlier Shaw had written a satirical pamphlet, 'Common Sense and the War', which lampooned the government's case in defending Belgium. Keir Hardie wrote to Shaw, 'Your article will produce an elevation of tone in the national life which will be felt for generations to come. . . . My heart throbs towards you with almost feelings of devotion.'[68] Shaw did not reply, but he publicly acknowledged in his mourning, 'Personally I owe Hardie a debt which I shall never be able to pay.'[69]

Frank Smith, who had shared Hardie's interest in spiritualism, contributed his thoughts; and Sylvia wrote a touchingly dispassionate tribute in which she described the hardships he experienced as a child and his difficulties in founding a Labour Party. Such hardships, however, had not left him bitter. An extract from Sylvia's editorial reveals a tender man who affirmed life: 'I remember his delight in the lovely and joyous movements in which plants grow and develop . . . He believed that some day the development of human life will be as beautiful and as good.'[70] In Sylvia's two long obituaries there was no mention of his wife and family. Added to the issue was a reprint from the *Labour Leader*, 'In the Light of Fifty Years', an address which Hardie had given his followers on the occasion of his fiftieth birthday. His wife had been present, one of the rare moments she shared in his triumphs; Sylvia had not attended. Keir Hardie reappeared in some of Sylvia's later writing, in *The Suffragette Movement*, and in *The Home Front*. His letters to her, and hers to him, were preserved. Whatever weakness Sylvia had, she did have a sense of history, and no doubt kept the letters not only as a symbol of her deep love for Hardie, but as a record of her relationship with one of the great men of her time.

Meanwhile, one bit of bureaucratic humanity established early in the war was the American War Relief Commission, headed by Herbert Hoover. In an effort to feed strangled Belgium, the Commission was working with German occupiers, and Dutch and Belgian officials. Hoover was in London dealing with British officials when Sylvia met him: 'How much,' she mused, 'of the humane and thoughtful spirit which appeared to dwell in the Herbert Hoover of these days remained when he ascended to the office of President of the United States?' (It will be recalled that Hoover experienced economic problems of his own in later years.) Hoover sent Sylvia some data on his relief work in Belgium, which she interpreted and used to show that people at home were paying more for rice than those in Holland and Belgium under the artificial economic system established by the War Relief Commission.[71] The news hardly surprised the War Cabinet; but it gave Sylvia ammunition for her propaganda campaign to nationalize food supplies at home. During much of the war she was to raise the issue repeatedly, but a single voice—especially Sylvia Pankhurst's—speaking to a bureaucratic government had little chance of being heard.

Hardie's death had removed the spiritual leader of the peace movement in Britain. MacDonald, Snowden and others kept the issue alive in political circles. Among the Liberals, the most respected opponent of the war was John Viscount Morley, who resigned from the Cabinet before the official declaration of war, but remained silent. For every Bertrand Russell there were many supporters, such as the Webbs and H. G. Wells. Shaw could never be counted on for a straightforward position, although his controversial pamphlet 'Common Sense and the War' indicated that he was a pacifist. E. D. Morel and the union of Democratic Control, another pacifist organization, attracted mostly intellectuals, some from the ILP.[72]

Pre-war suffrage organizations were divided on the issue. Within the NUWCSS, Mrs Fawcett personally opposed pacifism, but representatives from her democratic union were at the Hague for the women's peace conference. The WSPU, still under the control of Mrs Pankhurst, and with a significant drop in membership, supported the war wholeheartedly. Mrs Despard was a pacifist; the Women's Freedom League organized several programmes similar to Sylvia's, including 'Despard Hall', a former public house which served food at cost price. Mrs Pethick-Lawrence, who joined the United Suffragists after her dismissal from the WSPU was, like her husband, loyal to the ILP pacifists. Mrs Pethick-Lawrence, indeed, became the most prominent leader among the suffragists in the women's peace movement. Sylvia and Emmeline Pethick-Lawrence were again united, as they had been in the early days of the suffrage movement. Still committed to obtaining the vote, Emmeline looked to 'victory' on both counts—peace and suffrage.[73] In this dual goal, she was joined by Emily Hobhouse, who had gained public recognition in exposing the disastrous conditions in which Boer women and children suffered in British concentration camps during that war; and Jane Addams, a pioneer social reformer, from America.[74]

The peace movement in Britain brought former suffragists into an alliance with socialists who had not been concerned with votes for women. *Labour Leader* editor Fenner Brockway, Henry Nevinson and George Lansbury, who had helped to establish the United Suffragists, were joined by Ben Tillett, radical leader of the British Socialist Party, who actually supported the war; Tom Mann, a tough union organizer with extreme leftist sympathies; Sylvia, from the East End radical suffrage group, and the Pethick-Lawrences.

The key issue was conscription. Volunteers streamed in at the beginning, but they could not sustain the military's needs. As the government debated the Conscription Bill in 1916, radical Liberals, trade unionists and suffragists held public meetings against the draft in which Sylvia participated. The September 1915 Trafalgar Square meeting represented the largest numbers on a single platform, but other meetings were held regularly in Victoria Park under the auspices of the ELFS. The pacifists hired public halls around the capital for their meetings, but this became increasingly difficult as the war continued and people's patience with pacifists became exhausted. George Lansbury called a 'No Conscription Conference' in December 1915, but in January 1916, Parliament passed the first Conscription Act. Undaunted, the pacifists continued their campaign, using whatever means at their disposal to oppose what they regarded as an imperialist war under capitalist control.[75]

On the international scene, a network of women's organizations combined to form a Women's Peace party, with a reluctant Jane Addams as President. Dr Aleta Jacobs of Holland called for an international meeting at The Hague.[76] The International Congress of Women, held in April 1915, included women from belligerent nations (Hungary, Austria, Germany) and from war-torn Belgium and Italy, the Scandinavian countries, and North America.[77]

Britain was represented only by chance. Although nearly 200 British women, Sylvia included, had been designated as delegates, the Home Secretary, Reginald McKenna, contrived to keep them in Britain. Passports were unknown to British travellers before the war, but the fear of alien spies and other wartime nuisances led to a passport system. Women going to The Hague had to apply for the now official travel documents, and Sylvia was denied a passport.[78] The rest were still more frustrated; McKenna simply withheld permission for a ship to take them across the Channel.

Emmeline Pethick-Lawrence was in America for a speaking tour; she and her husband had joined the American delegation, which included feminist-pacifist Rosika Schwimmer of Hungary, Schwimmer being in America to lecture on the need for world peace at the time. Chrystal MacMillan, a Scottish lawyer, and Kathleen Courtney had been in Holland since the previous February, making preparations for the Congress.[79] On arrival, Mrs Pethick-Lawrence joined her British colleagues already at The Hague and the assembly of 'about fifteen hundred' women in calling for peace by negotiation, and in passing several resolutions for maintaining peace in the future. They also appointed a committee whose mission was to speak with the heads of as many governments as possible. In England they met Asquith and another of his ministers; and in America, Woodrow Wilson. While no concrete prescription for ending war resulted from these talks, a permanent organization, the Women's International League for Peace and Freedom did emerge.

In the autumn of 1915, the British section of the Women's International League held a conference at Westminster, which Sylvia attended on behalf of the ELFS. She helped organize an East London branch of the League, but failed to gain office in the League itself. There is no question that Sylvia was a devout pacifist in this period, but her commitment was too extreme for her to be of much help to the more temperate organizers such as Emmeline Pethick-Lawrence. Sylvia published articles in the *Dreadnought* by several prominent feminist-pacifists, such as Olive Schreiner and Jane Addams, but it is likely that she pirated them from elsewhere.[80]

Since Sylvia controlled the ELFS, she was able to be as active on the peace issue within her own organization as time allowed. She organized several meetings in Poplar, and in other areas of the East End where the ELFS had branches. Mrs Hercbergova, the manageress of the toy factory, enjoyed a passing fame when she was the featured speaker at Bow Women's Hall on the topic 'The Struggle for Freedom in Poland'. Thomas Masaryk, brother of the future president of Czechoslovakia, had come to tea with Sylvia and Norah as a result of his friendship with Mrs Hercbergova, giving the impression that the toy-maker was well placed in socialist circles. An insight into the manner in which Sylvia sometimes addressed serious issues is illustrated in a later mention of her meeting with Masaryk. She wrote that he was not a socialist because he 'preferred Christabel'.[81]

Other old associations which had suffered during Christabel's rise to leadership in the WSPU were re-established. Esther Roper and Eva-Gore Booth joined Sylvia on platforms in the East End, condemning the war and calling for an early peace.[82] And, always a supporter, never a spokeswoman, Norah Smyth joined the lists of feminist-pacifists in a brief message to the readership at the end of 1915. She advised that 'peace would be the overriding issue in the year to come'[83]— which was the case in 1916 with the ELFS.

In a continuing attempt to maintain a balance between suffrage and peace agitation the East London Federation of Suffragettes changed its name in March 1916 to the Workers Suffrage Federation (WSF), symbolically acknowledging its long-held goal of universal suffrage.[84] The times also called for a new image at Lincoln's Inn. *The Suffragette* was allowed to perish in Paris, but had been resurrected in London in April 1915, and in October the name was changed to *Britannia*, so reflecting Christabel's new patriotism.[85] Mrs Pankhurst and Christabel, funded on at least one occasion by the Lloyd George government,[86] gave all their energies in support of the war. Christabel 'moved into a role in which the Pankhursts were to excel—that of a recruiting sergeant.'[87]

Sylvia, in the meantime, defined pacifism for her readers in terms which generally described herself. A pacifist, she wrote, 'is a rebel against the present organization of society'. Olive Schreiner, however, saw in pacifism the means for taking 'the great step which humanity must take if it is to continue in its upward path—the step across the narrow bounds of nation and race in a larger and wider human fellowship.'[88] On a more personal level, Sylvia's activities and propaganda against the war could not hide behind the noble platitudes expressed by Schreiner. In her East End environment she 'felt sorrow in having to tell parents whose sons were at the front that war was wrong and its ideals false. . . . It required an effort to bring myself to do it . . . I lost old friends and subscribers to our movement.'[89]

The suffragists chose to close their ranks. When the International Women's Suffrage Alliance was formed, Mrs Fawcett of the NUWSS represented Britain. None of the Pankhurst women was included on its governing board. In Britain, when the National Council of Adult Suffrage was formed, Mrs Pethick-Lawrence was once more treasurer of a suffrage organization. Again, all the Pankhurst women were excluded from official duties.[90] Sylvia, representing the WSF, was affiliated. Indeed, even as a representative of the WSF on the committee, Sylvia talked of resigning, as she 'was generally a minority of one and could do nothing'.[91] Two months after complaining to her board she resigned, and the organization disaffiliated from the National Council.[92]

Always on the periphery of organized activity, Sylvia attacked the war from the borough of Poplar, often giving the impression that she was the sole inheritor of the peace mantle. She bombarded Cabinet ministers, in particular Lloyd George, with letters and requests to receive deputations. Not one of them replied. Her crusades for working women and children are legend in the East End, as are the toy factory, 'the Mother's Arms', and her 'Price Cost Restaurants'.[93] Her approach to the problems of her clients in Bow was not purely abstract, in the form of speeches and editorials. Nor did she involve the public only through the vehicle of processions and demonstrations; she gave considerable energy to the everyday issues which confronted her by way of personal appeal to 400 Old Ford Road. Sylvia, Norah Smyth and several professional women from the West End laboured for the individual mother, child and remaining men—those too old or frail or too young to be sent to the trenches. For a time they had the services of a woman doctor, but in 1917 she left her volunteer post with the WSF to give increasing time to paediatric medicine elsewhere.[94]

On Easter Monday 1916, an Irish rising in Dublin held sections of the city centre for more than a week until British troops were brought in and the rebels surrendered. The rebels had sought a propaganda victory through a strong gesture in favour of the suspended Home Rule Act. This produced a violent reaction in England, which regarded

Workers' Suffrage Federation: demonstration, Trafalgar Square, 9 April 1916

the rebels as traitors in the German cause rather than loyalists to their own. That gave Sylvia one more unpopular cause to champion (it will be remembered that she was arrested in 1914 for leading a demonstration in favour of Home Rule), and she wrote a long polemic called 'The Irish Rebellion: Our View'—that is, of course, her own.[95] The next week an Irish woman reported in the *Dreadnought* on 'Scenes from the Irish Rebellion',[96] but subsequently the paper dropped Ireland in favour of twenty-seven Russian followers of Tolstoi, who had been indicted in Russia for issuing a manifesto against the war.[97] Meanwhile the British had imprisoned some 200 Irish out of fear that they might be tempted to stage another rising. Sylvia later took up the matter in a pamphlet, which cast England at war in the role of villain.[98]

During the early years of the war Sylvia placed herself in opposition to so many things, it is hard to know what she favoured, other than peace and the vote. Even in circles where she was accepted, she frequently opposed people who generally agreed with her. At the Bow relief committee she 'threatened' to expose Lansbury and others in the *Dreadnought* for withholding food rations from a woman with children who had been caught drunk by a parson, also a committee member.[99] She seemed unable to compromise, never knowing how to win her point without direct confrontation. She, like her East End following, resented the authority of the government, the borough council, and the umbrella suffrage societies.

Yet the minutes of the ELFS reveal another dimension to Sylvia. It was she who understood personality conflicts among the organizers; and she, seemingly patiently, worked with her executive committee to defuse and dispel frictions. As combative as she was in groups where she felt she had no control, among her trusted circle she was regarded as a democratic, responsive leader. She was, on occasion, willing to share the limelight with her members, even, if less frequently, to let them claim sole attention. One member to whom she deferred, other than Norah, was Mrs Drake, who commanded Sylvia's respect and proved essential in keeping the members in line. Had Charlotte Drake and Sylvia fallen out, it is likely that Drake could have taken over leadership of the WSF. Her resolutions were almost always accepted; her voice was heard in the inner councils. And she was loyal to every scheme Sylvia devised over the years.[100]

Charlotte Drake, a spirited mother of five, had once been a barmaid; later, she joined the teeming ranks of women in East London who earned their livelihood in tailoring. As a worker's wife, she supported Sylvia on the feminist issue and remained friendly with her mentor after their crusades in the East End had ended. Sylvia paid her 'thirty shillings a week' so that she could hire someone else to take care of home and children—an unusual phenomenon—leaving Drake free to organize for the ELFS.[101]

Mrs Drake represented the WSF at the British Dominions Women's Suffrage Union in July 1916 where she spoke of the need for sex education among the working classes.[102] The women of East London, like working-class women generally, had little knowledge of how the human body functioned. Certainly they understood the sexual act; but many poorly educated women had no knowledge of birth-control methods, crude as they were. Home-procured abortion was the mainstay for preventing unwanted births. Sex was not a topic for open discussion. This attitude prevailed in much of the world at the time. In Australia, for instance, Adela was acused of 'pruriency' for staying in a courtroom while children testified on offences 'against little girls' perpetrated by men—men alone were supposed to hear such evidence—but Adela represented the Women's Political Association which brought these cases, and she stayed.[103]

If the middle and upper classes were beginning to discuss sex, it was usually through elaborate circumlocutions about 'racial health' (although *Married Love*, published in 1918 and written by Marie Stopes, was an outspoken and controversial primer in sexual instruction).[104] Working-class women remained silent on the issue, unless speculating among themselves as to whether a woman was pregnant, or piously condemning the husband of one who had many children. The WSF acknowledged this problem through Mrs Drake's lecture. Sylvia carried the theme further by reporting the hardships of ignorant young women who engaged in sexual relations and then, during the war, were left to fend for themselves and their offspring.[105] But in her newspaper, Sylvia was cautious. Reporting a conference on the growing birthrate, she quoted the Bishop of Southwark as saying sexual intercourse should only be performed for 'producing children'; any other motive was 'self-gratification', which he found unjustifiable. She also quoted a doctor arguing that the 'marital embrace' was an 'expression of mutual affection', but she passed over these views, only commenting that they represented one of 'deep and permanent interest to humankind'.[106]

Later, she was less equivocal in defining her own position. In 1918, when Stopes' book was first published, she committed this passage to her notebook: 'We are for free sexual union contracted and terminated at will. We are for free love because love is free and no one can bind it. We believe that loveless union should be terminated'. Concluding on an extremely radical feminist note, Sylvia believed that 'polyandry, if by agreement of consenting adults, is legitimate'.[107] Not even Sylvia's strongest female allies in the East End were ready for polyandry—to say nothing of their menfolk.

As the war ground on towards the end of its third year, WSF members were still energetically chalking pavements and announcing peace demonstrations, even as they had worked for the vote at the height of the suffrage movement. But there were fewer than previously, though Mrs Drake, Mrs Walker, Norah Smyth and the secretary had been mainstays from the first and were still fired with energy for the cause, whatever it happened to be. Mrs Minnie Lansbury, George Lansbury's wife, had joined them, and Edgar Lansbury briefly controlled the nearly empty funds.

The financial situation continued to be critical, as the statement for August, 1917 (the only one surviving) indicated:[108]

	Expenses	Receipts
Federation	£86 18s 10d	£42 19s 2d
Dreadnought	£114 6s 8¾d	£72 3s 10½d
Clinics	£48 8s 6d	£65 14s 11d
Crêche	£43 16s 2d	£10 14s 9d
Bow Rest	£56 3s 8d	£62 17s 1½d
	Expenses	Receipts
Poplar	£20 17s 6d	£14 11s 2d
Sundries	£10 0s 0d	£1 3s 6d
	£371 1s 4¾d	£270 1s 9½d

Loans (outstanding):   £263 14s 9d

Lansbury, citing the burden of commitments to his business, resigned as treasurer that month. The financial committee agreed that, in order to cut expenses, the secretary member should be given notice. She was unable to take shorthand, and Sylvia had been thinking of adding yet another person who could to the staff. Sylvia failed to recognize the precarious financial position into which her organization had fallen. Instead of dismissing the secretary (who solved the problem by giving notice herself) Sylvia repeated her call for an increase in the staff. This time the committee overruled her, and the burden of meeting over-drafts fell on Norah, who stressed 'the need to hold down finances'.[109]

The toy factory loomed large at this time due to decreasing sales and demand for higher salaries. Mrs Hercbergova now became a problem. When she was first employed 'she could not make toys and had no business knowledge'. In charity, Sylvia had employed her and helped in the early phases of her training. Before long, Mrs Hercbergova became manager of the factory. And when the factory began making money, Mrs Hercbergova threw out the profit-sharing plan and turned it into a business, reinvesting the profits. She also received a series of pay rises, going from a little over one pound a week to two pounds in six months. She was, however, 'always anxious to keep down the wages of the workers', and therefore had turned the socialist WSF members into employers of a sweatshop. When Hercbergova approached the committee for another pay rise, Sylvia drew the line and held her to her current salary. She did agree to a commission on orders received personally by Mrs Hercbergova. The concession lasted briefly, then the factory manager was back insisting on a further increase. Her assistant at the time was making thirty shillings but was thought to be 'unreliable' and 'stayed away' if there were air raids. The question before the committee was whether to keep Mrs Hercbergova, give her the rise, and continue the factory in hopes that it would return a profit, or close the factory down. They gave her the rise for two months only, until the issue of the factory and its management could be settled more definitively.[110]

Later, Sylvia wrote of her experiences with Mrs Hercbergova in *The Home Front*. Mrs Hercbergova, she wrote, was untrained, but because Sylvia felt sorry for her, she hired her. Uncle Herbert Goulden, a small businessman, was persuaded to make several trips to the factory as superviser until Mrs Hercbergova became competent at book-keeping. Soon Mrs Hercbergova was manager. She put the business on a profit-making basis, rather than continuing it as a cooperative: 'Karl Marx was now ousted in favour of "your great economists, Stuart Mill and Adam Smith",' was one of the lines in Sylvia's volume.[111] Mrs Hercbergova sued Sylvia's publisher, Hutchinson, for libel, who in turn asked Sylvia for proof. Not wishing to become finan-cially involved in defending the suit, Sylvia promptly hired a solicitor, who advised she disclaim financial liability. In order to keep the book in print, however, Sylvia was eventually forced to produce documentation for her statements against Mrs Hercbergova. She had some of the minutes from the toy factory committee meetings, but record-keeping was not her forte, and they were incomplete. The only proof Sylvia could produce was the discussion of Mrs Hercbergova's wages from the 'Minutes of the East London Federation of Suffragettes', which in the early years controlled the factory.

Sylvia then contacted Norah Smyth, who was staying with her brother at the British Institute in Florence. Sylvia explained her plight and asked Norah to send all records she had on the toy factory. What emerged from Norah was astounding proof of her financial sacrifices in the East End enterprise. By 1918, Norah had sold jewels, cashed bonds and even parted with an oak table in order to stave off a financial crisis at the toy factory. In all, Norah lent the factory £750; some of her investment took the form of shares in the company, the balance as straight loans. When the factory showed surplus profit, Norah was paid back roughly one pound per week. But she was never to recoup her entire investment. Indeed, between February 1915, and July 1916, Norah lent the East London Federation of Suffragettes a total of £1839 10s 4d for its various works.[112] She also deposited securities on additional loans from a London Bank, at one time forestalling eviction from the premises occupied by the factory because of default on bills.[113] Norah's corroboration of Sylvia's statements regarding Mrs Hercbergova's conduct, as well as her financial accounting, were incorporated into Sylvia's deposition to Hutchinson and Company. She also reminded Sylvia personally that while Mrs Hercbergova was receiving £3 a week, the two women were living in Old Ford Road on a diet of bread, margarine and tea[114]—£3 was a generous wage for working in the East End.

In March 1917, the news of the revolution in Russia and the formation of the New Provisional Government brought joy to WSF headquarters. The executive committee passed supporting resolutions, congratulating 'the Russian Duma on the overthrow of the autocratic dominion of the Tzar' and 'the Russian workers in their great fight'.[115] The *Dreadnought* joined in, chiding Lloyd George and Bonar Law for believing that the events in Russia were 'not serious'.[116]

The line adopted by the *Dreadnought* during the months that followed was not so much the victory of the Russian workers, which was far from clear at the time, but the possibility that the Russian Revolution would take Russia out of the war and enable Britain to withdraw as well. This was hardly a likely move politically, especially after the United States entered the war in April, but Sylvia continued her statements about peace, held demonstrations and processions for the cause, and called for a unilateral British withdrawal from the war to match the expected withdrawal of Russia. She kept the old link between hopes for peace and universal suffrage, but a new banner, 'Negotiate for Peace on Russian Terms', appeared in the summer at a procession to the House of Commons. But adult suffrage demonstrations could only get a turnout which Sylvia thought disgraceful, although stalwart WSF volunteers went as 'peace pickets' to the House of Commons, and another delegation chanted 'Give peace in our time, O Lord', when the Bishop of London ventured east to pray for victory at Tower Hill.[117] While it was important to keep the group's goals in the public eye, Sylvia's personal feelings illustrating the privations around her were manifested in a peace poem she wrote at this time:[118]

> The soldier's wife is like to faint;
> Today her children had no bread.
> The Under-Secretary said 'there's
> no complaint, there's no complaint.'

News from Russia through the spring and summer was sporadic and inconclusive. Even before mid-May, when the Provisional Government publicly repudiated the idea of a separate peace, Sylvia had dropped it from her May Day greetings in the *Dreadnought*. On 2 June, after the First Coalition, when Kerensky as the dominant figure agreed to stay in the war and even to take the offensive, she was prescient in stating in an editorial 'that Kerensky, too, will go, for . . . Kerensky has failed to realize the greatness of the movement that he would lead'.[119] Even before the show of Bolshevik strength in the great Petrograd demonstrations of 16 and 17 June (the 'July Days', following the Russian calendar) Sylvia had adopted a stance that would make her receptive to Lenin's slogan, 'All Power to the Soviets' and to the Bolshevik victory in October.

A Radical in Revolution

My own sympathies are a good deal with Sylvia; But she does not
stand for anything effective in England, and as she is a spoilt child
. . . she refuses to recognize or study anything that does not happen
to interest her temperament . . .
—George Bernard Shaw, to an unidentified correspondent (n.d.)

Throughout the years of 1918 and 1919, Sylvia moved from one radical
cause to the next, even more radical, cause: from peace at any price to
strong support for the Bolsheviks in the Russian Revolution, to organization of the first Communist Party in Great Britain—the Communist
Party, British Section of the Third International (CP – BSTI). The
utopian strain in her old socialist faith reappeared in her new one
—an attitude described by Lenin as an 'infantile disorder'.

By early 1917 all participants in the war were beginning to weary,
but Russia was falling into a state of new anarchy with defeat at the
front, strikes and riots in the cities. By early march the disturbances
had become the first revolution. The Duma demanded the Tzar's
abdication, and the Romanov dynasty came to an end. The events in
Russia seemed of immense relevance to all shades of British opinion.
Some, like Churchill, saw a danger that Russia might drop out of the
war, bringing the full weight of German and Austrian power to bear
on the Italian and western fronts. Those on the far left, like Sylvia, saw
the possibility of a socialist revolution that would end the war and
begin the triumphant march towards socialism throughout Europe.
Between March and November, Kerensky attempted to keep Russia
in the war, but war-weariness amid internal dissension was even more
prevalent in Russia than elsewhere.

British socialists, and female socialists in particular, received the
news of the revolution in Russia with many and diverse reactions.
Frances, Countess of Warwick, an eccentric supporter of George
Lansbury and of the revolution, reported reaction at Court: 'If you
could hear, as I do, the horror and hatred of the Russian Revolution
from King George, throughout the court, and in the aristocracy . . .
you *know* how little sympathy . . . exists with the real allies of the Proletariat—*fear* exists but *hatred*, too . . . The ordinary everyday talk of my
relations and those in court would amaze you . . . '[1]

Beatrice Webb, representing middle-class socialists, initially supported the Russian Revolution, writing that if it worked it would prove that democracy worked. But, when enthusiasts within the socialist movement, especially in the ILP, expressed their hopes that a similar revolution would come to Europe, Mrs Webb retreated. After the Bolshevik revolution she suspected Mary MacArthur, who had worked with the Webbs during the war, of 'sympathy with the lurid doings in Petrograd' and of entertaining Bolshevik ideas. When Russian agents tried to enlist Mrs Webb's support, she would have nothing to do with them, although she and Sidney travelled to Russia in 1920 with a delegation of British socialists.[2]

Mrs Pankhurst, still committed to the war and close to Lloyd George, wrote to the Prime Minister: 'We have come to the conclusion that it is the duty of our Union to send immediately to Russia representatives who will explain to the Russian people the opinions as to the war and conditions of peace held by us as patriotic British women, loyal to the national and Allied cause.'[3] Lloyd George responded to her request, arrangements were made for Mrs Pankhurst and Jessie Kenney to go, and in June 1917, they left for Petrograd. They travelled widely, met various Russian officials, and returned home in October unimpressed with what they had seen. Mrs Pankhurst's views reflected her move toward the right as well as the chaotic conditions in Russia. Committees directed everything: even the hospitals she had visited were run by committees of wounded soldiers, issuing directives affecting the conditions of other wounded men.[4]

The other Pankhurst women were divided. Christabel was anti-Bolshevik and pro-war.[5] Adela, in Australia, remained a socialist and pacifist, opposing even Australian participation. She was arrested during a demonstration in August 1917, appealed in December but lost. Meanwhile, in November, she had married Tom Walsh, a fellow socialist and pacifist. She wrote to Sylvia that she was very happy, 'though anxious about the four months' gaol which lie before me unless I am more lucky than I dare hope.'[6] The prison sentence interrupted her honeymoon, but Adela became the only one of the sisters to achieve the kind of marital stability their parents enjoyed. She wrote to Sylvia: ' . . . this is the life, isn't it, and I am happy—more than happy in it hoping that I shall have a son or daughter to carry on our father's work.'[7]

Adela was only in infrequent contact with her mother and Christabel, but she and Sylvia remained in touch during their communist years. Adela's son, Richard, was born in 1919; he died in childhood. Sylvia Walsh was next, followed by two more daughters, Christian and Ursula.[8] Walsh was a widower who had daughters by his earlier marriage and Adela wrote to Sylvia, 'they are very good children. They adore the little boy, but, you see, I have to be careful that they do not feel he has more love than they and as you are Auntie to him, please accept the position for them, too.' Given Sylvia's concern with the stepchildren of the world, it goes without saying that her response was a warm one.[9]

Sylvia, meanwhile, increasingly adopted the Russian cause as her own in the campaigns from Old Ford Road, but her involvement, and that of Norah Smyth and the WSF, in the pro-Bolshevik movement was complicated. The WSF minutes, which Sylvia kept, reveal very little about her activities in this period. The Home Office maintained surveillance of Sylvia, Norah, and George Lansbury, and other Bolshevik sympathizers, and reported on their movements regularly to the Cabinet.[10] Sylvia left an autobiographical narrative in the form of several drafts of a projected book, the 'Red Twilight'. The drafts differ from one another, from other published accounts of the period, and from the Special Branch reports.[11] The *Dreadnought*, which presumably reflected Sylvia's stand, took a radical line—indeed, Lenin's phrase, 'left-wing Communism', best describes Sylvia and her paper during this phase.

Even prior to the success of the Bolsheviks in Russia, Sylvia had run into trouble with the Home Office. In July 1917 she published a column calling on the armed forces to lay down their weapons and refuse to fight any longer. This was a clear call to mutiny, made in full awareness of the similar stand taken by the French anarchist-pacifist, Gustave Hervé, which had been responsible in part for French army mutinies in May and June. As a result, police raided the editorial offices of the *Dreadnought* looking for other subversive material. If the raid was designed to intimidate, it failed. Sylvia's subsequent speeches and writings were, if anything, still more provocative. It was partly a sign of defiance that she changed the name of the paper from the *Woman's Dreadnought* to the *Workers' Dreadnought*, seeking a more universal appeal.

Before the armistice ended the war, the women won an interim victory in the fight for suffrage. Sylvia paid little attention. She barely mentioned the passage of the Act in the *Dreadnought*. Her idealized position on universal suffrage, but above all the fact that the Act left her current constituency in the East End without the vote, gave it little meaning at the time. Furthermore, she was so wrapped up in Russia that the vote had become a side-issue.[12] Here is a further example of how quickly Sylvia could change causes, and in this particular case it raises the question of how committed she was to feminist issues like votes for women. Although headlines in the *Dreadnought* during this period centred almost entirely on Russia, Sylvia failed to mention that Kerensky and the Provisional Government had granted equal rights to women, including the vote, within a month of taking power. She did everything she could to compare Russia favourably to England, yet she failed to capitalize on the one issue that most concerned her following at that time.

In *Stepping Stones to Women's Liberty*, Les Garner, after a thorough reading of her papers pertaining to the suffrage movement, concluded that Sylvia and the East End Federation of Suffragettes (and later the WSF) had made one important contribution to the movement. This was 'their exposure of the limitations of suffragism'. It was inequality of the system, not votes, which kept women down. This may be the explanation for her seemingly incongruous switch from suffrage to communism. On the other hand, by studying Sylvia at this stage, rather than viewing her in life-long perspective, it is perhaps too easy to accept her account at face value. Sylvia had a penchant for speaking in the most revolutionary terms during these years, yet her behaviour after 1930 suggests she may have been less a genuine revolutionary than her speeches and writings at this time indicate.[13]

Christabel formed the Women's Party in November 1917, but she maintained her stand on segregation of the sexes: 'it would be wrong for women, with the special political contribution they have to make . . . to merge their . . . identity in the worn-out parties of the past.'[14] In December 1918, she stood for the Women's Party in the general election at Smethwick.[15] Sylvia was nominated by the socialists to a vacant seat in the Hallam division of Sheffield, but she declined to stand, and supported Arthur MacManus of the Socialist Labour Party for the seat.[16] In fact, her current political preoccupation was Bolshevik rule, and she told her *Dreadnought* readers that Parliament was an outdated machine. Her revolutionary zeal in this phase of her life was supreme: she was now working with the WSF to establish soviets in Britain, and it was illogical to stand for a seat in a body whose days she believed were numbered.[17]

Sylvia was silent on her sister's campaign. Both Christabel and her mother had great hopes for Christabel's election, which could have been regarded as a vindication and repayment for eleven years of committed effort on behalf of the suffrage movement. Christabel stood for equal pay, a shorter working week, and the right of women to hold office. She threw in a little anti-Bolshevism for good measure, pointing out that her proposal for shorter working hours was serious, while the Bolsheviks exploited similar issues to make trouble: 'if a 40-hour week were established', they would demand that 'workers strike for a 30-hour week'.[18] But Christabel lost. Countess Markievicz did win in that election, but she refused to take her seat. No woman entered Parliament in 1918.

For a time after her defeat, Christabel wrote a news column for the *Daily Sketch*, opposing Bolshevism as well as the newly proposed League of Nations. She believed that to retain national independence, Britain must keep up the Franco-British alliance. This meant exclusion of Germany and Russia from post-war influence.[19] In this, Sylvia was in agreement with Christabel, but on completely different ideological grounds. Sylvia said in one public stance: 'we are going to have revolution here just as they have in other countries . . . the League of Nations is only prepared for the one purpose of crushing liberty. . . . If the police came here tonight and killed some of us I think it would do a great deal of good.'[20] It is hard to reconcile policemen killing people in her audience (did she mean herself as well?) with the League crushing liberty: Sylvia seemed to have a less secure hold on reality at this stage of her political life.

Christabel soon withdrew from public life. Dame Ethyl Smyth, who was close to Christabel and her mother at this time, believed that she was unable to recover from the blow of electoral defeat. There 'occurred a change in her mentality which almost everyone except Mrs Pankhurst noticed and deplored.'[21] Leaving Christabel to lick her wounds, Mrs Pankhurst was forced to earn her living. With the four babies she had adopted during the war, she moved for a time to Canada, where she lectured against Bolshevism and on the dangers of venereal disease, which had increased to such an extent during the war it alarmed the health authorities.[22] She and Sylvia were on divergent paths. They did not see each other before her mother's departure, nor did Mrs Pankhurst keep in touch with her from Canada.

When the war ended in November 1918, the *Dreadnought* scarcely mentioned the armistice. Like the achievement of women's suffrage, which had at last been partially won, Sylvia all but ignored peace in favour of her campaign to revolutionize Britain.[23] Her polemical activities for Bolshevism were wide-ranging, and her workload must have been staggering. As in the anti-war campaign, her efforts appear superhuman. She thought her health was not good, but in her thirties and early forties, she rarely suffered from physical illness. Psychological strain was more of a problem, and it is possible that Sylvia's extreme statements gained much of their force from inner tension and overwork. On the other hand, Dora Russell described a Bolshevik friend in terms that would have fitted Sylvia: 'Like so many communists I was to meet then and later, she was totally convinced and dogmatic, willing to make any sacrifice for the cause'. Russell thought communism was a religion to the new converts, not a form of government. If this was the case with Sylvia, she brought all of the fervour to communist conversion that Christabel was about to bring to the Second Coming of Christ.

While some in Britain followed the Bolshevik experiment with interest, workers' councils on the Soviet model were actually established in France and Italy. Soldiers' rebellions in Austria and Germany had helped to end the war in its last weeks.[24] Meanwhile, in Versailles, European leaders and American allies were working to create a stable world for the future. New national boundaries were drawn in the Balkan states, and the Austria-Hungarian empire was dismantled. The conference declared Germany's war guilt, in spite of Lloyd George's protestations, and it punished Germany with heavy reparations and the loss of Alsace, Lorraine and her colonial territories. It was a time of major political readjustment, considerable instability and diplomatic uncertainty throughout Europe.

In Germany the voices of Rosa Luxemburg and Karl Liebknecht, stilled during the war, once more called the workers to revolt. Luxemburg, like Sylvia, occupied the far left of the socialist movement. Her views, however, were formed by years of study and devotion to Marxian scientific socialism. A founder member of the Spartacist League (precursor of the Kommunistische Partie Deutschlands—KDP), Luxemburg, of Polish-Jewish descent, was the intellect behind the movement.[25] Karl Liebknecht shared Rosa's views but, like Sylvia, he was more enthusiastic for the cause than embued with its underlying theory.

Rioting began in German city streets in December 1918, continuing into January 1919, persuading socialists that the chain of revolutions had begun. The German government, however, mobilized the army to quell the riots, and brought the violence under control. In mid-January, Luxemburg and Liebknecht were arrested and shot on their way to prison camp. The KPD was powerless to carry on without its leaders, and it went temporarily underground.

Italy was another anticipated locus of revolution; hunger, unemployment and discontent prevailed among the returning soldiers. Appearance suggested that the time had come to bring left-wing socialists to power. But socialists were divided among themselves, and they competed for the support of the working class with anarchists, syndicalists and Fascists—to say nothing of the continued hold of the Church. The Socialist Party did, in fact, affiliate with the Third International in 1919.[26] Mussolini, after splitting with the socialists, gained a large following of discontented soldiers who, instead of seeking a Russian solution, turned instead to the perverted nationalism of the Fascist movement.

In France, another link in Lenin's chain, the far left broke away to join with the newly formed Trotsky movement in 1920, with headquarters in Amsterdam, while the remaining radical socialists affiliated with the Third International in Moscow; neither group attracted enough influence with the French workers to bring about a revolution. Sweden, Norway and Finland were more important to Russia in the final analysis than the larger European countries. Socialist sympathy in all three was helpful to Russian propaganda. Stockholm became a centre for agents—including Norah Smyth—coming and going with messages for Moscow from Germany, Italy, France and England.

In England, Sylvia made contact with people who, like herself, were staunch supporters of Russia—men like Tom Mann, with whom she worked in the peace movement, and Harry Pollitt, a younger member of the British Socialist Party. Mann and Pollitt emerged in the fore-front of the Communist Party as it finally took form in Britain. Among Sylvia's old supporters, the Pethick-Lawrences and Mrs Despard were drawn to the Kerensky Revolution; but Frederick and Emmeline Pethick-Lawrence, staunch members of the Labour Party, abandoned Russia after the Bolsheviks came to power.

In the first months following the March Revolution of 1917, new friends appeared in the *Dreadnought*. G. D. H. Cole, leading Labour theorist, wrote about the relationship between the Russian workers' councils and the British trade unions. He focused on the potential importance of the trade unions as centres of political control, urging women to affiliate with the unions and to work from within to make the labour movement treat them as equal partners. R. Palme Dutt, a more radical theorist, also wrote on several occasions for the *Dreadnought*; but a split with Sylvia over the direction of the Communist Party in 1920 put an end to his association with the paper.[27]

Another new contributor to the *Dreadnought* was Silvio Corio, an Italian anarchist. Corio joined George Bernard Shaw in contributing to the Christmas issue of 1917, which focused on 'Italy and Her Future' through the eyes of the exile. Shaw, induced by Sylvia to provide additional comments on a speech he had recently made dealing with 'Democracy' advised: 'the truth is . . . the difficulty about governing with the consent of the people is that the people will not consent to being governed at all.'[28]

The Dreadnought began to carry political columns and propaganda from Russia, including translations of Lenin and Trotsky, and a column mysteriously labelled 'from our Russian Correspondent'. On occasion, Ludwig Martins, a communist leader in America, submitted mostly polemical copy about the purported strength of the Communist Party there.[29] Other contributors included the Zionist leader, Israel Zangwill, and an occasional article by an American radical, Max Eastman, whom Sylvia had met through the black poet and writer, Claude McKay. Sylvia first met McKay at the International Club, which according to McKay, 'was full of excitement, with dogmatists and doctrinaires of radical left ideas'. While foreigners—and among these Jews—predominated, McKay noted that Sylvia was among the 'Socialists, Communists, anarchists, syndicalists, one-big-unionists and trade unionists, soap-boxers, protesters, scribblers, and editors of little radical sheets' who comprised the English membership.[30] This helped launch Sylvia into the forefront of British radicalism. McKay, a Jamaican by birth, had lived in the United States and enjoyed the patronage of Frank Harris as well as Max Eastman before going to London to extend his perspectives and write a novel. At the time he met Sylvia he was unemployed, but had begun writing articles for a series of black publications in America. Sylvia took him on at the *Dreadnought*, where he covered dissident groups for the paper, including the London dockers. Sylvia never gave McKay a byline, although he worked for her for several months during 1920. He left the only account, partial that it is, of how she ran the paper and gathered materials.

It was McKay's function to 'dig up something from the London docks from the coloured as well as the white seamen and write from a point of view which would be fresh and different'. He noted that[31]

> ... I was assigned to read the foreign newspapers from America, India, Australia, and other parts of the British Empire, and mark the items which might interest *Dreadnought* readers. In this work I was assisted by one Comrade Vie ... [who] read the foreign-language papers, mainly French and German. ... The association with Pankhurst put me in the nest of extreme radicalism in London. The other male-controlled radical groups were quite hostile to the Pankhurst group and its rather hysterical militancy. ... But Pankhurst herself had a personality as picturesque and passionate as any radical in London. ... Her paper might have been called the *Dread Wasp*. And wherever imperialism got drunk and went wild among the native peoples, the Pankhurst paper would be on the job. She was one of the first leaders in England to stand up for Soviet Russia. ... Comrade Vie was a very young foreigner with a bare bland innocent face. He read and spoke several languages ... I suspected that Comrade Vie was a foreign revolutionist. ... We often compared articles. I criticized his English and he criticized my point of view, showing me how I could be more effectively radical.

McKay was assigned to cover a series of strikes at sawmills in the London area. He found that George Lansbury, who owned a sawmill in East London, was employing scabs. At that time Lansbury was 'symbolic of all that was Simon-pure, pious and self-righteous in the British Labour movement. As the boss of the *Daily Herald* he stood at the center ... with his right arm around the neck of the big trade-union leaders and Parliamentarians and his left waving at the Independent Labour Partyites and all the radical left.' Exposing Lansbury for using non-union labour would have been a major triumph for Sylvia. McKay wrote up his findings with the help of Vie. But Sylvia refused to print it, explaining 'we owe Lansbury twenty pounds. Besides, I have borrowed from the *Daily Herald* to print the *Dreadnought*. I can't print that.'[32] Her radicalism in this case was tempered by her wallet—one of several incongruities in Sylvia's behaviour at this time.

In the summer of 1920 while Sylvia was away, McKay wrote another article which dealt with the Trades Union Congress and centred specifically on the leader of the Miners Federation. The *Dreadnought* featured his article on the front page, probably with the approval of Norah Smyth, who was running the various enterprises that summer. When Sylvia returned she objected strongly, telling McKay it was the policy of the *Dreadnought* 'not to praise the official labour leaders but to criticize them'. McKay 'resented the criticism, especially as Pankhurst had suppressed my article on Lansbury'.[33] Yet, despite her attitude, Sylvia managed to keep McKay's goodwill. A year or two after he left London, McKay went to Russia. In Moscow he ran into Arthur MacManus, who had known and worked with Sylvia during her most radical days in the communist movement. MacManus 'felt venomous about her'—'intellectually dishonest' was his pet phrase to describe her. 'I said I thought Sylvia Pankhurst was as honest as any imperial Briton could be. And I really preferred Pankhurst to persons like Lansbury, and perhaps even to MacManus himself.'[34] McKay, the first black with whom Sylvia came into close contact, never mentioned any prejudice or racism on her part. It appears that even in these early days of her life she had none. But he saw her ultimate failing in all of her many campaigns: 'Pankhurst was a good agitator and fighter, but she wasn't a leader. She possessed a magnetism to attract people to her organization, but she did not have the power to hold them. . . . It was a one-woman show, not broad-based enough to play a decisive role in the labour movement.'[35]

Interestingly, when it became apparent that the Bolsheviks were going to win power, most of the press called for recognition. The failure of Winston Churchill's eccentric and abortive campaign against them was a foregone conclusion ridiculed in the press. A. G. Gardner, a radical Liberal and editor of the *Daily News*, supported Kerensky and wrote triumphantly, 'There is spring in the air and there is spring in the souls of men. . . . Russia is free.' But, when the Bolsheviks took over, he, like the Webbs, turned against them. They were, he said, 'wild men. . . . The Russian Revolution with which we were all so *enchanted* is turning out very badly, alas.'[36]

But Gardner opposed Allied intervention in Russia, while Churchill (a Liberal at this time) as Minister of Army and Air, was actively supplying the White armies with tanks and all the weapons he could get to them. The Labour Party, now growing in strength in the House, strongly opposed Allied intervention. For a while the *Dreadnought* was the only communist voice in England. Later George Lansbury and the *Herald* took up Russia's cause, joined by the British Socialist Party paper, the *Call*, and by the *Socialist*, the voice of the Socialist Labour Party. The *Worker*, under the editorship of John B. Clarke, represented the Scottish Workers Committee, another radical group with communist leanings. Except for the *Dreadnought* and the *Herald*, these papers represented a wide element of the working class, but the organizations were divided on communism. Lansbury and Sylvia, therefore, received the greatest share of funding and news from Moscow.

With the radicalization of the *Dreadnought* and repeated calls for peace with Germany on any terms, Sylvia met further printing problems. The government once again raided the Blackfriars Press, destroying the plates and 400 copies of her paper after the release of an issue which called for illegal action by the armed forces.[37] The Athenaeum Press agreed to print the paper, but only briefly, as an article by John MacLean, a quixotic radical from the Socialist Labour Party, brought a raid on its offices. A small printer in the East End finally agreed to take over publication and, possibly through the intervention of Philip Snowden in Parliament, the government ignored the paper for the time being. Eventually, with the help of Russian money, Sylvia purchased the Agenda Press on Fleet Street, and shifted all printing activities to the new headquarters.[38]

In September 1918, on the advice of the violinist and Russian agent, Edward Soermus, Sylvia opened the Russian People's Information Bureau. It issued pamphlets by Lenin, John Reed, Nikolai Bukharin and, of course, Sylvia. Her contributions included a range of attacks against the British government, in particular Lloyd George.[39] She accused the Prime Minister of deliberately disarming Germany to keep weapons from rioting workers and soldiers. In 'In Socialist Russia' Sylvia compared conditions in war-torn Petrograd with those in London. Another pamphlet dealt with the capitalist plague of 'Landlordism'. Yet another called for the 'Education of the Masses' in Marxist theory, which it is unlikely Sylvia herself understood.[40] And in the *Voice of Labour*, published in Ireland, she explained 'Why I Want the Soviets'.[41] All of these articles were based on pure utopian fantasy.

In February 1919, George Lansbury organized The National League Regiments to protect the interests of returning soldiers, sailors and their wives and dependants, with Sylvia as honorary secretary. In this capacity she had direct access to large numbers of soldiers and sailors, whom she hoped to convert to revolution. Speaking at the Labour Club at Rugby she said: 'It is very hopeful that the soldiers and sailors are beginning to feel the spirit of revolt . . . if we get the soldiers and sailors and policemen . . . we shall be able to take over the country very quickly and without bloodshed.'[42] Despite her hopes, conflicts within the league soon found Sylvia out of office and Lansbury in the chair. Her two months of activity among the returning soldiers and sailors stimulated the interest of the Special Branch, but the Home Office report concluded that, despite the seditious nature of her speeches, 'her influence is small . . .it is considered better for the present to leave her alone.'[43]

Sylvia and the Home Office agreed, however, about Lansbury. While the *Daily Herald* espoused a kind of radicalism which was suspect from the government's viewpoint, his own views were not easily discernible. The Home Office considered he played one side off against the other. He annoyed Sylvia for the same reasons: she could not count on him as an ally in her most advanced political views, yet he and his paper were at times useful to her. Lansbury travelled to Russia with the Webbs and other British socialists, returning as an admirer of Lenin.[44] The *Herald*, through the negotiations of Lansbury's son, Edgar, received Russian support in buying paper and shipping it from Sweden. The Special Branch notified the Home Office that 'It seems to be the first time in the history of journalism that a daily newspaper in England has been subsidized by a foreign government.'[45] But Lansbury's enthusiasm for Russia had waned by 1920 and when the movement was at its peak, the Special Branch described him as a Labour leader who played 'with the idea of Revolution' but was 'afraid to descend from the fence'.[46]

Sylvia, however, had no doubts. Always quick to settle on a hero, she abandoned her recent fascination with Ramsay MacDonald ('a golden tongued orator . . . his voice beautiful')[47] and focused her attention on Vladimir Ilyich Ulyanov—Lenin. 'Why was Russia ripe for revolution?', Sylvia asked. Because they 'are politically ahead. In Russia the politics of advanced politicians have long been more definite and scientific and above all more democratic.'[48] Russia, under the leadership of Lenin, was the utopia she had been seeking ever since she first developed strong anti-British government attitudes in the suffrage crusade.

In later years, Sylvia looked back at her initial enthusiasm for the Bolshevik Revolution with an accurate reflection of her feelings at the time: The 'long and bitter struggle which was to follow in Russia was not foreseen, it was a fairy-tale revolution of resolutions and cheers.'[49] And, Sylvia was first among the cheerleaders in England.

By 1919 a man known only as Fineberg was directly representing British communist groups in Moscow at the First Congress of the Communist International. His name does not appear in Sylvia's archive, nor in her publications, so we must assume that they were not then acquainted. In June 1919, her first writings appeared in the *Communist International*; 'Wake up! Wake up! oh, sleepy British people. The new war is in full blast, and you are called to fight it. . . . we in this country are actually in the revolution. Although the eyes of most of us are still shut to the fact!'[50] Few at the time would have questioned her final statement, but only Sylvia and a few others believed that the class war in England was 'in full blast'. Her grip on reality was failing.

From its inception, the *Communist International* carried a regular column on Britain, but it was certainly not written by Sylvia. The column, while radical, contained news of general information and featured no one single group. Had Sylvia been its British correspondent, she would have used the opportunity to push her own WSF, and would also have featured herself. The *Workers' Dreadnought* was, however, mentioned on occasion. One article referred to the *Dreadnought*, the *Call*, and the *Labour Leader*, saying that 'Every line in these substantial and growing organs . . . turns on one fundamental idea: all power to the proletariat.'[51]

In July 1919, Sylvia was listed with Angelica Balabanoff and Clara Zetkin as contributors to the paper; the only three women in a total of 23 contributors from all over the world. In that issue she wrote a column entitled 'Labour and the League of Nations' (which she still opposed); in August, another article, 'The Workers Again Betrayed' was a strong indictment of the British government and its exploitation of the working class who, according to Sylvia, had suffered in a war while the capitalists (the government officials) had grown richer.[52]

Sylvia's activities on behalf of Russia were carried out in Old Ford Road, where she continued to supervise the several arms of the Workers' Suffrage Federation. She attended the financial committee, which was still short of funds, and the executive committee; superintended the Mother's Arms, which was briefly operating on a government subsidy; and occasionally looked into the toy factory and other business operations. Norah Smyth, her deputy for Russian affairs, continued to invest money into various WSF causes. Some members who could not follow Sylvia on her shift to the left fell away, but a faithful few, now calling each other 'comrade', remained. Branches lost old members and gained new ones in the name of communism. Men especially began to swell the ranks, forming about half of the executive leadership.[53]

It is difficult to unravel the complexities of this period in Britain. The conservative press, especially *The Times*, adopted a hard line against Russia, calling for military intervention against Bolshevism. The government concurred. Among British socialists, who were virtually united in their reception of the March Revolution, there was dissent after the Bolshevik takeover. MacDonald was anti-Bolshevik but opposed to intervention. Snowden shared his views, but Henderson supported intervention. The extreme left of the ILP was opposed to intervention and supported the Bolsheviks. Within the Labour Party the range of views was wide, but the majority supported the government. But Labour's stand for a gradual change to socialism was seen as mere 'reformism' by those whose impatience carried them further to the left.

On the left, groups formed and reformed—as they had done since the 1870s. In short, the Social Democratic Party had been a syndicalist group resembling to some extent the American-based Industrial Workers of the World (IWW) or 'wobblies'. One group of dissenters broke away to join another from the British Socialist Party (BSP) to form a new Socialist Labour Party (SLP), which was larger than Sylvia's WSF and similar in its lack of trade union affiliates. The British Socialist Party was itself a spin-off from the old Social Democratic Federation (SDF), which had represented British Marxism in the late nineteenth century. The BSP was the largest as well as the most conservative of the radical left. The most radical were Sylvia's WSF and the South Wales Socialist Society (SWSS) consisting of groups of Welsh miners, but not a recognized political party. There were smaller but powerful organizations in Scotland, such as the shop stewards who reflected various degrees of radicalism but who were not in a position to organize workers' councils. Lansbury's Herald League was also radical, and was associated with the Third International for two or three years.[54]

Labour discontent, massive losses at the front, food shortages, high prices, lack of housing—all the discomforts and privations associated with the long years of war combined with a long history of pre-war misery for the British working class. It is difficult—from a sixty-year perspective that includes the Great Depression, another World War, and the anti-communism of the cold war period—to grasp the kinds of dangers and possibilities that seemed open to Sylvia Pankhurst and to British and European socialists at large. Britain had fought a 'War to end War' and built a 'Home fit for Heroes', but the reality did not reflect the promises. The far left was a mixture of old-fashioned malcontents, ideological Marxists or anarchists, and a large number of people who were inclined, at that juncture, to feel the weight of the world's injustice with peculiar sensitivity. Sylvia's brief period as a political leader in the British communist movement and her correspondingly larger audience was rooted in this discontent.

A priority was the need to unify the several organizations and groups —WSF, SLP, BSP, SWSS, the Herald League and shop stewards— into a single Communist Party.[55] Negotiations began in May 1919, but they quickly foundered upon two basic disagreements. The WSF and the SWSS, along with several members of the Herald League, refused to accept the idea of parliamentary democracy. They also balked at affiliation to the Labour Party. The Socialist Labour Party was divided on these issues. The British Socialist Party was firmly in favour of Parliament and affiliation to Labour. In fact, the BSP was already affiliated to the Labour Party. Throughout the summer and autumn of 1919 representatives of these groups negotiated, joined sporadically by the shop stewards, but no organization was willing to alter its position. All agreed to affiliate with the Third International as a condition for unity and most supported workers' councils, but that was all.[56]

To give her views the credibility she believed they deserved, Sylvia wrote to Lenin in Moscow in July 1919, asking him to express his views on Parliament and on the British Labour Party. She recognized that Lenin had led the Bolsheviks to victory; that he had studied vigorously the works of all past revolutionaries; and that he had dealt with a long succession of controversies of an international nature. For these reasons, his advice to the British would be advantageous in helping them work out their differences. Sylvia, however, had not approached him for what he *really* believed was possible in Britain; she had written to him expecting that, like Keir Hardie, Lenin would tell her what she wanted to hear. She mentioned the dissident organizations, then singled out the WSF, 'smaller and younger than the others'. It was a suffrage organization originally composed of women, but steadily gaining in male support, and she added 'more than any of the others . . . [it is] the party of the poorer stratum of the workers'.[57] Furthermore, the WSF had already voted to change its name to the Communist Party (implying that the movement should use her organization as a basis), but that it had withheld the use of the name in the interest of unity with the other groups. 'Why do I tell you all of this?', she wrote. 'If you were here, I believe you would say: Concentrate your forces upon revolutionary action; have nothing to do with the Parliamentary machine. Such is my own view.' In conclusion, Sylvia suggested that 'an address or an article from you would help us to concentrate our energies in this direction'.[58]

Living in a world devoid of political reality, Sylvia believed that the leader of the Bolshevik Revolution would support her party, and that she would then lead the forces of the left in Britain to the utopia she envisaged, when Parliament was replaced by soviets and the Labour Party was but a footnote in history. (The idea for the name change probably came from German Sparticists, who changed theirs in late 1918 or early 1919 to the German Communist Party.)

Lenin was a consummate politician whose adroit manipulations held together the disparate views within his own party. He was, of course, aware of Sylvia's work as a propagandist for communism, and he hoped that Britain would set the chain of revolutions into action. His response the following month seemed to offer some support to her notion of forming a communist party from the WSF, while at the same time advocating working within the system for the time being.[59]

> For my own part, I am convinced that the revolutionary British workers are mistaken in their refusal to participate in the Parliamentary elections. . . . The revolutionary workers who concentrate their attack on Parliamentarianism are perfectly right in so far as thereby they give expression to their repudiation of bourgeois Parliamentarianism . . . I should regard it as a valuable stage on the way towards complete unity to form two Communist Parties, both advocating the replacement of bourgeois Parliamentarianism by a Soviet Government . . . the simultaneous existence of two Communist Parties would be an immense advance upon existing conditions.

With unity seemingly impossible in 1919, Sylvia occupied herself with carrying out her communist mission to the people. In Glasgow she told her listeners that she 'expected the Revolution in the United Kingdom any day'.[60] In the Albert Hall she called for revolution in

England and read revolutionary poetry to her audience. A colleague, Edward Soermus, had been jailed under the Defence of the Realm Act. And in another flight from reality, Sylvia called on her audience to join her in storming Brixton prison where Soermus was imprisoned to remove him by force.[61] The fact is, however, that neither Sylvia nor members of her audience went to Brixton prison and she soon dropped her concern for Soermus.

According to the Special Branch, May Day 1919 passed quietly in England. Only in London was there an attempt by 'Miss Sylvia Pankhurst, whose funds are low, and who never neglects an opportunity for self-advertisement . . . to enter the House of Commons.' She was arrested, charged with obstructing justice, and detained overnight at Bow Street police station. At the end of May, Sylvia joined other radicals at a Trafalgar Square rally in their call for a general strike, a call which went unheeded by the workers. Instead of using the art of gentle persuasion on her audience, she concluded her speech in a frenzy of emotion calling on them immediately to seize the government and organize their own soviets.[62] This kind of hysterical rhetoric became more typical of Sylvia during her communist years; and, except for a few extreme radicals like herself, it fell on increasingly deaf ears.

The Special Branch was correct in noting that Sylvia's funds were low. Communists, especially those of Sylvia's extreme views, were not good candidates for middle-class donations. Small sums were sent by radical sympathizers such as Frances, Countess of Warwick, but for the most part friends and supporters from the West End who supplied her needs in the East End seemed unprepared to fund her revolution. In June, Sylvia and the WSF held a special meeting at 400 Old Ford Road to raise £200, part of which was to go 'in agitation in the docks to get men to refuse to load vessels carrying munitions to Russia'.[63] These munitions, sent by the British, would be *en route* to the White Russians. We do not know if the WSF was successful in its fundraising goal, but dockers did strike over loading vessels for Russia.

In her unpublished memoirs, Sylvia wrote that she received money from Theodore Rothstein, who she alleged was a Russian agent. Rothstein had been raised in England, worked for the British government, and turned to the Bolsheviks after the Revolution. The Home Office reported on her financial dealings with Russia and on Norah's. Norah often acted in the name of the paper or the Russian People's Information Bureau in raising money.[64] There was much talk in these years about Russian gold and jewels for the subversion of Western Europe and America. Confirmation comes from the memoirs of Angelica Balabanoff, another woman deeply involved in the Russian Revolution at this time.

Balabanoff was born in Russia and educated in Western Europe. She returned to Russia on the same train as Lenin—not the famous, if mythical sealed train, but one whose passengers were not allowed to disembark in Germany. Balabanoff had been active in international socialist circles from her base in Switzerland and, for a time, in northern Italy. Lenin assigned her to Stockholm as a representative of the Zimmerwald Committee (international socialists and workers for peace). There she disbursed funds for such purposes as buying presses and publishing newspapers favourable to Russia.[65] She told of sending money for a time to create 'Bolshevik movements and newspapers throughout the world'.[66]

She was also chief propagandist for Russia in the first year or so after the Bolshevik rise to power. Her knowledge of French, German, Italian and English made her useful as a translator. The Russians sent her material for translation in Stockholm, where she translated it into these languages and sent it on by way of Norway, or directly to Germany, Italy, France or England.[67] It was one of the curious coincidences of those years, that one woman in Stockholm fed information for distribution by another woman who hoped to lead the revolution in England.[68] As it turned out, both left the movement before Lenin's death.

Also in 1919 Sylvia made contact with the German suffragist, and now Bolshevik, Clara Zetkin, who invited Sylvia to attend a communist meeting in Germany. Zetkin lacked the stature of Rosa Luxemburg, but she was nevertheless important. Her desire for notoriety sometimes equalled Sylvia's, but Zetkin was taken more seriously within the German socialist movement than was Sylvia in Britain. Zetkin was born in Saxony in 1857 (a year before Mrs Pankhurst was born), finished high school in Germany, and attended university in Switzerland because no women could enrol in German universities in her day.[69]

After graduating, Zetkin met a young Russian emigré, whose radical political views she shared, and they produced two children. They never married because to have done so would have meant Clara forfeiting her German citizenship. Later, when her Russian partner was forced to flee Germany, Zetkin followed him into exile in Paris, remaining there until his death in 1889. After Ossip Zetkin's death, Clara (who had taken his name) returned to Germany with their two young children and again launched herself into the activities of the German Socialist Party.[70]

Like Sylvia, Clara Zetkin had been a pacifist during the war. Like Sylvia, and Balabanoff as well, the early promise of the Russian Revolution stirred her imagination. Her pacifist stance had helped Zetkin to maintain a strong and respected position in German socialism, unlike Sylvia's shaky status in British socialist circles. This made Sylvia all the more anxious to attend the projected meeting.

Unable to obtain a passport, Sylvia slipped quietly out of the country, making her way first to Italy, where she travelled around the country meeting socialist leaders. In Bologna she attended an All Italy Conference of Socialists where she met a Russian spy named 'Carlo', and he may have given her money for her journey, but there is no record of how she financed this extensive travel.[71] Lacking visas to enter Italy and Switzerland, she climbed the Alps from Italy to Switzerland at night, guided only by a friendly forester, walking on goat tracks and feeling her way across the terrain in her long ascent to the Swiss border. In Basel she retired to bed exhausted. At thirty-seven years of age, Sylvia, whose exercise rarely went beyond leading demonstrations in London, was not in the best physical condition for such strenuous exertion. She seems to have made a swift recovery, however, and with the help of Swiss socialists, she crossed the German border and made her way to Stuttgart.

On arrival in Stuttgart for her rendezvous with Zetkin, she found the communists had moved the conference to Frankfurt. The two women, with Sylvia's Swiss guide, made their way there and then waited an interminable (but undisclosed) time for the conference to begin. When the conference finally met, Russian agents mixed with socialists from Germany, Poland, Austria, Hungary and the Netherlands. Sylvia was fascinated by the international cooperation and the opportunity it afforded to meet the great names in European communism. The meeting also had its financial awards. The Russian agent known as the 'eye of Moscow' gave her £500 for her further work in England. As soon as possible after receiving the money, she bought appropriate papers in Germany and hastened back to England.[72]

7

Radical Politics in the Post-War Years

The lion will let you put your head in his mouth because the law says he must; but if you shake your hairpins in his throat, he is only too glad to have the excuse for snapping.
                                    —George Bernard Shaw to Sylvia (*c.* 1921)

The Peace Treaty of Versailles of June 1919 heralded a string of subsidiary treaties over the next few months and, despite the persistent civil wars in the new Soviet Union, the map of post-war Europe was drawn. Revolution had not swept through Western Europe as some had hoped and others had feared, and the need to create a united left seemed all the more important.

In Great Britain, groups to the left of the Labour Party were already divided on a number of issues, but two stood out as crucial. One was whether or not the small, far-left parties should affiliate with the Labour Party. The Labour Party had from the beginning been an organization of diverse and sometimes internally divided groups, and included the Fabian Society, the trade unions, and workers' cooperatives. It therefore encompassed a broad spectrum of opinion, including the fledgling communist groups, which would have not been possible in a party with a more narrowly defined ideology. The second problem confronting the far left was whether or not they should work through the parliamentary electoral system at all, or condemn parliamentary manoeuvring outright as a bourgeois tool.

Sylvia's stand was clear and uncompromising on both. She urged communists to repudiate the reformism embodied in the Labour Party, and she continued to be staunchly opposed to Parliament. Sylvia tried in early 1920 to win over the Socialist Labour Party (SLP) and the South Wales Socialist Society (SWSS), but she wanted to exclude the British Socialist Party (BSP) as too far to the right for true communism. Albert Inkpin of the BSP meanwhile began taking political aim at Sylvia in the *Call* and urging the far left to affiliate with the Labour Party, on the grounds that the communist movement should work with whatever organizational structure was available. Sylvia responded, as Inkpin must have known she would, by refusing any kind of reconciliation. She thus became more entrenched than ever, arguing that it was better to have a small Communist Party of sound doctrine than a large and diffuse organization. As the Party took form, she argued, 'We must persevere in communist propaganda, never hesitate lest we make it too extreme . . . the more extreme our doctrine is, the more surely we will prepare the workers for Communism.'[1]

In late February, she took her firm position on the two key issues into the international arena at a conference of the Communist International in Holland (set up to organize a sub-bureau for Western Europe). There she met firm opposition from Lenin himself, who sent a message urging parliamentary participation so that elected communists would be in a position to obstruct capitalist political processes from within.[2] Sylvia's faction nevertheless prevailed, aided by powerful support from Clara Zetkin and others in the German delegation, and from delegates from the Shop Stewards and Workers Committee. Meetings of this kind were still beset with police problems. Dutch police raided several times and deported some of the members whose documents were apparently not in order, but Sylvia, who had managed to secure a British passport in 1919, was able to come and go freely at this time.[3] Despite her extremist views she was not then regarded as a serious subversive by the Special Branch, which nevertheless kept a watchful eye on her movements.

At the end of the conference, Sylvia returned directly to London to follow up on her victory against the communists to her right. After Amsterdam, Inkpin and the British Socialist Party seemed willing to compromise in the name of unity. It agreed to drop affiliation with the Labour Party for the time being, though Inkpin intended to put forward his pro-parliamentary views once again at the Second Congress of the Third International, scheduled for Moscow in the summer of 1920.[4]

What Sylvia failed to recognize was that Inkpin's concessions were themselves a political manoeuvre to contrast his own desire for unity with her inflexibility. On 24 April, a unity meeting in London ended in *dis*unity. The Socialist Labour Party and the British Socialist Party voted for parliamentary action against the isolated stand of the Workers' Suffrage Federation. On the question of affiliation with the Labour Party, however, Sylvia's WSF was in the majority, with support from both the South Wales Socialist Society and the Socialist Labour Party, with the British Socialist Party now isolated.[5] But these supporters were fringe groups and unstable. The SWSS dropped out of the unity negotiations altogether; while the Socialist Labour Party split into a right-wing group and a communist unity group that supported Sylvia's position.

The Special Branch had its own theory on the underlying basis of disunity. Its agent reported, 'Miss Sylvia Pankhurst wants her own way. . . . She had already quarrelled with the Workers' Committee although it is recognized by Lenin.'[6] The unity group nevertheless moved ahead with plans for a national communist convention, but Inkpin was able to postpone it until after the Congress of the Third International. He also succeeded in setting ground rules which pledged delegates in advance to accept the convention's decisions on affiliation and parliamentarianism.[7] Sylvia was hardly likely to accept this kind of democratic centralism. She moved on her own with the Workers' Suffrage Federation and some associated support from other organizations. On 19 June, they met and formed the first official Communist Party in Great Britain (the Communist Party – British Section of the Third International (CP – BSTI)) with the *Dreadnought* as its official organ.[8]

The choice of name was the more curious because Lenin was already on record as having views much closer to those of the British Socialist Party. He had praised Sylvia's work in earlier statements, but he now sent a telegram to the BSP stating that 'the Tactics of Comrade Sylvia Pankhurst of the WSF are wrong'. Sylvia responded by asking for Lenin's support in travelling to Russia: 'If you, through the influence of the Labour Party or your parliamentary friends can obtain me a passport, I shall gladly meet you in debate.'[9] And while she was making preparations for Moscow, in Britain the CP – BSTI elected a provisional council to serve until a national convention could meet in September. Leaving aside the factions that were shortly to form the Communist Party – Great Britain (CP – GB)—the forerunner of the present British Communist Party—and against opposition from the *Daily Herald*, Sylvia's group decided to go it alone. It elected a chairman from the South Wales Socialist Society and a secretary from the Socialist Labour Party, moving beyond the narrow following of the WSF alone. It published a provisional programme in July, demanding the replacement of capitalism by communism; of rule by soviets; 'the establishment of the right of all human beings to the free satisfaction of their personal needs from the collective products of the working community'; the abolition of social classes; the end of colonialism; and all of this was to be achieved by winning the allegiance of 'the army and navy to the cause of the workers in preparation for the revolutionary struggle and the creation of a Red Army'. Sylvia saw to it that women were not forgotten: 'Communism and the Soviets will liberate mothers from their present economic enslavement and drudging. They . . . will elect their own representatives to the Soviets.'[10] Party spokesmen followed up with a firm line in the *Dreadnought*. The new treasurer wrote that the 'Communist Party refuses affiliation with the Labour Party; it has no use for Parliament . . . The Communist Party, which is the extreme Left Wing Party of this country calls for all revolutionary Communist workers to enlist in its ranks'.[11] At this time in her life, Sylvia was far removed from her father's radical politics. Dr Pankhurst had considered that parliamentary democracy was the only means of bringing about social reform, even revolutionary reform, without resorting to violence.

The Communist Party–BSTI had financial problems from the beginning. Sylvia had trouble getting on with Theodore Rothstein. In spite of her protests to Moscow, he withheld funds from her organization, perhaps on orders from Russia after she undercut the unity negotiations. As early as May, an air crash in England revealed mail bound for Moscow, and the Special Branch found one letter from Sylvia 'addressed in terms of extravagant eulogy', suggesting that gems ('sapphires for Britain') should be sent immediately.[12] Other fund-raising methods were far more prosaic, recalling some of the comparatively benign activities of the suffrage movement. The treasurer called for members to declare a 'Communist Saturday' each week after 10 July, to spend the time distributing literature, selling the *Dreadnought*, or otherwise helping the cause. The party also organized a middle-class phenomenon, a 'Garden Party and Musical At Home' in Woodford; as well as a more plebeian 'Social and Dance' at 400 Old Ford Road, both offering inexpensive refreshments that were to be kept within the means of the membership.[13]

Sylvia's other organization, the Russian People's Information Bureau (RPIB), was also in financial trouble at this time. The Special Branch reported that it was in arrears in both salaries and rent and Sylvia considered closing it altogether; but its supporters wanted it to continue. And, despite lack of money, Sylvia characteristically added new staff to solicit donations. In mid-summer the Communist Party–BSTI was losing membership as well as money, as Inkpin and the British Socialist Party began to regain support. It was at this stage of disorder on the home front that Sylvia left, still without a travel permit, to attend the Second Congress of the Third International. Her trip was paid for by more funds from Russia.[14]

Sylvia's journey to Russia was another grand adventure and even more dangerous than the earlier trip to Germany. Her physical energies were not so taxed, but her nerves were strained by the means she used to reach Petrograd. In the spring, while the unity meetings were in progress, the Special Branch reported that she was on the verge of a breakdown. The triumph of forming a Communist Party seemed, however, to have invigorated her; certainly the lure of Moscow and her forthcoming meeting with Lenin was sufficient to overcome any anxieties and gave her the courage to pass once again across international frontiers. Her travel plans seem to have been prearranged through Russian agents before her departure, with names and places established through the network used to pass agents in and out of Russia.

How she escaped the watchful eyes of Special Branch surveillance is unclear. She may have disguised herself, as she had often done during her suffrage period, or slipped unnoticed on a train to Harwich. There she stowed away on a Norwegian freighter with the connivance of communist crewmen. She left the ship at Copenhagen, arm-in-arm with one of the engine crew, passing the officers on deck as if she had been a recent arrival on board. She then went through Sweden and on to Norway, and across country to Vardo, where she boarded a small fishing boat bound for Murmansk. That part of the trip nearly ended in catastrophe; the seas were heavy and the boat small. It was forced to stop twice on outcrops of land, though sailing in the full light of the midnight sun.[15]

On her way to Petrograd, she encountered the Red Army and addressed the troops through an interpreter. She reached Petrograd, only to find that the Congress had moved to Moscow. Indeed, Sylvia reported that rumours were circulated that she was 'lying in a dungeon undergoing the tortures of Rosa Luxemburg'.[16] The rumours, however, may have been a figment of her overactive imagination, and the Congress was underway when Sylvia finally reached the new capital.

Before Sylvia's arrival in Russia, partly as a response to her disagreement with his politics, Lenin had written a pamphlet entitled *'Left-Wing' Communism: An Infantile Disorder*.[17] It was translated into several languages, including English; and much of it was directed against the German left wing, the Spartacists, as well as the British left opposition, with two individuals specifically in mind: Sylvia and William Gallacher.

Gallacher was a young, Scottish shop steward who had been active in Clydeside labour unrest. In the early stages of the search for communist unity, he had written Sylvia a long letter supporting her views, and she had printed the letter in the *Dreadnought* of 20 February 1920. It was this letter that Lenin chose as the basis of his repudiation. His pamphlet quoted the Gallacher letter in full and then went into reasoned counter-arguments in favour of parliamentarianism and Labour Party affiliation. He managed, however, to flatter Gallacher's ego while demolishing his arguments, praising the tone of the letter as that appropriate to young communists, deserving of appreciation and support, if not agreement.[18]

Lenin was an astute observer, and he may have recognized that Sylvia was so firmly entrenched in her views, lacking in the patience and discipline necessary to revolutionary success, that she had to be treated more firmly by one who was both father and leader of the movement. He accused her and some of her colleagues not merely of displaying attitudes inappropriate to young communists but of intellectual childishness, of not having 'the serious tactics of a revolutionary class'.

The errors of the Left Communists are particularly dangerous at present, because certain revolutionaries are not displaying a sufficiently intelligent, and sufficiently shrewd attitude toward each of the conditions. . . . In my opinion, the British Communists should unite their four parties ... into a single Communist Party on the basis of the principles of the Third International and of obligatory participation in Parliament.[19]

This statement was written before Sylvia had united the far left into a single party in Britain; but it still applied when she arrived in Moscow. Gallacher received the message Lenin intended for him in print and in person. Sylvia met the Russian leader in a head-on political collision. Speaking before the comrades at the Seventh Session of the Congress, Sylvia reiterated her opposition to affiliation with the Labour Party and her opposition to Parliament. Where Lenin had cautioned against extremism, she argued, 'I think one should be more extreme than one is. . . . Though I am a socialist, I have fought a long time in the suffrage movement and I have seen how important it is to be extreme. . . . In politics it is necessary to stand up for extreme ideas.' Furthermore, 'My opinion has proved to be right. . . . I therefore insist upon my point of view.'[20]

Sylvia regarded herself as Lenin's intellectual equal. Yet her educational background was limited; she lacked a broad exposure to ideas, an exposure that could have come from either university training or wide reading. As an activist, she had little time to read great books. She also had supreme self-confidence, a *class*-confidence, which ironically reinforced her views of equality during her dispute with Lenin; she was stubborn; and her behaviour was in line with her past, not with Lenin's tactical advice.

Lenin seems to have been tolerant—in public and in private—of Sylvia's behaviour, if not her ideas. No record of his thoughts on their debate remain, but he handled her gently at the Congress, while pushing his own tactical approach. Recalling that neither Gallacher nor Sylvia had a long history of revolutionary activity, he asked them to recognize 'that a good revolutionary will avail himself or herself of every opportunity of fighting against reactionary leaders', meaning the leadership of the Labour Party as then constituted. Yet he praised them for their enthusiasm and 'revolutionary agitation'.[21] Lenin later met Sylvia in private, and he encouraged her to join a united Communist Party in Britain. Sylvia, who had already expressed her grievances against the British Socialist Party to Gallacher, told Lenin as well that she had little faith that the other factions would deal fairly with her. Lenin advised Sylvia to trust Gallacher.[22]

After her conference with Lenin, Sylvia and other delegates made a brief tour of a factory operating under worker control about 60 miles from Moscow. She wrote that shortages, both at the factory and for workers as consumers, were openly discussed and accepted, the workers recognizing the problems of a new economic system and of bringing Russia industrially into the twentieth century. She took delight in 'How the Communist Party is Organized', idealistically noting its authoritarianism,[23] although at home her organization was built on the anti-authoritarianism of her East End followers.

Another visit took her to a 'House of the Mother and Child' serving women without male support. Illegitimacy, according to Sylvia, had lost its stigma after the Revolution, and this house, one of many, was supported by the state. Perhaps later personal decisions took root in Sylvia's views of marriage in Russia: 'marriage as we know it today, has grown up with capitalism and private property . . . abolishing Capitalism and making the community responsible for the burden of motherhood and childhood, will modify the marriage relation, as it will modify every feature of human life.'[24] Sylvia also claimed that, since the Revolution, 'it is believed that the Russian people have mostly forgotten the existence of alcohol'.[25] Whether this ideal was shared by the British working class is open to doubt, but it represents the kind of idealised picture of revolutionary Russia she wanted to convey.

Dora Russell was a communist sympathizer at this time. She and a friend travelled to Russia where they were supposed to meet a group of British officials. Russell confirmed Sylvia's memories of shortages which were accepted with a kind of pride. They were greeted in Murmansk with the same enthusiasm Sylvia encountered: speeches by all and a small band to greet them. They travelled by a slow, broken-down steam train to Petrograd (Leningrad), where they were taken on several tours, and found the Russians friendly and anxious to show off their country. Russell later went to Moscow where she mentioned a meeting was then in progress. That was undoubtedly the international meeting Sylvia attended, but there was no mention of meeting Sylvia in Moscow.

Dora Russell met anarchist Emma Goldman, Balabanoff and Kollontai while she was in Moscow that summer. Yet Sylvia, who should have come into contact with them at the Congress, never mentioned them in her memoirs.

The return trip to Britain was a near disaster. A fire on the train from Moscow to Petrograd might have ended in her death but for the bravery of William Gallacher, who awoke to choking smoke and rushed to Sylvia's compartment to find her nearly suffocating. Gallacher seized her and threw her over his shoulder as he jumped from the smoke-filled train. Sylvia recovered without damage from smoke inhalation. The crew put out the fire, and they continued their journey.[26] At Murmansk, however, they encountered even worse weather than Sylvia had met on the way over. Some of the French delegation, indeed, were drowned when their boat capsized. Sylvia and three British men embarked together in a small fishing boat, where they were soon tossed and flung about below deck. Sylvia, claustrophobic and terrified by the storm, insisted on going on deck, which was periodically swept by the seas. Once more Gallacher came to the rescue: he found a tarpaulin, got her to lie next to the hatch, covered her over, and held her in his arms all through the long night with the sea sending its pounding waves over them, as he described it, worse with each passing hour. The captain finally found safe anchorage at a small Soviet wireless station. Gallacher thought that in spite of the terror Sylvia experienced, she 'came through it very well . . . she wasn't long in getting back to her old lively self'.[27]

The Soviets assigned Sylvia separate quarters on the island, while they all bedded down for rest until the sea subsided. Sylvia, whose fear had been quietened by Gallacher's arms, rested briefly in her quarters, then set off with a sailor in a small boat despite the forbidding waves, leaving her comrades behind. Gallacher was understandably upset: 'You could have knocked me down with a twelve-pound hammer. . . . The names we called her, when I reported to the others! To slip off like that without a word—there's gratitude.'[28]

Sylvia later claimed that a message from the British to the Norwegian government called for her arrest.[29] But the Home Office reports at this time do not indicate that Sylvia was regarded as a serious threat, and it is doubtful that anyone actually tried to find and arrest her. Once in London, Sylvia lost no time in putting the advantage of her rapid return to work.

Lenin could hardly have expected sympathy from the British Special Branch, but, at Sylvia's announcement that Lenin had chosen her to unite the various communist factions in the United Kingdom, the Home Office official reporting to the Cabinet noted as an aside: 'He could scarcely have made a worse choice.'[30] Gallacher claimed that Lenin had actually sent *him* back to Britain on the same mission, and he may be right; or Lenin might have made a similar appeal or promise to each.

Sylvia's contacts with Lenin, and his hopes for her, can be more properly assessed in retrospect. Lenin was contemptuous towards women. In 1915, at the International Socialist Women's Conference in Berne, he appeared to support his wife Nadezhda Krupskaya, and his mistress, Inessa Armand. In fact he not only wrote their position papers, he sat at a table near the conference centre, dictating what they should say throughout the conference.[31] One can only infer that Lenin initially saw Sylvia in a similar light—as someone he could manipulate. Once he encountered her formidable rejection of his tactical plans, he turned to Gallacher and other men for the serious work of building a party.

According to a Special Branch report in 1918–20, some Russian money went to the *Dreadnought*, which provided at this point the widest available circulation for Soviet views—particular for encouraging dockers to refuse to load ships carrying military supplies to the counter-revolutionary forces. Other small sums went to the free distribution of communist literature. But the largest sum, £15,000, went to settle the debts of the Agenda Press; £500 more went to the Workers' Suffrage Federation; and the Russian Peoples' Information Bureau received £300 in grants and £250 to help settle old debts.[32] It seems unlikely that a distribution of funds so singly concentrated on Sylvia's personal causes was quite what the Russians had in mind. This is especially so since the Communist Party–Great Britain was closer to Lenin's tactical ideas while the British delegation was in Moscow. The Russians, however, had no knowledge of the new party when they handed over the money, which helps explain why Sylvia received such a large sum.

Others in the British delegation to Moscow had been won over by Lenin's persuasiveness. John Clarke, editor of the *Worker* and a former extremist, returned from Moscow urging fellow communists to show 'less egotism, less vanity, less personal ambition, less personal injustice for those who agree with us nine-tenths of the way'.[33] Both Clarke and Gallacher promptly joined the CP–GB, along with others from Sylvia's CP–BSTI, deserting her in the process. Sylvia did not quite see the handwriting on the wall; but, having given Lenin her promise to work for unification, and having dispersed the Russian funds to her own organizations, she set off to Manchester for a secret conference of all shades within the communist movement—one, it was hoped, that would finally combine all believers under one umbrella.

A reporter from the *Sunday Express* described her arrival in Manchester: 'A frowsy-headed woman with a pale, drawn face, tremendously lined . . . jumped off a train, passed the obvious policeman . . . went into the building where the meeting was held. The woman was Sylvia Pankhurst, and the revolution in England had begun.'[34] Not quite. Again an official in the Home Office predicted the final outcome. The secret conference at Manchester, he wrote, was of no serious concern. 'No one has yet ever succeeded in working amicably with Sylvia Pankhurst, and her paper is now to be controlled by a committee of three.' The Home Office prediction was correct: boxing Sylvia in with controls was not the way to force her to capitulation. Conflict, according to the Home Office, characterized the Manchester meeting. Sylvia was accused by some of being a secret agent of the government, by others of being a spy for the Special Branch. The charges were false, but they set the stage for Sylvia's loss of personal followers. The cleavage in fact, continued after the Manchester meeting. In late September Sylvia pre-empted the others by announcing in the *Dreadnought* that the Communist Party–British Section Third International had been received into the Third International.[35] John McLaine, another radical in the movement, who had been to Moscow, immediately wired the *Communist* that 'It is untrue. . . . Her reference to so-called united party [hers] makes me regret my magnanimity. I should have denounced her double dealings [at Manchester]. . .'[36] Still not acknowledging the true situation, Sylvia advised Lenin in a letter intercepted by the Special Branch and published in part in *The Times*, 'The situation here is moving in a revolutionary direction more swiftly but of course we are far away yet.' Instead of setting his mind at ease that she would compromise with her fellow communists, she advised him that she was again on the warpath —this time against George Lansbury and his more conservative views.[37]

There was unrest at this time among the East End dockers. Sylvia saw an opportunity to bring them into her organization, but she was headed off by their leader, Ben Tillett. Tillett was a staunch anticommunist who had been elected to Parliament in 1917. But when he saw that the dockers were leaning toward the left, he changed his rhetoric to support for the Bolsheviks, 'hoping to head off revolution by keeping friendly with those union officials on the left' (who, of course, did not include Sylvia).

Tillett also faced competition for leadership within his own union from Ernest Bevin, who rose from the ranks during the war. Bevin had supported the 'Hands Off Russia Committee' which Sylvia also praised in issue after issue of the *Dreadnought*. When in 1920, the East End dockers refused to load the *Jolly George* (a munitions ship with arms for Poland, which was fighting Russia), Sylvia again ran banner headlines congratulating the strikers and calling for them to join in the revolution. It was in this connection that Sylvia, on the sidelines, ended up in jail; while Bevin, who stayed clear of communist infighting, eventually took over from Tillett.[38]

Sylvia was arrested on 20 October and charged with sedition under the Defence of the Realm Act for publishing in the *Dreadnought* two articles inciting members of the armed forces 'to mutiny and lawlessness'. Both articles were written anonymously, but Sylvia, as editor of the *Dreadnought*, accepted responsibility. One, 'Discontent on the Lower Deck', urged men in the navy to rebel; the second, 'How to Get a Labour Government', told her readers, 'Parliament is an institution of the capitalist state for doping the workers, and it can never become anything else'. Such open opposition to Lenin's party line could hardly earn much sympathy from her fellow communists.

Nor was her arrest a surprise. The offices of the *Dreadnought* had been raided repeatedly since May. Her managing editor had already been arrested under the Defence of the Realm Act on a similar charge, and was in jail.[39] He had moved among soldiers and sailors in the pubs, distributing communist materials—in the naive belief that all members of the armed forces shared his 'political' views. Some soldiers passed his pamphlet, 'Soviets for the British', to Scotland Yard and testified against the editor at his trial. Sylvia made a similar error in judging that readers of the *Dreadnought* shared her views. One of the many sailors she was anxious to convert wrote: 'Idiot . . . as regards the Royal Navy to revolutionize, well as far as I can see about 99% would screw your neck around if they had the opportunity'.[40] Clearly, opinion was divided on the subject of revolution, but subtle persuasion was not Sylvia's method. Nor was caution part of her normal armoury. The Home Office reported that, while 'the Communists . . . believe in hitting a man when he is down, . . . In point of fact, she is one of the very few British revolutionaries who really believe the doctrine which they preach.'[41]

The author of 'Discontent on the Lower Decks' was a young British sailor named Springhill. Claude McKay made contact with Springhill while Sylvia was in Russia. A radical malcontent himself, Springhill submitted an article to McKay for publication in the *Dreadnought*; McKay passed it on to Sylvia on her return from Russia, and after changing names of people as well as the ship on which Springhill was serving, Sylvia published it.[42] Two days after the article appeared, the police raided their offices. According to McKay;

> I was just going out, leaving the little room on the top floor where I always worked, when I met Pankhurst's private secretary coming upstairs. She whispered Scotland Yard was downstairs. Immediately I thought of Springhill's article and I returned to my room, where I had the original under a blotter. Quickly I folded it and stuck it in my sock. Going down, I met a detective coming up . . . 'And what are you?' the detective demanded. 'Nothing sir,' I said with a big black grin. Chuckling, he let me pass. . . . I walked out of that building and into another, and entering a water closet I tore up the original article, dropped it in and pulled the chain.

Sylvia was arrested and charged, however, as she 'did not want to risk having the youth's identity discovered by the authorities'. And she thought he could serve the cause more excellently by remaining at his post.[43] Indeed, she may have seen her arrest and subsequent trial as a rallying force for all radicals; she seemed not to recognize her fall from grace within party circles.

A former suffragette, Rachel Ferguson, published a cutting commentary on Sylvia in the *Daily Sketch* the day she was arrested. Ferguson described her as she had been in the suffrage movement, 'her soft hair parted in the middle . . . her misleadingly weak face that was pretty in the pussycat manner . . . Sylvia is a very clever woman with her share of the Pankhurst brain. . . . Herself of the people, she understands them well.' But, Ferguson continued, changes had altered the former suffragette:[44]

> I know you and your kind, Sylvia. You are of the authentic martyr stuff. Where your convictions lead, right or wrong you fight . . . I shall be easier in my mind when you are arrested by the Government as a dangerous character.

It was ironic that her former friend should call for her arrest on the day it happened. But, eight days after her arrest, conviction and sentencing to six months in jail, Norah Smyth had mortgaged Agenda Press to secure the £1000 bail for Sylvia's release on appeal. To gain her freedom she had promised not to assist in the publication of the *Dreadnought*, nor to speak at any public meetings. A hush fell over 400 Old Ford Road while Sylvia put her considerable energies to work preparing her appeal, which was set for January 1921.

Norah Smyth, always in the background, remains an elusive figure. She was apparently as committed to communism as Sylvia, although the Special Branch kept few records of her activities. We know that she made several trips to Sweden to collect money for Sylvia's communist enterprises; and one can suspect that she continued contributing her own funds when there were none from other sources. She was a socialist-feminist before she was swept into the communist tide and she remained a feminist in the years to come.

At the time of her arrest, Sylvia's various enterprises again lacked funds. Smyth and Edgar T. Whitehead (about whom we know only his name) ran the CP – BSTI; and Whitehead sent a steady stream of instructions to the *Dreadnought*. Lenin also came through with a final instalment of Soviet assistance, part of a promised £3000. Some of the money came through Russian agents, though Smyth had picked up one instalment in Sweden.[45] With Whitehead in charge, it may be that the Russians now expected better propaganda value for their money than they had under Sylvia's regime.

On Armistice Day 1920, Sylvia was still quiet, but an angry crowd attacked the *Dreadnought*'s Fleet Street office when its staff marched outside, keeping a silent vigil for the war dead.[46] At about the same time, still another communist unity conference drew fourteen representatives of the CP–BSTI, including Norah Smyth, but not Sylvia, and one subject of discussion was the communist press. As in the past, when Sylvia was forcibly relegated to the sidelines, Smyth emerged to take the helm. Throughout this period the normally reticent Smyth demonstrated her loyalty by attending meetings, running the enterprises—in so far as she was able—and trying to rally support for Sylvia. The *Communist* was by now the official organ of the CP – GB, but the *Dreadnought* was still a cause for concern. Joe Thurgood of the CP – GB wrote to Sylvia expessing his anxiety. Money from the revolutionary workers in Moscow had been used to buy part of the Agenda Press, of which Sylvia, Norah Smyth and Silvio Corio were trustees. But Thurgood believed that Corio, printer as well as manager for £5 a week, had mismanaged the press, refused orders, and opposed printers who might have joined the Communist Party. For that matter, Corio, a long-term anarchist, was not a member of the Party.[47] Lenin himself had sanctioned non-communists on the editorial staff of communist papers, but the Party in Britain would not accept a non-communist editor.

By January 1921, when Sylvia went before the Court of Appeal, her party was crumbling away, and her paper had lost its support from Moscow. Her days of glory in the revolution were behind her. But her few loyal allies—Norah, Corio and the faithful few from the suffrage days in the East End—remained. The radical, exciting associations in the movement had passed her by, choosing to unify on the instructions from Moscow.

Sylvia argued her own case before the judges, and she was clearly a disturbed woman at this juncture. Instead of discussing the two articles for which she was convicted, she read long rambling excerpts from other *Dreadnought* articles. She quoted Karl Marx and Frederick Engels. She interrupted the judges when they attempted to focus her attention on the articles under question, but she stood firm for communism telling the court that the only possible solution for Britain was 'violent revolution'. And she was dramatic: pleading frail health (which was true of her mental state) she threatened that putting her in prison 'may be a death sentence . . . but it will give currency to my views and I am going to take the risk.' This stand was reminiscent of her earlier encounter with Asquith, when she threatened death unless he saw her deputation. As might be expected, her conclusion was defiant: 'you may put me in prison but you cannot stop the cause.'[48]

The Times reported that 'when she sat down, exhausted after addressing the bench for one and one half hours, her hair had fallen down over her shoulders. Her outpourings were lost on a mostly hostile audience, some of whom cheered when her appeal was dismissed and she was sentenced to six months in the second division.'[49] But George Bernard Shaw wrote a consoling note, 'I am very sorry your appeal has not succeeded, though like all people in the movement, I am furious with you for getting into prison quite unnecessarily. . . . However there is no use in scolding you now; so keep up your spirits and look forward to the day of your deliverance.'[50]

Sylvia, having once again assumed she had the last word with the Communist Party, went to prison to serve four of the six months to which she was originally sentenced. Entering Holloway in 1921, Sylvia was considered a statistical habitual offender. That year 1128 of the 11,043 women committed had been in prison over eleven times. Sylvia fell into that category. Dr Mary Gordon presented an interesting analysis of the habitual criminal, which fits Sylvia at the time of her imprisonment: 'The habitual offender seldom takes the trouble to deny what she did or to conceal the facts. She argues that the main use of liberty is that you may do as you please.'[51] Sylvia entered the second division of Holloway with thieves and prostitutes, as she had done during her suffrage imprisonments, though Norah and others tried to get her moved to the first division as a political prisoner.

Sylvia complained bitterly, but she remained in the second division until her health deteriorated to such an extent that she spent her final month or so in the prison hospital. She complained, too, of the poor food and clothing, of the persistent cold, and inadequate blankets.[52] Every Sunday afternoon Norah and a small coterie of followers from the East End lined up outside the prison walls to cheer Sylvia and call attention to her presence in Holloway.[53] As often as was allowed, Norah visited her, always reporting on her condition—usually pale—in the *Dreadnought*. No member of her family visited her during those months. At this time she was a political pariah to Mrs Pankhurst and Christabel. (Adela, in Australia, also committed to communism, was equally rejected by her mother and oldest sister.)

As a second division prisoner, Sylvia was not allowed writing material, and the cells were frequently searched for forbidden items. Library privileges were few and the cells were dark, so reading put a strain on her eyes. She was forced to work as a cleaner; she washed windows and interior walls, cleaned up when things were spilled, and at times carried buckets of coal—heavy work for one unaccustomed to manual labour.[54] The old routine of chapel in the morning was still observed, as were the walks in the yard for exercise. But despite the personal hardships she encountered in prison, Sylvia was overwhelmed by two strong passions—compassion for the women occupying the cells alongside her and anger at her jailors and the intolerable conditions of the prison.[55] She later wrote several poems and short vignettes of the troubled women with whom she shared the daily gloom of prison life.

> A curious hatred doth her door awake
> Its spyhole centered in an iron disc,
> whence hidden faces stealthily gaze in.

Pregnant women and nursing mothers with babies most stirred her feelings. In those days, mothers were allowed to keep children born in prison until they were ten months old. In the yard, these mothers and their babies were part of the general prison scene, though they were otherwise segregated from other women. And here, at last, we see a genuine feminist emerge in Sylvia, as expressed in her concern for her fellow prisoners. Her solution to their plight, however, was as utopian as ever. Only the revolution she sought through communism would prevent poor women from stealing trifles for bread or from selling their bodies to survive.

On motherhood and pregnancy Sylvia wrote:[56]

> In lofty scorn she bore her pregnant state
> which marred her beauty not, but seemed to add
> Yet sombrely she swelt nor ever smiled
> nursing aloof in dreary prison yard.

Her lack of pen and paper moved her to lament:[57]

> Only this age that loudly boasts reform
> hath set its seal of vengeance against the mind,
> decreeing nought in prison shall be writ
> save on cold slate and swiftly washed away.

In an angrier, less humane, mood she attacked the judge's prejudice in her case:[58]

> He hath the power, and he will vengeance take;
> that was decided ere the case was called.

None of her poems, including those she wrote in prison and later published as *Writ on Cold Slate*, was prize-winning material, but writing verse provided an outlet for her, much as her infrequent attempts to draw and paint did when she found the time to pursue her art.

Bolsheviks in Russia used her imprisonment for propaganda purposes despite her fall from grace in those circles. The Moscow workers sent 'warmest and sincere greetings' to 'our brave and courageous sister in arms'. Moscow also used the occasion to call on the English workers to 'Rise up! Begin at last to fight your enemies.'[59] The French and German communist women also sent greetings to Sylvia, which no doubt gave her a sense of celebrity even as she was locked away from political activity.[60]

In May 1921, Sylvia was released from Holloway. A large crowd gathered at the entrance and sang 'The Red Flag'. But *The Times* reported, 'she looked unwell and appeared to find it difficult to walk'.[61] She had indeed been ill with colitis, and had suffered for some time before she had been granted a special diet of milk and eggs.[62] But on the eve of Sylvia's departure for Holloway, the Executive Committee of the Communist Party–British Section of the Third International sent her an official letter repudiating the *Workers' Dreadnought* as the voice of the Party.[63] Busy with her appeal and unable to speak out between the sentence and the appeal, Sylvia lost control of her organization to Edgar Whitehead.[64] Along with Whitehead, there was also a new male honorary treasurer thus bringing male domination to the CP–BSTI in the knowledge that Sylvia's jail sentence would allow the new leadership the time it needed to transfer power. Since the *Dreadnought* was run by Norah Smyth and others of Sylvia's remaining faithful, the paper was more easily disposed of than brought under control. Whitehead's letter also promised a boycott of Agenda Press, at that time run mainly by Silvio Corio.

The Communist Party–British Section Third International was now fragmented. Whitehead and his group were courting alliance with the Community Party–Great Britain, while Norah and the old faithfuls from the East London Federation, as well as the radical dockers, still favoured an independent course. The *Dreadnought*'s funds were almost exhausted now that Moscow had ceased financing Sylvia, and sales were almost non-existent.[65] Over the summer of 1921, she resumed her editorial position and begged constantly for funds. Next, in August, she turned the paper into a corporation, offering to sell stock (an uncharacteristic capitalistic approach) for one pound per share. In order to 'put a little ginger in the movement', the shareholders were to 'have a voice in the management and control of the company to give supporters and friends a more intimate relationship with the Communist Party.'[66]

Finally, in September, other attempts to raise money having failed, Corio turned to George Bernard Shaw. By this time, Corio was carrying his name on the paper as printer and listing his shop as the address of Sylvia's Agenda Press—10 Wine Office Court, Fleet Street.[67] At this stage Shaw was unsympathetic as well as unwilling to admit he had any money. He wrote:[68]

> I have known for some time past that Sylvia is in difficulties; ... though I am quite as much disposed to make a spoiled child of her as the rest of her friends I am not really sorry that she should lose a toy so expensive and dangerous as a printing press, and have a spell of total abstinence from *Weltverbesserungswahn* [the illusion of world improvement].

Shortly after Shaw wrote to Corio, Sylvia announced that the 17 September issue of the *Dreadnought* would be the last. It was not merely a matter of low circulation and mounting debts. The CP–BSTI had finally merged into the CP–GB, and the united party expelled her. In a candid statement, she explained that the controversy centred on her lack of discipline within the Party and her position on the *Dreadnought* as an independent, left-wing paper. Admitting that she was tired, she wrote, 'and so I leave the Party', but stated categorically that she was staying with the movement and drew parallels with conflicts within the communist movement in Germany and Holland, where in each case the far left had broken from the centre. In Moscow, indeed, in her opinion, the Third International had come under control of the right-wing, and this was as abhorrent to her as the movement to the right-of-centre within the British Communist Party. 'The Communist Party of Great Britain is at present passing through a sort of political measles called discipline.'[69] Sylvia for one, was not likely to succumb to that disease.

In a *Times* interview, she discussed her expulsion from the Communist Party–Great Britain, attacking the leadership for its 'zeal to serve the Communist Party by controlling me and bringing to an end the pioneer communist paper that . . . is known to the Communist movement throughout the world.' She declared her continued commitment to run an independent newspaper on principle, but in fact she was out of money. She refused simply to hand the paper over to the united Communist Party (in spite of the fact that its major source of funding had been the Soviet Union), but she hinted that she might be willing to sell the paper to the Party in a 'comradely spirit'. And she concluded by saying: 'I do not regret my expulsion . . . I desire freedom to work for Communism with the best that is in me.'[70]

At the time, she was also inclined to reverse her actions. Three weeks after announcing the end of the *Dreadnought*, Sylvia told *The Times* that she had changed her mind. The paper would continue: 'It was vital that there should be an independent Communist newspaper untrammelled by party bias.'[71] Norah seems to have come forth with enough money to bail her out once again, and in the autumn of 1921, she managed to align what remained of her personal following with the Fourth International. Herman Gorter, a Dutch left-winger and ideological opponent of Lenin, was temporarily supportive because of her anti-parliamentarian stance and her recent criticisms of Lenin. It is unclear whether her new Communist Workers Party was ever granted formal affiliation with the Fourth International, but the Home Office found that Gorter sent her at least £50 to support the *Dreadnought*, and possibly more in 1922 and 1923.[72]

Ironically, 39 years later, on Sylvia's death, her son protested to *The Times* about its obituary, which reported her expulsion from the Party. *The Times* replied: 'Dr Richard Pankhurst informs us that his mother, Sylvia Pankhurst, was never a member of the Communist Party and was therefore never expelled from it'.[73] Apparently she kept this most flamboyant of her involvements buried in the recesses of her mind and never admitted to her son that she was as responsible as anyone for getting the Communist Party off the ground in those early post-war years. Indeed, she quickly reversed the action in her own mind, and by 1923 she was telling people that she had left the Party, not that the Party had left her.[74] In one autobiographical draft for a book edited by Margot Asquith, she wrote that she found herself 'not fully in agreement with the Communist Party created here under the influence of the Revolutionary Socialist Government and the Third International. I had done, I knew it, more than any single individual here to pioneer the way which made such a movement possible here . . .'[75] But this never got into print. Another draft for an article showed Sylvia in a complete about-face. In describing a meeting of the early enthusiasts for communism in Britain, in which we have seen how dedicated she was from the first days, Sylvia wrote: 'For my part, I contributed, I think not a word to the discussion; I listened in complete amazement to sentiments so revolutionary . . . and wondered what the world could

be coming to when some of those present, who had been shocked by
.the mild militancy of the Suffragettes, should be discussing such a tremendous step.'[76] There was every reason for Sylvia to deny her
involvement with left-wing extremism but in fact she was one of the
most extreme, if irrational advocates of revolution—indeed violent
revolution—in England during the early organizational period of the
party. But in time, just as she enlarged her role in winning votes for
women, she conveniently distorted the truth with regard to her role in
the politics of the far left.

PART 3
Motherhood and Journalism

8
Motherhood and Family Life

The boy looks a jolly little arrival, and is still, I hope, trailing
clouds of glory. I trust you selected an eligible father for him.
  —George Bernard Shaw to ESP, 29 July 1929

Silvio Corio was born to Luigi and Chiara Domenica Corio in Turin
in October 1875.[1] He had been a rebel since youth. His father died
while he was a teenager, which perhaps explains why he was sent to a
technical high school to become a printer instead of being given a more
formal academic training. He left before completing the course, took a
job, and soon became active as a socialist propagandist among the
other printers. He progressed quickly from socialism to anarchism,
continuing as a propagandist, lecturing and writing on anarchism.
When he was twenty-two, he entered military service under Italy's
universal conscription law, but a year later he was assigned to the first
Compagnia disciplina for his propaganda activities.[2] In 1899 he finished
military service with the equivalent of a dishonourable discharge, and
rejoined his former anarchist circle on the outskirts of Turin.

In 1900 Corio went to France, where anarchism enjoyed wider
popularity. In October he was arrested by the French police on suspicion of being involved in a bomb plot. Subsequently he was banished
from Paris, but, because he refused to leave, was sent to jail. On his
release he escaped to England. The following year his socialist mistress, Clelia Alignani, joined him, and in 1902 she gave birth to Corio's
second child (the first by her), a son. Later that year Corio, who was
penniless and unemployed, was hunted by the British police on the
charge of stealing a sewing machine. Apparently he went undetected,
and the charge was eventually dropped. He and Clelia were living
with an Italian couple in London when Clelia made the first of several
abrupt departures, taking her son and going off to live for a short time
with a socialist.[3]

When next the Italian agents in London reported on Corio, in September 1903, Clelia had returned: then, a year later, their baby died.
Corio left for Paris in October 1904 on what was described as private
business,[4] apparently supporting himself by printing menus for
various restaurants and hotels. He spent his free time in agitation, in
distributing propagandist letters and circulars, and in other anarchist

activities. He wrote then, as later, under the pseudonyms 'Crastinus' and 'Virginus'. In 1904 he briefly worked full-time as a waiter at a London restaurant, and he also worked for a Dutch firm doing some unknown job—possibly printing.[5]

In 1905 the Italian police noted another trip to Paris; this time Corio returned with his eldest son. The mother's name is not known, but she was probably Italian, since her son travelled back and forth between England and Italy. By this time, Corio and Clelia had produced a daughter, Beatrice Roxanne, who also spent much of her childhood in Turin. By 1907, Italian police reports indicate Corio, Roxanne, Clelia and Corio's son were all living together in England when Clelia and the children again left abruptly for Italy. Rumours in the London Italian community had it that she left because of Corio's behaviour, which included affairs with other women. Some anarchists went further and accused him of being both a spy and a pimp.[6] Not all was comradeship among the anarchists, any more than it was among the communists.

In the autumn of 1908 Clelia and the children came back to London, where they remained until 1920; then they left again. She and Corio continued this pattern of quarrelling and reconciliation, although he seems not to have contributed much to her support or that of his children in those years. He increased his status among his fellow anarchists between 1911 and 1915, when he was involved in making Italian translations of radical literature, such as the works of Hyndman of the Social Democratic Federation and Russia's Bakunin. He wrote for the *Daily Herald* as Crastinus, and for the Italian socialist paper, *Avanti*. Some of his work appeared in the period when *Avanti* was edited by Benito Mussolini.[7]

In mid-1912 Corio became associated with the anarchist and later martyr, Errico Malatesta. This was probably the peak of an otherwise peripheral career in London anarchist circles. He translated several of Malatesta's speeches and articles into English and, in 1913, shared the rostrum with the socialist hero, who was an old acquaintance of the Pankhursts when they lived in Russell Square. In 1915 Corio spoke in favour of Italian participation in the European war.[8] In 1916, however, he reversed his views and joined Malatesta in opposing the war.

He apparently had no further demands for military service by either Italy or Britain. He was a foreigner resident in England—though harmless enough not to be deported—and because of his political activities he was not desirable for conscription again with the Italians. Furthermore, he was too old, having turned forty in 1915. And he had a heart condition. He was thus able to travel quite freely between England and France, and he may have been one source of foreign news for the *Dreadnought*.

It is possible that Sylvia and Corio first became acquainted as fellow pacifists in wartime England, although Sylvia certainly knew anarchists in the East End. When Sylvia met him, Corio was stocky and prematurely bald. His first by-lined article in the *Dreadnought* appeared at the end of 1917, and he followed that with a long historical piece on 'Karl Marx in Fleet Street, 1865 – 1867' in May 1918.[9] At the end of 1918 he went to Paris as a correspondent covering the peace conference for *Avanti*, and Sylvia was there, representing the *Dreadnought*. In 1919, Sylvia and Corio were both in Italy, Corio for the first time since 1900 to attend a socialist congress in Bologna and to help arrange for Malatesta's covert return.[10] Corio probably introduced Sylvia to Italian socialists in several cities before she left for her rendezvous with Clara Zetkin in Germany.

The Italian police monitored Corio's movements in 1919 and 1920 with close interest. His ability to travel widely and frequently—especially for someone who was chronically short of money—may have been facilitated by the Soviet funds that flowed through Sylvia's hands in these years intended for a variety of radical causes. He passed back and forth between London, France, Switzerland and Italy. At one point he was jailed in Paris for fifteen days for possession of brass knuckles. The police at another point located him in the company of an Italian communist (possibly Antonio Gramsci) on his way to Russia. Later, the Italian police, who followed him closely whenever he was in Italy, lost him for more than a month, which resulted in acute embarrassment for those responsible as well as a good deal of dashing around to known anarchist circles to try to pick up the trail. Corio finally surfaced while visiting a sister in Palermo before returning to England.[11] This same sister reported in 1925 to the Italian police that Corio had become a British subject. Sylvia, on the other hand, told her friends that Corio was unable to take a regular job because he was an illegal alien in Britain.

After this spate of activity, Corio returned to London; Clelia left for reasons that are unclear; and he became more regularly associated with the *Dreadnought* and the Agenda Press but always a little on the periphery of the socialist, anarchist and anti-Fascist groups within the London Italian community. Apparently most, including the Italian police, regarded him as something of an eccentric, and with reason. In the early 1920s, Corio converted to Islam and joined the *Ahmadiyya*, an Islamic brotherhood with headquarters in India, but one which had the unusual policy of sending out paid missionaries on the model of a Christian missionary organization. One of these establishments was a mosque on Melrose Road in Wimbledon, run by F. M. Sayal. In 1922 the Corio family was on such good terms with the mosque that the family members—Corio, Clelia (then back) and Roxanne—all moved into the mosque with Mr and Mrs Sayal.

But the original friendship turned sour. Sayal loaned Corio £50, which Corio could not return when it came due. Sayal's wife then evicted the Corios but held their personal property as security for the unpaid loan. Corio took Sayal to court but achieved nothing except a solicitor's bill for a further £15. The London Ahmadi Committee tended to blame Clelia for these troubles, but it was itself passing through a period of financial stringency. In the end, His Holiness the Khalifatul Masih Qadcan intervened from India, saying that Sayal should have used more 'perfect patience' but refusing to pay Corio's claims against the mosque.[12] Corio may have left the *Ahmadiyya* around this time, although he continued in later years to show an interest in non-western cultural groups in London.

Sylvia and Corio probably became lovers in 1925 or 1926. Corio was living alone in slum conditions and had withdrawn from active political life. He was in financial trouble, and the Italian police suspected that he was helped or partly supported by his children.[13] In fact, before 1924, Roxanne wrote to Sylvia (who never met her mother, but knew the girl through Corio), saying that she had done sufficiently well in entrance examinations to qualify for a night scholarship at the London School of Economics. Roxanne pointed out that fees 'for this, the last session, will not have to worry me, or you...I seldom see my father now and the money he gives me is less than negligible...I am wondering if you can give me a little financial assistance.'[14] Sylvia was then living on Norah's kindness and probably did not have much to offer.

In a letter to Corio, Roxanne mentioned that her brother, Percy, was coming to live with her and that they needed to find housing. Corio was clearly not then living with his children, but Roxanne hoped for support to carry the responsibility of her brother and her own schooling. She continued as an occasional student at the London School of Economics until she finished her BA in 1930 and went to work for a London business firm. Rejecting her father's anarchistic views—and possibly the memories of her own unhappy youth as a victim of politics—she settled into married oblivion.[15]

Meanwhile, Corio had so mastered the English language that, on occasion, he was more precise, and certainly more eloquent, than Sylvia. He displayed this skill in a long, sometimes flirtatious, letter to her in the early 1920s. Apparently they had quarrelled (Corio was said to have a bad temper). He wanted to patch up their differences which had involved, among other things, her objection to his writing under a pseudonym, and her charge that he was despotic in his management of the paper. Corio began thus: 'Apologia being a Fragmentary Essay on Politics, Technicalities; Editorial Rights and despotism; The Alphabet, its values and importance; names and anonymity.' He wryly observed that 'I sit and consider as you advise me to do...'. Where others often found her unkempt and frumpish, Corio praised her as 'willowly' and called her 'graces pleasant to behold'. Turning to their similarity of names, he was half-mocking. Moving next to serious problems, Corio explained why he chose to write under a pseudonym. He was proud of his name but concerned for those he loved still in Italy if, as a propagandist, he openly signed himself as Silvio Corio. And he wanted to be considered more than a mere foreigner by English readers.[16]

It is difficult to judge a person by one letter, especially when the bulk of other evidence consists of unflattering police reports of undesirable behaviour; but Corio, at this time, seemed more able than Sylvia to submerge his identity into the cause. It was 'torture' to him to write, yet, 'if I ever venture to set down a few lines, I do so under the illusion that they may, even in a small way be useful to the cause I have at heart.' Corio ended this long letter with the wish that they could visit Richmond Park once more (where in earlier days Sylvia had often met Keir Hardie). Finally, 'I miss you, you do not know how much.'[17]

What began as love—if it ever truly existed for Sylvia—soon became a working partnership that lasted until the end of Corio's life. Both were difficult. As the years passed, he seems to have lost his earlier capacity for abuse and sexual infidelity. Instead, Corio settled into the role of prince consort to Sylvia Pankhurst. She, in turn, provided an erratic form of financial security for him, something he had not known since before his earliest days as a socialist propagandist.

As the fortunes of the *Dreadnought* waned, Corio, with Sylvia's approval, planned a new quarterly journal 'to tilt with outworn standards and conventions in all fields'.[18] The first notices concerning *Germinal* appeared in the *Dreadnought* in 1921, but the journal was not actually published until April 1923. The idea of a political and literary magazine featuring leftist writers, past and present, probably came from an earlier publication; the name originated in Zola's novel *Germinal*. The first publisher to use this title for his journal was Rudolf Rocker, another anarchist with a base in the East End. Rocker was a German gentile living with a Jewish woman, and he was prominent in the mostly Jewish anarchist movement at the turn of the century. His 1900 *Germinal* was published in Yiddish, and its circulation was thus limited. Corio would have been aware of this earlier publication from his East End anarchist associations. His *Germinal* came out in English, though also with a very limited circulation and a short life—only two issues ever appeared.[19]

Corio, as editor, was barely in control of the enterprise. The first issue led off with a translation of Maxim Gorky's short story 'Comrades'; H. D. Harben, heir to the Prudential Insurance fortune provided a poem in free verse entitled 'Friends'. Another contribution was signed by Richard Marsden, Sylvia's pen name, taken in honour of her father. But the honour was doubtful, for it was an immature and uncreative short story called 'Utopian Conversations', and it must have pained Corio to print it. Sylvia, in fact, dominated the two issues. Her poetry was interspersed throughout, unpublishable except through such channels. In the first issue, however, she briefly assumed the role of literary critic, a role for which she seemed more suited than either poet or short story writer.

A magazine of this type was out of tune with the non-literary interest of the *Dreadnought* readers—mostly East End dock workers and a few still faithful women from the East End Federation. It required the talents of a man like Robert Blatchford to inspire such an audience. And *Germinal*'s lack of literary merit disqualified it from a broader or better educated audience.

With *Germinal* extinguished, the *Dreadnought* on its last legs, and no more political credit among either the communists or her old middle-class associates, Sylvia was dependent on the faithful—but long-suffering—Norah's dwindling inheritance. So too was Corio, the only remaining employee. Needing something to sustain her, Sylvia advertised a series of lectures she was prepared to give for a fee. The eight topics ranged from 'Lessons of the French Revolution' to readings of her own poetry.[20] No record remains of her success in these ventures.

Sylvia and Norah had found an old, four-roomed cottage[21] at 126 High Road, Woodford Wells, on the London-Essex border, across the street from a public house which attracted crowds of people who came out to Epping Forest at the weekends. They originally intended to use the house as both a residence and a meeting-place where they could form a growing discussion circle with what remained of their following. They still considered themselves as communists, and they named the restored house 'Red Cottage'. It was shielded from the street by a screen of trees and shrubs behind which they placed tables and chairs for their discussion groups.

Sylvia had already moved to the renovated cottage when the *Dreadnought* folded. It proved unsuccessful as a meeting place and she therefore turned the new liability into an asset by following the example of her mother and Christabel's tearoom in the south of France (which they briefly and unsuccessfully ran) to turn the Red Cottage into a weekend tearoom. She was thus in competition (of sorts) with the pub across the way. Sylvia did not drink, and did not seek a licence for the sale of alcohol. Instead she offered a family-style service at her tearoom. The project had only one drawback: Sylvia could not cook. In the early days, Annie Barnes' husband once stopped by and found Sylvia in the kitchen *boiling* a rasher of bacon to serve with liver.[22] But Annie Barnes and a few old friends from the East End came on weekends to help out. Norah was still on hand at the beginning of the enterprise; and Corio, who could cook, may well have helped too.

By Christmas 1926, Norah was in Italy, and Corio had moved into the Red Cottage. Sylvia was then writing the first of several books that were to occupy her time over the next few years, and was running the tearoom at weekends. She used paid help when she could find it, along with volunteers from among the loyal East End following. During the General Strike in 1926, she took in miners' children from Wales, some of whom were farmed out to friends in the East End. Sylvia kept others at the Red Cottage where they helped out in the tearoom in return for board. She made a practice of bringing in poor girls to work for her—presumably in exchange for a room and board—but relations soon soured and she could never keep help for long.[23]

Sylvia had been anxious to bear a child ever since she recovered from the arduous suffrage campaigns which had wrecked her health. In 1926 she phoned Charlotte Drake announcing she was pregnant. However, that 'pregnancy' was wishful thinking, and examination by a doctor proved otherwise. Sylvia believed she might now be too old to conceive, but she was mistaken, and in December 1927, she gave birth to a son. Whatever the trials she and Corio suffered in adjusting to each other and running the tearoom, a third person had now permanently entered their lives, and at rather a late date. Sylvia was forty-five, Corio fifty-two.

Sylvia wrote to keep herself occupied during her pregnancy. Emmeline Pethick-Lawrence helped make arrangements with a hospital and nursing home. She also met part of the expense. Sylvia discussed the birth of her baby and the problems surrounding motherhood in *Save the Mothers: A Plea for a National Maternity Service*. She never undertook any task without sharing it with the public at large. The first people, however, to share in the event were her doctor and three attendants. It was a somewhat remarkable feat for a woman of her age to give birth to a first child and suffer no ill-effects. She recorded that after a slow start, she had a fast labour. Soon after it began her 'little son nestled his rosy face against her chest'. Corio was a proud, loving and experienced father, but Sylvia still lived with memories of old attachments and named her baby Richard Keir Pethick Pankhurst, after her father, Keir Hardie, and Emmeline Pethick-Lawrence, because of her help and life-long friendship.

Neither Sylvia nor Corio believed in marriage. He had at least two child-producing liaisons in the past, both without benefit of marriage and with scant parental responsibility. She was still a radical product of her times and believed in free love, though she had never practised it indiscriminately. She remembered unhappy marriages from her youth and had seen the crippling effects of marriage on many a woman in the East End. She had read widely on successful women who rejected marriage—her heroine, Mary Wollstonecraft, for example, and Clara Zetkin, had both been unmarried mothers. Sylvia was also reluctant to submerge her identity as a Pankhurst, although she might have made

Sylvia Pankhurst *c.* 1925, before the birth of Richard

Sylvia Pankhurst with her son Richard, April 1928

Annie Barnes, as a young East London Suffragette

an exception for Keir Hardie, had he not been married. She was proud of her father's successful career and her mother's prominence in the suffrage movement; and, above all, because of her self image during the suffrage period when she frequently enjoyed headlines in the press. She would not have considered losing this identification by marrying an Italian immigrant.

Her penchant for self-justification in delicate situations surfaced again when she became an unmarried mother. In a published article, Sylvia wrote, 'Like most idealistic young people, . . . [she had begun] with the notion that true love can only come once in a lifetime, and invariably, endures forever.' Hardie was dead; she had seen other young women lose their loved ones during the war. She was also 'compelled to see that true lovers are not always good judges of character . . . though I happen to be one of those persons who are not swift to fall in love, and are tenacious and constant in their affections, I early became convinced that no man or woman should be chained for life . . . ' In fact, few people had Sylvia's single-minded pursuit of causes, or flair for gaining publicity, good or bad. She believed she was correct to the extent that these affections centred on a tiny baby. She also believed that she and Corio had 'the same economic obstacles', and again she was correct; though she did not put it quite that way, neither of them had ever, except briefly, held a full-time job.[24]

Dora Russell would have supported Sylvia's right to have an illegitimate child, although they may not have been well acquainted at the time. Both Bertrand and Dora were advocates of free love and each had affairs. Dora gave birth to one child by another man, and was pregnant for a second time by the same lover, when Bertrand divorced her so that he could legitimize the child his mistress was carrying. 'Sound motherhood', Dora wrote, 'should not be subject to social and legal conventions.'[25]

Corio was alone at the Red Cottage for some time after Richard's birth, and he used some of this time to build a small shed-like structure in the garden, which the family was to occupy. Sylvia and the baby left the nursing home and went to a farmhouse in the country for further care and convalescence. Emmeline Pethick-Lawrence and H. D. Harben agreed to pay the costs of building the hut. Harben also accepted responsibility for the household expenses during Sylvia's long confinement. Corio, however, spent more than the £100 Emmeline had promised, and he overspent Harben's household money as well. Emmeline Pethick-Lawrence—who was serving as a go-between while Sylvia was away—was angry, thinking she had been deceived. Several drafts of Sylvia's letters to Emmeline trying to explain the circumstances have survived, and they are revealing. Corio was as irresponsible about money as was Sylvia. He had underestimated the expenses. Sylvia had not intended to deceive. She explained that she had avoided discussing money matters when Corio approached her in the nursing home; she had been tired, Richard was not well, and Corio visited infrequently. In one draft she pleaded with the older woman to realize 'my circumstances in all those months. I was almost as much in the dark as you . . .'. In another draft she stated that she 'was not capable'; and that she should have had Emmeline 'keep the money and dole it out to Silvio . . . he was always worried, nervous, excitable . . . and getting more nervous if I opposed anything he said.' Indeed, 'I did nothing wrong—only anticipate Mr. Harben's cheque . . . It was my intention to pay the bills as soon as you sent Mr. Harben's money.'[26]

Richard's birth caused consternation in other circles. Mrs Pankhurst was back in London, having been chosen by the Conservative Party to stand for election at Whitechapel and St George's. She had been ill and was living in a poor, dingy flat in the constituency she had hoped to represent. Sylvia saw her mother once after her return, but before Corio moved into the Red Cottage. The greeting was affectionate, but the differences between the two women were by this time too great to overcome.

Political differences were one thing; however, the disgrace of her daughter as an unmarried mother was more than Mrs Pankhurst could bear. According to Mary Gordon, one of Mrs Pankhurst's adopted children, Sylvia tried to visit her mother once during her pregnancy, but Mrs Pankhurst ran to her room 'like a sulky girl and refused to see Auntie Sylvia when that scarlet woman dared to call'.[27] Helen Moyes, who saw Mrs Pankhurst in London shortly after the baby's birth, said that she was 'horrified and greatly distressed when Sylvia had her son . . . she really looked quite ill about it'.[28]

In fact, Mrs Pankhurst was ill. She was depressed and in failing health by the time Sylvia gave birth. Christabel is credited with having kept Sylvia away from Mrs Pankhurst during her final illness.[29] But whether this was Mrs Pankhurst's or Christabel's decision, Sylvia was never allowed to see her mother or show her the grandchild who was named after her husband.

Always defiant, still jealous of Christabel, and now completely shut out of her mother's life, Sylvia hit back at both women by going to the *News of the World* (generally regarded as a scandal sheet) in April 1928, to announce the birth of her 'eugenic baby'.[30] More sensationalism followed this act of open defiance. Newspapers around the world, especially the tabloids, headlined the 'Eugenic Baby Solution'. Sylvia got the attention she sought, but the revenge and sheer vulgarity of the publicity proved too much for her mother. Several members of the family and former WSPU members believe that Sylvia's public announcement sent the already weakened Mrs Pankhurst to her death.[31]

On 14 June 1928 Mrs Pankhurst, the queen of the militant suffragettes, passed away before the election which might have brought her

Portrait of Emmeline Pankhurst, 1927, by Georgina Brackenbury

to Parliament. She had lived long enough to see the Bill for universal suffrage pass its second reading in the House of Lords but she died a month before its actual passage into law. (Winning universal suffrage that year was a subject on which Sylvia did not comment publicly.) Mrs Pankhurst never saw any of her grandchildren. (She had repudiated Adela over her pacifism in the First World War, and the two never completely reconciled.) She rejected Sylvia when her daughter needed her most. A woman with such steel-like qualities would hardly seem the type to die because of yet another of Sylvia's forays into the public eye. A follower who first met Mrs Pankhurst at the age of seventeen described her as delicate and frail, with violet eyes and lovely skin, but as to her gentle appearance: 'it seemed incredible that such gentleness could hold so much steel.' A subdued Sylvia attended her mother's funeral but, still defiant, she brought the baby with her.

The *News of the World*, in publishing Sylvia's story, heralded 'Sylvia Pankhurst's amazing confession' that she gave birth 'to a child out of wedlock—a ''Eugenic'' baby, she prefers to call it.' During the interview Sylvia reiterated her views on marriage but emphasized that she 'was very much in love with her ''husband''' whose identity she refused to reveal. That he was fifty-three (fifty-two actually) and foreign was all she would say. Since 'he is of a retiring disposition and hates publicity, I will not bring him publicity by naming him'.[32] Holding her baby, she told the reporter, 'I suppose you think I am awfully silly don't you, . . . This is him.' She explained that she was running a tearoom for support but 'I have another problem now . . . this boy. The tearoom will enable me to support him. Since his father, although a most brilliant man, is unable to contribute much towards his support.'[33]

The fact that she 'had long desired a child' is also confirmed by Annie Barnes, who was nevertheless shocked when Sylvia confided that she was pregnant. Despite Mrs Drake's apparent support, many of her old friends and supporters in the East End shared Annie Barnes' chagrin that Sylvia had openly admitted she was not married. They were equally annoyed that she called the child 'eugenic', knowing that the anarchist Corio was the father. But Barnes also recalled how tender and loving Sylvia had been with the children on Old Ford Road.

For the sake of the child's health, Sylvia told the reporter, she planned to 'live in a little hut in the garden behind the tearoom'—Corio's financial folly. 'My union with my husband is entirely free', she said. 'The tendency of the future is in the same direction and . . . posterity will see nothing remarkable in our decision.' As to the 'eugenic' baby which had captured all the headlines:[34]

> it is good eugenics, I believe, if one desires parenthood, to consider if one is of sufficient general intelligence, bodily health and strength, and freedom from hereditary diseases to produce an intelligent and healthy child. I believe that of myself. I believe that also of my baby's father. Indeed I consider my 'husband' has many gifts with which to endow our child, and aptitude and patience as a teacher.

For many years Sylvia's attention had been drawn to the plight of the married mother, usually poor working-class women who could barely support their children. She claimed an interest in both mother and child, but she seemed in this case only to see the child as an extension of the unmarried mother. Whatever 'hate mail' she received she mostly destroyed, but she kept a number of sympathetic letters. Most of them praised her courage in attacking an evil society through her personal example, although quite a few wondered whether having eugenic children was something with which working-class women could cope. And George Bernard Shaw came through with the light touch, in words quoted at the beginning of this chapter.

Yet Sylvia's leap into the headlines brought repercussions, in her neighbourhood, among friends, and in the press. Her article 'My Baby and Me' published in the Manchester *Sunday Chronicle*, hastened to explain that 'I thought it necessary to reply to statements connecting myself with the view that a eugenic baby may be produced by a woman who seeks out a man merely because he is healthy and intelligent and induces him to make a mother out of her without either affection or friendship.'[35] Referring to letters she had received, Sylvia further explained that she believed 'the enthusiastic love of the parents for each other to be an important factor'.

In order to quell the storm of criticism, she talked about her childhood. She read a lot of poetry; she was romantic: 'My father was a very prince among lovers, and his abiding affection for his wife and children' influenced her finally to have a family. She thought her youth had been too complicated by the suffrage movement, war and East End activities. She left out her communist years which could hardly have helped her cause of the moment. But she explained that, in recent years, she had yearned for the quiet, peaceful countryside and a family. She had turned to literary pursuits, further suggesting that the peaceful nature of her new interest was conducive to child-bearing.

Love, too, had been elusive. Referring to her past love for Hardie, she wrote: 'Great love can seldom cease without great sorrow. To me it still seems that the greatest love never ends and that only the death of the loved one can render possible another equally close relationship.' Perhaps these words were meant for her mother. As to Corio, 'Life has taught me what love is . . . a faculty which so far from being exhausted from employment, grows and grows with usage . . . I learnt a great tolerance for love of every sort. It is not love but indifference and hate that should be feared. . . . Regarding our union I do not seek extraordinary press publicity which has been thrust upon me.'[36] She thus recognized the folly of her original announcement, and her response was to try to turn the tables so as to become the victim rather than the perpetrator.

Christabel visited her sister only once, to plead with her 'for the sake of the family and of the child . . . to allow Richard to bear his father's name'.[37] Sylvia turned a deaf ear to this request. This was the last time the two sisters met, for Christabel remained in London only a short time after Mrs Pankhurst's death. The meeting ended on the same sour note that had come to characterize their relationship since WSPU days, only this time it was Sylvia who held the upper hand.

Christabel lectured frequently in the 1920s and 1930s, published books and articles dealing with the Second Coming of Christ, and travelled widely, mainly between North America and London. In 1924 Helen Moyes happened to be in New York when Christabel was lecturing in the Calvary Baptist Church. Moyes attended a service where Christabel spoke, and recalled 'she looked very little older when I saw her, beautifully gowned and wearing a big, becoming, softly-feathered hat . . . the same upward fling of long, eloquent hands, unbelievably the same, incredibly different, she enunciated her new faith.'

In her evangelism, she directed the 'scorn she used to pour on the politicians' against the non-believers, warning her audience that because of man's unchanging ways, 'within the next half century an Armageddon would come . . . I am still a politician but I have abandoned worldly politics for the politics of God.'[38] Mrs Pankhurst, always a declared atheist, never expressed herself publicly on Christabel's crusade in the last years of her life.

In 1936, Christabel was honoured by the Tories with the female version of knighthood, and became Dame Christabel. In 1940 she published another religious work, again heralding the end of the world.[39] She slowly disappeared from public view, retiring to Santa Monica, California, staying in touch with only a few friends and former suffragettes, among them Grace Roe. Sylvia and Christabel had little—if any—contact in the intervening years until 1957, when Sylvia's fighting instincts emerged in connection with Roger Fulford's *Votes for Women*, which was published that year. Although Fulford claimed to have drawn largely on Sylvia's published works on the suffrage movement, his basic sin was to have published works on the topic at all. In 1957 Sylvia was in Ethiopia and unable to muster the kind of attack she believed Fulford deserved. She turned instead to Christabel, writing that he had distorted 'everything I have written',[40] and trying to cajole Christabel into taking up her cause. Christabel was publicly mute on the subject of Fulford's book, as she had been whenever words, including Sylvia's, were published about the movement.

Christabel died in February 1958, at the age of seventy-seven. She was mourned by feminists in America and Britain[41] and honoured by a memorial service sponsored by the Suffragette Fellowship in London. No public word about her death came from Sylvia.

Sylvia's contacts with Adela were also infrequent because Adela and Tom Walsh lived in Australia, but the relationship was not strained, and they were in substantial agreement on most political issues. In the waning days of the *Dreadnought*, when Sylvia badly needed material, Walsh contributed a column 'From Australia', mainly concerned with Australian labour and shipping, as might be expected from one of the leading organizers of the Federated Seaman's Union of Australia.[42]

In 1926, Sylvia and Walsh were in contact regarding a projected new London dockers' union, in which Sylvia was briefly involved. Walsh contributed a sixteen-page, closely-typed letter describing his experiences in Australia and New Zealand and giving tactical advice on ways to use the vehicles of parliamentary politics, the courts and the strike. He was proud of his role in obtaining conditions for Australian seamen 'second to none on earth today', mainly through the intervention of the judicial system.[43] In spite of this generous advice, there is no evidence that Sylvia played an active role in the dockers' cause at that time. It is likely that she used her brother-in-law's name and connections in an attempt to have her own organization again. There was even talk of the Walshs coming to England, but they lost a child that year and the project fell through.[44]

Sylvia wrote more frequently than usual to the Walshs during her pregnancy, which suggests that she may have been lonely. Adela became an admirer of Japan during the 1930s, calling publicly for an Australian-Japanese alliance just as Japan was preparing for aggression in the eastern hemisphere. Like all the Pankhursts, Adela developed a fixation for her cause of the moment and ran for the federal senate in 1940 in her campaign for the alliance. After her predictable defeat, she became involved with pro-Axis forces. In 1941 she was active in founding an 'Australian First' group, which was similar to Oswald Mosley's blackshirts in England.[45]

Her wartime activites were less tolerable to the Australian government than her previous radical activities. She was interned as a security risk in 1942, leaving at home an ailing husband—Tom Walsh died in 1943. Adela, alone and friendless during the war, was forced to take a series of menial jobs after her release. Her daughter, Sylvia, also died during the war, leaving Adela with one surviving son. Her own death came in 1960, after years of near obscurity.

Richard's birth put an end to Sylvia's loneliness. When the early joys of motherhood were replaced by the child's needs for total care, she was overwhelmed. She had writing obligations and a new book to finish. The Red Cottage tearoom occupied her at weekends. Corio added to the burden, being ill with sciatica, and demanding care and attention himself. Sylvia turned for help to Nora Walshe, a former suffragette who had helped out at the East End clinic and one of the few middle-class friends still loyal in 1928. She could afford to pay someone to help with Richard, but hated to hand him over to strangers. 'It would be too much to hope', she wrote, 'that you could do it for me even four or five afternoons a week. . . . Actually I find myself so irritable and jaded when I sit down to write I am often unable to frame a sentence for some time.'[46] And finances were again tight. Nora Walshe helped out with clothing, but the only substantial income was from Sylvia's writing, and neither the loyal Mrs Pethick-Lawrence nor the generous Henry Harben could be counted on to keep the family going in the long run.[47]

Sylvia probably did not nurse her baby. If she did, it was not for long. Goats' milk was thought to be the best substitute for mother's milk, so the family soon bought a goat, tethered it in the garden, and let it serve the dual purpose of supplying nutrition for Richard as well as keeping the lawn in trim. As the child grew older, Corio paid close attention to him, and apparently became more of a father to him than he had been to his other children.[48] Sylvia's tender feelings for the boy are expressed in this verse:

> Baby, Baby, O Baby dear
> What is before us in the New Year?
> You will be bigger, I shall not grow
> Shall we go sailing in a big ship
> Shall we see Red men, shall we see Black?

It is interesting to see the notion of race introduced to such a young child. But the poem not only conveys her gentle love; its underlying message is her uncertainty about the future.

Life with middle-aged reformers would have been a burden for any only child. But Corio and Sylvia recognized Richard's need for companionship. When he was nearly three, Sylvia organized another Montessori nursery school in association with Vera Brittain, a socialist and professional writer. They formed a committee from the middle-class world Sylvia was beginning to re-enter.[49] Soon Richard and three others began classes, including Vera Brittain's daughter, Shirley (Williams) later a politician and co-founder of the British Social Democratic Party. The school had thirteen pupils at its peak, and Sylvia herself participated by teaching morris dancing.[50]

By the 1930s, life at the Red Cottage was out of harmony with the social environment. Corio was still unemployed, though he was busy with his translations of anti-Fascist tracts and often absent during the daytime. He kept up his contacts with the Italian exiles and maintained his anarchist associations, but the Italian police, who still followed his activities, reported that he kept a low profile. His profile at home was even lower. People who frequented the Pankhurst house in those years report that he was often seen in the garden or kitchen, but seldom introduced to guests. Annie Barnes said that most people thought that he was some kind of handyman.[51]

Sylvia's return to the middle-class socialist world of her youth met a psychological need to escape from her self-imposed isolation. Even Corio, with his foreign background and sometimes unstable temperament, was not really close. Only the baby offered her emotional security. But important new contacts like Vera Brittain helped to counter the scorn of the former suffragettes who still blamed Sylvia for her mother's death.

Conflict with that group, however, continued into 1930. Old followers of the WSPU had joined the survivors of similar organizations to form the Suffrage Fellowship. Among its other activities was a campaign to establish a permanent memorial to Mrs Pankhurst. By 1930 they had raised enough money to erect the statue that now stands on Parliament Square, just west of the Houses of Parliament, but this group made no effort to include Sylvia in their plans. When the statue was unveiled in early March, Mrs Flora Drummond, presiding, read a telegram from the absent Christabel but refused to acknowledge Sylvia at all, although she was present in the audience.[52]

Outraged at being ignored, Sylvia sent blistering letters to various women whom she regarded as responsible for the intended slight. An anonymous suffragette wrote to Mrs How Martyn, 'In confidence I have had *sheets* of irate Explosion from Sylvia asking me why . . . she was not notified of the last suffrage Dinner and of the unveiling of her

mother's statue.'[53] Another former suffragette sent batches of congratulatory letters with the notation, 'so nice to have them after Sylvia's
onslaught'.[54] Sylvia contracted with the *Star* (a London tabloid) for an
article about her mother. As might be expected, the article mixed vine-
gar with honey. Although Mrs Pankhurst 'had none of the qualities of
the student. . . . Her appeal was to common experience and common
humanity. . . . The Suffrage cause . . . gave free scope to her
dramatic power, without demanding from her the difficult task of
discovering precise solutions.'[55]

Reminding her readers first of her father's initiative in the struggle
for women's enfranchisement, Sylvia turned to the Pethick-Lawrences
and their contribution to the movement. She reopened the issue of the
split, which she regretted. Turning back to Mrs Pankhurst, she wrote:[56]

> She could do the outrageous thing without appearing outrageous, or losing
> her charm. A detective confided in after years on the ex-militant: 'Mrs.
> Pankhurst was my idea of a queen' . . . Her interest in dress . . . her
> desultory reading, mainly confined to novels, were surprising in one whose
> life was so largely given to public causes. . . . Her greatness was in her
> courage to meet all hardships. . . . That she lost the reformers quality in
> her declining years and became a reactionary . . . will not be recorded
> against her. That failing has been a common one amongst reformers . . .

Sylvia's mixed portrayal of her mother was not entirely a reflection of
the old quarrel. Emmeline Pethick-Lawrence saw Emmeline Pankhurst in terms that were not very different; in fact, they were slightly
more negative. She conceded that Emmeline Pankhurst had been a
'*great force* in human history', but said that her total immersion in her
cause had become an obsession, and that in order to win,[57]

> she threw scruple, affection, human loyalty and her own principles to the
> winds. The movement developed her powers—*all* her powers for good and
> for evil. Cruelty, ruthlessness or you may say—I should add *betrayed*—
> courage, resourcefulness and diplomacy. She was capable of beautiful
> tenderness and magnificent sense of justice and self-sacrifice. These things
> in the course of the struggle became damaged. We all sacrificed many
> things—she sacrificed her very soul.

In another letter, Emmeline wrote to Sylvia:[58]

> I wish you could have written your mother's life because I feel that you
> would have made for it a work of art. Her life and character present mater-
> ials for a deeply human story . . . Christabel's idea of mother and also of
> herself is that of ultimate triumph of a vindicated . . . benevolent despot.

Sylvia did write her mother's biography, and she proved Emmeline wrong, as—in the circumstances of Sylvia's poor relationship with her mother—she would be unlikely to regard her mother in an objective light.

The first years of the 1930s were especially difficult for Sylvia. She still found life and work at the Red Cottage tedious. In the summer of 1931 she was able to take advantage of an offer from Dora Russell to spend her time during the vacation at Beacon Hill School. The Russells were then living in Telegraph House on the West Sussex Downs. Dora was continuing her affair with the American father of two of her children while Bertrand was involved with a governess. They had started their Beacon Hill School on the 'MacMillan' method of progressive education, believing the Montessori approach to be 'too rigid'. In 1929, when Sylvia was staying in their guest-house in the small village of East Marsden, Richard attended classes for a time. Dora remembered him as 'a very determined small boy; we used to say that he was the only male who succeeded in bullying his intrepid mother'.[59]

While tension was building up between the free-thinking Russells, things were not going well for Corio and Sylvia at that time. He stayed behind to manage the tearoom. His letters are full of intense affection for his son, but he added at one point: 'I am very sad: I really hope I could go away and try my luck elsewhere.'[60]

The bad times continued into 1932. The Russells abruptly disappeared from the Pankhursts' lives, perhaps on account of their divorce. In January 1932, Bertrand declined Sylvia's request to write a preface to *The Home Front*.[61] In the summer she and Richard again went away with assistance from Emmeline Pethick-Lawrence. Sylvia was suffering from dental problems; Richard had been ill, contributing to her worries; and she came close to a nervous breakdown. At one point, Sylvia, her nerves on edge, lashed out at the generous Emmeline, who replied in character: 'I can't think how you can be so naughty as to suggest that I am not concerned about your danger of a crash! I care supremely—I can understand how easy it is to lose every kind of hope ... I understand and can smile at your little outburst.'[62]

And the grim financial situation continued, though Mrs Pethick-Lawrence helped out a great deal, and small unexpected windfalls turned up. In 1931, Sylvia sent Corio to auction all of her letters from George Bernard Shaw through Sotheby's.[63] Annie Barnes recalled the hardships in an amusing story. Sylvia was in her study, before her breakdown, when Annie, who was helping at the Red Cottage, answered the door. It was a man from the GPO who had been sent to disconnect the phone because the bill had not been paid. Sylvia, told that her phone was being cut off, shrieked over and over, 'It's inconvenient', while she grasped the man by his jacket and eventually succeeded in throwing him out the door. After he left, Sylvia turned to Annie and in quite serious tones asked: 'Can you imagine coming when it was so inconvenient?'

With those words she returned to her study and the phone remained connected.

One cause of Sylvia's nervous stress in 1932 also turned into a financial windfall. Cecil Bishop published a book in which he alleged that in her suffragette days Sylvia had plotted to kidnap the Prince of Wales (later Edward VIII). Supported by Emmeline Pethick-Lawrence, Sylvia brought a libel suit against the author and his publisher, the Hutchinson Company. The publisher decided to settle out of court by withdrawing the book and paying Sylvia £300.[64]

The following year it was her turn to be under attack in a libel suit also involving Hutchinson, her publisher for *The Home Front*. Mrs Hercbergova (who had been manageress of the wartime toy factory in the East End) sued Sylvia and Hutchinson for libel. Norah Smyth, it will be recalled, was able to produce enough evidence to make it possible to keep the book in print, though the Hutchinson Company had to settle with Mrs Hercbergova.[65]

Then things began to improve. That same year, the family moved to a large, rambling, detached, three-story house called West Dene, in Woodford Green. Sylvia rented the house, and later bought it. At times the top floor was rented out, but was later turned into offices for Sylvia's staff. For a time, also, they rented out the Red Cottage.[66] Corio settled in as cook and childminder to his son, occasionally doing odd printing jobs, mostly anti-Fascist propaganda, with the Walthamstow Press.[67]

9
Author and Journalist

...that you had this specific literary talent for rhyming and
riding over words at a gallop has hitherto been a secret.
 —George Bernard Shaw to Sylvia, *c*. 1930

From 1924 to 1934, Sylvia devoted much of her attention to the publication of books and articles. She produced a steady stream of works,
some of them autobiographical, like the small volume of poetry published
on her release from prison. Writing poetry was not uncommon among the
utopian socialists of her generation, but Sylvia was not a writer of
uncommon ability and she often used an old-fashioned, nineteenth-
century style which serious poets of the 1920s and 1930s had long since
abandoned.

Much of her poetry was concerned with nature and visual images—
trees, sky, birds—as seen through the artist's eye. She wrote too of
cities, a poem each on Russia and Petrograd during her post-war love-
affair with Russia. And her dedication to the working class and the
revolution were recurrent themes expressed in poems like those in
memory of Rosa Luxemburg and Karl Liebknecht.[1]

Sylvia's problems as a poet were similar to those which she experienced as a serious writer. Ideas came to her and she wrote them down;
serious editing seldom followed. Art, not journalism, had been her
calling and she lacked the formal education which Christabel had
received in her legal studies and Adela had been exposed to in teacher
training.

Keir Hardie launched her in her career as journalist. He, too, was
poorly educated but, like Sylvia Pankhurst, Hardie's name was prominent and he was a welcome contributor to papers and journals on the
left. Hardie was not a great thinker; nor was Sylvia. Both were caught
up in the arena of political activism and it was this that dominated
their writing: their causes were primary, the way they articulated them
secondary. Hardie had more natural ability as a writer than his pro-
tegée but she wrote much more in the course of her long life. Hardie's
book on India was based on a series of articles he wrote in the *Labour
Leader* which he later strung together; many of Sylvia's books resulted
from the same sort of process—linking facts and figures together with
an overlay featuring her convictions on the subject at hand.

After her slim volume of prison poetry, *Writ on Cold Slate*, Sylvia turned to a massive (638 page) study of India which she published in 1926 as *India and the Earthly Paradise*.[2] The subject of India loomed large in the 1920s. Lord Curzon's memoirs were published that same year, as was Annie Besant's *India Bond or Free*. (In 1915 Besant had published her first India volume, *How India Wrought for Freedom*, which was the result of her years in India and her fascination with Hindu religion and philosophy.) Both of these books strongly argued the case for Indian nationalism but their value is best explained by the label 'romantic nationalist' which was applied to Besant by a later Indian political theorist.[3] In the case of Sylvia and her contribution to Indian nationalism, she might well be called a 'romantic communist'; indeed, this study of India may have been the last result of her contacts with fringe elements of that movement.

After the failure to extend communism across Europe, Russia turned its attention to areas under colonial domination and India, with increasing nationalist sentiment, seemed a likely target. By the early 1920s British officials in India feared that the Bolsheviks would play on this nationalism and took steps to outlaw the Communist Party. Nevertheless a local party was formed, and in 1924 moved its headquarters to Bombay, where Sylvia's book was published two years later. Sylvia, it will be recalled, clung to communism even after she was expelled from the Party. While she and Nora were living in the Red Cottage they attempted to organize seminars and study groups, and may have attracted some like-minded Indians into their circle. Corio had contacts with members of the Indian community which dated back to his days with the *Ahmidiyya* when he was a brief convert to Islam. But if Indian communists were responsible for the publication of *India and the Earthly Paradise*, they barely got it through the press before members of the Communist Party–Great Britain (who would have quashed any attempts to publish Sylvia) moved into Bombay and began working directly with their Indian counterparts.[4]

Another explanation for Sylvia's turning to India at this time may have been the inspiration of her former art teacher, Walter Crane. Crane and his wife had gone out in 1907 and, while his socialist principles reacted against the authoritarianism of the British Raj ('it is not a comfortable thought for an Englishman loving freedom . . . to realize that this vast empire is held under the strictest autocratic system'), he was charmed by the people and the country. On his return to England he wrote a travel book which featured his capricious drawings.[5]

And, of course there had been Hardie's visit in 1909 which had had repercussions in England when he spoke publicly of British oppression of Indian nationalists. In a widely publicized telegram from Bengal, Hardie said that the people of India were 'at the mercy of the corruptest police in the world.'[6] The viceroy at the time contemplated having him expelled but found, on meeting him, 'a warm-hearted enthusiast with fixed ideas.'[7] Hardie certainly discussed his Indian findings and opinions on colonialism with Sylvia: her father, too, had been strongly opposed to colonialism.

Many of the points covered by Sylvia in her book had been raised earlier by Hardie. Corio's input seems to have been inspiration for her long discourse on Indian religions. And as she regarded herself as a feminist, she criticized the treatment of Muslim women, but seems to have had only surface knowledge of the culture, and therefore little to say about the condition of women among other Indian ethnic groups, primarily the Hindu. There was no theoretical structure to this book (as was the case with her 'political' works), but her utopian communism shines through in a variety of positions, including strong anti-British statements calling for a return to village councils based on the Russian commune (the 'true village' which 'was, and unless it is to lose its essential character, must always be, the product of a communist society'.[8]) In the case of India, Sylvia was on less firm theoretical ground than at home.

The sources for this rambling volume were those which suited Sylvia's notions of Indian history and politics: Hardie, Crane on people and places; Corio on Islam and Indian politics (he was at that time a member of the Muslim League, more a political than religious body); Indians living in London; and various travel accounts she had read. She looked for the perfect society to be reconstructed out of Indian history and therefore used history as a tool to glorify the Indian past. Her reading was insufficient for genuine historical understanding and she was, after all, writing with a purpose: 'Our goal is the end of all exploitation: the world-wide abundance, mutuality and fraternity of the Earthly Paradise' which, in this case was a communist India.[9]

The book's superficiality was further indicated by the quality of printing. There are errors throughout the book which quite clearly show that the printer was in as much of a hurry as Sylvia. No English or American edition followed, but with Sylvia *persona non grata* among organized communism that is not surprising. One reviewer, in the Glasgow *Forward*, took the book seriously enough to suggest factual errors in her discussion of the Indian peasantry. Her response came from her source, R. N. Chaudry, who submitted further documentation to support his claim.[10]

But the reviewer for the Manchester *Guardian* captured the spirit of her book:[11]

> One can easily see that when Sylvia Pankhurst is vicereine she will change the face of India in a year or so. But one is not quite sure whether she will begin by abolishing child marriage, the caste system, private property and the monetary system, or by granting full adult suffrage and full liberty to

India to govern herself according to her own ideas. And will Sylvia Pank-hurst's empire be a land of self-governing, self-contained villages each pro-ducing its own needs, or will her experts distribute the products of monster coal mines over an endless network of railways, while the cultivators are instructed to preserve the droppings of their cattle to fertilize the fields commanded by gigantic irrigation works which shall bring the snows of the Himalayas to water the sands of Cape Comorin? In spite of her forceful intellect, Miss Pankhurst fails to keep in touch with the hard conditions of the India problem.

Her next work was even more utopian. This time she championed international language as the vehicle for world harmony. This need for harmony seemed to grow from her personal situation. Her life as she approached middle age was not particularly happy: the break with her mother was almost complete; she had lost friends and supporters from the East End; the Communist Party had expelled her. This left only Corio, and later the baby, to provide the support she had once received from so many, and then from a faithful few in the final years before she sank into oblivion. It is hard to believe that Sylvia found internal harmony until her old age in Ethiopia, but she sought it constantly as an escape from inner turmoil and political controversies.

Shortly after she was expelled from the Communist Party, Sylvia became interested in Esperanto. In an issue of the *Dreadnought* she dis-cussed the need for an international language, especially the need for communists the world over to communicate in a single tongue. And as the *Dreadnought* reached its final days, she wrote constantly about Esperanto for want of other copy.[12] But the Esperanto boom was not con-fined to communists. The American industrialist Andrew Carnegie, among others, was fascinated with the prospect of an international lan-guage and donated large sums for its support. But Sylvia soon lost interest in Esperanto, and turned to 'Interlingua' instead. This international language was developed by Giuseppe Peano, an Italian mathematician. Corio learned it through his Italian connections: Peono too was from Turin. The support organization was the *Academia pro Interlingua*, which issued a bi-monthly journal in Interlingua as well as select pub-lications in the new language. Corio, in one of his rare moments of leadership, was honorary secretary of the British section of the *Acade-mia* and one of the pioneers in bringing the language to England.[13]

Sylvia offered herself as lecturer on the language and began serious research for a book to introduce it to the English-speaking world.[14] *Delphos: The Future of International Language* appeared in 1926. In it she proclaimed a need emerging from a particular human failing: 'the horses whinney by the roadside, the dogs exchange courtesies of nose and tail'; humans, however, lack these basic modes. But Esperanto was now rejected 'for its barbarity and lack of precision'. Peono's method was preferred for its 'definite scientific principles'.[15] She cited historical precedents—such as the attempts to unite Europe through universal adoption of Latin in the Middle Ages—and declared that, where those had failed, Interlingua in thirty years would 'be as familiar as the mother tongue'. Her conclusion was utopian: 'The Interlingua will play its part in the making of the future, in which the peoples of the world shall be one people . . .'.[16] *Delphos* was published as part of a series by Kegan Paul. (Among the other titles in the series were *Orpheus, or the Music of the Future*; *Midas, or the United States and the Future*; *Narcissus: An Anatomy of Clothes*; and *Hypatia, or Woman and Knowledge*, by Mrs Bertrand Russell.) Sylvia's short volume doubtless yielded a small advance and small—if any—royalty payments. It was not reviewed in any of the major English journals.

Sylvia's next venture into print was even more esoteric and hardly more rewarding financially, though it brought some satisfaction. She translated the Romanian national poet, Mihail Eminescu, into English. How she came upon Eminescu's poetry, only available in Romanian, is a mystery, although she may have been introduced to it by I. O. Stefanovic in the British section of the *Academia*. In any event, Stefanovic was her co-translator. Eminescu himself had been a romantic and a nationalist who had died at the age of thirty-nine, towards the end of the nineteenth century, after producing a number of epic poems. He had been educated at several European universities, where he came under the philosophical influence of Schopenhauer's subjective realism, but his greatest influence on his Romanian audience was an ardent nationalism which began in his lifetime and continued for decades after his death.

Sylvia knew Italian and French well and, of course, Interlingua. She did not know Romanian, but Corio may have helped. She deserves credit, however, for her translation of the Eminescu poems, with or without the assistance of Stefanovic. It may be that he translated into French the poems she then translated into English. The result, in any case, was a small but praiseworthy volume. The most difficult for Sylvia, and the best example of Eminescu's debt to Schopenhauer, was 'The Emperor and Proletarian', an epic poem following the style of Tennyson, which dramatized the conflict between the nobility and the masses during the French Revolution.[17]

Sylvia believed there was a universal appeal in the poet's writing, in spite of a specific Romanian quality. She wrote, 'His themes, clothed with art in picturesque trappings of this or that time or story, are the fundamental problems of human existence which never grow old . . .'[18] It is easy to see why his poetry appealed to her—it touched her artistic sense while dwelling on the theme of humanity.

The need to live by her writing—she now referred to herself as 'Author and Journalist' on her letterhead—was a source of difficulty. She anticipated that sales in the English language would be small and appealed for help from her old friend, George Bernard Shaw, asking for his comments and a Preface. Shaw was uninterested at first, but he read the typescript in response to Sylvia's prodding telegrams. He was not optimistic. 'If I were one of these young publishers with printing presses of their own who dig up impossible old books . . . I would jump at this amazing book. . . . The translation is astonishing and outrageous; it carried me away. . . . that you had this specific literary talent for rhyming and riding over words at a gallop has hitherto been a secret.'[19]

If Shaw was mischievous, so was Sylvia. He refused to write the requested Preface on the grounds that Eminescu's poetry was 'not the stuff that crosses frontiers'.[20] Undaunted, and very much aware of the value of Shaw's name, Sylvia took his earlier letter and had it printed at the front of her book with the heading 'Preface by George Bernard Shaw'.[21] With the stolen 'Preface' and an introduction by the historian N. Iorga, Sylvia's translation was released in 1930. It was well received in Romania, with much praise for Sylvia.[22] The British reception was cooler, but Sylvia blamed the publisher, Kegan Paul for that. She told a Romanian admirer that Eminescu 'has been well received, though undoubtably his reputation would have been greater had the publisher been equipped with the funds to advertise the book in the press'.[23]

By 1929 money seemed less of a problem than before, perhaps because of the combined Harben–Pethick-Lawrence support. Sylvia had a secretary for the first time since her East End organization collapsed, and she could afford a summer holiday with Richard at Gloucester.[24] But she was already busy on another book, *Save the Mothers: A Plea for a National Maternity Service*, published in 1930. Sylvia's interest in this topic was inspired by her own recent pregnancy, her varied experiences with poor women in the East End before the war, and also from a general socialist concern with the plight of poor women, which had been the focus of various studies in the early part of the twentieth century. Another woman, Eleanor Rathbone, had written a well-received economic treatise on the family, *The Disinherited Family*, in 1924, following the discovery of appalling malnourishment in young men called up for war service. Rathbone's work differed from Sylvia's in that she emphasized the family; but her advocacy of economic reforms was as far-reaching as those Sylvia called for in her national maternity service.[25] *Save the Mothers* treated the problems of women in pregnancy, childbirth and lying-in. She characterized the discomforts of aching body, swollen legs, and nausea. (She herself had experienced difficulty in the later stages of pregnancy, no doubt complicated by her age.) The government offered little assistance to poor women who, despite their pregnancy, carried heavy loads, and shouldered their domestic responsibilities as usual without help. Basically, having a baby was women's business, and any comfort they received came from their own families.

Elsewhere she provided a different version of her pregnancy: in her unfinished autobiography 'The Inheritance', she also recounted Richard's birth. But the contradictions in the account may be explained by her age. After her baby was born, she wrote, 'The doctor stood beside me: If you had not come into the home when you did, the baby would not have been.'[26] That made her aware of her good fortune. An unmarried, unemployed, middle-aged woman was unlikely, in Britain of the nineteen-twenties, to enjoy the facilities of a nursing home and a doctor, as well as loyal friends to pay the expenses. These were privileges of a Pankhurst, and she recognized them as such. The debt she felt she incurred was to the less fortunate and it was repaid in her new campaign for a national maternity service which was to be added to the projected National Health Service already part of the Labour Party platform.

In preparation for her book, she wrote to Ramsay MacDonald and to Labour's Foreign Secretary, Arthur Henderson, for information on natal and post-natal mortality for both mother and child. She also asked Henderson and MacDonald to support her proposal for a national maternity service, and their responses were supportive, if noncommittal.[27] She also called for 'free house-help service' and relief from employment during the final months of pregnancy.[28] These proposals were too utopian to be practical in 1929 and 1930. But to Sylvia it was 'a sad solution for a nation in which five-sevenths of the national expenditure is for war and military purposes'.[29]

Her statistics were too arid to convince, but in one descriptive passage after another, many about the East End, she encapsulated the burden of approaching motherhood for the poor. Writing partly from personal experience, she devoted a chapter to 'The Unmarried Mother and Her Child'[30] but this time without personal reference. She drew attention instead to legal problems and social pressures. Inheritance laws, for example, made it impossible for the child of an unmarried father to inherit, unless his will specifically named the child.[31]

As she had done in her suffrage days, she looked elsewhere for a successful model. In Scandinavia, she wrote, 'the unmarried mother and her child have not to meet the grievous social boycott often directed against them here'. Fathers in Scandinavia were forced to recognize their financial responsibilities whether married or not. 'Briefly put, sexual union is in effect marriage, whether registered or not, as regards responsibility for its results.'[32] One can only ponder Corio's possible reaction, since he had not pursued his obligations in his relations with Clelia, the first two children, or even with Sylvia.

After Richard's birth, Sylvia desired nothing more than to move back into middle-class circles and thus give her baby a more respectable upbringing. She grew puritanical at this time—so much so that one wonders if she continued sexual relations with Corio even though the two shared the same bed for years to come. One woman who knew her in her solid middle-class Ethiopian crusade suggested that she thought Sylvia engaged in sex only to produce her child. That comment seems to say more about Sylvia's image of the moment than about her early years. And, progressive as she was on health, Sylvia opposed abortion. It was, in any case, against the law in Britain, and she was most concerned about careless, illegal practice by unscrupulous doctors, midwives or untrained practitioners. She did not attack the issue of abortion in her brief crusade for a national maternity service. She did, however, favour birth control, and called for wider public education, as had been the case earlier when her East London Federation had attempted to educate the poor on birth control.

Following established habit, Sylvia tried to promote her book by turning to friends. She contacted Mrs Walshe in the autumn of 1930, when both the Eminescu translation and *Save the Mothers* were published: 'Thanks for passing on *Save the Mothers*. The publishers want names and addresses for sending out prospectives.' The publisher in this case was Knopf, who, Sylvia claimed, 'are never done with the jobs they give me'.[33]

Shaw was probably bemused when he received a copy of the Eminescu translation carrying his 'Preface', but he was enthusiastic about *Save the Mothers*. It had apparently been his suggestion that Sylvia look into this problem. He believed that 'the poor, who have a much higher infant mortality than the rich, have a lower maternal mortality'.[34] Sylvia had proved him incorrect, if her figures were accurate; but as with the *Dreadnought* and in her books, she often chose data because they supported her theories, and she had no statistical background. Mrs Pethick-Lawrence wrote that she was pleased the book was well reviewed: 'I think it is simply wonderful the way you are able to link your personal life and your life of public service and make the one equipment do for the other.'[35] This is exactly what Sylvia did with so many of the works she published during this period and later.

Among the responses she received came this cryptic but mostly congratulatory note: 'I expect most readers will feel that if you and your friends had not worked for that freedom twenty years ago, people would still not be bothering in the least about what happens to women or how many of them died . . . '. Concerning Sylvia's own pregnancy, the writer could not 'help wondering whether you yourself did not have a worse time than many mothers'.[36]

This book, like her others, appealed first to the emotions; it was, after all, a 'plea'. The research and writing of *Save the Mothers* called for sophisticated use of medical terminology, which Sylvia mastered with stern self-discipline. (Among her papers were notes defining medical terms for different parts of the body, in particular those confined to females.) There are no records as to sales, but its message was regarded as important by women like Vera Brittain, who placed Sylvia along-side Eleanor Rathbone and Beatrice Webb as champions of women and children.[37] And it also helped to nudge Sylvia into the more respectable social circles she was trying desperately to reach despite her notoriety. Attention and praise from people like Vera Brittain helped to lessen the sting of neglect she felt from former suffragettes, many of whom were still hostile towards her.

But, aware as she was of rejection by former WSPU members, as early as 1928 Sylvia began looking for a publisher interested in her version of the history of the suffrage movement. Perhaps part of her motivation was to redefine herself in relation to the movement by writing her version of it. Lapsing into the language of the East End she wrote to Sir James Marchant that she intended to write 'about me life', and enclosed a synopsis.[38] 'The book I have in mind to write', she told Marchant in another letter, 'is the inner history of the Suffrage Movement and those who made it and the environment from which they sprang.'[39] What she really meant was the history of her own and her family's involvement. The outline showed a clearly autobiographical account of the heyday of the suffrage movement. She claimed that:[40]

> It is the sort of book which can only be written by one who was in the inner circle of the drama; who, having gained by time and temperament a meditative detachment from the struggle . . .

What she produced in *The Suffragette Movement* was highly personal; there was an account of her tragic childhood (as she saw it in comparison with Christabel's), with Adela and her brothers getting scant attention. The promise of 'meditative detachment' never materialized. It was replaced by bitter recriminations against Christabel and, at best, ambivalence toward her mother: some praise, some reproach, but never detachment. Sylvia concentrated on her own prison experience, the hunger and thirst strikes, and especially on her work in the East End. She graphically described her own feelings in Holloway, but she ran her two trips to America into one. She ignored Mrs Pankhurst's American triumphs and only mentioned that she had left poor Harry to die in England. Family matters, unconnected with the suffrage movement, were treated in detail: Harry's death, the marriages of Pankhurst servants, and aunts. Sylvia was especially hard on Christabel's later political stands, for instance her support of the war and her joining the Conservative Party, both of which she saw as slights to Hardie's memory as well as to Sylvia's own stand. Sylvia also supported Adela who 'was regarded by Christabel as a very black sheep amongst organizations because the warmth of her Socialism did not always permit her to comply with actions guaranteed.'

Sylvia regarded the book as an autobiography. She relived her own triumphs—which were never as successful as she suggested—while exaggerating her role. The son to whom she dedicated it,[41] and others as well, later mistook it for objective history. Richard Pankhurst wrote a new introduction to a later edition accepting his mother's account, already nearly a half-century old in the telling, as though nothing had appeared in the meanwhile to modify it.[42] Looking back on his mother's writing days he wrote: 'One of my last childhood memories . . . was on waking to go to my mother's room in the morning to find her still at her desk where she had been writing since dinner the previous night. This was by no means an infrequent occurrence.' That Sylvia had vast stores of energy is certain. Reading *The Suffragette Movement*, one attains insight into the intense drive she poured into the movement, as well as into the book. Others, closer to the events, received *The Suffragette Movement* quite differently. Ray Strachey, a member of the Bloomsbury group, reviewed it from a participant's perspective. Strachey was Mrs Fawcett's biographer and a member of the NUWSS, but her review in the *Women's Leader*, in retrospect, presented a fair-minded assessment.[43]

> The account of the militant movement for women's suffrage . . . is crammed with drama and incident, with personalities, prejudices, enthusiasms, and quarrels, and is, in its way, as complete a revelation of its author's character as the most exacting student of psychology could desire. There is much bitterness and misrepresentation in its pages, much inaccuracy and misstatement, and an evident and undisguised animus against Mrs Pankhurst and Christabel which is almost tragic in its intensity. But after all, bitterness, inaccuracy, misstatement, and animus all lay on the fringes of the militant movement so that they are in a deep sense appropriate to its historian; and though they do not tend to edification, neither did these aspects of the suffragette campaign itself . . .
>
> Miss Pankhurst attributes the rise of the women's movement to the same political unrest which led to all the radical and revolutionary movements of the end of the last century. . . . Political changes do not come in this country through mass turbulence and . . . occasional rioting of small groups. The change of opinion which carried women's suffrage through to victory is a much larger and more important thing than Miss Pankhurst describes.
>
> When she turns to politics proper, Miss Pankhurst is a very erratic guide. Many details of the story of which I have personal knowledge are incorrectly described, and her comments upon the non-militant movement, and upon the Labour Party are as unjust and as misguided as they well can be . . .
>
> Miss Pankhurst . . . appears to believe that nothing but her own activities in the East End was of any political significance, though she admits that when the first suffrage bill came forward her society was the only one of them all which opposed it . . .
>
> She gives the picture of her own childhood which is in many ways distressing, and her treatment of the characters of her mother and sister is anything but kind. No doubt that was how she saw and felt it all, but it can hardly have been how it actually was . . .

Even though the Strachey review was not glowing, it was a tribute to her effort to be just in trying circumstances—especially since Sylvia herself had forced Strachey's publishers to withdraw the original edition of her own book in 1928. By that time Sylvia had adopted the role of spokesman for all the Pankhursts, in spite of differences within the family. When Strachey's *The Cause: A Short History of the Women's Movement in Great Britain* appeared in 1928, Sylvia threatened legal action. The offending passage referred to 'enormous sums rolling' into WSPU coffers, and 'as fast as they rolled in, went out again'.[44] Mrs Pethick-Lawrence wrote to Sylvia privately: 'From what I know I think your mother's financial affairs would not be easy to explain', but she backed Sylvia's action, and the book was withdrawn.

A new edition, suitably amended, appeared in 1929, but Sylvia continued to pursue the issue. As late as 1953, she threatened Vera Brittain, who quoted from Strachey's first edition in her book *Lady Into Woman*. As Brittain later described the incident:[45]

> I quoted (in order to criticize them) some tendentious strictures on suffragette account-keeping in Ray Strachey's *The Cause* which reflected the constitutional movement but was singularly unobjective in its treatment of the militants . . . unknown to me, the first edition had been withdrawn. . . . Although my quotation had been used to illustrate Mrs. Strachey's prejudice, I found myself the astonished target of Sylvia's indignation. On that occasion Pethick himself nobly came to my rescue and persuaded Miss Pankhurst to accept an erratum slip in my book, instead of the libel action which she clearly thought I deserved.

Sylvia's proprietory feelings towards the suffrage movement were again illustrated in 1944 when Jill Craigie, the first woman to direct films in Britain, explored the possibility of writing and directing a film on the movement. She wrote to Sylvia in more than complimentary terms: 'I have a very great admiration for your past achievements . . . '. At the same time, she mentioned her projected film. Sylvia replied with stipulations she wished to comment on any film written and produced by Craigie. Whereupon, Craigie responded: 'As you know, I have embarked on this subject in a spirit of enthusiasm and admiration for everyone who has done so much to win for women their present position . . . '[46]

Sylvia's response was to interject herself:[47]

> My feeling . . . boils down to the fact that I do not think a film about the Suffragette Movement can possibly be a success without one who took an active part in the Movement having a considerable share in the production . . .
>
> You of course said to me that you would be pleased for me to come down . . . but I do not think a mere occasional visit to see what is going on and to offer advice . . . from the outside, whilst a dozen or more persons were also paying visits and giving advice, would be at all effective . . .

Sylvia outlined several arguments for not producing a film on the suffrage movement at that time, including the fact that, with the war just ending, the recent suffering of the soldier would pale the equal, earlier tortures endured by the suffragettes, although 'the Suffragettes definitely went into something which was not forced upon them . . . and that is the case of the minority who are engaged in the present struggle.' In conclusion she stated:[48]

> It was for all these reasons I thought it would be worthwhile to talk the matter over further with you and a member of the firm undertaking the production. . . . I may add that it has always been my intention that there should be a Suffragette film. . . . As I have written the history of the Movement it was of course quite natural that I should present the Movement in another medium, I had the best possible reason for wishing to do so, and I have the necessary experience of the Movement.

This was not the last of Sylvia's forays into the world of cinema. In 1948, Rosamond Silkin, then a young professional actress, was making *Fame is the Spur* by Howard Spring, playing a suffragette being forcibly fed in prison. Mrs Pethick-Lawrence ('a wonderful woman') was brought in as a consultant. According to Mrs Silkin, Mrs Pethick-Lawrence told them that she wore her own clothes in prison and the actress was dressed accordingly for the part. Then Sylvia Pankhurst arrived:[49]

> [She] found fault with everything—including my lack of prison garb. She was so vociferous in her criticisms that Ray Boulting [the director] said 'get that woman out of here' which they did. I met her by chance, later, leaving the set, and she vouchsafed that she had forgotten. 'Of course Mrs. Pethick-Lawrence did wear her own clothes—she would!'

While making the film, Silkin had read a great deal about the suffrage movement and 'was astonished at how different the facts were from the myths that survive. Nobody mentions that in every country after women were given the right to vote, legislation on behalf of children was vastly improved.' Here, we can again credit Sylvia with her pleas on behalf of mothers and children which arose from her involvement in the movement, no matter how proprietory she was towards efforts to revive it on film.

In 1958, Sylvia once more took up the battle, this time against Roger Fulford's *Votes for Women*. Now she turned to Christabel: 'In the case of Ray Strachey's book and that of Vera Brittain I was in England; you were abroad . . . I am much further outside the world than you are . . . at the moment I cannot even think of a suitable lawyer. . . . I would put it to you that you should take a strong objection to the allegation that the Pankhurst family were subsidized by the WSPU funds. . . . I consider it your duty to act.'[50] Sylvia revealed a more distressing aspect of her personality in the same letter to Christabel. Fulford had called their mother an autocrat; Sylvia wrote: 'Definitely mother became the ''autocrat'' at the request of the Pethick-Lawrences. I told her at the time it was quite unnecessary. . . . She accepted the Pethick-Lawrences' proposal.'[51] In this case, as with her unkind comments to Rosamond Silkin, Sylvia was prepared to do battle against all comers.

In spite of various squabbles, *The Suffragette Movement* was generally well received, and it brought Sylvia an improved public reputation. The *Spectator* observed, 'Every praise is due to Miss Pankhurst for the manner in which she has unravelled a piece of history so complicated.'[52] On the other hand, the *New York Times* observed, 'As Greek meets Greek, so do these Pankhursts praise one another',[53] and *Current History* found 'the style of the book . . . loose and somewhat patternless. The writer is not chiefly concerned with the philosophy of feminism. . . . She is more at home in the field of action than of idea.'[54] Here the reviewer unwittingly captured Sylvia's weakness in all of her books; and correctly noted that she was not intellectually concerned with the philosophy of feminism—or any other 'ism'. She was an activist and essentially a propagandist—which is why much of *The Suffragette Movement* fails to satisfy our requirements for historical accuracy.

The *Times Literary Supplement* thought that Sylvia wrote with 'affection and understanding about all her family. . . . The character studies of Richard Marsden Pankhurst and his friend Keir Hardie are two of the best things in this very interesting book.'[55] *The Times*, however, observed correctly that 'the author of this book shows little knowledge of the non-militant suffrage movement, but her account of the scenes and people she knew carries conviction and is often of moving interest.'[56]

The Prime Minister, Ramsay MacDonald, pleased Sylvia by placing a volume in the library at 10 Downing Street, especially when he told her, 'you realize the space available is very limited'.[57] But George Bernard Shaw created the biggest splash for her book. He had already referred to her in the 1924 preface to *Saint Joan*. Now he returned to a comparison between the two women in a BBC lecture on 6 June, 1931, and he recognized the publicity value of the book, writing to Sylvia: 'I gave it a tremendous boost in my broadcast on Joan of Arc'.[58]

Shaw's first Preface, dated August 1924, was written at a time when Sylvia had left the Communist Party and was foundering in desperation. As Shaw saw the similarities then, 'Joan was persecuted essentially as she would be persecuted today. . . . If Joan had to be dealt with by us in London she would be treated with no more toleration than Miss Sylvia Pankhurst, or the Peculiar People . . . who cross the line we have to draw, rightly or wrongly, between the tolerable and the intolerable.'[59]

The 1931 BBC broadcast included several parallels between Sylvia and St Joan. Shaw told his listeners:[60]

If you want an example from your own time, if you want to find what women can feel when they suddenly find the whole power of society marshalled against them . . . then read a very interesting book . . . by Miss Sylvia Pankhurst describing what women did in the early part of this century in order to get the . . . vote. Miss Sylvia Pankhurst, like so many other women in the movement, was tortured. In fact, except for burning, she suffered physical torture which Joan was spared . . . If you read Miss Pankhurst you will understand a great deal more about the psychology of Joan . . .

Sylvia never commented publicly, but a friend wrote excitedly: 'I didn't hear myself . . . I am told Bernard Shaw compared you to Joan of Arc in his speech on the wireless. . . . Will it help your book, I wonder?'[61] Shaw used his talk to bring Joan into a contemporary setting; he also showed more than a touch of admiration and sympathy for Sylvia.[62] Dame Margaret Cole, who knew him well from their Fabian days until his death, believed Shaw would have been drawn to someone like Sylvia, who was troublesome to the government; but she added that 'Shaw had no affection for anyone . . . he may have liked Sylvia. . . . He liked people who stirred things up.'[63] Christabel, urged by friends to speak out on the book, refused to review it, or to comment on her sister's blatant hostility towards her.

Sylvia was at last back in the public eye. Her suffragette antics helped drown the memories of her communist days. Many now thought of her as merely an eccentric; her living arrangements were not generally known, and Richard, who was obviously dear to her, seemed an extension of her eccentricity. As an author of some note, Sylvia applied in 1931 for membership of the PEN Club.[64] She was already struggling to finish another autobiographical volume, although she told Mrs Walshe she feared the publishers 'may think it too anti-war and try to break contract with me when they read it'. As for Mrs Walshe's contribution, 'If you feel inclined to write and say you saw a notice of it in some paper and want to know is it ready to Hutchinsons . . . Please don't let them think the author suggested it. . . . That would not do.'[65] *The Home Front*, another long (447 page), hastily written volume, appeared in 1932. It was appropriately dedicated to Emmeline Pethick-Lawrence, 'whose generous appreciation encouraged penning of this record'.[66] An appreciative patron, Emmeline wrote for extra copies; but she was 'sorry that the book leaves out your many adventures during the war, crossing frontiers and getting to Russia. .. . But no doubt you have decided against using in the circumstances.'[67] In a later letter, Mrs Pethick-Lawrence suggested it should have been called 'My Life Till the End of the War. . . . In any case the present title is, in the opinion of nearly everybody I have consulted, both misleading and dull and has prejudiced many. . . . I have been surprised at the complete cessation of advertisement.' Apparently this book did not get the publisher's blessing, probably because of Mrs Hercbergova's threatened lawsuit. Sylvia wrote several different drafts of a third, partly autobiographical volume, and these remain among her papers. She may have shown it to publishers, as she certainly did to Emmeline Pethick-Lawrence, who thought it 'extremely attractive. Russia, in spite of all attempts to boycott it, is now becoming a subject of deep interest'.[68] But it never appeared in print.

In *The Home Front* Sylvia described the various enterprises in the East End (including the story of Mrs Hercbergova and the toy factory). It included case studies of people—mainly hardship cases—in the East End. But most of it concerned Sylvia. She discussed her pacifism, her travels with Norah, and her own endless struggle to make the government respond to the needs of her constituents. And, like all her published works, it was largely humourless and dull. Her father's admonition to work for humanity had left her without the ability to see the bright side of life, except as dramatic revelations.

A Shavian incident brought one of the few traces of amusement. Shaw had consented to judge some essays written by children at Sylvia's Poplar Christmas parties. But, to each of the participants, he presented a bill, not an award. Miss Mollie Beer, the winner, was charged a penny for 'correcting two mistakes in grammar'; $1\frac{1}{2}$d for his having counted '22 kisses for Miss Pankhurst'; and, he concluded: 'I award Miss Beer a special prize of three pence for laziness. She was in such a hurry to get to bed that she wrote the shortest essay...'[69]

Ray Strachey had detected Sylvia's psychological make up in *The Suffragette Movement*; he could have used *The Home Front* just as well. Sylvia was generous, warm, loving and tender in her concern for people. The book was emotional in tone, nostalgic in memories of her East End followers and self-promoting in detailing her accomplishments, and it showed the frantic and frenzied activities which characterized her life.

Three years later Sylvia took Emmeline Pethick-Lawrence's suggestion and wrote a biography of her mother. Attention was focused on the suffrage movement, and she allotted considerable space to her own role in it. But by the time she wrote *The Life of Emmeline Pankhurst*, Sylvia seemed to have purged her deepest hostilities and this time she repressed her ambivalent feelings toward her mother.[70] She did not refer to her mother's personal weaknesses or the transitions in her personality so poignantly captured by Mrs Pethick-Lawrence. Tinges of bitterness towards her mother and Christabel crept in, as might have been expected considering Sylvia's real feelings. What is missing is the fire, drama and pageantry of Mrs Pankhurst's *actual* participation in the suffrage movement and the human dimension of the woman who was both wife and mother before she became national heroine. Mrs Pankhurst appears as stiff, formidable, and politically inept—a tragic-comic figure devised by Sylvia's imagination. The narrative recalls that Mrs Pankhurst was jailed thirteen times, went on hunger strikes, was forcibly fed, was, indeed, the most militant of the militant—a sort of female David to the government Goliath. What motivated Mrs Pankhurst, what burning fires inside her sent her to prison, to hunger strike, kept her going when she was being attacked in the streets, are questions never raised. Yet Sylvia, so much like her mother in these respects, might have brought insights as no one else could.

Emmeline Pethick-Lawrence may have been partially accurate when she predicted that if Christabel wrote Mrs Pankhurst's life it would be a 'me and mother' approach. She was wrong, however, in believing Sylvia could be more objective. Sylvia's approach was also 'me and mother', but in opposition both in distance and attraction, like poles of a magnet. One account dealt with Mrs Pankhurst's return from Canada and the south of France, when the old suffragette was in her late seventies: 'Ignoring repudiation and estrangement, I hastened to her; with a pang of grief I saw she had grown old . . . in speech she would light again with remembered fire. . . . Then as the first rush of joy and sadness passed, a gulf remained.'[71] It was not Mrs Pankhurst that Sylvia was describing, but her own feelings for her mother.

Sylvia wrote several more articles about her mother for various newspapers. Some sold, some did not. In one, 'The Importance of Emmeline Pankhurst', Sylvia believed the answer was 'in her persistence'.[72] Sylvia inherited this trait from her mother and was therefore a reliable interpreter of it.

As was her custom in the past, when the volume was published Sylvia set out to promote it. She sent Herman Ould, Secretary of the PEN Club, a copy, with an accompanying note. 'The book', she wrote, 'unfortunately came in the height of the General Election, so I am afraid that instead of being very widely reviewed . . . it may have been partially snowed over.'[73] Ould, by now accustomed to dealing with Sylvia, responded: 'You know, we cannot actually review books; it would be rather invidious in an organization like ours.'

The hard times to which Sylvia referred were not due to lack of effort. She wrote articles on every imaginable topic, in addition to the long books she produced between 1926 and 1935. Two brief articles concerned Richard: 'Goatie' and 'Dog Land'. She also wrote extensively on Romania; but English readers showed very little interest in Eastern Europe. In a prescient pamphlet soon after the *Dreadnought* closed down, Sylvia had written 'The truth About the Oil War', predicting in the 1920s what the world discovered fifty years later: that oil was going to be a source of world tension, affecting Russia, Holland, Britain and the United States.[74] During her period as author and journalist, she founded and published a new paper on the anti-Fascist cause. *Humanity* was the organ of 'The Women's International Matteotti Committee', but only two issues appeared, in November 1933.[75] And, like her father before her, she wrote letters to the editor on every issue which caught her eye.

I have no regrets!

Sylvia Pankhurst's announcement that she had become a mother without a legal marriage shocked the world.

She was criticised—severely.

Here, in this frank article specially written for the "Daily Mirror," the famous suffragette delivers her own verdict on her daring experiment in parenthood . . .

By E. SYLVIA PANKHURST

I ALWAYS loathed Mrs. Grundy. Her gossip, heard in drawing-room and kitchen, about the inmost personal affairs of which only those intimately concerned can know the first essentials, her avid curiosity, lascivious leers, and sly, smirking innuendoes, disgusted me before I had a hint of her vicious cruelty.

As I grew older I saw that vicious cruelty itself—everywhere, all around me. And I began to understand the tragedy of the unmarried mother and her child.

As a Suffragette in prison, I met young expectant mothers serving sentences for having attempted suicide in fear of a censorious world.

During the war, when I worked in the East End among war sufferers of every sort, girls came to me with their "war babies." Many had been dismissed by irate employers, some had been driven from home by angry parents.

In all those years of public activity, busy as I was with other matters, I had formed my own conclusions on matrimony, parenthood and the rights of children.

I resolved very emphatically that I would always stand against classing any children as illegitimate, and insist that all must be entitled to equal respect and equal opportunities.

"No secrets. He knows . . . and he understands"

both as regards their parents and the community.

No man should be released from the duty of bringing up his children at his own social and economic level, whether he has married their mother or not.

It seems to me that the law which encourages fathers to evade their responsibilities towards certain children, and places those children in an inferior position as regards inheritance, is totally wrong.

It was to help to banish these grave injustices that I decided to champion the cause in a practical way. It was, I realised, a difficult

tenacious and constant in their affections, I early became convinced that no man or woman should be chained for life to another without the possibility of escape.

I also became convinced that the only persons able to judge that a marriage is unhappy and harmful are those most intimately concerned. I was, and am, convinced that the Divorce Court is not the way.

I believe that so intimate a question as marriage should be determined by the two most intimately concerned. The children, of course, should have the strongest possible claim on their parents and on the community.

I do not believe that the average marriage is kept together by the force of law, but by community of affection and interest. Therefore, I do not believe that if marriage were an entirely personal and free union homes would be ruined and marital constancy at an end.

These being my opinions, I naturally carried them through to their logical conclusion in my own case.

In practice, my life at home is just the same as other people's. We have the same economic obstacles to face in maintaining our home, the same community of interests, the same affections, the same anxieties, the same joys.

My boy is learning music and swimming now, and is taking carpentry lessons. I watch his steady progress with eager interest. In his spare time just now he is studying morse.

I have no secrets from him; he knows, and he understands

cannot serve his offspring as faithfully and earnestly as his legal counterpart?

We are firm friends, my child and I. Our mutual comradeship is based upon natural love and not upon an ancient statute.

Like most idealistic young people, I began with the notion that true love can only come once in a lifetime, and invariably endures for ever.

Even the re-marriage of widows and widowers appeared to me contemptible; these people, I felt, had never really loved.

I should have preferred to believe that only marriages of convenience prove unhappy, but

An article by Sylvia Pankhurst from the *Daily Mirror*, November 1935

The topics were so wide-ranging and the letters so many, it is impossible to assess them all. In 1935, for example, she wrote to *The Times* about getting women admitted to all meals at Oxford—including High Table at the male colleges. As her interests turned towards anti-Fascism in the mid-1930s, she wrote more on Italy and Ethiopia. And she was always free with advice to the government in power, regardless of party.[76] She kept up her interest in women, children and education, deploring the decline of feminism during the Depression, but predicting a resurgence when 'our womanhood will again be stimulated to great end'. Sylvia was wide-ranging and forward looking in her interests. They even extended to housing and urban planning which excited the attention of very few in those days.[77]

In 'Now That I Am Nearly Fifty' she was uncharacteristically optimistic. 'I am enthusiastic for life', she wrote: her motivation for living was to serve. Referring to marriage, she thought most were happy. Sex 'was one of the great mysteries: there is nothing in it and there is all in it.' Her religion was to be a 'citizen of the world'. She sought 'assurance that my separate, individual ego will continue after death'. Ending on a self-congratulatory note, she hoped 'By the work I have accomplished, by the opinions I have helped to create, the people I have influenced, I shall live on when my name has been forgotten.' Here again we see an example of Sylvia presenting herself to different people at different times, in different ways. Her capacity for self-deception and her ability to give to others were equal and unlimited.

Her new enthusiasm for life and her sense of immortality were all centred on Richard, in whom 'I am content to live on when my end comes'.[78] Causes came and went; loyalties were made and broken; the one constant, after 1927, was her dedication and devotion to Richard.

New themes combined with old in the mid-1930s. Sylvia began a history of socialism which she never finished. The rise of Fascism on the Continent put socialists on the defensive. In 1933 she wrote to her old opponent George Lansbury:[79]

> I do feel this that the Jews have taught us socialists a lesson by their solidarity. . . . Even now the terror is in Germany. We are not awake to it as the Jews are—yet for the terror against the Jews, awful though it is for them to bear, is largely camouflage to mask the reactionary class dictatorship against the Socialists and ultimately against the worker. . . . If it were you, I, my little Richard—none of us would be safe.

With these words, Sylvia was laying the foundations of her next crusade. As an opponent of Fascism, she found herself for the first time in the company of much of the world community, even though in this crusade, as in others, she was a step or two ahead of most and would be more committed than all but a few. Her period as 'editor and journalist' overlapped her communist years; indeed, after the birth of her son it enabled her to move back into middle-class circles, and gave her some income with which she could help support her family. With the exception of *The Suffragette Movement*—which we know is an idiosyncratic document at best—none of her works in this period has stood the test of time. While each amused her in its preparation, they represent little more than a stop-gap in her life. Sylvia did not write for the pleasure of setting ideas on paper; she was much more comfortable in putting her ideas into practice. With few exceptions, her books were long editorials: a plea for maternity services; a call for communism in India; an appeal for an international language; and, of course, long discourses containing critical views of the British government which made their way into her poetry as well as her prose.

PART 4
Anti-Fascism and Ethiopia

10
Multiple Causes

My friend Sylvia Pankhurst...lives in a tempest of virtuous indignation.
—George Bernard Shaw, *Sunday Referee* 21 July, 1935

One might suppose that running the tearoom, raising her son, and producing a stream of literary outpourings were enough to keep Sylvia busy at West Dene. In fact between the Depression and the Second World War she also pursued a variety of political causes. The content of her campaigns showed a transition from mainly domestic to foreign issues. Her old republicanism and pacifism gave way to a cry for military action—and that in favour of one of the few remaining 'unconstitutional' monarchs wielding real power.

One remaining domestic preoccupation grew out of *Save the Mothers*. In the mid-1930s, she continued to agitate and lobby for a national maternity service,[1] as did Eleanor Rathbone, whose earlier book became the blueprint for later action. Sylvia's zeal on this single issue presents a strange contrast to her relative neglect of other damage done by the Great Depression. At its peak there were more than 3 million Britons out of work at one time, including many of her former constituents in the East End and the Welsh miners who had been her loyal allies in communist days. For that matter, when Marxism and the Communist Party finally gained the attention of British intellectuals, Sylvia made no effort to reaffiliate. She had turned her back on that phase of her life; and from the mid-1930s she saw Stalin's persecutions as an extension of the repression already at work in Italy and Germany.[2]

Peace was a dominant issue at that time, and Sylvia returned to the peace movement, partly through involvement with the International League for Peace and Freedom (where Emmeline Pethick-Lawrence was international president in the early part of the 1930s). She also joined the International Women's Peace Crusade, recruiting friends in support of her new venture,[3] and affiliated with the International Peace Press Bureau, run in Amsterdam by J. B. Hugenholtz, a minister of the Dutch Reformed Church. Hugenholtz collected printed material like articles or messages from different organizations, edited them, and distributed the mimeographed material to peace groups all over the world.[4] Sylvia's protracted correspondence with Hugenholtz began about 1932, and she continued to work with him on Ethiopian issues, a collaboration which led him to form an Ethiopian Society of the Netherlands.[5]

The Women's World Committee Against War and Fascism, of which Sylvia was treasurer (the only group in which she held that particular office), stood mid-way between the cause of peace and violent opposition to evil in the world. Few records of its activities survive, however, beyond copies of protests to the German government about unspecified mistreatment of women.[6]

By 1935 Sylvia's activities in the International Women's Peace Crusade again attracted the attention of the Special Branch of Scotland Yard. A police agent reported that among 'the two people who seem to take the lead in the Society are Miss Sylvia Pankhurst . . . who has taken a lively interest in the affairs of the Society for the Promotion of Cultural Relations with the USSR.'[7] He thought the society seemed harmless enough; yet, even with the best of intentions, it might 'be used for purposes other than the one for which it was originally intended'. Sir Samuel Hoare believed the crusade was one of those organizations which, though 'supremely innocent and laudable', can 'ultimately be traced back to the Soviets'. Queen Marie of Romania turned down Sylvia's invitation to become honorary secretary.[8] Whatever else, Sylvia was no longer pro-Russian. Other than her brief affiliation with this society her only activity involving Russia in the 1930s was occasional aid to Jewish refugees who escaped to England. We do not know exactly what role she served in this connection—perhaps she met these refugees through other Jews she knew in East London. Anti-Semitism was still a cause for concern; and Sylvia had always opposed it.

In 1936 Sylvia joined Clement Attlee, later Labour Prime Minister, on the platform of a major peace demonstration in Cardiff. There she urged that Britain support sanctions against Italy, even at the risk of war. For the first time she spoke for a large segment of the British Labour government. Pacifism was strong, as was Labour support for sanctions against Italy. It was not simply a move to punish Italy; it was concern for the survival of the League of Nations, which Mussolini had openly defied when he invaded the African Kingdom of Ethiopia.

Before the Italian aggression, Sylvia's pacifism had been virtually absolute. She warned, 'Never were peace efforts more needed. The tremendous war-building programmes by every Government, including our own, are sufficient indication of this.' What, she asked, was there to fight for? Germany had already rearmed, but nothing should be done to alter that. She rejected a current theory which stated that France would fail without British support on grounds that Germany would be too exhausted defeating the French 'to tackle the undamaged British Empire'. As for Russia, 'I am convinced that her greatest strength and safeguard is to remain out of any alliance . . . I hope that she has not committed herself to . . . France'.[10] If Russia did become involved, Sylvia hoped that her people would not honour the commitment. If war came, Sylvia believed that England should remain neutral and negotiate a quick settlement. France was, in any event, responsible for Germany's rearmament and German hostility. In conclusion, 'one principle stands forth as a clear policy for every nation—the refusal to enter war. . . . Our slogan should be "no more war".'

But war in Ethiopia triggered a new attitude towards Germany as well. In the Second World War she reversed her pacifist stand, writing, 'As a woman, I hate war, I have worked for peace throughout my adult life'; but she felt that it was essential for women to oppose Hitler. Hoping for a resurgence of female power, she called on the 'suffragettes who led the world struggle for women's citizenship' to 'aid our sisters in other lands to regain their lost freedom and stoutly defend our own'.[12]

In the midst of this major shift in attitude, Sylvia built further on her concern for Romania. Beginning in 1930, some citizens at Constantsa on the Black Sea organized a commmittee to celebrate Eminescu with a statue. Valerian Petrescu, a judge with literary interests and one of the leading figures, proposed editing a volume in Eminescu's memory, to be published in 1934 to coincide with the dedication of the statue. He located Sylvia through the British Consulate and approached her for an article as first English translator of Eminescu's poems.[13]

Sylvia replied enthusiastically and also requested an invitation to the ceremonies. This caused a stir in the sponsoring committee and raised some political problems for Judge Petrescu. Sylvia was known to Romania as a communist and a republican; there the monarchy was threatened in 1934 from both left and right—Fascist sympathizers and communists within, and a frontier with the USSR. After some discussion the committee decided to issue the invitation, billing her as a suffragette and passing over her more awkward politics.

Sylvia's family made this the occasion for a rare holiday together. Corio applied successfully for an Italian passport, though he was still under surveillance. Romanian authorities in London granted him a visa as interpreter for 'Dr. E. S. Pankhurst'.[14] Exactly who paid for the trip is not clear, but Sylvia was less than candid when she wrote to the editor of *PEN News* that 'as translator of Mihael Eminescu, I am invited to go to Constantsa as a guest of the Romanian government'. The sponsoring committee may have paid her travel expenses.[15]

The family travelled through Europe, across Germany, 'sombre and large, flying the swastika', to Poland, and south through Hungary before they woke 'to verdant paradise' in the heart of 'Eminescu's dreamland, this jewel of the Carpathians, fairyland and home'.[16] They arrived late in Bucharest and missed those who were to meet them. They woke early the next day and spent it touring the city on their

(*far left*) Corio, with (*centre front*) Richard and Sylvia, Judge and Mrs Petrescu and their son Arcadiu at Constantsa Romania, 1934

own. After a siesta, Corio hired a boat in a nearby park and rowed Richard around while Sylvia rested in the shade. This idyllic-sounding family outing seems to have been an unprecedented event in their lives. Resting in the shade was wasted time and so Sylvia must have been fatigued from her travel—or she may have acceded to the demands of her little boy. Furthermore, this trip seems to have been very special, in that it included Corio. In all the manuscript material Sylvia left behind, she mentioned Corio by name—or identified him as part of her life—only twice; and both mentions were made in her unpublished memoirs of the Romanian holiday.

After a few days in Bucharest, the family went on to Constantsa for the Eminescu celebration. It was a minor comedy of errors. Sylvia had not contacted Judge Petrescu, her host, in Constantsa, so the family arrived unexpected at the station. They hailed a horse-drawn coach, leaving their baggage, and set out for the Petrescu residence. A surprised Mrs Petrescu answered her front door to be greeted with 'I am Sylvia Pankhurst . . . '. The judge was not at home, and no hotel had been reserved.

The Petrescus provided a room for the night, and Mrs Petrescu phoned the station to prevent their luggage from being sent back to Bucharest. The adults communicated in French. Richard, at six-and-a-half, spoke only English, but, by using gestures, held his own with eight-year-old Arcadiu Petrescu. We have little information about the family's behaviour, but Arcadia Petrescu remembered that they were not the easiest of guests. Sylvia made a surprise announcement that she was a vegetarian. Richard refused coffee served with cow's milk rather than the goat's milk he had at home. Corio presumably ate whatever was offered since he was spared cooking and he liked meat. After breakfast the family went to a hotel overlooking the new Eminescu statue, where, incidentally, they could solve their dietary problems.[17] Sylvia introduced Corio as her husband, and he accompanied Sylvia and Richard to the ceremonies; this was one of the few occasions where they appeared together publicly as husband and wife.

Sylvia spoke at length; the family was given souvenirs, including stamps for Richard's collection; and they left with a guide to tour Romania, including the ancient monasteries in Bucovina. In all, they spent nearly a month in Romania, touring, meeting people, and sometimes being entertained by government officials and important members of the academic community. Sylvia made the most of her role as English translator of their great national poet—hence the invitations from the kinds of people with whom she had little association at home.

On her return to England Sylvia launched into a host of activities on behalf of Romania and its national poet. She had already offered *PEN News* a series of articles 'on art, literature, or social questions of interest'.[18] The Romanian PEN Club had invited her to 'a very interesting dinner' in Bucharest and asked her 'to convey certain matters to the English PEN Club and to the International Committee'.[19] Herman Ould, the Secretary of PEN, replied cautiously that if she had 'special news to communicate' she could send it to him before the next international committee meeting.[20] *PEN News* would, in addition, be glad to accept a paragraph or two from her regarding her trip.

The special news Sylvia promised was an offer to organize a concert consisting of her translations of Eminescu's songs and her reading from translations of his poetry.[21] Mr Ould was gracious but firm, and Sylvia found another sponsor, Mr C. M. Laptew, Romanian chargé d'affaires in London.[22] 'The Rumanian Concert' at the Lyceum Club on 17 January 1935, featured Sylvia, who reported to Valerian Petrescu:[23]

> It was a tremendous success . . . I read . . . 'Ghosts'. That, too, was a great success, though the poem was rather long. The final part was tremendously well received, but I attempted to read the whole thing without a break, which I now see was a mistake. I should have made a break at the end of each part, walked off the platform, had a few bars of Rumanian music, and come on again, in order to revive the audience, as people in this country are not accustomed to having things read to them.

Sylvia tried unsuccessfully to organize other 'Rumanian evenings', but she did finish the promised article, 'Hail to Thee Blithe Spirit', for inclusion in *Omagiu lui M. Eminescu* (Homage to M. Eminescu).[24] Even that brought some discord to the Eminescu committee, since her theme was on the anti-monarchist poem 'The Emperor and the Proletariat'. The committee favoured editing her copy, but Petrescu stood firm, and her contribution was printed as submitted. Nevertheless, Sylvia's sympathies were those of the poet. As she saw it, the intent of the poem was to level society, the king being brought to the level of the least, as all must be 'at last . . .'.

Her subsequent outpouring of articles on Romania was typical of her earlier fascination with people and places beyond Britain. She praised Romanian womanhood, excusing the fact that they had not yet received the vote because they 'never had to face in Romania the obstacles to the study and practice of law and medicine which were experienced here'. She also concluded that peasant women had 'proved the best and most efficient Mayors which Romania has had'. Romanian women—few of whom she actually met—were generally self-reliant, patriotic, talented in craftsmanship, and loyal to each other.[25] In Romania she briefly found a new utopia.

But her romance with Romania was short-lived. In 1935 Sylvia turned wholeheartedly to fighting Fascism. Corio, the silent partner, supplied her with the fuel for her campaign, and, in his quiet way, continued his own activities on the fringes of the anti-Fascist movement in Britain. In September 1922, before Mussolini became Italian leader, Sylvia had already pointed out in the *Dreadnought* that the Fascists might be a threat to Britain.[26] Two months later she issued a prophetic statement: 'Thousands of Fascists who shed the blood of their Italian fellow workers are likely to lose their lives in imperialistic overseas adventures.'[27] When the *Daily Herald* published an article about the bloodless revolution in Italy, Sylvia wrote to its editor: it may have been bloodless, but 'its victims succumbed to superior force as an unarmed man obeys the orders of "Hands up".'[28] To Sylvia, passivity in the *Daily Herald* was akin to approval for Mussolini. This time she was right to point out the danger of Fascist Italy at a time when few indeed recognized Mussolini's rise to power for what it would later represent.

In February 1923, she linked Hitler's *putsch* in Bavaria to Mussolini's ideology and tactics, also commenting in the *Dreadnought* that no one in Bavaria, Germany, or abroad was willing to go against the Fascist Hitler.[29] Just as her paper was folding, she found a cause to justify further publication. She advertised anti-Fascist meetings in the *Dreadnought* in 1923 and 1924, offering herself as a speaker on Fascism to any group interested. In the early 1920s few could regard a small-time, erratic Italian dictator as a threat to Great Britain. A few Italian anti-Fascists—mostly socialists, communists and a few anarchists like Corio—were then in exile in London, and they made up an occasional audience. But she only re-inforced what they already knew and her influence on the larger public was negligible.

While Sylvia was gradually becoming immersed in anti-Fascism, Britain was emerging from the Depression. By 1934–35 when Fascism was making an impact, economic recovery was becoming a reality. The National Government (a Conservative/Labour coalition) led by Ramsay MacDonald was still in office. There was some Fascist sentiment among Tories (who would later offer appeasement to the Fascists), and some anti-Fascist sentiment in Labour circles. Jews, who were alert to the dangers of Fascism, began to join the Communist Party which was the most anti-Fascist in its approach at that time. The Communist Party, in an attempt to gain credibility, approached Labour in a move towards unity. The Labour Party, however, was not yet ready to declare itself anti-Fascist, nor was it interested in a communist affiliation. Except for a few raised voices in those years, Fascism—or any other external threat—took a back seat to home affairs.

After the gap of eight years for writing and child-rearing, Sylvia emerged as an anti-Fascist leader to form the Women's International Matteotti Committee. Giacomo Matteotti had been secretary of the moderate Unitary Socialist Party, and one of the few dissidents to speak openly against Mussolini. The legitimacy of the Italian election in 1924 had been open to question, the Fascists having claimed their first electoral majority by means that Matteotti, among others, thought and said were fraudulent. After his challenge, Matteotti disappeared. A few days later he was found dead, and was generally believed to have been murdered on Mussolini's orders.[30]

In 1932 Sylvia's information from Corio's Paris contacts was that Mrs Velia Matteotti and her children were being held as virtual house prisoners. In order to enrol her eldest child in school Mrs Matteotti had had to change his name. The secret police followed her wherever she went, and her movements were restricted.[31] Sylvia hoped to call world attention to Mrs Matteotti and her children, with the ultimate aim of getting them out of Italy. With her customary vigour she inundated friends and acquaintances with literature outlining the tragic circumstances, including American friends of suffrage days and active public figures such as the British Ambassador to Rome, and Ramsay MacDonald.[32] Sylvia's letter was circulated in the Foreign Office to determine if MacDonald should receive a delegation from her committee. Ultimately they decided against it. They also advised against the kind of answer 'that might be sent to a reasonable person' on the grounds that 'she might make mischief with a straight reply'. She therefore received a polite refusal and no more.

It was this kind of attitude on the part of the British bureaucracy which dogged Sylvia for the remainder of her career. There is no question that some of the uncomplimentary commentary on Sylvia was the result of the anti-feminism which dominated government opinion during her lifetime. But, in fairness, Sylvia was a strong-headed, but naïve, radical. She was not astute politically (a Pankhurst characteristic shared by all three women), and because of this weakness she did not know how to approach politicians. Her outrageous communications to British officialdom sometimes provoked wrath among those who had to deal with her; sometimes (and probably for anti-feminist reasons) her directives provided a source of amusement.

It was at this time that Sylvia founded her short-run (two-issue) newspaper, *Humanity*. While civil servants in Whitehall regarded her as a pariah and ignored her considerable efforts on behalf of Mrs Matteotti and her children, concerned citizens of the world lent her their support. Professor G. Salvemini (who would himself later make fun of Sylvia) wrote to tell her that 'it is fine work you are doing to help Mrs Matteotti'. Alice Paul, a former American suffragette, supported this cause (as she would not later in the case of Ethiopia), writing that she was trying to get American newspapers interested in the Matteotti case. Angelica Balabanoff, who had broken with the Bolsheviks, wrote a supporting letter as did Henrietta Roland Holst, a dutch poet. Mrs Holst, in fact, had had her own difficulties with the Fascists in 1931, and was knowledgeable about Mrs Matteotti's plight from other sources.[33]

Sylvia, Norah (now back from Italy) and Mrs Drake from the East End led public demonstrations in Hyde Park and Trafalgar Square with placards calling attention to Mrs Matteotti's circumstances. Sylvia also sent off her usual flurry of letters to newspaper editors, but only the Manchester *Guardian* published her plea that all of Britain rise as one and confront the Italian government, demanding freedom for the widow and her children from the Fascists.[34] One woman among the many that Sylvia contacted went to Italy to plead personally but unsuccessfully for Mrs Matteotti's release.[35] This crusade illustrated the best of Sylvia's character: nobility and unegotistical service to a suffering woman and her family.

Sylvia and Corio also printed pamphlets translated from or based on Carlo Rosselli's paper *Giustizia e Libertá*, which was published in Paris.[36] Richard Pankhurst recalled that his mother saw much of Carlo Rosselli before he was murdered in Paris in 1938 by Italian agents.[37] Sylvia had met Rosselli in Paris, where she saw him several times before he went to Spain during the Civil War.[38] She later published in the *New Times and Ethiopia News* everything written by Rosselli that Corio could locate and translate.[39] Apparently Rosselli made himself available to Sylvia and Corio on occasional visits to England, and she in turn tried to use her PEN contacts to provide him with a forum.

Corio was never prominent in anti-Fascist circles, but he was useful as a translator and sometimes as a printer at the Walthamstow Press. As early as 1926, when only a handful of Italian anti-Fascists were in

England, he had served briefly as secretary of an anti-Fascist committee, Comitato di Milano. The Italian secret police suspected at that point that he was a spy for dissident factions at home[40] and they received reports in the 1930s that he was printing a 'subversive paper' *Il Comenta*, edited by Dr Galasso as well as other pamphlets.

In 1934, just before the family left for Romania, the Italian police reported that, 'supported by Miss Sylvia Pankhurst', he was still circulating anti-Fascist propaganda 'among Englishmen'.[41] At one point, possibly in the 1930s, Corio started writing a book, 'Critica Sociale Milano, 1894–'[42] which he never finished. There was little hope for a publisher in those days; a handful of impoverished exiles were all that could be relied upon for financial support.

Busy or not with his anti-Fascist work, Corio always found time for Richard. When the boy was away, Corio wrote him loving notes. On his return to London to see Italian anti-Fascist friends, Corio would often bring him presents. One acquaintance wrote that there was 'quite obviously a deep affection' between him and Sylvia. Her friends remarked they had never seen her so happy. Corio gave her a sense of security, he supplied the intellectual support which enabled her, in middle age, to 'blossom with glorious intensity'.[43] That support remained well in the background and her name—not his—was the more prominent.

Her concern with her famous name suggests that Sylvia was something of a snob. She declined an invitation to a rally staged by the Women's Committee Against War and Fascism on grounds that 'as a general rule I only attend meetings at which I have to speak'. Her causes were selected in a way that appears idiosyncratic. She spent far more energy opposing Fascism in Italy, for example, than Nazism in Germany, or even Sir Oswald Mosley's English version of Fascism.

In 1931 Mosley formed the Fascist New Party. His followers adopted the symbolic blackshirts and shared his admiration for Benito Mussolini. Mosley's blackshirts were xenophobic—'Britain for Britons'—but not obviously anti-Semitic at first. After 1933, however, Mosley became more anti-Semitic in response to Jewish opposition, especially in the East End. He incited the Irish in particular against the East End Jews, and the conflict increased until by 1936 anti-Semitism had become his single message.

In the East End, Sylvia witnessed a particularly ugly scene when some Fascist youths nailed a pig's head to a synagogue. She was alarmed, especially because those involved came from an ILP background. 'I was told', she wrote, 'that the young people are growing up and know nothing of politics and these are the young people who are joining the blackshirts. What is the matter with us?'[45]

The political turmoil of the period also soured Sylvia's epistolary relation with Bernard Shaw. In 1928 Sylvia accused him of fostering

Fascism. She wrote to George Lansbury that Shaw approved of the 'Soviet and Fascist Corporate State. What a thing for a socialist to say, alas!'[46] Or again: 'My old friend Shaw for some time had been suffering from an all too widespread epidemic of ethical influenza which has caused him to sneer at democracy.'[47] Shaw refused to sign a petition for Mrs Matteotti because, he said, 'This memorial will make Mrs Matteotti's situation worse . . . What the memorialists, including your incorrigible, pugnacious self, are doing is making an attack on the Fascist regime in Italy under the cover of sympathy with a distressed widow and her orphans.'[48] By mid-1935, however, Sylvia thought she detected a change of heart and published an open letter of 'congratulations':[49]

> In view of the correspondence on the subject of Fascism which you and I have had over a period beginning in 1928 . . . I was surprised but deeply interested to learn you had accepted membership in the International Committee of Writers against Fascism. . . . I trust this means that at last you have understood Fascism to be a totally reactionary movement. . . . Your change of front will probably occasion as much surprise as did that of Asquith when he came out for Votes for Women after his long resistance to it.

Shaw replied a week later:[50]

> My friend Miss Sylvia Pankhurst has never been able to follow what she calls my changes of front . . . I have not 'accepted membership of the International Committee of Writers against Fascism'. I have refused it . . . I am not a Fascist. I am, and have been . . . a Communist. . . . Miss Pankhurst's indignation at the murder of Matteotti are not discreditable to her; but she will never get anywhere in a revolutionary movement if she lets herself be turned aside to Red Cross work. . . . I . . . add that Nazi anti-Semite ethnology is balderdash and its biology a recipe for degeneration . . .

Refugees constituted a problem of the 1930s. A few Italian anti-Fascists like Corio had been around London in the 1920s; others came in the 1930s. Jews came from Germany; republicans from war-torn Spain; and many more. Sylvia was especially concerned to help Austrians and Italians. She took some into the house at West Dene as she had done with the Welsh miners at the Red Cottage during the General Strike in 1926; and she turned to her few remaining friends in the East End to place some of the homeless victims.

Annie Barnes tells how Sylvia arrived at her door one day with a frail young man who spoke very little English. Sylvia called him 'William Morris' because he was an artist; he was also an illegal immigrant and Sylvia had no room for him at her home. Annie and Albert Barnes agreed to take him in, and he stayed more than eighteen months, never employed; the only money he had was given him by Albert

Barnes. The only friend he made outside the home was a British girl he met on one of his outings to paint.[51]

Early one morning, with no previous warning of illness, 'Morris' came to Annie's bedroom telling her he was violently ill. She went to call the family doctor and returned to find Morris already dead. Complications developed on two fronts. The police were called in to investigate his death, which caused them to investigate his life as well. An inquest showed he died of natural causes, but no identity papers were found in his possession.

The Barnes insisted to the police that 'Morris' was a lodger, worked somewhere unknown to them, and had lived a quiet, solitary life during his brief residence with them. Annie recalled being very nervous during the several interviews with police officers and coroner's officials. Sylvia tried to calm her fears, insisting it was perfectly reasonable to have a lodger about whom one knew nothing, so long as he paid the rent on time.[52] The police soon lost interest, but later Annie was surprised to find an official from the Italian embassy at her door. Identifying 'Morris' by another name, he warned that Morris was an 'Italian socialist and dangerous'. Annie answered that he was dead and therefore no danger.

Richard Pankhurst remembers a houseguest who had fought in the Spanish Civil war, but not large numbers of others moving in and out of West Dene.[53] The house was a good way out in the country, about an hour from London, and not easily accessible by public transport. Corio may have known that he was under occasional surveillance, which would increase the risk for illegal immigrants.

Sylvia also did what she could to help dissident Italians jailed in their own country. Sylvia approached Herman Ould of the PEN Club with the case of Mario Vinciguerra and Renzo Rendi. As journalists, she claimed it was the responsibility of the PEN Club to take up their cause. Ould investigated and found that the men had been convicted for political activity having nothing to do with freedom of the press.[54] Sylvia refused to believe the report and sent him Italian sources to substantiate her claim. She went on to warn that 'a day will come when the inequity of the present Italian regime will be exposed to all, and when that day comes, those who have failed to do anything in their power to assist the oppressed writers of Italy, after that matter has been brought to their notice, will survey that failure with feelings of regret and shame.'[55]

A few months later Sylvia sent Ould a letter from Professor Gaetano Salvemini, then teaching at Harvard, and a leading scholar of anti-Fascism, confirming Sylvia's account of the convictions, and refuting the 'report' from Italy.[56] Still PEN did not get involved in the case and Sylvia abruptly dropped the issue in favour of something else.

Sylvia's involvement with anti-Fascism inevitably led to her final and greatest crusade, the public defence of the Ethiopian cause before, during, and after the Italian conquest of 1935 and 1936.[57] The issue was natural for her. She was already involved in activities opposing the Italian government. Her attempts to use the League of Nations as a peace-keeping body reflected her old pacifist interests. In the Emperor Haile Sellassie, eight years her junior, she was nevertheless to find a hero and father figure to whom she would be loyal for the rest of her life. On 5 May, 1936, her birthday and the day the victorious Italian army entered the half-deserted capital of Addis Ababa, Sylvia launched a new weekly, the *New Times and Ethiopia News*, which was increasingly to occupy her time.

Like the *Woman's* (later *Worker's*) *Dreadnought*, the *New Times and Ethiopia News* was a tabloid, usually comprising one folded sheet, and featured pictures of members of the imperial family or pirated prints showing atrocities committed by Italians during the Ethiopian campaign. Sometimes it featured illustrations, again usually by someone other than Sylvia, and these always illuminated the horror stories she carried in her paper—some of which were true, some of which were exaggerations provided through her several but often questionable sources, including the Ethiopian embassy.

In fact, the Ethiopian crisis is not quite so clear in retrospect as it seemed at the time. Italy was certainly an aggressor, trying to resurrect in the 1930s the scramble for Africa, which the other great powers had given up. The reasons were mixed but included a desire to avenge the Italian defeat by the Ethiopians at Adowa in 1896; to find living space for an expanding Italian population; and to bring Mussolini glory as a new Roman emperor.

Ethiopia was the one remaining truly independent country in Africa, but the empire ruled by Haile Sellassie I was itself the product of conquests carried out by the ruling Amhara over their neighbours in the late nineteenth century. In the Europe of 1935 and 1936, few knew or cared about Ethiopia; but the people's direct interests were touched by international power relations, of which the League of Nations was an essential experiment in the inter-war years. Ethiopia had joined the League in 1923, and it was the League's responsibility to ensure the territorial integrity of each member-state. Italy was directly flaunting its challenge to the League. France and England—whose colonies bordered Ethiopia—by silent acquiescence in Italian aggression, weakened the League. The British public was enraged by Italy's breach of League principles and demanded sanctions. Ethiopia stood alone against Italy. British and French official policy was to object, but never to cut off vital supplies such as oil, thereby keeping Italy's goodwill. Within the Labour Party a few, especially the ILP group, cried 'sell-out', but Labour was divided. Fenner Brockway, one of the few voices of dissent, called for sanctions against Italy in the *New Leader*, but was ignored.[58]

A sympathetic few in London joined to form the Abyssinia Society under the leadership of Professor Stanley Jevons, son of the well-known economist. Sylvia was one of the early members, but from her first encounter she tried to exercise leadership in ways that soon precipitated her departure to form yet another group under her own control. Meanwhile, the events which led to the Second World War were already in motion. Within months, General Franco launched his attack on the new Spanish Republic, with support from Italy and Germany quickly forthcoming. Sylvia could hardly ignore these events which occurred comparatively close to home, although she kept her emphasis on the Italian issue. Corio apparently took the threat in Spain more seriously; he thought, as many others did, that Germany and Italy were using Spain as a proving ground.[59]

But the *New Times and Ethiopia News* did carry news of Spain, beginning with a column by Nancy Cunard in September 1936 signed 'An Englishwoman in Barcelona'. Cunard also covered the Spanish Civil War for the American Associated Negro Press, and later for the Manchester *Guardian*.[60] Nancy was the rebellious descendant of the famous and wealthy Cunard shipping dynasty. Although much of the family wealth was gone, and Nancy's mother kept her on a tight allowance, there was no question about the aristocratic class this hard-drinking, sexually liberated woman represented. Sylvia—by strong contrast—hailed from Manchester's middle class. None of the men in her family had attended public school—a social cachet that was far more important than Dr Pankhurst's academic achievements. Sylvia's suffragette background, while recognized as a good cause, also projected images of violence and unrest—not a tradition to which the best people subscribed, even if some few were active in the movement. In spite of the scandalous reputation that Nancy Cunard enjoyed within her social milieu, she was still at the top of the social ladder.

Nancy was devoted to republicanism in Spain. As 'roving reporter' from 1936 until the war's end in 1939, she submitted irregular copy to the *New Times and Ethiopia News*, mostly personal analysis, at times suggesting the same kind of overstatement that Sylvia used for her causes. She also wrote dramatic accounts of Fascist bombings of schools and playgrounds and the fall of Madrid.[61] From a distance Nancy and Sylvia worked to help the Italian anti-Fascist brigade, which they believed was forbidden entry into France after the republican defeat. Nancy tackled the French authorities, while Sylvia took the cause to Parliament, seeking admission into Britain for anti-Fascist foreigners.[62] In fact, France was not automatically excluding everyone but was admitting them on an individual basis, though most were placed in internment camps[63] and it is unlikely that the efforts of either Sylvia or Nancy were helpful in this instance.

Sylvia mourned the fall of Spain in an editorial. She saw French and

British recognition of Franco's government as a sign of worsening conditions for all Europe. The Japanese invasion of China had already begun—a fact she covered in her paper. In Spain, she said, people were fighting on behalf of Ethiopia and China as well as their own country. She wrote that in Spain international justice was threatened; patterns for the future were being drawn; and 'justice, peace and liberty . . . grievously threatened'.[64] She also wrote that rioting had broken out between the Palestinians and the Zionist settlers. Sylvia saw this as a threat to world peace, yet: 'The conflict between the Arabs and Jews is tragically sad and unnecessary. These two races must agree to live together'.[65]

Another incident, this time involving the arrest of Arthur Koestler in Spain, shows some of Sylvia's determination in pushing issues in which she had an interest. She was very persistent in letters to Ould at PEN, demanding action from him to incite the British government to action, without realizing that Ould had already raised a petition signed by 'Forty Famous Writers'—she was not among them.[66] This might have been a deliberate snub on Ould's part. Sylvia was not a 'popular' writer; nor was she regarded as a literary figure of significance. He may have adopted the same attitude as those in the Foreign Office, who decided not to give her an opportunity to make 'mischief'. He had had his troubles with her sometimes imperious ways in her earlier period as a journalist and author.

Earlier, in January 1931, Sylvia was included in a peace deputation to the Foreign Secretary which included some of the leading women of the time: Rebecca West, Mrs Clement Attlee, Mrs Dingle Foot, Vera Brittain, and Mrs Corbett-Ashby, who had taken over the Fawcett suffrage society. Instead of working with the delegation, however, Sylvia took over. She was so aggressive and talkative that the other women sat quietly until Sylvia exhausted herself and they were all dismissed. After that, she was not invited to future meetings and lost this group of potential allies. She made much the same mistake in protests to the government especially through Winston Churchill, the Member of Parliament representing the constituency that included West Dene. Churchill usually referred her letters to the appropriate department and got appropriate answers, with an occasional tone of exasperation, such as the time the Foreign Office felt called upon to warn that 'Mr Churchill . . . should not be led by Miss Pankhurst's letters into thinking the situation is anything like she says it is.'[67]

Sylvia's service to one king wronged by Mussolini spilled over into the service of King Zog of Albania—an unsavoury tyrant by any liberal judgement, at that time or later. She devoted lengthy columns to Albania in the *New Times and Ethiopia News* as the Italian invasion loomed. She was associated with the Friends of Albania, a group the Foreign Office dubbed as having 'no political colouration though probably dominated by Miss Pankhurst, an ardent Zogite'.[68] Her ambivalence towards British royalty came in her remark, on the abdication of Edward VIII in 1936, that: 'It's the first time I ever heard of a man giving up something for a woman.'[69]

Just as opposition to Fascism drew Sylvia to the Ethiopian cause, support of Ethiopia brought her into the quite separate forment of Pan-Africanism, a rising movement, especially in West Africa and among Africans in Europe and Afro-Caribbeans. Ethiopians, the emperor included, regarded themselves as Christians with an ancient tradition that was racially and culturally superior to the rest of sub-Saharan Africa. But other Africans saw only that Ethiopia was a black state fighting for its life against European imperialism.

Sylvia already held a record of protest against colonial wrongdoing in Africa, and she maintained this stance.[70] Her propaganda in the Ethiopian cause brought her to the attention of Pan-African circles. She came to know C. A. Davies, Arthur Creech-Jones, the Colonial Secretary, and I. T. A. Wallace-Johnson of Sierra Leone; and the *New Times and Ethiopia News* was widely quoted by the West African press, especially in Sierra Leone.[71] Sylvia came to be associated with the League of Coloured Peoples, founded by Sierra Leonian Harold A. Moody. At times she was the only European he was willing to consult.[72]

Among other London Pan-Africanists she also worked with George Padmore, a West Indian, sometime communist, and ultimately advisor to Kwame Nkrumah in an independent Ghana. In 1935 he founded the International African Service Board with the cooperation of Wallace-Johnson, but with a mainly West Indian following. Sylvia was a member of his board for a time. C. L. R. James, the Pan-Africanist intellectual, novelist, essayist, historian and Trotskyist, was editor of the bureau's newsletter until he left for America at the beginning of the war.[73] Padmore, later writing on the Pan-African movement, referred to the Italo-Ethiopian war as 'the most stimulating and constructive in the history of Pan-Africanism'.[74] Furthermore, people who were to be prominent later supported Sylvia, although not necessarily directly. Jomo Kenyatta became honorary secretary of the International Friends of Abyssinia Society, with J. B. Danquah of the Gold Coast and Muhammad Said of British Somaliland on his executive committee.

With the outbreak of the Second World War, Sylvia redoubled her aid to refugees, especially to those the British interned as enemy aliens without regards to previous political stands,[75] such as anti-Fascist Italians and German Jews. Several became, in turn, some of her warmest supporters in her Ethiopian causes. Professor Ruth Schulze-Gaevernitz was active, and contributed occasional articles to the *New Times and Ethiopia News*. The Hungarian exile Bela Menczer, a friend and supporter after initial contact through the Abyssinia Society, contributed to her paper and became an unofficial advisor to Haile Sellassie's sometime personal advisor, Lorenzo Taezaz, a member of the emperor's delegation to the League of Nations.[76]

While Sylvia responded warmly to the security she found through her relationships with Ethiopians, she was occasionally piqued by the ingratitude of other clients. In 1941 she wrote to Piero Treves: 'I gave more than six months of the best part of my time working for the Italian internees. The majority, whose release I procured, did not take the trouble to send me a postcard and let me know of their release.'[77] Until 1942, however, she kept in touch with Piero Treves' refugee work, but at a respectful distance. Then Treves excluded both Corio and Sylvia from the Free Italy Committee that he and others set up in April.[78] Rejection was never easy for Sylvia, and in this case, Corio may have been even more severely wounded, since he had so little involvement with the outside world. He wrote to several newspapers and to Professor Salvemini, accusing the Free Italy movement of being a Fascist plot. In fact, the movement was a straightforward, anti-Fascist propaganda organization. Salvemini did not bother to reply to Corio, but in writing to a friend in New York, Salvemini warned that in the case of Corio, whose letter he enclosed, 'we can do nothing with such people except have nothing to do with them.'[79] Sylvia was earlier described by Salvemini as '*di quella seccatrice di* Miss Pankhurst' (a troublesome nuisance).[80]

Neither Sylvia nor Corio managed to enjoy for long the goodwill of others with whom they were united in campaigns, until Sylvia found Ethiopia. Corio then further receded into the background of organizational activity, writing for the *New Times and Ethiopia News* and handling printing details. Sylvia not only antagonized the Italian anti-Fascists, but, according to her, the strong position she took against Fascism brought repeated threats of violence. She received and published letters from Italian Fascists in London advising her 'not to go out at night' or she 'would be murdered'.[81] Nothing in the Italian secret police reports indicates that these statements reflected that government's attitude toward her activities. In fact, the Italian officials reported little on Sylvia, and when they did, it was usually in connection with Corio. And, as time went on, the reports were but perfunctory follow-ups on where he was living. He seems not to have been regarded as a threat to Italian interests in Britain (or elsewhere).

When it became clear that war was inevitable, Sylvia founded another organization, the Women's War Emergency Council, which began lobbying for virtually the same issues she had reported during the First World War in the East End. An unknown benefactor helped underwrite the costs of the organization, and Sylvia enlisted the support of several well-known women, including Lady Mary Barton, wife of the former British Ambassador to Ethiopia. With adulation for the emperor of Ethiopia filling the pages of the *New Times and Ethiopia News*,

Sylvia's considerable but brief involvement with the Women's War Emergency Council went almost unnoticed except by various Members of Parliament and the Ministry of Health, whom she repeatedly urged to come to the relief of London's poor.

An unsigned, unfinished letter, bearing only the address of 17 Somerset Terrace, dated 17 December 1939, chastised Sylvia for her irresponsibility in signing a seven-year lease for Council offices and criticized her failure to keep her accounts straight.[82] Sylvia was once again spending other people's money with abandon. This practice gathered momentum in the Ethiopian campaigns, but did not amount to much in the case of the Women's War Emergency Council because her involvement was limited to a year or so before she dropped out to pursue other interests. Sylvia's forte, in the case of the Women's War Emergency Council, was initiative. She quickly formed organizations to meet any cause that appealed to her emotionally. Her ability to bring people together was unfortunately offset by her inability to relate to those who shared her goals but disapproved of her radical method of problem-solving which, in the case of the Women's War Emergency Council, consisted of repeated attacks on the government.[83] Sylvia criticized food shortages and lectured government officials on rising costs, both of which affected the poor most severely. In the end, however, she was forced to acknowledge that no parallels would be drawn between the First and Second World Wars, and in so doing she probably withdrew from the Council, choosing instead to concentrate her energy on pleas to the Foreign Office on behalf of Ethiopia and other victims of Fascist and Nazi aggression. Thus she gained a sense of worth, of contribution with the mainstream that she had not experienced in the suffrage movement, during her communist days, or even in her surface relations with the anti-Fascists. As a rebel, she had been accepted by the communist outsiders as an insider, but that relationship collapsed when she was unable to conform to their nonconformity. Turning to Corio, another rebel, she found a modicum of comfort and support. Her final, long-lasting, security came from the Ethiopians, who appreciated her devotion to their country. From 1936 onward Sylvia, her clothing in disarray, her hair flying out beneath a hat thrown on her head as an afterthought, developed what can be referred to as familial relationships with many Ethiopians—young and old—first in England, then in Africa. Her last crusade brought her the sustained love and appreciation she had been seeking throughout her many past campaigns.

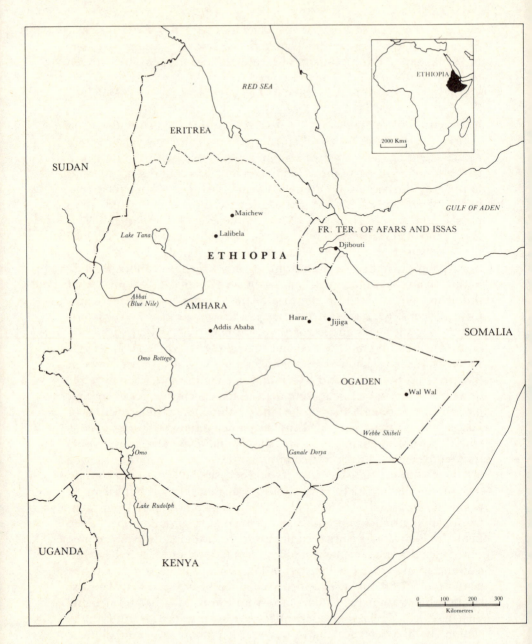

Ethiopia *c*. 1955

11

Sylvia and the Emperor

I pray to God that he may keep the nations of the world from the torment that has been inflicted on my people. . . . the issue today before the League of Nations . . . is a question of the very life of the League of Nations
—Haile Sellassie I to the General Assembly of the League of Nations, 30 June 1936; quoted in *My Life and Ethiopia's Progress 1892–1937* (trans. Edward Ullendorff)

In 1935 the Ethiopia Sylvia Pankhurst was determined to defend was just emerging from centuries of isolation. There had been periodic contact with Europe over the centuries, but very little prior to the twentieth century and much of the contact had been detrimental to Ethiopian interests. The third quarter of the nineteenth century had witnessed European expansion into Africa south of the Sahara, with British influence in Egypt and the Sudan on Ethiopia's northern and western boundaries, and in Kenya and Uganda to the south and west. France established a tiny fuelling station at Obock to the East.

Earlier in the nineteenth century an independent Egypt had taken control of Massawa, Ethiopia's Red Sea port, and in 1872–74 war between the two countries ended with Egypt's sovereignty in the area. It was not until 1884 that Egypt withdrew and Ethiopia once again had an outlet to the Red Sea, but it was short-lived because Italy, already in Assab (a corner of Eritrea), took over Massawa in 1885 with the encouragement of the British. Britain, in her quest for control of the Horn of Africa, occupied the Somali coast to the east of Ethiopia. France, in competition, expanded her presence from Obock on the Horn to form French Somaliland. In short, by 1895, when Italy decided to move against her, Ethiopia was surrounded by European 'protectorates'.

Internally Ethiopia, led by strong kings from the 1830s, was being centralized through a series of military manoeuvres. King Teodros (Theodore), who came to power in 1855, began the process of centralization but tried to accomplish too much too fast: fighting intruding Galla from the south; trying to subdue the powerful Ethiopian Coptic Church; and reducing the power of the regional nobility. Combined operations on all these fronts caused him to lose peasant support. In addition, he imprisoned many foreigners in the capital through irrational fears of outside interference. As a result the British mounted the

Napier expedition from the Red Sea and defeated the Ethiopian forces in 1867–68; Teodros committed suicide.[1]

Teodros was succeeded by the Emperor Yohannes IV (John), who ruled from 1871 until 1889. It was under his influence that Italy established herself first in Assab and later at Massawa. While continuing to unify the empire Yohannes was forced to deal in the 1880s with the Mahdist invasion from Sudan; his successor, Menelik II, later used the Mahdist threat in his own interests, thus increasing problems of unification from within. Yohannes originated from Tigre, one of the oldest areas in Christian Ethiopia and located in the Italian-influenced north, while his opponent Menelik came from Showa in the central highlands.

When the Italian forces took over Massawa, Yohannes initiated a two-year campaign (1887–89) against them. He was at first successful, routing Italy at the battle of Dogali, but before he could proceed decisively against the Italian incursion he was forced to move south to fight the Mahdist challenge. Here Menelik delayed delivering his considerable army and in February 1888 launched a revolt against Yohannes with Italian support and arms in return for a promise to cede more territory in the Italian-named province of Eritrea. Although the revolt was unsuccessful, Yohannes died in battle against the Mahdists and Menelik ascended to power in Ethiopia. Despite wars and revolt, Yohannes had extended Teodros's moves toward centralization.[2] Menelik continued the unification process, but he had also to deal with the Italians.

In 1889 Menelik signed the treaty of Uccialli with Italy: in the Amharic text this guaranteed Italy's right to Massawa and Assab. In a later agreement Italy made a substantial loan to the Ethiopian government with Harar on the east put up as security. Unknown to Menelik, in the Italian version of the Treaty (which he had also signed) was Article XVII which made Ethiopia a virtual dependant of Italy, and gave it rights over Ethiopian foreign policy. In the meantime, and again with British support, Italy had in 1889 secured from the Sultan of Zanzibar rights to a considerable area of land giving Italy the Benadir coast from Kismayu to Cape Guardafui. This brought Italy to the Horn as a neighbour to Britain, which had established rights over British Somaliland in 1884; and to France, which had extended her small fuelling station to Djibouti. Djibouti came to be the chief caravan route in landlocked Ethiopia until camels were replaced by the French-built railway to Dira Dawa (Ethiopia) after 1902.

When Menelik discovered he had been tricked by the Italians not only on the two versions of the Treaty of Uccialli, but also on boundaries in the north ceded to Italy by Ethiopia, he attempted to fight back —first by appealing unsuccessfully to the other powers in the area, then in direct confrontation with Italy. In 1895 Italy, prepared for war, launched her attack. Fighting continued for almost a year before Ethiopia successfully wiped out the majority of Italy's forces at the Battle of Adwa. At each successful battle the Ethiopian army had amassed thousands of weapons and rounds of ammunition which would be the vanguard of their military stores when the Italians reinvaded in 1935.[3]

France first backed Ethiopia, with Britain behind Italy. As the war progressed, however, France gave in to Italy and stopped supplies from Djibouti. Ethiopia, nevertheless, later joined France in her efforts to claim part of the Nile in competition with Britain. When France and Britain met at Fashoda in 1898, Ethiopian forces were on their way under French leadership. It was at Fashoda that the two major powers reached the apex of their rivalry and after 1898 Ethiopia negotiated over boundaries on the northern front with Italy and on the Somali borders with Britain. Menelik feared Italy's further designs in Eritrea, but he also regarded his win at Adwa as mostly good luck and decided not to tempt fate by further military conflict.[4]

Within his empire, Menelik marched south and, before he died in 1913, managed to bring together much of what constitutes present-day Ethiopia. After his death the problem of the succession was eventually settled by placing his daughter Zawditu on the throne with *Ras* Tafari (Haile Sellassie I) serving first as her regent, later as Crown Prince. Before his death Menelik had suffered a series of debilitating strokes which forced him to rely on a number of advisors, including his wife. The old emperor became more dependent on his wife's counsel and was unaware of factions lining up to seize the throne when it became vacant. Despite his illness, Menelik managed to appoint his thirteen-year-old grandson, Lij Yasu, as his successor with a regent to govern in his name until he came of age. *Ras* Tafari, having twice been passed over for his father's old governorship at Harar, was regarded by some supporters of the young king as a potential threat and had been forced to take an oath that he would never attempt his removal. After three years of what some regarded as misguided rule, rival factions over-threw Lij Yasu (his regent having died earlier), and while *Ras* Tafari was not directly involved his supporters were backed by Tafari's considerable army. A compromise finally resulted in the appointment of Zawditu as Empress and Tafari as her regent. From 1916 to 1930, the years of Zawditu's reign, Tafari gradually assumed more and more power for himself; in 1928, after a considerable confrontation with the Empress he became Crown Prince.[5]

When in 1930 *Ras* Tafari ascended the throne as Haile Sellassie I, the emperor had authority that was theoretically autocratic, but in fact limited by important residual powers in the hands of the priesthood and of secular authorities whose control over their own regions was often greater than the emperor's. These lords with the title *Ras* gained power in a variety of ways. Some, like *Ras* Kassa, claimed descent from the same Solomonic dynastic line as Haile Sellassie himself. Others were elevated to princedoms through appointment, such as some provincial governors. In all cases, the *Rases* were appointed by the emperor.

Haile Sellassie was born into royalty; his father had been a cousin and loyal lieutenant to Menelik as well as governor of Harar. The family came from the Amhara ruling class, whose language was Amharic, a Semitic language similar to Hebrew and Arabic. The emperor's early schooling had been by French tutors in Harar and later he attended a small private school established by Menelik in Addis Ababa. He never mastered English although he lived in exile in England for five years. And, prior to taking the throne his only foreign travel had been a tour of Europe in 1924, during which he stopped in Italy to receive an honour ironically bestowed by Mussolini.

Haile Sellassie's model of government was the European monarchist version, with heavy emphasis on the centralization of authority that had characterized the reigns of his predecessors in the nineteenth century. In order further to weld together the empire Haile Sellassie used his personal life as a manipulative tool. He divorced his first wife (an Amhara), whom he had married when he was a teenager and by whom he had a daughter, to marry a woman who was partially of Galla descent. The Galla were African invaders from the south who had variously played a role in earlier governments or had been in conflict with them. The Empress Menon gave her husband six children (three sons and three daughters) and lived with him as a close and faithful advisor until her death in the 1960s.

Addis Ababa, the capital since 1891, was in the 1930s an anachronism. A few modern buildings, including the emperor's palace, were surrounded by shacks with corrugated tin roofs. The only serious attempt to modernize the city took place for Haile Sellassie's coronation in 1930 when new roads leading nowhere were built out from and around the palace. The French-controlled railway had been extended from Dire Dawa to the capital and was the only source of outside supplies. Vinigi Grottanelli, a young Italian anthropologist who visited Addis Ababa soon after its capture, recalled the lack of a sewage system in his hotel, 'a sort of shack with no sink or bathtub for washing'. The modern embassy buildings were 'small islands in the sea'. Small stores run by Yemenis or other outsiders already supplemented the African open market but Ethiopians in commerce were rare.[6] George Steer, a British intelligence officer who was in Addis Ababa during the war, described hyenas howling in the evening as they waited to invade the town by night, scavenging for garbage.[7]

Yet there was progress. Haile Sellassie had moved to bring his isolated country into the twentieth century with the introduction of several reforms, including a constitution that was drawn up in 1930 and which provided for a Parliament appointed by the regional governments, and he established a criminal code for the first time.[8] While still regent he established a few primary schools in the capital and in the provinces. And since education called for books, he arranged for two printing presses to replace the costly and rare handwritten manuscripts which the priests had supplied to the élite for centuries.[9] During his regency he had also seen the need to involve Ethiopia in international affairs and had sought and gained entrance to the League of Nations in 1923, sponsored by Italy. One purported 'reform' followed affiliation with the League: slavery was partially abolished in 1924 but remained an issue in the empire for decades to come.[10]

In spite of Mussolini's apparent support of Haile Sellassie and Ethiopia, the Italians smouldered over Menelik's defeat of their army at Adwa for decades. And Italy's meagre empire was limited to Libya in North Africa, and Eritrea and Italian Somaliland on the Ethiopian border, making her a small colonial power in comparison with France, Britain, Germany and even backward Portugal. Dreams of the restoration of Roman glory combined with an ever-growing population at home made Italy ambitious for expansion: Ethiopia seemed the natural area into which to move. Men and supplies were quietly moved into Eritrea and Italian Somaliland but hostilities did not begin until December 1934 and even then under questionable circumstances.

The borders between Italian Somaliland and Ethiopia had not been clearly defined in the 1880s when the Sultan of Zanzibar ceded the territory to Italy. In order to clarify the boundaries between the two countries, two British surveyors in company with a group of Ethiopians (including soldiers) travelled to Wal Wal, commonly regarded as being well within Ethiopia's territory, where they planned to camp for the night. There they came upon Italian soldiers who refused to allow them to strike camp. The British surveyors withdrew, but the Ethiopians stayed on. Someone started shooting; no one knows who fired the first shot, but the incident gave Mussolini the opening he wanted. He immediately demanded excessive reparations from Ethiopia, labelling it the aggressor. Haile Sellassie appealed for help to the League of Nations; the League rejected the appeal but requested a peaceful settlement between Italy and Ethiopia. Peace, however, was not Mussolini's goal and he launched his attack on Ethiopia from Eritrea. A weak attempt to impose sanctions on Italy came from the League, forbidding arms sales, but permitting the purchase of oil. It was oil, not arms, that Italy needed in this war.

Ethiopia was ill-prepared for war; the empire's resources had been assigned to modernization schemes. Many Ethiopians were armed, but the weapons were mostly those taken from dead Italians in 1896 and therefore no match for the modern arsenal employed by Mussolini's forces. The imperial army had little artillery and its air force consisted of only eight planes and insufficiently-trained pilots. Italy had easy command of the air and a modern army that numbered nearly half a million, partly Italian, but also Somalian and Eritrean under Italian command. But, in spite of their numerical superiority, the Italians used mustard gas against the people Mussolini called 'barbarians'. They bombed hospitals and Red Cross facilities indiscriminately, and poisoned water supplies with yperite causing painful death to men and animals alike.

The new emperor followed the Ethiopian tradition of going into battle along with the nobility. An American on the scene later wrote of the emperor's bravery. 'For Haile Sellassie I cannot say too much. . . . for dignity and courage I have never met his equal. He actually worked a machine gun against the Italians then was down amongst the wounded . . . [but] the old reactionary group here are hard against him'. Although he took personal command of this unsuccessful mission, he was quoted later by a British diplomat as saying, 'je ne suis pas un soldat'.[11]

The draft call issued by the emperor illustrates the state of military unpreparedness in Ethiopia when the Italians invaded:[12]

> When this order is received all men and boys able to carry a spear will go to Addis Ababa. Every married man will bring his wife to cook and wash for him. Every unmarried man will bring any unmarried woman he can find to cook for him. Women with babies, the blind and those too aged and infirm to carry a spear are excused. Anyone found at home after receiving this order will be hanged.

(This order was translated from Amharic and sent to J. Edgar Hoover, of the American Federal Bureau of Investigation. Hoover forwarded it to Roosevelt's aide-de-camp, Major General Edwin M. Watson, with the notation that 'it at least represents a simplification of our draft problem which at times may seem somewhat confused.')

Haile Sellassie was a religious man, an intensely private man, who listened to his advisors but kept his own counsel. One remaining puzzle is his escape even before the final Italian victory when, by traditional values, he should have fought to the finish. Explanations vary. Good sense and awareness of inevitable defeat was the prime motive, but it left him a leader without honour among his nobles (some already in opposition to him) and the patriotic soldiers who continued to resist in his absence. He claimed that he left to go to Geneva to plead Ethiopia's case in person before the League of Nations even though his advisors believed the cause to be hopeless within the context of the major European powers' attempt to contain Hitler. In fact, France had closed the railway in Djibouti to arms importation before the emperor left. (Pierre Laval, the French Foreign Minister, had made a secret agreement with Mussolini renouncing French interests in Ethiopia and ceding some of her Somali territory in exchange for Italy's promise of support if Germany attacked France.)

Running from Mai Ceu in northern Ethiopia to Lalibela, site of the famous rock-hewn churches where he stopped to pray, the emperor reached Addis Ababa ahead of the advancing Italian troops. In Addis he stopped long enough to collect his wife and some of his children and loyal followers, and boarded the train for Djibouti in French Somaliland. From there he took the British ship *Enterprise* (which was waiting for him) to Jerusalem, where the Ethiopian Church maintained a monastery and the emperor later bought a home.[13] In his entourage were his son, the Crown Prince (Asfaw Wassan), Princess Tänagna Warq (his daughter and wife of one of his generals), *Ras* Desta, Prince Makonnen (the Duke of Harar and his favourite son), Prince Sahle Sellassie and Princess Tsähay, his youngest daughter. In addition, he took several grandchildren and a support staff that included secretaries and servants—altogether a sizeable entourage.

From Jerusalem the emperor, Asfaw Wassen, *Ras* Kassa and staff members travelled direct to England, where there was considerable public sympathy for him and his country.[14] John H. Spencer, an American foreign affairs advisor to Haile Sellassie at this time (and for many years thereafter), praised the British press and the BBC for calling public attention to the Italians' use of poison gas and other inhumane acts toward Ethiopians. While still in Ethiopia it 'was the strong reaction of British public opinion that became most apparent to us ... far more than in the case of Sweden or Norway which had substantial numbers of their Red Cross personnel in Ethiopia, some of whom were direct casualties'.[15]

Sylvia Pankhurst was also doing her best to alert the public to the gas attacks and the hospital bombings. While her efforts were not on the scale of the BBC, she and her anti-Fascist friends carried huge placards on their backs, and stationed themselves in public places where large numbers would see them, such as underground stations in rush hour. Sylvia was among those who greeted Haile Sellassie and his courtiers when they arrived in London and before their intended departure for Geneva. Spencer remembered that although he had come incognito at the request of the British government 'London streets were lined with cheering crowds shouting "Haile Sellassie".'[16] The emperor was in London from early May until late June when he went to Geneva to plead his case before the League. During that time Sylvia saw something of him. Because of her recent friendship with his ambassador to Britain, Dr Charles (Workeheh) Martin she had an easy entrée to his wider circle, and was among those 'advisors' who accompanied him to Geneva.[17]

Spencer remembers meeting her: 'I would say that it was in the afternoon of Thursday or Friday, June 25 or 26, 1936 at the Hotel Richmond in Geneva that I first saw Sylvia. . . . They [Sylvia and Professor Jevons with whom she was then working] had been received by the emperor and were full of suggestions not only for the forthcoming speech before the Assembly of the League, but also with plans for the future.'[18] Haile Sellassie, however, politely declined to follow their advice on his dealings with the League. When the emperor stood before the combined assembly the hall was filled with catcalls and other heckling which came from the 'Fascist journalists in the gallery', but Spencer pointed out that despite his small size 'he so instantly summoned up the majesty of presence'.[19] Sylvia was in the visitors' gallery. Not only had she been his strong supporter because of his victimization by Fascist Italy, but she was won over completely by his standing courageously, surrounded by the hostile sounds, yet unflinching in his argument against Italian aggression. Sylvia's recollections of the emperor at that time corroborate those of Spencer: 'One did not know that he was small and frail of stature, though he stood on the carpet before us . . . he seemed to tower above . . . embodied in him we saw Ethiopia.'[20] The fact that he was ultimately sold out to European interests only re-enforced her dedication while at the same time it increased her anger at her own country, as well as her hatred for Italy.

On the emperor's return from Geneva after unsuccessfully but eloquently stating Ethiopia's case before the League, he stayed first in a hotel, but later rented a house in Bath, where he was joined by his wife and other members of his family. Supporting the large retinue was expensive, and reports as to how much money he was able to extract from Ethiopia vary considerably. British Foreign Office reports indicate he was not financially well off. A few months after his arrival he approached the British agent for the Bank of Ethiopia, stating that he was thinking of breaking into his children's trust funds (totalling about $270,000) and wanted to know the legal problems involved.[21] The bank's agent advised him to buy a house with a mortgage and to get rid of the hangers-on he was supporting.

One member of his group that he was not supporting was Dr Martin. Martin was thoroughly westernized and, among Ethiopians, he best knew the British. By the time he made his way to England and had been appointed to his post, he was elderly, married to his second wife, an Ethiopian, and suffering from chronic asthma.[22] Even before Haile Sellassie left his country, Dr Martin had begun a fund-raising campaign for Ethiopia—apparently an independent action on his part. He seems not to have shared the proceeds with the emperor. Foreign Office reports indicate that Dr Martin's efforts caused friction between himself and Haile Sellassie. Martin, like Sylvia, was adept at getting money, but not at keeping records. Dr Martin also made it hard for the emperor to keep his promise to the government not to engage in political activities during his British exile. Spencer noted that Dr Martin was not among the advisors who accompanied Haile Sellassie to Geneva in June, although he did take him along when he returned in

September 1936.[23] One suspects that Martin was in the entourage more to keep him from activities in London than for any serious advice he might offer.

Back in London the emperor played cat-and-mouse with the Italian government, sometimes indicating he would return as a puppet ruler, sometimes intriguing with the Foreign Office through British friends. The Foreign Office resented Dr Martin for his meeting with 'various groups of individuals who had no knowledge of the situation in Abyssinia and whose sentimental enthusiasms on the subject led them to adopt an attitude which did not facilitate the task of His Majesty's Government'.[24] Sylvia was one of these sentimental enthusiasts: she was also personally close to Martin, who fed her much of the Ethiopian propaganda which found its way into her paper during his stay in Britain. Ethiopia retained its legation during the Italian occupation even though the British government eventually, in 1938, recognized King Victor Emmanuel as the new emperor of Ethiopia.

In the summer of 1935, Sylvia took a brief holiday in Beccles in Norfolk, leaving the paper to Corio and the draft of an invitation to a fundraiser for Ethiopia with Dr Martin. Martin approved the invitation and added that while he appreciated her advice on investments, he preferred 'looking into other possibilities'. The emperor perhaps had cause for concern about Martin's fund-raising.[25] The Foreign Office certainly did. Its first mention of Sylvia was to report that Haile Sellassie did not approve of 'certain of Dr Martin's activities, notably his close contact with such bodies as the "Friends of Abyssinia League of Service" run by Miss Sylvia Pankhurst'.[26] Dr Martin soon became a frequent contributor to the *New Times and Ethiopia News*, and Sylvia regularly advertised for donations for the Ethiopian relief fund that Martin ran.

The *New Times and Ethiopia News* announced in September 1936, that its editor was attending a peace conference in Brussels 'carrying a message' from Dr Martin, not the emperor. Sylvia stayed two weeks, until it was clear Ethiopia would retain its membership of the League in spite of the Italian conquest. She then joined the emperor in Geneva where he had gone to try once more to influence the League, again unsuccessfully.

During 1937, Sylvia overworked on Ethiopia's behalf to the point of illness. Dr Martin wrote an intimate note to her at Beccles, where she was again on holiday: 'You are very precious my darling to millions of people, so please take special care of your dear self . . . get well soon my dear and return to yours'.[27] By the summer of 1938, Dr Martin had been dropped by the emperor's camp, but was still in touch with Sylvia, helping raise funds for the *New Times and Ethiopia News*.[28] He no longer wrote for the paper, but was on hand for one of Sylvia's 'International Fete and Bazaar' fund-benefits, now under the patronage of the emperor himself.[29]

From 1936 to 1939, when war broke out in Europe, Sylvia was single-minded in her service to Ethiopia as a victim of the Fascist plague. Wherever Fascism seemed to be spreading in Europe—Austria, Romania, Albania—she attacked it for the disease it was. But Ethiopia stole the headlines in her newspaper. She became gradually better acquainted with Haile Sellassie, her new idol, and his family. Every possible tribute to the royal family was front-page news in the *New Times and Ethiopia News*. Henry Fry, a former colleague in the peace movement, commented, 'She became very, very immersed in Ethiopia. She imagined that the atmosphere that existed when she campaigned in East London for women's suffrage also existed in relation to Mussolini's occupation of Ethiopia, but it didn't.'[30]

To the British, Ethiopia was an anomaly. Sympathy did exist for the diminutive emperor and his ancient Christian country, but Britain in 1936 was the largest imperial power in the world. Her African colonies arguably re-enforced an element of racism that had existed since slavery and the slave trade had been intertwined with the development of British capitalism. This racism affected some aspects of the emperor's relations with the Foreign Office, and especially his dealing with the officers in the Egyptian Department. England's active defence of Ethiopia, however, was out of the question on political grounds until World War II made the two countries allies.

The emperor's position was an interesting one. In Ethiopia loyal supporters such as *Ras* Emru with his army of patriots were fighting the Italians, preventing a complete takeover of the countryside. Other *rases* deserted almost immediately to the Italians and offered to help pacify the country for financial gain or territorial power. The Italians had originally planned to make use of local warlords to subdue the country and aid them in the conquest they were never able to complete. After an assassination attempt on Marshall Graziani, the Italian viceroy in Ethiopia, they abandoned those plans and began deporting important nobles to Italy where they were kept in detention from 1936 until 1939 when most were returned.[31] In fact one of Haile Sellassie's daughters and the wife and children of Dr Martin were among the detainees. Some came back to serve the Italians in Ethiopia—in effect abandoning the emperor in England for power in their own right at home.

In England, however, the emperor was playing a game of his own with the Italians. Sellassie was surrounded by three groups of advisers, each with a separate set of recommendations. The first group, and those whose influence was at first dominant, proposed abdication with financial compensation from Italy. The second group, composed of Dr Martin and members of his family, urged the emperor to return home and lead the rebellion against Italy. The third group, of whom his daughter Princess Tsähay was one, as well as various members of British intelligence and British politicians, advised a 'wait-and-see' approach.[32] At one point the emperor established contact with Italian officials and even had a letter of submission signed (in his name) by his representative at the League of Nations. In return for submission he expected to be paid handsomely. The letter, however, was never acted upon. During the negotiations back and forth between Haile Sellassie and the Italians, the Vatican seems to have acted for Italy (on at least one occasion), in the person of Eugenio Cardinal Pacelli (later Pope Pious XII) offering the emperor a million pounds sterling to abdicate.[33] In 1938 when Britain and France recognized Victor Emmanuel as emperor of Ethiopia, Italy felt less inclined to pay the emperor off, although haggling continued into 1939.

The British authorities meanwhile kept a tight rein on their guest and eventually the recommendations of the second and third groups— to wait and see on one hand; and to lead the patriots on the other— were put into effect in that order. After unsuccessfully negotiating with Haile Sellassie, the Italians turned to the Crown Prince, who was known to be in dispute with his father. A series of indirect contacts through third parties eventually produced nothing. The Crown Prince was greedy and with events in Ethiopia seeming to produce sufficiently greedy and disloyal *rases*, the Italians decided they could ignore both the Crown Prince and his father.[34]

Despite some of the emperor's negotiations with Italy having made the British press,[35] Sylvia made no mention of them in the *New Times and Ethiopia News*. No doubt she disregarded press reports as anti-Ethiopian propaganda fostered by the British government. Richard, in a memoir of his mother, stated that Sylvia had informed the emperor 'frankly as a Republican that she supported him not because he was an emperor', but because of his cause.[36] A thorough reading of the *New Times and Ethiopia News* and of archival documents of the period, as well as interviews with participants in Ethiopia and London, cast doubts on this statement. Sylvia was overwhelmed by Haile Sellassie. Her republicanism departed from Waterloo Station in June 1936, when the emperor's train rolled in. By July of that year she had had her first audience and 'exclusive interview' with His Imperial Majesty. At about this time he must have begun to appreciate her potential usefulness. He insisted, she wrote, that he was not a refugee: he left Ethiopia 'in the service of his country'. He described himself as a soldier in battle, with people falling around him. The fact that his cousin *Ras* Emru was still in Ethiopia as regent meant that in law and in spirit the emperor was there too. His mission to the League of Nations required his departure. Sylvia swallowed every word, every argument, and made no attempt to balance the account.

The emperor knew the paper was smuggled into Ethiopia through Khartoum and Djibouti. Whenever it served Haile Sellassie's purpose to address his people, however indirectly, his messages were dutifully printed in the *New Times and Ethiopia News*, translated into Amharic, and smuggled across the border. One official of the Foreign Office blamed the *New Times and Ethiopia News* for the deaths of *Ras* Kassa's sons at the hands of the Italians.[37] For Sylvia, however, the emperor was 'profound in grief and anxiety but in good health' despite his exile and the continued bondage of his people. Another 'exclusive interview' in August 1936, found the emperor expressing himself on Ethiopian womanhood—by this time someone on his staff had done his homework and knew who Sylvia was. She, too, had learned more about Ethiopian court etiquette: all the emperor's words were printed in bold type.[38]

The *New Times* also interviewed empress Mänän, with her daughter, Princess Tsähay, acting as interpreter. She expressed her own concerns about Ethiopian women and spoke of her sadness about the war and their subsequent exile.[39] The princess was a favourite of her father, and Sylvia found her more approachable than other members of the royal family, and hence an effective route to the great man. With permission from her parents, Tsähay became the first member of the royal family to move out of comparative seclusion and begin training for a job. She rapidly learned English and began training as a nurse at the Children's Hospital, Great Ormond Street. In 1937 her sister, Princess Tänagnä Warq, lost her husband, *Ras* Desta, in the continuing war with Italy, but remained with her children at Bath.[40]

The Abyssinia Society, which Sylvia joined, took an active role in supporting the patriots in exile and publicizing the emperor's forced retreat from his country. It gathered in Members of Parliament, prominent citizens, and cause-oriented people like Sir Norman Angell (the World War I pacifist), several of whom, like Professor Jevons and Sylvia herself, had had an earlier interest in India.[41] Jevons, according to the Foreign Office, became British advisor to the Ethiopian embassy in London. Sylvia had sought that role and grew jealous of Jevon's close contact with Haile Sellassie, in spite of her services to him through the paper. It was not long before the conflict erupted into public battle, though Sylvia stayed on for the sake of Ethiopia and briefly joined the executive committee. Her paper remained the association's unofficial voice. Much of the money raised for publicity went to Geneva to support Ethiopian claims to the League, until the League collapsed.

In this crusade, as in others, Sylvia acted independently. She organized demonstrations in Hyde Park, Trafalgar Square and in front of the Houses of Parliament, using a few of her old friends from the East End, occasional new sympathizers with Ethiopia, or those more specifically anti-Fascist. Huge placards described Italian atrocities; front-page headlines from the *New Times and Ethiopia News* were blown up to alert the public to mustard gas and yperite attacks on the Ethiopian people. Sylvia used any method she could, and in so doing broke ranks with the more conservative members of the Abyssinia Society. Her demonstrations and undocumented 'news' in the paper were constant sources of friction. But not all her news was undocumented: in 1945 she published through the *New Times and Ethiopia News* a pamphlet which graphically illustrated Italian atrocities in Ethiopia in 1937. The cover, for instance, carried the reproduced photograph of a smiling Italian soldier holding up the severed head of an Ethiopian patriot. Other pictures showed Ethiopian soldiers hanging from trees or with their bodies badly mutilated. Included was an appeal 'to all Christian Churches' from Haile Sellassie, which indicates that Sylvia was working directly with the Ethiopian embassy and, through it, the emperor in producing the pamphlet. Francis Beaufort-Palmer, honorary secretary of the society for a time, recalled that the majority, who were also appalled at Italian atrocities in Ethiopia, 'wanted to do things in an orthodox way and go along with the Foreign Office.... Sylvia never wanted to wait, and never gave a damn.... She had no respect for authority.'[42] In this case, the authority was Professor Jevons and the Abyssinia Society; Sylvia's respect was for a higher authority—the emperor—who found her lack of patience an asset in publicly promoting his cause in England.

The final split left the Society to Jevons and his colleagues. Sylvia kept the paper. Beaufort-Palmer joined the emperor in fence-sitting. When Sylvia went to Brussels and Geneva, Beaufort-Palmer took over the paper in her absence, joining Corio, who was also left behind. The Ethiopian legation sent or phoned copy daily. Beaufort-Palmer believed Haile Sellassie was behind some of the news stories, but of course no one ever spoke directly to him. Nor did anyone check for accuracy with other papers or with the Foreign Office, and Sylvia could not afford to subscribe to a news service.

Throughout this period, Sylvia and Corio worked closely together. Or rather, as Beaufort-Palmer recalled, 'Corio worked for *her*'. While Sylvia was away, Corio and Beaufort-Palmer ran the paper and, in the process, became friends. At that time, Corio was 'stocky [with] just a fringe of white hair. He looked Italian, although he wasn't dark'. And he still spoke with an Italian accent. He once told Beaufort-Palmer about Clelia and the children but said he was bored with them. But of Sylvia, Beaufort-Palmer recalled, 'you couldn't be bored. She was a great character'. In her fifties and early sixties Sylvia continued her old habits of dress: she was dynamic, 'but she wasn't good looking ... it was all frightfully nondescript'. And Sylvia and Corio still had their dietary conflicts. Corio was a good cook, Sylvia was not ('a bit heavy on the soya sauce, but what can you expect from a vegetarian?') This sometimes bothered Corio: once, when he and Beaufort-Palmer went to lunch and Corio was asked what he would like the answer was immediate—'Steak. Miss Pankhurst is a vegetarian.'[43]

Family life had settled into a routine. Some of Sylvia's associates in the 1940s recalled the press release on the 'eugenic baby' so many years before, sometimes with tolerance if not approbation. Mrs Beaufort-Palmer thought the release was terrible ('People never think on a child's being born that they will become an adult') but her husband doubted that Sylvia would have permitted herself to have a baby by a traditional sort of man, it might have meant marriage and, 'I cannot imagine her married, too independent. . . . in an odd sort of way, Richard had a mother and a father. I don't know that you would call it normal—I mean, a vegetarian mother—but in a way they adored him'. But, 'Corio must have been an extraordinary man to stay', and 'Richard was devoted to his mother'.[44]

The Beaufort-Palmers remained in their country home and let the emperor use their town house, at 2 Rosalie Gardens, Kensington, as his office. Sylvia was always trying to get to the emperor through Beaufort-Palmer, whose own contacts were weak. She tried to get the emperor to the International Court at The Hague to appeal before the League of Justice for the restoration of Ethiopia's name and status. Dr Martin influenced the emperor, who sent for Sylvia, Beaufort-Palmer and Colonel Sandford, a former British farmer in Ethiopia and staunch supporter of the emperor in London. Haile Sellassie outlined his plan, but Sandford explained that it was impossible without Foreign Office consent, which was not forthcoming—the Foreign Office preferred to keep the emperor out of the limelight. Sylvia, according to Beaufort-Palmer, 'was absolutely furious'.[45]

One of Sylvia's habits was out of character for someone as energetic as she; she talked for hours on the phone. Beaufort-Palmer recalls an occasion when she rang him up on Ethiopian business. His doorbell rang. With no one else at home, he tried to excuse himself to answer the door. Finding it impossible to stop the torrent of words, he set down the phone, walked downstairs, opened the door, accepted a package, and went back to the phone: 'Sylvia was still going on—oblivious to any absence.' Others confirm her habit of talking endlessly about Ethiopia on the telephone; when she finished, no matter how long she had been talking, she rang off abruptly.[46] Another view of Sylvia at the height of her Ethiopian crusade comes from Mrs Tedros, a woman of mixed West Indian and English descent who was married to an Ethiopian waiter. Mrs Tedros became involved with Sylvia's demonstrations and helped with her bazaars. She found Sylvia 'a fantastic woman' and Corio a 'hardworking, very nice man who used to wait on her hand and foot. Whatever she said, he did.'[47]

Outsiders' views on a relationship reflect in many ways their own values and judgements rather than those of the parties involved. In this case, as in most other insights offered on the relationship between Corio and Sylvia, we have no picture of how they themselves saw the partnership. We know that Corio at one time contemplated leaving Sylvia, and we suspect that because of his strong attachment to his son he conquered his ambivalence. The couple had in common a mutual interest in anti-Fascism—although overlaid with Sylvia's devotion to the emperor and his country; and both loved Richard. If Corio was relegated to the background more than he might have wished, and forced into a subservient position, he may have chosen to accept the role because the options otherwise were worse. He was after all an unemployed illegal immigrant with no place to go, except to his daughter Roxanne from whom he seems to have become alienated.

When the war broke out, Emmanuel Abraham was a student in England. A Galla of humble origins, he had grown up in the outlying provinces of Ethiopia. His story is part of Ethiopia's development: even before he became emperor, *Ras* Tafari had begun a programme of limited education for the rural non-Amhara, and Emmanuel Abraham was one of the first to be brought to Addis Ababa to attend a missionary school. After six years of intense schooling, his education was curtailed by lack of higher education facilities in Ethiopia. The government sent him to England, where he became secretary to the legation under Dr Martin while still intending to further his education. Instead, he became increasingly involved in the legation. As Haile Sellassie's mistrust of Dr Martin mounted, Emmanuel Abraham's responsibilities increased, and he found himself in frequent contact with Sylvia, who telephoned the legation for news at least once a day.

Seated in his office in Addis Ababa in 1974, a few weeks after his release from prison under the military government, Emmanuel Abraham chuckled with amusement over anecdotes about the feminist propagandist who sought to save Ethiopia. He remembered Sylvia as 'very radical, a very militant person'. His major problem was controlling the news he passed on—'She published everything she got, so I had to be careful'. On one occasion, after Haile Sellassie's return to Ethiopia, there was some difficulty between the emperor and the British government, and news from Ethiopia was scarce. When news finally arrived, Emmanuel Abraham passed *part* of it to Sylvia, which she immediately published in the *New Times and Ethiopia News*. 'It upset the authorities in Ethiopia and upset the Foreign Office because the war was still on.' As a result, relations between Emmanuel Abraham and the Foreign Office became strained, and on future occasions he was circumspect in what he allowed Sylvia to know. She, however, was very impatient: hearing any snippet of information about Ethiopia, she would ring Emmanuel Abraham and press for confirmation.[48] Memories of visits to her West Dene house were especially amusing: 'Her house was so cluttered with books and periodicals you hardly had a place to sit, and no one gardened at all'.[49] At one point Corio got a horse and tethered it in the garden, presumably to crop the tall grass.[50] Emmanuel Abraham's career took him home after the war, later to Rome, and then back to England. Throughout the years he maintained his correspondence with Sylvia, and when she visited Ethiopia in 1944, he was among the group of old friends waiting to greet her.[51]

When Sylvia left the Abyssinia Society, she forfeited their financial help for the *New Times*. Other support, always somewhat mysterious, came from several sources. Paid subscriptions were never significant. She circulated the paper free of charge to people she believed should be kept informed on Ethiopia—Members of Parliament, people who wrote in response to her letters in the press, members of organizations to whom she had spoken in the last several years, and a number of women, including pacifists she had known in the early 1930s. At public meetings of any sort someone was on hand to sell copies of the *New Times and Ethiopia News*, and Sylvia began 'poster parades' in which at least two women were daily kept at Whitehall, wearing large placards and offering the paper for sale.[52] The Ethiopian bank, under instructions from the emperor, gave 'generous aid' which enabled her 'to make the paper bigger'.[53] Partly for that reason it became unnecessary to beg for funds as she had done for the *Workers' Dreadnought*. Other contributions came from Beaufort-Palmer, Nancy Cunard, Henry Harben, the Prudential heir, and other persons of wealth sympathetic to Ethiopia.

Submitted articles came from some of these financial contributors, from Bela Menczer, the Hungarian exile and, from time to time and in spite of other disagreements, from Professor Jevons. George Steer, who often wrote for *The Times*, was also published in the *New Times*, probably because copy was pirated from *The Times*. Sylvia kept her old habits of publishing anonymously, of taking whatever pleased her from other papers, and of writing endless impassioned editorials, all in support of Ethiopia and its emperor. Corio, still under a pseudonym, submitted mostly anti-Fascist, anti-Italian copy; and Richard appeared with an infrequent by-line, writing on, among other things, stamps from Ethiopia. An example of Sylvia's journalism was a headline in 1938: 'ETHIOPIA IS UNCONQUERED AND WILL REMAIN UNCONQUERED'.[54] On Italy: 'The facts we publish week by week are facts Rome wants to suppress.'[55] The *New Times and Ethiopia News*, she wrote, is 'read and quoted all over Africa, all over Europe . . . '.[56] There is some evidence that this claim was at least partially true, but, good propagandist that she was, it was in her interest to suggest the widest possible circulation. The paper was named the *New Times*, she said, because of its opposition to *The Times*, which Sylvia believed was tied to the government. She was not at first tied to any legal government, but she was as firmly tied to the Ethiopian government in exile as any house organ could be.

When Italy finally declared war on England on 10 June 1940, Richard recalled: 'Our salvation was getting Italy in. We were happy.'[57] The columns of the *New Times and Ethiopia News* had barely reflected the fact that Britain was at war, but now she stressed what British participation meant to Ethiopia. The appearance of German bombers over London, however, brought Sylvia a new concern: even before the battle of Britain in September 1940, she thought of sending Richard to Canada for safety. But Emmeline Pethick-Lawrence commented, 'I do not even know whether you and Richard could live in any happiness apart from each other. . . . You and Richard can never be parted in the inner and spiritual reality. Your lives are mentally, morally, and spiritually interwoven. My conviction adds *forever*'.[58] Richard stayed in London, but during the air raids 'the family often spent night after night in the two tiny Anderson shelters dug in the garden'. His mother, in the interest of the war, also ceased being a vegetarian.[59]

Sylvia did not exactly ignore the war, but the soldiers marching to their deaths in Europe and North Africa were justified because Ethiopia would be saved for its emperor. Her banner headlines reflected this single-minded point of view with her usual adulation of Haile Sellassie. Her role as propagandist for Ethiopia was dominant, and she paid scant attention to the devastation on her own doorstep, including the massive bombings of the East End. The *New Times* said nothing about Pearl Harbour or America's entry into the war.[60] The emperor was back in Ethiopia, and his news was her only news.

Because of Sylvia's inability to suppress dangerous information, Emmanuel Abraham waited a month after the emperor left for Khartoum before he told her that Haile Sellassie had joined the Ethiopian patriots and that, with the support of British forces, he was leading an army against the Italian aggressors. Banner headlines then proclaimed the emperor's arrival in Khartoum. When Haile Sellassie returned to Addis Ababa on 5 May 1941, five years after it fell to the Italians, Sylvia rejoiced with such exuberance one might have supposed the war was over.[61] But her paper also carried such esoteric items as a history of Fascism[62] and several versions of Ethiopian history over the years. She took occasional swipes at statesmen with whom she did not agree, including the American Ambassador, Joseph P. Kennedy, who opposed aid to Britain early in the war.[63]

In 1941 the advisory board of the *New Times and Ethiopia News* consisted of Isabel Fry (a wealthy Quaker), Nancy Cunard, A. Eidenschenk-Patin (general secretary of the International League of Mothers and Educators), Dr Hugenholtz of Holland, Rosika Schwimmer (the feminist-pacifist Hungarian) and three lesser known men, including the president of the Union of the Young People's Evangelical Association of Bulgaria.[64] Sylvia's talents for bringing together disparate people for a common cause—even though they rarely stayed together for long—is clear. It is inconceivable that her 'advisory board' ever did more than lend their names. Richard recalled only one editorial meeting: 'She proceeded to observe that the paper, having always urged the need to resist the aggressors, would of course be whole-hearted in supporting the Allied cause, but would, at the same time, continue its opposition to Mussolini, who at that stage had entered the conflict.'[65] Then, 'my father assented without discussion, and the "editorial meeting" ended as abruptly as it had begun.'[66]

Some stories in the *New Times and Ethiopia News* have their light side in retrospect. In Churchill's first year as Prime Minister, Sylvia thought the 'sincerity of his voice' would qualify him to be 'an admirable Minister of Information'.[67] She spent much time and effort getting the BBC to play the Ethiopian national anthem at its daily conclusion, along with those of other Allies. But such recognition of equality was important; it was still feared that the British colonial pattern might prevail, and the emperor would return to office as a puppet of Britain, as opposed to Italy. Sylvia had a rare occasion to praise the government when Anthony Eden announced that the British government supported the independence of Ethiopia and the emperor as its ruler.[68]

On the other hand, when Margery Perham, the noted authority on colonial government in Africa, was quoted as saying that Haile Sellassie would not be able to control Ethiopia even if he were restored, Sylvia counterattacked vociferously, pointing out that Perham 'has never stepped foot in Ethiopia'[69]—neither, for that matter, had Sylvia. And indeed, a majority of patriots who still fought Italy after the emperor fled agreed that Haile Sellassie should not be allowed to return to the throne. He and the army had kept the empire together before 1935, but his political manoeuvres were legendary and resented. His departure had made it easy for some dissident factions to support the Italians. The patriots who suffered the consequences never forgave him for leaving. Ethiopian internal politics were far more complex than Sylvia imagined.

In fact, the reconquest was not as one-sided as Sylvia indicated in her paper. She believed that all of Ethiopia rose in a chorus to greet him and to give support to the British Commonwealth troops accompanying him. What happened was that some turncoats, such as *Ras* Seyum of Tigre, deserted the Italians he had joined and with whom he had become disillusioned, sending word to the emperor that he would use his forces to help with the invasion. *Ras* Seyum was fully aware of the British presence and its re-enforcements in Sudan; in addition, he was the father of Asfaw Wossen's wife and would have wanted to insure his future in a restoration government. Another traitor to Haile Sellassie, *Ras* Haylu, turned his back on the Italians when the British paid him 300,000 Maria Theresa dollars (the currency of pre-war Ethiopia).[70]

Some played for time, weighing the advance of British and Ethiopian patriot troops before they joined forces with the emperor. The Italians had appointed new *rases* whose loyalties were tied solely to their fortunes and there was no glory to be had in realigning themselves with Haile Sellassie. Unfortunately for the occupiers, they offered too little too late, but they did have their defenders among Ethiopian dissidents. Sylvia was not informed of any internal conflicts. As Emmanuel Abraham made clear, news fed to her was closely censored and it was always presented to put the best light on the emperor—a fact that never seemed to have occurred to her.

In 1948 Sylvia once again took on Margery Perham in the *New Times* with a hostile, at times irrational, review of her *The Government of Ethiopia*. So intense was Sylvia's resentment that she continued her review in successive issues and referred critically to Perham in later months. Perham's book was in fact a scholarly effort at an unbiased picture of the country, its recent history, its internal schisms, and its political and constitutional problems. Perham's Preface, however, was the real source of Sylvia's anger. Perham wrote, among other things:[71]

> I am aware that I have been influenced by a desire to correct the distorted picture of this country which it has been the object of some propaganda to build up in Britain. I see in this illusory picture a danger to the formation of sound policy. But for this it would not be necessary to point out at intervals that Ethiopia is not to be confused with Utopia . . .

It was precisely Sylvia and the *New Times*, plus a few others less vocal in the same opinion, that Perham had in mind. Sylvia's portrayal of a benevolent king's benign rule over a worshipful population was a serious concern to anyone who believed in supplanting myth with fact. By that time Sylvia had visited Ethiopia, albeit briefly, and could more justly criticize Perhams's lack of first-hand knowledge, 'It is noticeable that people who have made but a short visit to a country, or have simply read of it from a distance, are, in general, readier to write a book about it than those who have lived there for a long period.'[72] In her Preface, Perham warned that although she had not lived in Ethiopia, she had consulted a wide variety of sources and authorities, checking one against the other in the light of twenty years' experience as a scholar of Africa.[73]

Sylvia's thoughts on the government of Ethiopia seemed blindly influenced by her employer, the emperor and members of the legation. In 1942, for instance, Sylvia defended the first Ethiopian constitution of 1930 as 'the gift of the Emperor, granted of his own free will without agitation' and, she argued, it 'did have something to do with running the country'.[74] The 1955 constitution, which called for an elected Lower

House and an appointed Upper House was more form than substance. Haile Sellassie appointed the Upper House, but all power over the state purse and foreign affairs remained firmly in his own hands. John H. Spencer was deeply involved in the creation of the 1955 constitution. In the preliminary stages of producing a document that would confirm a constitutional monarchy, the emperor and his assistants indicated they supported his efforts. On completion, however, the emperor was far from happy with the results. In the final analysis, Spencer realized Haile Sellassie saw the revised constitution 'as a screen behind which conservative positions could become entrenched'.[75] Again, Sylvia, in London, with no knowledge of political manoeuvrings in Addis Ababa, hailed the 'new, democratic constitution' as another example of modernization. Sellassie's critics in Britain knew that this new imperial legislation was a facade.

But in August 1942, with the British still in Ethiopia and Haile Sellassie not yet back in control, Sylvia wrote complaining that she was not getting enough news for her paper. The emperor's private secretary responded on behalf of His Imperial Majesty promising news would be forthcoming and adding that 'His Majesty was also very pleased to hear that you immediately challenged the misleading statements about Ethiopia which appeared in the British press.'[76] The misrepresentations in question were the suggestions that Haile Sellassie was not running his country—that peace was kept by the British, who were there in occupation. There were discordant notes in Ethiopia about which Sylvia was ignorant or, if she read about them in the British papers, she dismissed as mere propaganda for Britain's colonial intentions. Shortly after Haile Sellassie was restored to his throne, an area in south-east Tigre revolted, and it was only with the aid of British troops that the emperor was able to restore power.[77] Haile Sellassie kept news of such incidents from Sylvia, while encouraging her reaction to published accounts unfavourable to Ethiopia.

Sylvia also ran an Ethiopian information office, first out of her home in West Dene, later from quarters in London, modelled on the Russian Peoples' Information Bureau. It produced and sold 'information' pamphlets about Ethiopia. She also organized and served as honorary secretary of the International Ethiopian Council for Study and Report, mainly run from home, but with some meetings at the House of Commons. The council's chairman was Peter Freeman, a pro-Ethiopian Member of Parliament, who often raised questions in the House, some of which were drafted in the Ethiopian embassy, submitted to Sylvia, and then passed on to Freeman. He was a true friend of Ethiopia, but, like many people Sylvia knew over the years, he had a naive trust in her dedication and her sources.[78]

Sylvia used the Council as a base from which to write letters to Members of Parliament, government ministers (mostly the Foreign

Office) and international leaders like Franklin Roosevelt in the United States, Josep Tito in Yugoslavia and, after 1945, the Secretary-General and members of the Security Council of the United Nations. The time and energy spent in writing letters to public officials and to the press (her letters to the editor probably ran into the hundreds each year) must have taxed her, but she found strength to produce a weekly paper with her own editorials, attend meetings on Ethiopian affairs, write books, histories which required at least minimal research, talk to supporters at length on the phone, run an office with a staff in her home, spend some time with Richard, and, in the late 1930s, after the war began in Europe, spend time with the Women's War Emergency Council. Fo a woman in late middle-age, Sylvia was indefatigable. Her output hardly altered with the passage of time—only her causes changed.

In the circumstances, it may be expected and even excused if she often overestimated the extent of her influence. On 1 May 1943, with a curious forgetfulness of other May Days in her political past, she printed a glowing description of the way Ethiopian villagers carried copies of the *New Times and Ethiopia News* in the folds of their garments. This was another of her periodic lapses from reality: imagining as she did that illiterate peasants (as virtually all Ethiopians were, other than the priesthood, who would not of course be literate in English) could be reading her paper: such was the nature of her imagined Ethiopian idyll.

In 1946, on the tenth anniversary of first publication of the *New Times*, Sylvia reached into her store of supporters soliciting high praise for her paper, which she used as front page copy.[79] She also had her critics. Brendan Bracken, formerly Minister of Information, had felt called on to issue a public complaint in 1944.[80] Even earlier, Foreign Office personnel in Addis Ababa had occasion to question the image of Britain Sylvia was trying to foster in Ethiopian circles. Some of Sylvia's articles claiming British exploitation of Ethiopia were finding their way into that British-occupied country to the embarrassment of the occupiers. And indeed, many Ethiopians even today look back on the British occupation as somewhat less benign than the Italian once the first violence had subsided.

C. G. H. Gill of the British Legation in Addis Ababa was warmly exercised at the 'news' printed in her paper. With regard to an especially offensive despatch from the *New Times* he said, 'We shall be delighted if you will rub it with a large handful of salt into Miss Pankhurst's backside. It might help her to sit in the editorial chair with more uprightness.'[81] His Foreign Office superiors answered with a combination of moderation and realism—'Miss Pankhurst is quite incorrigible on the subject and I don't think any direct communication to her would do any good'.[82] Here again the Foreign Office treated Sylvia as a wilful child with whom communication was impossible—as indeed it could be. Sylvia's history of irrationality in any cause with which she was associated often worked against her. The Foreign Office had little choice but to contend with her and her paper as best they could. This they did in the years to come as she continued—indeed enlarged—her crusade on behalf of Ethiopia.

12
Radical Propagandist

When the struggle for Eritrean independence and federation with the motherland occurred, Miss Pankhurst worked unremittingly until the day when Eritrea joined Ethiopia in freedom.... We must remember that she served Ethiopia in the country's darkest hour.... Therefore Ethiopia's friend, the great Englishwoman...should be called a true Ethiopian patriot.
—*Ras* Andargatchew Massai, quoted in *Ethiopia Observer*,
5 January 1946

Sylvia's growing importance as a propagandist for Ethiopia left her with an exaggerated view of her importance in Britain. She became an imagined and self-appointed advisor on Ethiopian affairs to Winston Churchill, and to Anthony Eden in the Foreign Office. She favoured Churchill, whom she came to believe was acting on her advice. His secretary, at least, responded dutifully to her letters. The stream began in 1936; she wrote to Churchill that Ethiopia needed a loan from Britain to buy aeroplanes. Churchill, in turn, wrote to the Foreign Office and learned that the emperor had not requested any such loan.[1] In 1940, after Churchill became prime minister, she thanked him personally for the decision to recognize Abyssinia as an ally.[2] A few months later, she wrote about the resistance movement in Ethiopia, claiming that it was 'effectively unified'.[3] In May 1941, she launched her campaign to call the country Ethiopia, following the emperor's preference, instead of Abyssinia, instructing Churchill to see that the change was made in government usage.[4] In June she wrote thanking him and continuing with advice about Ethiopia's future, including plans for independence.[5] In July she sent a booklet published in Addis Ababa to celebrate the country's liberation from Fascism. She suggested it 'should be circulated in the press and also broadcast'.[6] In August she wrote a six-page letter saying in part: 'I venture to hope arrangements are being made to remove all Italians from Ethiopia at the earliest possible moment.'[7] In Addis Ababa Haile Sellassie was by now simultaneously assuring the Italian settlers that they could live in harmony together with the Ethiopian people.

In September, Sylvia dispatched another long letter reporting on recent events in Ethiopia. She noted: 'You will be delighted to learn ... that the Emperor and his government have abolished by decree the legal status of slavery'—when slavery had been abolished *de jure*, if not *de facto*—and she reminded Churchill that Ethiopia expected immediate independence.[8] Later in September she chided him for his failure to follow through her earlier instruction that Ethiopia should be invited to all Allied conferences. Even after Mr Eden's assurances that this would be the case, 'another conference had gone by and Ethiopia was again absent'.[9] In October she prodded Churchill to restore diplomatic relations with Ethiopia, noting that a graduate of Yale was now Foreign Minister in Addis Ababa.[10]

In December Sylvia wrote a stronger letter, copied to Eden, warning Churchill that he would 'be in trouble when the facts are known'. If nothing were done, she herself would reveal Britain's intentions to 'maintain all Ethiopian people permanently in a subordinate position to destroy the only remaining independent African state'.[11] A week later, another veiled threat on the same topic arrived at 10 Downing Street: 'His Majesty's government may not be able to carry this policy through for the moment, but if so, serious trouble will undoubtedly result.'[12]

In January 1942, Sylvia shot off a five-page directive outlining what Churchill should say in a forthcoming speech on Ethiopia. But in Feruary, of the systematic defeat in North Africa, she wrote apologetically: 'I regret to approach you in the grave anxieties of the present time. My desire in so doing is to assist in the war effort on the present emergency . . . '—and so on for another four pages to the punch-line that Britain might ease its military burden by accepting the 'help offered us by Ethiopia'.[13] But the military and naval crisis was not serious enough to deflect her concern about the disposition of Italian property in Ethiopia,[14] and she enclosed press cuttings from the *New Times and Ethiopia News* as an accurate assessment of the folly of 'respecting Italian properties'.[15] She addressed Churchill several times on matters of a more practical nature. When Churchill announced 'the list of the United Nations' in the summer of 1942, Sylvia lashed out at him for failing to mention Ethiopia and Albania: 'It is the colour bar, or is it the desire to appease Italy . . . Just these two—is it not strange?'[16]

Sylvia's only success in her many communications with Churchill came when the BBC included the Ethiopian national anthem in its closing minutes along with those of other Allied anthems. She triumphantly noted this success in the *New Times and Ethiopia News*. Sylvia's elation on the question of the anthem did not necessarily reflect the views of the British public at large. Journalist Keith Irvine remembered, 'as the war went from bad to worse, and Hitler entered more and more countries, the list of anthems got longer and longer until it was most top-heavy. They finally shortened the anthems to just a few bars of each. But the whole thing had overtones of musical comedy.'

Anthony Eden too received his share of scolding, but Sylvia preferred to go directly to the top and often sent him copies only. On Ethiopian independence, however, she ensured that the Foreign Office was fully informed of the emperor's desire to get on with governing his country, incidentally revealing a total ignorance of the actual complications of re-establishing centralized power in an African kingdom.

The emperor himself was acting on a larger stage on the matter of Britain's intentions towards his country. Soon after his return he sent a series of letters and telegrams to Franklin D. Roosevelt in which he stressed that Ethiopia and America were allies, thereby re-emphasizing himself as leader of an independent country. He declared war on Italy, Germany and Japan, re-enforcing the notion of independence, if not the fact. In 1943 he sent an emissary to the White House for a personal interview with Roosevelt.

There was genuine fear within Ethiopia that Britain intended staying on as a colonial presence. The Anglo-Ethiopian Agreement of 1942 recognized Ethiopia as an independent state, but also forced the emperor to submit to a series of humiliating measures; most importantly, he could not make any imperial appointments without British consent, and all major appointments had to be British subjects. A further Military Convention between the two countries placed Addis Ababa and all major cities under the authority of British police forces. It was, of course, in the emperor's interest to keep Sylvia well informed of these circumstances so that she would continue whipping up sentiment against them.

Sylvia had been sending copies of the *New Times and Ethiopia News*, levelling accusations of Britain's colonial intentions, to the American Secretary of State as well as to the White House. She also wrote to Eleanor Roosevelt, who in turn, passed on Sylvia's letters to her husband. Roosevelt, unlike his successors, was staunchly opposed to colonialism. He and Sumner Welles both suspected British colonial motives in Ethiopia. While Sylvia's correspondence did no more than remind him of Ethiopian concerns when he was occupied with the larger war effort, he sent a note to Welles asking him to look into her charges of British intentions permanently to colonize the African nation. Welles responded that 'there have been various indications that the British Government intended to seize the present opportunity for establishing what would be tantamount to a protectorate over Abyssinia'. He requested that Roosevelt notify Britain of America's policy 'with regard to the first victim of Axis aggression' and suggested that a strong letter of support be forwarded to Ethiopia, with a copy to Eden at the Foreign Office.[17] Here at last, Sylvia played a successful, if minor role, in bringing pressure on the British government.

Sylvia frequently wrote to Eden about the Italian properties; he answered with the ambiguous approach the Foreign Office had already decided on: 'His Majesty's Government had no intention of interfering

Sylvia Pankhurst in front of her
West Dene home in the 1940s

Sylvia Pankhurst at her
bookstacks in West Dene,
during the early years of
NTEN *c.* 1940–2

with actions of future Ethiopian governments'.[18] Eden was also a favourite target on the issue of slavery. A well-publicized report on slavery in Ethiopia suggested that, after the emperor's return, bondage had been legalized, reversing its abolition in the 1920s. Sylvia wrote to Eden that the report was full of unfounded allegations, and she insisted that it be withdrawn from circulation.[19] In 1941, when Eden told Parliament of the government's intention to move towards an independent Ethiopia, the Abyssinia Society sent a message of gratitude. Sylvia waded in with a letter to the Manchester *Guardian* complaining that the promised independence was not immediate and that 'other rights were not made as clear as they should have been'.[20]

Sylvia was so persistent that the Foreign Office had a case file entitled 'How to Answer Letters from Miss Sylvia Pankhurst'. It was easier to send no response at all, or, when Churchill's office intervened, to send a brief, noncommittal statement. One Foreign Office official complained: 'Miss Pankhurst is quite irrepressible: there is no satisfying her. . . . We really cannot be expected to provide her with refutations— which in any case she will not believe—of every rumour'.[21] The Foreign Office knew that she was being fed stories from the Ethiopian Legation, and printed them without verification. One civil servant wrote in exasperation: 'I do not know to what extent this unbalanced and fanatical lady is politically important. . . . I would prefer that we not get involved in an exchange of correspondence with her.' His fear was that Foreign Office statements would find their way into print out of context in the *New Times and Ethiopia News*.[22] Simply through her nuisance quality Sylvia did bring pressure to bear on Foreign Office officials. In publicizing their intentions (whether confirmed or not), she exposed the duplicity toward Ethiopia which characterized contemporary British policy.

In 1943, one Member of Parliament demanded that the Foreign Office shut down Sylvia's newspaper as a security risk. The government decided, however, that 'Miss Pankhurst and her paper have long been thorns in our side . . .', but that to close the paper down 'might have repercussions; the circulation is small and she might do more harm unchained than as it was'.[23] Her campaign had some effect: even in provoking negative responses she was calling attention to Ethiopia.

Early in her Ethiopian campaign Sylvia was well regarded by West African nationalists within their home countries. Her paper provided the most frequent, although often inaccurate, accounts of the Italo-Ethiopian conflict that were available. Youth League members read and discussed the *New Times and Ethiopia News* and frequently reprinted articles in the Youth League newspaper. Because of Sylvia's strong identification with Ethiopia and her coverage of the patriots' guerrilla warfare, British influence in Sierra Leone eventually forced a ban on the *New Times* as 'undesirable literature'. Sylvia raised a storm of protest, but the Colonial Office was worried about discontent in the African colonies and held its position.[24]

Although she depended most heavily on the Ethiopian government, Sylvia had other sources of information. One of these was Hiwot Hidaru, a civil servant working for the British during the war years and based mostly in Khartoum. He was in touch with the patriots who crossed back and forth between Sudan and Ethiopia, and was in an ideal position to gather information about the underground. For a time he himself crossed the border and joined the Ethiopian patriots fighting near Gondar. In 1975 Hiwot Hidaru published one of the first patriot books of the Ethiopian war, describing his experiences as a guerrilla. The volume was published only in Amharic and therefore not widely read or distributed outside Ethiopia, but it included references to Sylvia, with whom he corresponded both as a civil servant and later during his brief career as a patriot fighting the Italians. The connection began in 1938, when Hiwot Hidaru read of Sylvia's activities in London and wrote to her about his cousin, then a refugee interned in Kenya: Hiwot Hidaru hoped to have him freed. Sylvia wrote to friendly Members of Parliament on his behalf and secured his release.[25] Hiwot became a regular correspondent, sending any news he obtained through hearsay or observation. When, in 1941, it appeared that Sylvia would lose her Djibouti correspondent, she wrote to Hiwot Hidaru imploring him to send more news, and she included money for postage: 'Though we are terribly short of means to bring the paper out.... facts must be known. That is the way to keep the cause alive and secure redress for the wrong.'[26]

As a former patriot, Hiwot Hidaru was one of the few Ethiopians who could, and did, criticize Haile Sellassie in the post-war years and escape retribution. He was also among a group of educated Ethiopians who were dismayed at the behaviour of the British occupation forces in Ethiopia. Although he never gave Sylvia news of the occupation—she published anonymously the accounts she did receive—he recalled the discrimination against Ethiopians, especially by the South African forces, and the sexual harassment—including rape—of married women by the allegedly friendly occupying force. As the emperor reassumed his power, began to appoint ministers and govern the country, Hiwot Hidaru approached several ministries with complaints about this misconduct. Although not long in Ethiopia under Italian rule, he was in and out of Gondar and knew many who stayed. His is one of several Ethiopian opinions that the Italians, whatever their faults, were no worse than the British who followed them.[27]

What men like Hiwot Hidaru failed to recognize was that the emperor could not control the British forces. The Anglo-Ethiopian Agreement of 1942 placed Ethiopia firmly under British rule.[28] The second agreement, made in 1944, granted freedom to most of Ethiopia, with Britain still retaining all of the Ogaden including the Reserved Area and the Haud. These two regions were kept back specifically because they had never been securely under Ethiopian control and their ultimate future would have to be a part of a broader decolonization of the Horn of Africa comprising Eritrea, and French, British and Italian Somaliland. Gradually, by further agreements, Britain withdrew from the country, but Hiwot Hidaru—like most Ethiopian citizens—was kept in the dark about foreign policy. Hiwot Hidaru, and many of the élite in pre-war Ethiopia, had looked on Haile Sellassie as 'my second Christ'. After the war, and especially during the years of British occupation, as Hiwot Hidaru observed: 'He cared for nothing: cared only for his crown'.

Other of Sylvia's correspondents in Ethiopia were less reliable and perceptive. Ali Baig, who covered North-West Ethiopia, was described by the Foreign Office as 'originally a letter writer, pleader, and general hanger on and busy body . . . at Harar'. During the Italo-Ethiopian War, however, 'he had the time of his life retailing sensational and mostly quite fictitious news to various Ethiopian news agencies. . . . most of his customers saw through him fairly soon, but he is still a mainstay in the *New Times* of which Miss Sylvia Pankhurst is the editor.'[29]

It was during negotiations for the Anglo-Ethiopian agreement of 1944 that Sylvia made her first trip to the country whose cause had been her overriding concern for nine years. Accepting an imperial invitation, Sylvia asked permission to take Richard, then seventeen, but the Foreign Office refused him a visa. Her own problems with the Foreign Office rose to haunt her, and she too barely secured a visa; it was only on the contrived pretext of looking for a hospital site in connection with a fund she administered that permission was finally granted. Soon after her departure, Lord Vansittart wrote to the Foreign Secretary saying that he had received numbers of indignant complaints 'inquiring why Miss Sylvia Pankhurst was given a visa' for Ethiopia 'when infinitely more deserving people have not been able to do so. Indeed Miss Pankhurst seems to have done a great deal of mischief out there . . . Who is responsible?' The Foreign Office replied that, alas, she went out 'not in her personal capacity' but at the invitation of the Emperor.[30]

Leaving Corio and Richard to run the paper, Sylvia set off in October by train, ship and plane—her first experience of flying—for Ethiopia. She stopped briefly in Asmara, in Eritrea, where British forces were in occupation, and henceforth the fate of that former Italian colony became one of her major concerns. Even then, she was lobbying vigorously in England for the reunion of Eritrea and Ethiopia. There she toured schools, accompanied by a British educational officer. She met and was entertained by local officials and spent a considerable time questioning various British officials about British policy. She encountered difficulties with a 'Dr Ullendorff [sic], a very young Jew from Palestine, who is Editor of the *Eritrean Weekly News*', the first weekly paper in Eritrea published in Tigrinya, the local language.[31] Someone, perhaps Ullendorff, criticized the *New Times and Ethiopia News*, suggesting that it was biased in its coverage of Ethiopia. Sylvia, of course, denied the charge and switched the conversation to her cause of the moment—unification of Eritrea and Ethiopia. 'I was', she wrote, 'surprised to find the Editor of the *Eritrean Weekly News*, himself a member of a Semitic people . . . opposed to this solution and desired Eritrea to be placed under a European government, preferably British . . . he is in fact, more pro-Britain than the British, except as regards Palestine . . .'[32]

Sylvia commented that she had not yet had the opportunity to study the *Eritrean Weekly News*, but promised that she would do so at the first opportunity. In fact, Sylvia could not read Tigrinya, and any reading she did was through a translator. Ullendorff eventually learned of Sylvia's criticism, including a statement that he did not understand Tigrinya. As a linguist whose speciality included Tigrinya, he was appreciably upset and he called for an apology in *The Times*. Ullendorff went on to become one of the most distinguished British Ethiopian scholars, with a Chair in Linguistics at the School of African and Oriental Studies at London University. Over the years Sylvia continued to level attacks at Ullendorff's work, though he remained publicly silent through respect of her dedication to Ethiopia.[33]

One of Sylvia's journalistic difficulties was her inability to understand any local languages, including Amharic, the official language of the Ethiopian government. The interpretations she relied on were those her translator chose to clarify. In Eritrea she met numbers of carefully selected people who supported unification. The few dissenters she encountered, again with a translator, heard her lecture on the benefits of unification and promised their support under certain conditions. The conditions were not defined.[34] As might be supposed, British officials disliked her meddling in what they regarded as their affairs. Her Eritrean visit was reported to the Foreign Office thus:[35]

> Miss Pankhurst clearly set out on her journey with her mind already made up. She was going to visit a citadel of freedom populated by brave, virtuous and wholly admirable defenders who were beset by the machinations of European imperialists. She began briskly in Eritrea by referring to all non-European inhabitants as Ethiopian . . . her most ungracious act—and she frequently lapses through her zeal into bad manners—was in addressing uninvited an audience of English-speaking Eritreans at a Ministry of Information lecture, when she suggested that the methods employed in the women's suffrage movement to attain their ends might usefully be emulated by other political movements.

While the Foreign Office statements reflected the official—and male—

view of Sylvia, Rebecca West, the feminist writer and journalist, and some suffragettes also found her 'off-handed and bad mannered'; her greatest problem seemed to be in dealing with people of her own cultural and class background, when she exhibited arrogance and intolerance.

Sylvia finally landed in Addis Ababa and was met at the airport by the emperor's private secretary. The monarch assigned her a car and chauffeur to take her to a villa in the former Italian compound, which the emperor made available to her for the duration of the stay. Her exhilaration was boundless:[36]

> I could hardly believe it—I was in Addis Ababa, seen for the first time: strange yet familiar . . . Ethiopian people in their traditional dress, with their donkeys and mules . . . straw umbrellas. . . . I was enchanted and bewildered; I seem to be living in a dream.

The officials of the British Foreign Office perceived her arrival otherwise: 'Miss Pankhurst's sense of her own importance . . . shelters inadequately behind an affectation of modesty.'[37] After her ride in the countryside, which was covered by eucalyptus trees, maskal daisies in bloom, and other lush, semi-tropical plants, Sylvia recorded that 'it all seemed like a dreamland'.[38]

Her first visit to this 'dreamland' was sufficient to make even the most staunch republican seek conversion. At the palace she had an audience with Haile Sellassie and the empress: 'I entered the room where you have so often seen photographs of the Emperor sitting . . . like a dream I walked toward them . . . they were so kind, so real and friendly, they almost waked me . . . '[39] At a dinner party some nights later, she sat at the head table with the royal family. This was a signal honour in Ethiopia where, until the war, the emperor was regarded as a demi-god. The occasion was to celebrate the Anglo-Ethiopian treaty (which she had opposed). Later, she attended a private dinner with the royal family, the prime minister and other Ethiopian officials, during which she had the opportunity to 'discuss all matters of importance'[40] —mostly her propaganda campaign in England.

But there was also the memorial hospital Sylvia was sponsoring in memory of Princess Tsähay, who had died after returning to Ethiopia. This was the official reason for her visit, although it appeared secondary to her desire to meet Haile Sellassie in person and ascertain what else might be achieved in England as well as discuss continued support for her paper. So obvious to his Imperial Majesty was Sylvia's blind loyalty that Sellassie had confidence that any small sums sent to her were more than well spent. First, there was the question of Eritrea. With its outlet to the sea, the colony was important to Ethiopia, and the emperor used every avenue to achieve unification or, more accurately, an Ethiopian takeover. With Sylvia in England, circulating her

Sylvia Pankhurst wearing the Order of Sheba and Patriot Medal

paper worldwide, Sellassie had a propaganda vehicle which no small country could equal. Her loyalty and her energy were so wrapped up in him and his country that she felt no sacrifice was too great for the achievement of his goals. At first her impulse had been voluntary, but now she received strong encouragement from Addis Ababa.

Grateful for her achievements in Ethiopia's interests, and in keeping with his habit of rewarding supporters, Haile Sellassie awarded Sylvia the Order of Sheba, an extremely high honour for a commoner. The Order had been established by His Imperial Majesty as a way of paying tribute to foreign queens. At the British embassy there was some consternation because the emperor did not observe protocol, but simply called Sylvia forward and decorated her during a major ceremony. She received, in addition, a Patriot's Medal with Five Palms—one for each year of the war with Italy.[41] The Foreign Office queried whether Sylvia should be allowed to retain her awards after this breach of protocol. After stalling for some time, Eden's secretary advised that she should keep her medals. But Sylvia had already—and to the irritation of the Foreign Office—gone directly to the press and announced the honours.[42]

She spent Christmas Eve 1944 with Princess Tänagnä Warq and her family at a lengthy Ethiopian Orthodox Church service. It was the custom to fast until after the service, so Sylvia, now an ageing woman, joined the family at a 4 a.m. feast before retiring to her villa. On Christmas Day she accompanied the emperor as he dispensed gifts to the many children who came traditionally for the occasion, and had another audience with the royal family. 'Christmas in fairyland with Prince Charming' was the way Sylvia described the experience in the *New Times and Ethiopia News*.[43]

Dr Martin, now back in Ethiopia, had bought some land and was running a corn mill: Sylvia visited her old friend at his home, and ate the traditional *injera* (bread) and *wat* (a very peppery stew). Just as she was leaving, a group of peasants came to grind their corn. Her account of the peasants' relationship with Dr Martin indicate a *volte-face* in her political ideology: the peasants, 'one by one, came forward' to Dr Martin, where, in the most traditional Ethiopian form of peon greeting lord, they 'kissed his feet . . . he bent and laid his hand on each one's head in an affectionate deprecating way'.[44] Sylvia found herself carried away with the ritual of subservience.

Her travels included a trip to Dire Dawa and Harar, in the eastern highlands where the emperor had once been provincial governor. This was part of the territory disputed with Somalia for it was occupied largely by ethnic Somalis. Ethiopia claimed it as part of its ancient Christian kingdom. The emperor hoped to acquire all of Somalia and bring an end to Greater Somaliland agitation, which had support in official British circles. Sylvia naturally supported him in this territorial quest, as she also supported his designs on Eritrea. A Foreign Office report described some of her activties in Jigjiga, a border town she visited on the same trip. She had informed the British Legation that she was going to the disputed areas and she told the Somalis with whom she spoke that British administration of the Reserved Areas ought to cease. The report concluded: 'In a brief stopover she collected all the stones and general information possible which could be turned into sticks with which to beat His Majesty's Government. Her conduct even disgusted the Ethiopians'.[46] Ethiopians working with British officials would of course have been constrained to speak out against her, and it seems unlikely that Moslem Somali leaders regarded her statements as reflective of any government—women did not speak officially (or unofficially) on geopolitical matters.

Unaware that her actions were being reported to London, Sylvia had the *New Times* forward to the Foreign Office several articles damning British policies in the Ogaden, adding fuel to the flames. Rather than respond openly, the Foreign Office denied her 'the opportunities for publicity which she craves' and continued receiving information on her from Ethiopia. She had a problem with her chauffeur, who, she complained, was always late. (The car later broke down, provoking further complaints to British officials.) She did not see as much of the emperor as she hoped, because he was occupied in meetings with British officials negotiating the second Anglo-Ethiopian agreement. Furthermore, she became violently ill, took incompatible medicines, deserted her British doctor for a Czech (whom she greeted with a zesty, if anti-British, 'Oh, you are not a colonizer').[47] None of these incidents appeared in the columns of the *New Times*.[48]

The Foreign Office in London was also deluged with letters criticizing Sylvia's anti-British reports from Ethiopia in the *New Times*. These were a source of embarrassment even to Ethiopians who knew of them. One wrote to the Foreign Office that 'Her news of Ethiopia is mostly [sic] incorrect and her comments and criticisms conveying relations between Ethiopia and Great Britain are unjust and unfounded.'[49] Members of Parliament and officials in the Foreign Office denounced her statements as 'half-truths, almost wholly (and apparently), deliberately misleading'. When she denounced the Anglo-Ethiopian agreement demands came for Ernest Bevin, the Labour Foreign Secretary, to discipline her newspaper. But the Foreign Office held to its policy of benign neglect, as expressed to a concerned Member of Parliament:[50]

> The militant Miss Pankhurst has been defending for years what she believed to be the Ethiopian cause. Her paper . . . has negligible circulation and is subsidized by the Emperor. Her constant harassing of her country consequently lost Ethiopia friends here and Miss Pankhurst is anathema to the Abyssinia Society.

On Sylvia's return to England early in 1945, she at once sent Bevin copies of two reports of her trip and raised the issue of British mal-administration in Eritrea and the Reserved Areas.[51] Sylvia had become critical of Churchill even before he left office in 1945, believing that he was responsible for the continued British presence in Eritrea and the disputed areas. Therefore, when Labour won the general election in 1945, she wrote to Bevin of her relief that he was now Foreign Secretary: 'This is a very critical hour and I for one am devoutly thankful that the late government has been removed.' Shortly after her congratulatory note, Sylvia wrote to Bevin suggesting that he send a commission of three Labour Members of Parliament to Ethiopia, with herself as secretary, to investigate the charges against Britain that she carried in the *New Times*. It was her belief that Ethiopians would not reveal their feelings to anyone, but that they would speak freely to her. Someone in the Foreign Office filed her letter with the remark that one trip to Ethiopia was quite enough for Sylvia Pankhurst.[52] Subsequently Sylvia wrote repeatedly to Clement Attlee, the Prime Minister, often including petitions on behalf of Ethiopia's claims to Eritrea and the Somalian territories. Her petitions were variously signed by Vera Brittain, Emmeline Pethick-Lawrence, Isabel Fry, the Archbishop of Canterbury and T. R. Makonnen, the self-appointed West Indian emissary for Ethiopia in Britain. The Foreign Office files are clogged with editorials and cuttings from the *New Times and Ethiopia News*. She also forwarded all of her pamphlets on Ethiopia which, if unread, were duly catalogued, filed and retained.

Unaware of how her correspondence was received by members of the government, Sylvia approached Attlee in the vein of self-sacrifice: '. . . the work I have done for Ethiopia has entailed a considerable sacrifice and compelled me to put aside work which I should have preferred to do and which would have been very much to economic advantage had I so done.'[52] (But as we know, it was her Ethiopian work which gave her her principle income.)

Returned to England Sylvia pursued the new cause—the emperor's desire to unify Ethiopia and the old Italian colony of Eritrea. The question of 'proper' boundaries for the independent countries of post-colonial Africa was at best tangled. The European powers had drawn lines by mutual agreement, often with little regard for existing African political and cultural divisions. Thus, in the Horn of Africa, they had marked out Italian and British Somaliland and Eritrea after Adwa but before the end of the nineteenth century, and none of these boundaries corresponded more than roughly to an ethnic or political reality. They were to this extent 'artificial', as were the boundaries of the Ethiopian empire marked out at the same period and by the same process of conquest. Sylvia argued that the Eritreans and Somalis were ethnically Ethiopian. All people in the Horn of Africa shared aspects of a common culture. Most were either Christian or Moslem. Most spoke either Semitic or Cushitic languages. For Sylvia, this made them Ethiopian, though they themselves often saw their loyalty to a smaller subdivision of the greater whole, such as Oromo Galla or Amhara within the core area of the Christian kingdom; or Somali, Tigreans or Afar outside it. Such ethnic identifications might appear capricious or irrational, but they were nevertheless real. In the circumstances, it might have been argued, as the Somalis were later to argue, that Ogaden, with its Somali majority, should belong to them. Or it could be argued, as Sylvia was inclined to do in all instances, that the presence of any ethnic group within the Ethiopian empire constituted a claim by Ethiopia over all similar people as a kind of *Ethiopia irredenta*. These statements on Sylvia's part conveyed the actual claims of her employer, His Imperial Majesty.

The campaign followed her usual pattern. She wrote to and visited Members of Parliament; dispatched a stream of letters to the Foreign Office; wrote pamphlets distributed by the *New Times* bookshop and later by the Lalibela Press which Sylvia founded; and carried out the emperor's instructions in banner headlines in the *New Times and Ethiopia News*.[53] She gave speeches wherever she could find a platform, including at times, at Speaker's Corner in Hyde Park. The issue was referred to a committee in the United Nations, and Sylvia quickly issued letters to the Secretary General, to the Security Council members, and to various members of the Eritrea committee.

Most of the few Eritreans Sylvia knew were followers of the emperor who had left the province after obtaining a rudimentary education under the Italians. They came to Ethiopia in search of government preferment and jobs. During her short stay in Eritrea she met Moslem leaders; they were anti-British and on these grounds seemed pro-Ethiopia. Some Eritrean Moslems actually favoured unification but these were a minority, and Sylvia did not stay long enough to meet a sufficiently wide spectrum of political opinion. In retrospect the plan for federation forced on the emperor gave way to unity by vote of an Amhara-controlled legislative body; Ethiopia ultimately swallowed Eritrea in 1962, two years after Sylvia's death.

When in 1950 the General Assembly of the UN recommended Eritrean federation with Ethiopia, Sylvia was elated. She rented a hall in London to mark what she viewed as her victory—a celebration which was in fact a sombre meeting with speakers. Although Ernest Bevin was unable to attend, she advised him by letter that the solution was 'the best that could be obtained in the interest of all concerned . . . I believe that with cooperation and goodwill from all, we shall succeed.'[54] The Eritrea solution did not, of course, work out as smoothly as Sylvia had predicted. But the 'we' to whom she referred was indeed the Imperial One, and to some extent Haile Sellassie was able in his lifetime to keep Eritrea within the framework of the Ethiopian government.

A survey of Sylvia's publications from 1941 until 1956 shows her views to be anti-Italian, anti-British to the point of hostility, and pro-Ethiopian beyond reasonable interpretation. One article, published in the *Tribune*, then under the editorship of Michael Foot, dealt with British atrocities Sylvia said she had personally witnessed at Massawa, the Red Sea port. Though it is not likely she actually saw atrocities, on the subject of Eritrea her imagination was unbounded.[55] On the other hand, articles she wrote in the *New Times and Ethiopia News* which accused Britain of dismantling and moving Italian-constructed floating docks were correct. Before the British moved out of Eritrea they managed to dispose of all Italian properties they could move. For instance, AGIP (Italian oil) installations in Eritrea were transferred to Shell Oil (British Shell). And, in a move which perhaps best illustrates the pettiness of the British officials then governing Eritrea, they ordered that the railway the Italians planned from Agordat to Gondar be dropped and materials sold to Sudan for scrap. Sudan was, of course, a British colony. This final disgrace was stopped by John Spencer, the American foreign affairs advisor to the emperor. Sylvia raised these issues (except for the railway) time and again but in Parliament her complaints fell on deaf ears.[56]

Britain, according to Sylvia, was guilty of producing a situation in Eritrea which forced everyone to live in squalor, with few jobs and few schools. Here Sylvia reverted to propaganda without facts. During the occupation Britain had more than doubled the number of primary schools (from 24 to 59) and had managed to increase public services while imposing less taxation than the Eritrean population had suffered under the Italians, who had established only a few primary schools.[57] As part of her campaign, she published a pamphlet by an Eritrean, Alazar Tesfa Michael, called *Eritrea Today: Fascist Oppression under the Nose of British Military*.[58] Richard's Preface described the background for unification which Ethiopia was then still seeking, while the author wrote from his own knowledge of atrocities committed against Eritreans under Italian rule. It was questionable, however, if Italians were still committing brutalities in Eritrea after the British took over.

After her second trip to Africa, Sylvia researched and wrote a massive study, *Ethiopia and Eritrea*. She had witnessed the emperor's triumphant visit to Massawa after the federation. Richard contributed as last-minute co-author when his mother was stricken by a heart attack and unable to complete the volume.[59] Another book on the area was *Eritrea on the Eve*. John Spencer, then negotiating for Ethiopia on the question of the federation of Eritrea remembered that the book came out 'at a particularly opportune time demonstrating textually and photographically the sabotage measures adopted by disgruntled British authorities'.[60] There is no evidence on the sales of the books, but it is clear their publication was subsidized by the Ethiopian government. The style of both is that of a documentary anthology linked by explanatory passages, including letters from the editor of the *New Times and Ethiopia News*. Sylvia condemned both Italy and Britain, but in *Ethiopia and Eritrea* the British bore the brunt of the blame for a harsh and racist occupation. On the issue of racism her facts were at least partially correct and no doubt came from the Ethiopian embassy. The images of poverty, lack of sanitation, and privation were, for the majority of the Eritrean people, true, but the same conditions prevailed in Ethiopia at the time—not because of British occupation, but because both areas had barely emerged into the modern world. Sylvia's interpretation of political events was that she and her committee in England were the major force behind federation for Eritrea. What actually happened was that Sylvia agreed with an independent consensus of the United Nations supported by Britain—and not totally acceptable to the emperor.

Years later, in the *Ethiopia Observer* of 1956, Sylvia apologized for the emperor's suppression of Eritrean opposition to his rule. By that time he had suppressed political parties, but Sylvia explained that it was better for candidates to run without an affiliation so that the electoral struggle could concentrate on issues and personalities, not parties.[61] For once in these years, her stand recalled her early anti-parliamentary opposition to Lenin.

Sylvia's aim nearly to double the area of the Ethiopian empire by the addition of Somalia was less successful. On her return to England in 1945, she proclaimed Somalia's wish to 'return' to Ethiopia. In fact, the Somalis she saw were anxious to get the British out, which she interpreted incorrectly as a desire to bring the Ethiopians in. She promised them, in any case, to do what she could 'to forward their cause in Britain'.[62] True to her word, she embraced the new campaign and brought out the old tactics: she wrote to anyone in power, anywhere she could think of, and produced another large and hastily written book, *Ex-Italian Somaliland*, to demonstrate the historical arguments for Ethiopian control and to decry once again the Italians and the occupying British.[63] The volume was not reviewed in any British scholarly journals, but its American edition, published in 1951, was noticed in several. *Current History* called it 'a detailed and fully documented history of the colony'.[64] Edmund S. Munger, in the *Annals of the American Academy* thought Sylvia had made 'a strong case for Ethiopia, or at least non-Italian control of the territory'. But, 'many people who agree with her conclusions will find her argument disorganized and emotional'.[65]

The 'fully documented' character of the work was its publication of long, often unexpurgated official reports by UN committees studying the disputed areas. Whatever the merits of its documentation, it is flawed by her bias: for example, she describes an Italian on the United Nations commission as 'lynx-eyed for all chances to advance the border' of Somali to the detriment of Ethiopia.[66]

The Somalian situation was even more complicated than the Eritrean. Italy had occupied and loosely controlled the Indian Ocean coast of Somalia since the last decades of the nineteenth century. On the coast, the mainly fishermen population was ethnically diverse; inland, most people were nomadic camel herders; in between, the Wabe Shebelli and Juba rivers carried down water from the Ethiopian highlands to create ribbon oases that provided the only significant arable land in the country. Italians seized the best land, but immigration from Italy was never significant outside the cities. In the semi-desert, nomadic herdsmen needed enormous tracts of land to roam in search of grass and water. Camels were the main form of transport, and a centuries-old caravan traffic stretched west into Ethiopia. The border between the countries was neither marked, effectively policed, nor respected by the nomads—then or now. Indeed, on both sides the people were ethnically Somali.

Before the Second World War, culturally similar people speaking various dialects of a common Somali language were scattered among a variety of jurisdictions. Italian Somaliland was one of them; in addition, the British had taken over the north coast bordering the Gulf of Aden. The north-east corner of Kenya also had a substantial Somali majority under British rule. Finally, and most significantly in this context, Ethiopia controlled a large territory that contained a Somali majority in the Ogaden comprising perhaps one-third of the total land area of the Ethiopian empire, though it contained far less in terms of population. The final colony, French Somaliland or Djibouti, was somewhat different. The French had acquired their port as a means to harass British ships on their way to India. Later they became a colonial presence in Somaliland. Its importance was therefore mainly strategic, and the population of Afar and Issa peoples were related to the Somalis, though not necessarily close enough to share Somali national sentiment in all circumstances. For all of these Somali people, the political objective was not centred on Ethiopia, but on a desire for cultural unity for the national group on open lands over which nomads could roam freely with their livestock.

Ernest Bevin, as Foreign Secretary in 1943, proposed a Greater Somaliland which would fuse northern Kenya (with its substantial Somali population) Italian, French and British Somalilands into a whole. In this respect Bevin seems to have had greater colonial ambitions than the Conservative Churchill government because he wanted to place the newly forged Somaliland under British dominion, or alternatively place it under British trusteeship. Italy, on the other hand, wanted to return to colonial control over Italian Somaliland and was interested in reclaiming its territory in the Ogaden as well.

Sylvia's position—uniting Somalia with Ethiopia—links her to Haile Sellassie in a most interesting manner. His Imperial Majesty was singularly alone in his desire to unify Somalia. Others in his government opposed the notion altogether. There were no roads nor was there a railway between his country and Mogadiscio, the coastal port in Italian Somaliland. There were roads, built by the Italians, between Addis Ababa and Massawa; and there was the railway between Addis Ababa and Djibouti.[67] The emperor had at times in the past entertained the hope of linking Ethiopia with Zeila, the port city in British Somaliland, but Zeila was close to Djibouti and the French were not interested in losing potential business from their port. Yet, the issue was under discussion in the early 1950s; and Haile Sellassie suggested unification on several occasions.[68]

Musa Galaal, a young Somali student in London in the 1950s, heard of Sylvia and her championing of unification and arranged a meeting with her in West Dene on the pretext of using her extensive library. He found her to be so 'pro-Ethiopia that she considered all Africa to be Ethiopia'. He remembered her as 'a very old woman . . . [whose] hard life put a footprint on her features'. He admired her: 'Historically, [she was] a great woman because of suffrage in England. In that case she worked for all the women in the world and my mother was a woman. . . . But she was a woman who opposed all Somali causes.'[69] According to Musa Galaal, Sylvia was irrational in insisting that all Somalis were Ethiopians. At one point she asked him, 'What could you be that is better than being an Ethiopian?' Her insensitivity towards other ethnic groups could be crude, and Musa took great offence. As their arguments grew louder, he noted that people passing outside stopped and peered into the big, dark yard and through the windows, trying to see what was going on between the tall, youthful black and the ageing English woman. Seeing that he could not penetrate her closed mind on Ethiopia-Somali differences, Musa concluded that 'she was taking the Amhara version of history—not trying to balance her view with study and inquiry.'[70]

Apart from these differences of opinion, Musa recognized 'a number of valuable characteristics'. She was 'a person, who, if they form an opinion, they strongly keep it . . . a person, who, once she believes it, she almost worships it. The problem is that such persons are difficult to deal with. . . . hard to fit into a community—too rigid.' Indeed, these are the traits Sylvia manifested in her relations with most people throughout her life. Musa saw *Ex-Italian Somaliland* as Sylvia's way of giving 'advice to world powers', but he, too, recognized the value of the many documents she had amassed. As an artist, even Sylvia could be brought around on the value of Somali culture: 'In the *New Times and Ethiopia News* she used to give excellent studies of Somali people. They were accurate when she was describing scientific aspects of the culture . . . correcting some colonial studies which depicted Somalis as having no art . . . I am aware of the good and bad sides of Sylvia Pankhurst.'[71]

How much effect did Sylvia have on Britain's policy toward Somalia, Ethiopia and unity? Bevin favoured ethnic unity for Somalia. *The Times* was in favour, as were a number of voices in Parliament.[72] Sylvia argued for a more general ethnic unity within a greater Ethiopia.[73] At least one Member of Parliament argued in the House for Sylvia's plan, calling for all ethnic Somalis, even those under Ethiopian rule, to vote, thereby choosing between a sovereign independent state and federation. And, once again she bombarded Members of Parliament, the Colonial Office and the Foreign Office with her plan for federation, conducting a commendable one-woman campaign, but meeting only partial success. The Reserved Areas, the Haud and Ogaden were returned to Ethiopia by negotiated agreement. Former British Somaliland and Italian Somaliland were united to form present-day Somalia, and the Somalis in northern Kenya remained where they were, politically attached to Kenya, now independent. But this Somali solution worked out by the United Nations in 1955 left the same potential for conflict as had the earlier Eritrean settlement. Even then, Sylvia continued her efforts to unite Somalia and Ethiopia; demanding that Britain 'free' Somaliland and 'return' the area to Ethiopian rule.[74]

Despite Sylvia's concentration on Ethiopian affairs, she kept in touch with old friends and, on occasion, engaged in miscellaneous feminist activities. She tried to draw feminists into her Ethiopian campaign, writing, for instance, to Alice Paul in America. But Paul declined to lend her name to this particular crusade.[75] Faithful Emmeline Pethick-Lawrence did give her support—at least in name, as sponsor.

In 1955 Sylvia was invited to participate in an Oxford Union debate. The proposition was 'That this House regrets that woman having risen up in Emancipation, is once again sitting down and being dictated to'. Sylvia opposed, but the debate carried against her. However, according to the Oxford Magazine, she 'received one of the biggest ovations the Union can ever have given a guest'.[76]

When Autherine Lucy, a black woman, tried to enter the University of Alabama in 1955, Sylvia supported her in the *New Times and Ethiopia News*. She lambasted American racism and quoted the Birmingham, Alabama, *Post*: 'The cause of integration in the southern states seems to have produced its Pankhurst in Miss Autherine Lucy.'[77] Soon after her heart attack in the early 1950s, Sylvia spoke against apartheid in Trafalgar Square, and in the *New Times and Ethiopia News* she ran columns opposing South African legalized racism. Sylvia opposed racism unequivocally wherever it existed.

Racism was one issue; sexual equality in Ethiopia was another. Women had some traditional rights, after divorce, for example, they were allowed legally to keep half of the marital property. But they had few rights over their children. Because education was even more deficient among women than among men, few were in a position to seek positions of leadership even had they been available to women. In 1951, His Imperial Majesty proclaimed equal rights for women when presiding over the opening of a private boarding school for girls. His speech was made available to Sylvia in England and she immediately rejoiced in the *New Times and Ethiopia News*. The new constitution of 1955 gave women the vote and also the right to sit in Parliament; and in 1957 the headmistress of a girls' school was elected to Parliament. But John Spencer found that in comparison with the earlier limited constitution of 1930, 'there gradually emerged a recognition that the reforms were meagre indeed and that the Emperor was in reality opposed to anything suggestive of a parliamentary regime. . . . concentration of power and form rather than reform and liberalization remained at the centre of Haile Sellassie's interests'.[78] So, while Sylvia praised the election of a woman to Parliament in 1957, the Emperor of Ethiopia bypassed that elected body altogether.

As correspondent for the *New Times*, she went to Paris to cover the peace conference in 1946. Corio dutifully printed her description of her 'Paris Journey' and her diatribes against Italy.[79] She had trouble with accommodation, travel connections, and suffered small discomforts such as being forced, because of large crowds at the stations, to carry her own baggage. The trip was not pleasant. Her real intention, in addition to gathering material for her long, rambling columns in the *New Times*, was to lobby for Ethiopia among the delegates from the major countries. It seems unlikely that the emperor, knowing her weaknesses as well as her strengths, chose that assignment for her. A reporter for the *Evening News* wrote, 'She has taken up Ethiopia's claims for the return of the ex-Italian colonies. . . . All day long she is lobbying at Luxembourg Palace, carrying an enormous briefcase stuffed with pamphlets. Then she sits up until two or three in the morning writing letters and petitions. . . . She told a colleague of mine that she had intended to retire and reflect and write books. "But", she added, "there is so much to be done in the world".'[80] A curious quality of Sylvia was this ability to drive herself relentlessly: on the larger public stage, however, she failed to win converts to her cause because, convinced she was right, she was uncompromisingly rigid. But this reporter, like many others who dealt with her on a one-to-one basis, was sympathetic to Sylvia's commitment and attracted by her personal magnetism.

In 1947 Richard visited northern Europe.[81] Most of the travelogues on Holland, Denmark and Germany in the *New Times* were written by Richard, but Sylvia contributed an article on Sweden because of her contacts with former missionaries to Ethiopia. In October 1951, Haile Sellassie invited her to return to Ethiopia for the dedication of the hospital she had sponsored—it was on this visit that Richard accompanied her, and she did some of her 'research' for *Eritrea on the Eve*.

Complications delayed the opening ceremonies for the hospital, so Sylvia was able to enjoy seven months in her fairyland before returning to England.[82] As ever, she wrote long columns for the *New Times*. As before, the emperor's staff carefully arranged for her to meet Eritreans and Somalis friendly to Ethiopia providing ammunition for her campaign at home. She noted the presence of buildings new since 1944, including the Haile Sellassie theatre and the new airport terminal. She dealt at length with the hospital, its staff, its new equipment, and its plans for future growth. Richard, who that year received his Doctor of Philosophy degree, remained with her through much of the trip. Sylvia's second visit only fuelled her desire to serve the emperor, 'probably the most wonderful man I have ever met ...under all circumstances, so calm and collected, and gentle.'[83]

Her earlier friendships and associations with other Africans and Afro-Caribbeanists had dissipated during the war years. C. L. R. James had little respect for her.[84] Padmore was preoccupied with West African interests; Jomo Kenyatta attended a few of her bazaars, but seems to have stayed politically detached. A West Indian had taken the name of Haile Sellassie's father, *Ras* Makonnen, and served as an unofficial representative of Ethiopia at various Pan-African meetings. Because of Sylvia's official ties to the emperor, they might have been friendly. *Ras* Makonnen did attend a London conference on Ethiopian affairs in 1945 where Sylvia reported on her first trip, and signed several of her petitions; but in 1946 when he was largely responsible for organizing the Pan-African Congress in Manchester, she was not invited.

In 1950 Seretse Khama, an hereditary chief from Bechuanaland, was banned from returning home because he had married a white woman. Sylvia was outraged and protested in his defence. 'Everyone is shocked', she wrote, 'everyone is ashamed' at the open display of racism. Sylvia believed, correctly, that the British action was taken to placate South Africa. What she did not know was that many of his own people also opposed the marriage, and looked unfavourably on his return to assume the chieftainship. Eventually, however, Khama went home and abandoned the hereditary position for a new role in national leadership. As Sir Seretse Khama, he brought Botswana to independence.

In the late 1950s, other African countries began to move towards independence. Ghana under Kwame Nkrumah gained its independence in 1957, and George Padmore and *Ras* Makonnen, his old friends and supporters, entered the government. By then Sylvia seems to have lost contact with her former Pan-Africanist allies. She had not known the Afro-American W. E. B. DuBois well, but the two had corresponded after the Fifth Pan-African Congress in 1946. Sylvia asked DuBois to use his influence among Afro-Americans to rally support in the United States for Ethiopia's claim to Eritrea. In this respect she highlighted her claim to be operating, however fervently, independently of the Ethiopian government: 'We never ask for any official approval for what we do for Ethiopia. The Legation is perfectly able to tell the Foreign Office, if it chooses, that we are acting independently and cannot be controlled.'[85] DuBois replied in a long letter, part of which outlined the frustrations of black Americans:[86]

> Whenever we try, as of course we must try, to help our fellow Africans in other parts of the world, our work is looked upon as interference and with that attitude goes usually the assumption that we are busybodies who must be ignored. . . . No one has appreciated more than I the long and courageous effort you have made for the freedom of Ethiopia; but I strongly believe that you would be helped if your alliance with American Negroes and your understanding of their efforts were more complete. The Ethiopians them-selves for a long time have been misled by the idea that any appearance of sympathy between them and American Negroes would be unwise.

Understanding that Sylvia had influence with the emperor, DuBois wrote again in 1954, before Haile Sellassie's visit to the United States that year. He asked her to intercede on behalf of black Americans, whom, he thought, should be allowed to meet the emperor.[87] Sylvia hastened to respond:[88]

> I will write to the Emperor . . . but perhaps I might mention to you that Ethiopia does not recognise the term 'negro' as applied to the whole of the African people . . . I promise that I will put the matter to His Imperial Majesty, and I am sure he will do what he can to meet the desire of the Afro-Americans, or Negroes, if you prefer to call them so.

Since he was on a state visit, Haile Sellassie did not meet DuBois and his fellow Afro-Americans. *Ras* Emru, the emperor's cousin and Ethio-pia's ambassador to the United States, met DuBois in connection with his fears that the emperor would be subjected to American racism during his visit (which he did not because he met high government officials only). *Ras* Emru, indeed, spoke out critically on race relations in America and gained a measure of popularity with Afro-Americans because of his open stand on the issue.

In 1954 Haile Sellassie returned to England, thirteen years after his original exile. Sylvia was ecstatic; as his chief propagandist and supporter in England, she was invited to many official functions, including the ceremony at which Sellassie received an honorary doctorate at the University of Oxford. She also went to a reception given by the citizens of Bath where he had lived in exile, but was not invited to the state dinner he gave for the Queen.[89] Her moment of triumph came when Haile Sellassie invited her and her Princess Tsähay Hospital committee to the Ethiopian embassy. Lord Amulree, the committee's chairman, presented the emperor with some new equipment. Haile Sellassie publicly thanked Sylvia and her committee. Even such small praise for her stupendous efforts were gratefully received and printed in the *New Times and Ethiopia News*.[90]

Sylvia meanwhile continued as though she was the sole supporter of Ethiopia in Great Britain. When the Manchester *Guardian* mentioned Ethiopian unrest in 1954—and there was in fact a great deal of it—she lashed out in defence.[91] Since she refused to publish anything but praise in the *New Times*, the Ethiopian news became tiresome and the paper became more of a glamour publication, featuring pictures of Haile Sellassie and his family and fantasies about his popularity at home.[92] When the *Economist* pointed out, among other things, that the Ethiopian Parliament had no real power, she waded in: he had been 'elected to the imperial throne by the will of the people' as an absolute monarch, and that later, 'of his own free will', he had limited his own power by creating a constitution and a Parliament.[93] Again, these are paradoxical words from a woman bold enough to quarrel with Lenin in favour of the abolition of the British Parliament.

Was Sylvia's loyalty to Haile Sellassie blind, or was she, by the mid-1950s, so deeply in his debt that she had psychologically locked herself into an unrealistic defensive position? Perhaps the answer is a little of both. Mrs Ivy Tims, a tiny, energetic woman, in 1942 answered Sylvia's advertisement for volunteer workers on her Princess Tsähay memorial fund. Her acceptance began a long and close working relationship. Her affection for Sylvia, however, may have biased some of her memories; she is the only informant intimately acquainted with Sylvia at this period who was alive and willing to be interviewed for this study. Nevertheless, Mrs Tims was well acquainted with Sylvia's financial dependence on the Ethiopian embassy in London. Each month Sylvia drew up and submitted a projected budget. Each week Sylvia, and sometimes Mrs Tims, went to the embassy and collected the allowance. Each month £1000 went towards household and personal expenses. Up to £2000 more was for secretarial staff, the *New Times*, and other publications, but usually the personal and expense accounts were equal at £1000 each. Sylvia was also in direct contact with Haile Sellassie through his personal secretary and sent him special requests for extra funds.[94]

'Sylvia didn't always get the money she requested and was quite frantic,' Mrs Tims recalled. She kept her old habits of spending money when there was none, which Mrs Tims thought was a weakness: 'She just didn't think.' Once Corio persuaded Sylvia to stage a benefit concert for her hospital fund. Corio hired orchestra and soloists and the event lost £300. The embassy refused to underwrite the loss and Sylvia had to make good the deficit.[95] In time, Mrs Tims took over much of the financial side of Sylvia's operations as well as Sylvia's personal accounting, insisting that Sylvia note down every expenditure, even if she removed a five-pound note from the cash in hand. Corio also received a small allowance by post once a week. No one knew from where or how much.

Mrs Tims described Corio as difficult. It is not hard to see why, working on a paper which produced empty paeons of praise to the emperor of Ethiopia each week, first at the Walthamstow Press, later at Manchester. He was remarkably skilled as a printer; there were fewer printing errors than factual ones in the *New Times* during the long years he handled the work, and was effectively editor as well. He worked from copy full of Sylvia's last-minute changes and scraps of paper pasted into columns.[96] Towards the end of his life, his position became even more difficult.[97] His role as partner had been reduced to little more than employee. Mrs Tims also thought he placed too much pressure on Richard, insisting on knowing about his activities. But his fatherly contribution was emotional, not financial. H. D. Harben, whose generosity kept the family in the immediate period after Richard's birth, also paid the school fees. Sylvia was never embarrassed to ask for money, and Harben's contribution increased as the school fees increased.[98]

Although there is little in Sylvia's makeup to suggest that she and Corio maintained a sexual relationship beyond the early years of their partnership, or even after the birth of the long-desired child, Mrs Tims indicated that the couple shared a bedroom up until Sylvia's return from her second trip to Ethiopia.[99] By this time Corio was nearing eighty, suffered from a severe smoker's cough, and was in declining health.[100] His study was his retreat, where he spent long hours alone reading. And in contrast to Sylvia's workplace, his was the model of neatness.

Many who knew them felt sorry for Corio, but Mrs Tims believed he treated Sylvia less than courteously: 'He was always shouting at Sylvia, but she never blinked an eye.' Was she stoic or, in old age, uncaring? He, too, remained financially irresponsible, often asking for money and then disappearing, never concerned about shortages in the budget. If 'he didn't have his way, he would storm, make a scene'; if an incident disturbed him, he 'would make a fuss about it, indicating that in his late seventies he had little patience. Mrs Tims was fond of Richard, who even as he reached adulthood was often 'caught between two strong, often opposing personalities'.[101]

Sylvia's devotion remained to Ethiopia and her work. Her greatest work of homage was her massive *Ethiopia: A Cultural History*, brought out by her own publishing company, Lalibela House, in 1955. Sylvia's book was appropriately dedicated to 'His Imperial Majesty, The Emperor Haile Sellassie I, Guardian of Education, Pioneer of Progress, Leader and Defender of his People in Peace and War'.[102] The huge volume consisted of many of the articles she had published in the *New Times*, just as *The Suffragette* had earlier contained much from *Votes for Women*. Newly discovered plates of historical Ethiopian art and architecture found their place alongside the recent art of Ethiopian students Sylvia had known in London, including several studies by her protégé, Afä Warq Tekle.

The historical sections ran from ancient pre-history to contemporary Ethiopia; current events were emphasized in laudatory style. One chapter, 'A Bird's Eye View of Some Schools',[103] based on Sylvia's observations and travels during her seven-month sojourn in the country in 1951/52, listed numbers of students and numbers and locations of schools, with much praise for the advancements made in education since the war. Her chapter 'Addis Ababa University College'[104] might have been lifted from the college prospectus; courses and requirements are listed in full.

Had Sylvia confined herself to ancient and contemporary art, her book would have been valuable. The art, ranging from pictures of monasteries to beautiful reproductions of traditional Ethiopian painting and handcraft, was new and of interest to the English public, but Sylvia passed her own weaknesses on to her book. She could not control her enthusiasms, and the volume became too unwieldy to serve any practical purpose, for scholars or the general reader.

Edward Ullendorff reviewed *Ethiopia: A Cultural History* in *Africa*, referring to her 'industry, resilience, and remarkable enthusiasms'— hallmarks, in fact, of every volume she wrote. But Ullendorff also saw another characteristic in the 'errors and factual mistakes' as well as 'the many half-truths' which pervaded the volume.[105] It was these 'half-truths' which cast a shadow over the credibility of most of her writing. Ullendorff complimented her on the art sections and must have reminded Sylvia of her earlier criticisms of him as a linguist when he wrote: 'She lacks the equipment, linguistic, historical, etc., required for such a task' as writing about all aspects of Ethiopia. 'Nor is she at home in either a Semitic or African civilization.' The result is 'lacking in scholarly discipline and judgement.' 'It is a pity that ever since 1941 Miss Pankhurst has been engaged in fighting imaginary foes of Ethiopia, for without the propagandist overtones, with a lot of judicious pruning, and with knowledge of the cultural history of Ethiopia rather than dedication to the politics and aspirations of the present time, this could have been an important book.'[106]

The anonymous reviewer in the *Times Literary Supplement* wrote along the same lines: 'The labours of Lalibela House. . . have brought forth a monster of 747 pages (plus plates XXXVIII). . . . But was it really necessary to know the name of the school electrician in 1925 – 26?' There were no words of praise to balance the criticism. In all, the useful parts of the book, especially the art, were buried in the hyperbole that ultimately exhausted the reader's confidence.[107]

The vigour Sylvia displayed between the emperor's return to Ethiopia in 1941 and the publication of her 'history' defied her increasing age: in May 1953 she turned seventy-two. The last eighteen years had been spent in the service of Ethiopia. She had first adopted the country as a result of her fierce anti-Fascism. Later she threw herself into righteous combat for its ruler, becoming more of a spokesperson for Haile Sellassie himself than for Ethiopia. Visiting her fairyland, she joined her mother and Adela as an apologist for the trappings of monarchy—noticeable in the coverage of her visits both to the palace and to Dr Martin. In old age, too, we see her starting to tire—the young Sylvia would never have complained about petty problems such as carrying baggage or a late chauffeur. In fact, a chauffeur would have been anathema to her in earlier years.

On an individual basis, Sylvia maintained some of her charisma, but among the Africans with whom she had worked for independence from colonialism she was regarded as a puppet of Haile Sellassie, unable to see the complexities he faced at home or the international problems his country confronted. With her credibility among African freedom-fighters diminished, her only outlet remained her imagined position of past glory in the suffrage movement. Having previously been the object of suspicion and surveillance by the British government in her earlier causes, she became an object of ridicule (although sometimes a successful nuisance) to British bureaucrats.

Recognizing these changes in her life, it is with a measure of pity that one reads *Ethiopia: A Cultural History*. Here is not history as historians know the discipline, but a gigantic gift of love to Haile Sellassie and to his people.

13

A Radical in Fairyland

You are whitemailing me. I can't afford it. . . . Hospital-trained
nurses kill most of their patients by untimely washing.
—George Bernard Shaw, NTEN, January 1948

Sylvia's tireless campaigning on behalf of Ethiopia eventually took its
toll. In the early 1950s she showed signs of nervous strain, the begin-
nings of a breakdown, the result of overwork. As an alternative to hospital, she moved into the Royal Forest Hotel, a few miles from West
Dene, where she stayed for several weeks. Mrs Tims made daily trips
between the office and the hotel, bringing her papers to read, and
carrying back instructions to the staff. Corio, according to Mrs Tims,
was worried about Sylvia's condition, but was not allowed to visit her.[1]
Relations between the two seemed to have disintegrated, at least from
Sylvia's point of view.

In April 1953, Sylvia was again struck. She collapsed outside her
home with a heart attack. Corio immediately summoned a doctor and
Mr and Mrs Tims. Despite urgings by family and friends, Sylvia
again refused to be hospitalized. She rested in her room but continued
her massive correspondence. The only concession she made was to
allow Richard to take over some of her writing—for example, the book
on Ethiopia and Eritrea then in progress. By late May, Sylvia was well
enough to contribute columns to the *New Times*, and to plan a mid-
summer garden party in support of the Princess Tsähay Hospital.

Richard was now moving more into family projects, writing more
for the *New Times and Ethiopia News* and helping his mother with her
research. In 1953, when called up on conscription, Richard asked to
be classified as a conscientious objector and refused to submit to a
medical examination. As a member of the United Nations, Britain was
contributing to the combined forces then fighting in Korea. In Kenya,
the so-called 'Mau Mau' rebellion required national service conscripts
to help put down the revolt. Richard was opposed to fighting against
the 'Mau Mau'. Sylvia was also opposed to the Korean War. She
testified at his trial pointing out the folly of fighting in Korea. He lost
the case, however, and was fined £5 for refusing to obey the National
Service Act.[2]

At the trial's conclusion, Sylvia met the press to give her views on war and Richard's pacifism. *The Times* reporter described her: 'At seventy: Sylvia has a vaguely 1910 look: grey hair, scooped back, an ancient black corded coat over a drab cardigan, no nonsense, no jewelry, not so much as a ring. And, of course, no lipstick.' To the reporter, 'who passed her tongue over her own pinked lip', Sylvia said she abhorred lipstick, 'not only does it spoil the shape of the mouth . . . it also reveals the slave mentality.'[3]

Most of her contacts, interests and associations were focused on Ethiopia. But an American historian, Arthur Dudden, researching the life of Joseph Fels, managed to gain an interview with her to discuss the former supporter of Henry George and the single tax. Invited for tea, he found a house 'crammed with books and papers'. Sylvia was reluctant to talk about Fels, did not mention her brother Harry and his experiences on the Fels' farms, and believed the suffrage movement was more important than Fels' involvement with the single tax, which never got off the ground in America. Sylvia also complained about Americans gaining the vote before the British did because, as she saw it, 'we suffered more'.[4] Sylvia, it seems, measured success in terms of input.

After the war many young Ethiopians came to England to schools and universities. Sylvia's home became the centre of London Ethiopian activity. Michael Emru, Mary Tadesse and Afä Wärq Tekle saw her frequently. All found their way into the pages of *Ethiopia: A Cultural History* as leaders among the Ethiopian students (in the case of Michael Emru and Mary Tedasse) or as artists of promise (in the case of Afä Wärq and Menghestu Lemma). Menghestu was also a poet, which appealed to Sylvia, who continued writing poetry into her old age. Michael Emru, son of Haile Sellassie's cousin, briefly became Foreign Minister in 1974 after the *Derg* (a group of soldiers) overthrew the emperor. Mary Tedasse's father had been among those massacred by General Graziani in the early days of Italian rule in Addis Ababa; she returned home to become a civil servant. Afä Wärq and Menghestu spent more time at the Pankhurst home than did other Ethiopians, although most of the students came into contact with Sylvia either through letters of recommendation she wrote, Ethiopian parties held at her house, or the school vacations she arranged for them to spend with her friends.[5]

The public radical—which is how most knew Sylvia—became a warm, loving mother-figure to the many Ethiopian students she encountered in the post-war years. Mary Tadesse thought one of Sylvia's major contributions to Ethiopia after the war was her availability to young Ethiopians struggling to come to terms with an alien environment. Sylvia often helped the new arrivals find an appropriate school and then sought their admission either directly or through intermediaries. In most cases, the Ethiopian government supported the students financially in Britain, depending on Sylvia to serve as liaison.[6]

When Afä Wärq Tekle arrived in London he intended to study mining engineering, even though art was his major interest. He met Sylvia on the day he arrived, staying for some time in her home. She persuaded him to change his mind and concentrate on developing his artistic talents. Perhaps through him she was acting out her own desire for a career as an artist. Afä Wärq's personal situation was complicated by disfiguring scarring on his face. Through one of her many contacts, Sylvia arranged for Afä Wärq to go into a London hospital, where plastic surgery successfully removed the scars. He recuperated in her home, where she cared for him, and where Richard became his close friend—indeed, more like his brother. For Sylvia, Richard was the child of her life; Afä Wärq was her spiritual son who would carry on the artistic tradition she had abandoned in her youth.

She followed closely Afä Wärq's progress through high school, into art school, and later at the Slade School at the University of London. Looking back on those years, Afä Wärq recalled: 'She never really praised my art. She criticized my art . . . gave advice to me . . . arranged for me to meet the right people.'[7] Memories of his many visits to her home re-enforced impressions given by others: Sylvia was always up early to work, never leaving her desk until Richard or Corio announced lunch. When time permitted, she reminisced about her early years in art school, the Royal College, and in Venice. Her career in art, Sylvia told him, ended when she was forced to abandon painting, first for the suffrage movement, and then for later crusades. Afä Wärq saw her as a dedicated woman who, with her interest in humanity, became an inspiration: she gave him the discipline he needed for success: 'I have always considered her my spiritual mother . . . and I have also considered her as a guiding light and a torchbearer . . . '[8]

As Sylvia's father had admonished her to serve, so she guided Afä Wärq to create. When his training in England was complete, Sylvia arranged for him to tour Europe, making provisions for further study in Italy, following her own course. But she believed that eventually he would return to Ethiopia, and encouraged it. Afä Wärq quickly established a name for himself in artistic circles and, though tempted to stay in Europe remembered Sylvia's advice and went home: 'When I am critical about my country,' he recalled, 'she would not hear it. When I am very critical about the Emperor she would say "shame", "disgusting by you. What do you know about what he has been through".'[9]

Afä Wärq remembered Corio as 'a gentle man. It was a happy home . . . a house of work.' But, 'I always looked forward to my holidays' when Corio would read to Afä Wärq and Richard from the classics. 'He was the one who took us to the corner and bought us ice cream. He was the one who said you must go to the museum to relax.' When Sylvia arrived, however, 'he was subdued and quiet. That is why I don't know if he was the husband, when people asked me. I always said he was a household member.'[10] Other Ethiopian students in London during those years shared Afä Wärq's fond memories of Corio rather than the negative ones of Mrs Tims. He seemed to have been a man's man; criticism almost invariably came from women. Even so, according to Afä Wärq: 'Miss Pankhurst was the head of the family. There was no question about that.'[11]

Sylvia shared some of her art with Afä Wärq. He saw a portfolio of her early drawings as well as a few pieces she had managed to finish in recent years. As an artist, he believed, she 'had talent . . . you cannot judge the greatness of her work by the work she has done . . . painting is such an affair that you have to live long with it.' Sylvia never asked Afä Wärq who later became artist laureate of Ethiopia for an assessment of her work, but she always encouraged him, and shared his progress with those who knew him in England in his early student days.[12]

Sylvia's close ties to the emperor brought her into contact with another set of Ethiopian students in England—Sellassie's own grandchildren and other young relatives. The emperor sent money to cover their tuition and personal needs, and Sylvia dispensed it fastidiously.[13] Among the grandchildren under Sylvia's guardianship were two descended from Haile Sellassie's first marriage. These became a problem, especially in the light of Ethiopian court etiquette, because to report their juvenile pranks and misdemeanours was to cast aspersions on the crown. One of the grandchildren was accused of having sexually assaulted his roommate, the son of a British doctor, at boarding school. The doctor complained to the school and directly to the Ethiopian embassy. The embassy did nothing, no doubt for the same reasons Sylvia was reluctant to report the incident, but the school immediately notified Sylvia. The grandson in question denied the charges. The doctor persisted. Eventually, after a scolding from Ethiopian authorities in the embassy, the boy was briefly allowed to return to school. He remained a troublemaker and a bad influence on the other Ethiopian boys. The headmistress wrote to Sylvia: 'My complaints about the boys are not so much about what they did, as about what they did not do. They were all completely uncooperative. . . . A certain café near here was forbidden ground and he [the eldest] told me he did not frequent it, but I am still being asked why he was allowed there'. The boy continued to be aggressive and rude to the staff and the headmistress, but the sexual misdemeanour was conclusive. The two errant grandchildren were quietly returned home. After this, Sylvia's only unhappy experience with her chosen people, she delegated much of her responsibility as informal guardian to Mrs Tims.[14]

Sylvia entertained other members of the royal family. Alexander Desta, son of Princess Tänagnä Warq, was one of the students she had contact with. The Duke of Harar, Haile Sellassie's most favoured son, visited her at West Dene.[15] He later died in a car accident in Ethiopia. It was the premature death of the Princess Tsähay, however, that moved Sylvia to embark on her last major campaign for Ethiopia and it was to be her most successful of all.

Princess Tsähay was born in 1919, spent five years in exile in England, and returned to Ethiopia committed to building a European-style hospital in what was then a medically barren country. Soon after her return her father arranged to marry her to a patriot of substance, and the princess accompanied her new husband to take up a provincial governorship. Four months after the marriage, Princess Tsähay suffered a haemorrhage and died. The death served to emphasize Ethiopia's need for diagnostic treatment centres, not only in the provinces, but in the capital. At Corio's suggestion, Sylvia decided to build and equip a hospital in Addis Ababa as a memorial to the princess.[16]

In October 1942, Sylvia launched a memorial fund in the *New Times and Ethiopia News*, with the emperor and empress as its patrons. Nurses at Guy's Hospital in London, where the princess trained, had already contributed to a fund to help Tsähay begin her drive for improved public health units in Ethiopia. This became the seed money for Sylvia's memorial fund, serving to help pay workers on the larger campaign. With much of the public credit in Ethiopia and England going to Sylvia, Ivy Tims worked behind the scenes directing the fund drives and providing an organizational base in the West Dene headquarters.[17] According to Lord Amulree, who worked on the hospital committee for over ten years, 'Mrs Tims took care of Sylvia, and Sylvia wanted someone to take care of her.'[18]

Anthony Eden turned down the invitation to become honorary president of the Princess Tsähay Memorial Council[19] but Sylvia was successful in getting a number of other influential people involved. Dame Elizabeth Cadbury, of the chocolate family, joined the council. Lord Davies, a wealthy Welshman noted for his pacifist views, agreed to be chairman. Lord Horder, the queen's physician, became honorary treasurer, and Sylvia was honorary secretary. Emmeline Pethick-Lawrence joined with Lorna Wingate, wife of Orde C. Wingate who had been attached to Haile Sellassie's forces in the liberation of Ethiopia in 1941. The hospital was a cause both pacifists and those committed to the war effort could support.

During the push for donations, Sylvia reinstated an early practice from her East End days. She published the names and amounts of contributions from each donor, no matter how large or small each week in the *New Times and Ethiopia News*. She and Dame Elizabeth toured the country lecturing on Ethiopia's need for modern health care and on the hospital as partial solution.[20] Sylvia sent volunteers to collect money at cinemas, and contacted groups like the YMCA, first through volunteers and later through her paid staff. They sent press releases to all major publications, asking their readers for donations. They made a direct appeal to all registered doctors and nurses in Britain, and to all Members of Parliament.

Sylvia set her goal at £100,000, a very considerable sum. Her first trip to Ethiopia, which caused such consternation in the Foreign Office, was undertaken in part to choose a site for the hospital. Haile Sellassie donated a half-built building in a very dilapidated condition. Emmanuel Abraham thought it 'a derelict building', but workers refurbished it as part of the emperor's contribution. Sylvia dreamed of sending a team of doctors from Britain to train Ethiopians in medicine. Nurses' training was also part of the project, along with facilities for outpatients, a maternity clinic (in keeping with her earlier concerns for women in childbirth), and a paediatric unit with new and modern equipment. Her dreams were vast: no one but Sylvia believed they could be realized in a lifetime.

Ras Emru formed an Ethiopian branch of the fund, again with the emperor and empress as patrons. Emmanuel Abraham was treasurer and busied himself raising funds from among the emerging middle-class.[21] Those who sought favour with the emperor no doubt contributed generously, but the bulk of the contributions came from England. Sylvia solicited contributions from, among others, Lord Lugard, former governor of Nigeria, Pearl Buck, Rebecca West and George Bernard Shaw. Shaw turned her down, telling her to sell his letters and give the proceeds to the hospital funds.[22] Little did he realize his letters had long since gone under the auctioneer's hammer.

Lord Horder, ageing and probably finding work with Sylvia too taxing, soon asked his friend, Lord Amulree, to become assistant honorary treasurer. Amulree, a physician and humanitarian, was surprised to receive an invitation from Sylvia asking him to take over the financial affairs of the fund. Her note 'took me back to my childhood, with the suffragettes and the mobs', and, flattered to be noticed, he arranged to have lunch and discuss the hospital. Expecting a flaming modern feminist, Amulree invited her to a fashionable hotel, where she could have 'a two-martini lunch'. Instead, 'This funny little creature came in and announced, "I never drink at all".' With that introduction the two settled into serious discussion of the hospital. Amulree accepted her invitation to join the council, and a firm bond was formed between Sylvia and the calm, dependable gentleman doctor.[23]

Lord Amulree often convened meetings at the House of Lords, eventually took on financial responsibility for the fund, and for all practical purposes served as chairman. The control was badly needed; Sylvia no sooner began receiving money than she started spending it. Before the hospital was ready she bought and sent off expensive equipment of all sorts. She ordered beds, nursing supplies, sanitary supplies, towels and bedding. Every necessity was secured and shipped, even when there was no money to pay for them. Amulree said he could always tell when Sylvia was in financial trouble: 'When she entered a meeting with her hair coming down, you knew she had done something awful ...like spending money that was not there'. 'She was terrible to work with, always spent more than we had'. Yet he regarded her as 'a very remarkable character' and 'one with whom it was a pleasure to talk'. As to her newspaper, which as a member of the House of Lords he had long received, 'It was awful. Full of lies.' The tall, handsome and patrician Amulree thought Sylvia looked 'like a cottage loaf'. But hers was a winning personality for the hospital enterprise: 'If you were somebody Sylvia got hold of and were asked to build a hospital, you simply helped build a hospital'.[24] According to American-born Princess Rosalie Viazemsky, another friend of Amulree's and long-time supporter of Sylvia, Amulree often bailed Sylvia and the fund out of their financial crises. As a sensitive man who had great sympathy for developing countries as well as a dedication to medicine, Amulree found Sylvia's own commitment irresistible.[25]

Dark-haired, graceful and slender, Rosalie Viazemsky had an unusual, if revealing, first encounter with Sylvia in 1947, five years after the hospital drive had been launched. Her father, Sir Gordon Selfridge, founder of Selfridge's department store in London, had just died. Sylvia sent her a note of condolence saying how good Sir Gordon had been to her. Although Princess Viazemsky and her Russian emigré husband had lived with Sir Gordon and were especially close to him in his last years, they had never heard of Sylvia: 'He was very generous, but he never mentioned her...he didn't know her'. About a week after Sylvia's first note to the princess, another arrived, asking her to join the hospital committee. Princess Viazemsky, touched by Sylvia's note of condolence, accepted and began a great adventure in which she met an odd, but equally dedicated assortment of fellow philanthropists. Rosalie had been born in Chicago, where her father was a partner in Marshall Field & Co. She was accustomed in both America and England to a life of culture and sophistication; being part of Sylvia's enterprise was a wholly new experience and brought her into contact with the East End, Ethiopian and other African supporters, eccentric members of the Labour Party, and the miscellaneous assortment of people that Sylvia attracted to the support of the Princess Tsähay Memorial fund. Princess Viazemsky found herself variously stationed behind baskets of strawberries for sale at Sylvia's fund-raising bazaars, watching a demonstration to raise money for Sir Seretse Khama, or attending a lecture by Jomo Kenyatta at a local hall.[26]

Interestingly, and perhaps surprisingly in the light of her earlier idealization of Russia, Sylvia now appeared to want to suppress that period of her life. Prince Viazemsky, though an aristocrat, had been sympathetic to the Russian Revolution in its first phase, but Sylvia never mentioned either to Rosalie or Prince Viazemsky that she had been an active communist, nor that she had visited Russia in 1920. Her Bolshevik past was behind her, and she preferred to forget that particular crusade even with close friends.[27]

Rosalie found Sylvia 'extraordinarily clever . . . someone always interested in everything to do with women . . . and a very good artist'.[28] But in the frenzy of her many Ethiopian activities Sylvia now had little time for art, though she completed at least one pastel which may well have been in tribute to nurse Princess Tsähay—two long brown arms stretching toward a white gauze-like material against an otherwise black background. Because Rosalie appreciated her art and became a patron of sorts for Afä Warq Tekle, Sylvia presented her with the pastel. As a result of the hospital campaign, a bond developed between these unlikely allies —the unrestrained radical, and the genteel, warm aristocrat.

Another woman entered Sylvia's life during the hospital campaign and remained a staunch friend until her death. Elsa Frankel, a sculptor and artist, met Sylvia during 1950. By 1951 she was helping organize cultural events featuring Ethiopia. She helped with and contributed her own work to a huge artistic celebration held in London when the Princess Tsähay Hospital was about to be dedicated. She sculpted and exhibited a bust of the princess, later placed in the hospital. Sylvia also contributed, loaning her portrait of Keir Hardie, which ordinarily hung prominently in her own house. Afä Warq Tekle showed some of his work, and Ethiopian students helped Rosalie run the associated bazaar. The actress Wendy Hiller, among others, spoke at the dedication, praising Sylvia for her tenacity in maintaining the fund despite the pressure of inflation and competing claims for attention from the Korean War.[29]

But the ceremony was not the end of the campaign: even after nine years of fund-raising and reckless spending on the hospital, the £100,000 goal had not been met, nor was the hospital ready to open. It was not until November 1951 that the emperor invited Sylvia, Lord Amulree, and others to the official opening in Addis Ababa. The delay resulted partly from personnel problems. After an extensive interview with several committee members, including Lord Amulree and Sylvia, a medical director had been hired in London. Sylvia alone detected what she regarded as serious personality flaws, and although she had a reputation for swift and astute character assessment, and was critical in this case, the overall judgement was to engage the candidate and send him to Ethiopia. According to Lord Almuree who was there, the new director was an alcoholic, and his wife too proved a liability in Ethiopia. The appointment was a serious embarrassment to the emperor and to the fund organizers, and the doctor was soon dismissed.[30] By early 1952 other problems were resolved and the Princess Tsähay Hospital was opened as the first fully-equipped training hospital in Ethiopia.[31]

Back in London, funds continued to be needed to pay for equipment sent out at the last minute. Mrs Tims and other staff made a frantic effort and brought in just enough to keep the creditors at bay; the need for extra funds was to continue for some time. The committee itself raised money for more equipment—the first elevator in Addis Ababa, in 1953; a complete physiotherapy unit through Lord Amulree's efforts, in 1955; and still more in the years which followed. In all, more than £90,000 was raised, and the hospital stands today, now considerably expanded, a monument to the memory of a young woman's dreams and a tribute to an old woman who made the dream come true.

In all, Sylvia probably received less credit than she deserved, and met with a certain amount of criticism from missionary societies and church groups. The Colonial Office and the Foreign Office themselves voiced many complaints, especially about Sylvia's fund-raising BBC broadcast. The critics alleged that the focus on the Princess Tsähay Hospital gave the impression that no one else in England was providing medical help to Ethiopia. In fact, several groups had contributed smaller clinics which were already working during Sylvia's long campaign for her hospital.[32]

As she reached her seventies Sylvia began to lose some life-long friends. George Bernard Shaw died in the autumn of 1950. Although never close friends, the two had been friendly antagonists at certain times, and supporters in mutual causes at others. Sylvia wrote a warm eulogy in the *New Times and Ethiopia News*:[33]

> I have fond memories of Bernard Shaw's outspoken support to the suffragettes, at a time when the voices were raised against us. . . . I remember gratefully his help during the First World War, when I and others from our headquarters in the East End of London were striving to obtain fairer dealings for the mothers, wives, and children of the soldiers. . . . Shaw emerged as a protagonist of social welfare and reform when English socialism wore the numbers of its early glory, proclaiming the brotherhood of mankind.

The loss of her dear friend Emmeline Pethick-Lawrence in 1954 brought a much stronger emotional response. Emmeline had been in failing health for some time. Crippled from an earlier fall, and nearly deaf, she was too frail to survive the heart attack which ultimately killed her. She and Frederick had recently celebrated their fiftieth wedding anniversary, and Sylvia had been among the speakers at the occasion. Emmeline had supported Sylvia through her many crises and was, in many ways, a surrogate mother. Her death brought great distress: Sylvia needed the emotional security and support Emmeline had always provided so generously. The *New Times* announced her death on the front page, referring to her as 'a friend of Ethiopia', (though Ethiopia had in fact been only a passing interest of Emmeline's). Sylvia then traced her active life as a reformer, as a founder of the Women's International League of Peace and Freedom, and as a humanitarian. No mention was made of the personal aid given to Sylvia or, earlier, to her mother's Women's Social and Political Union.[34] In the following weeks, Sylvia mourned Emmeline in several issues of the paper, linking her to Ethiopia so as to keep the cause alive. She also wrote a long letter of tribute to the Manchester *Guardian*, though mentioning only those among Emmeline's many contributions in which Sylvia was involved. There was no mistaking Sylvia's grief, but her self-centredness deepened in old age and she failed to recognize much beyond her own concerns. At a memorial service for her old friend, however, when Sylvia rose to give her eulogy, she was so overcome she broke into tears. She paced up and down the stage, hysterical and incoherent. Much of the audience—many former members of the WSPU—found her outburst unseemly but in character.[35] Emmeline's affection for Sylvia survived her. In her will, Richard and his mother were each remembered.

Earlier in 1954 Corio had died, but Sylvia took this loss more calmly. In recent years his health had been poor, and although his condition seemed stable, he must have had an awareness of trouble to come. A week before he died, he wrote to Mrs Tims, thanking her for her many kindnesses to Sylvia.[36] A cleaning woman found Corio dead one morning, apparently of a heart attack. Richard was immediately sent for. Mrs Tims remembered how little outward show of emotion Sylvia displayed. She made the funeral arrangements, but only Richard could attend. No memorial service was held, and an obituary on the front page of the *New Times* identified him only as one who laboured 'steadfastly for Ethiopia' —not as husband and father. There followed an inaccurate, but nevertheless admirable, potted history of his life as a reformer.[37] In contrast to Sylvia's poetic outpouring at the death of Keir Hardie, Corio's obituary was a mere chronicle. Several of his earlier anonymous articles were also included in this final tribute to her comrade of over thirty years. The only public expression of grief came from Afä Wärq Tekle, far off in Ethiopia, who wrote, 'I was deeply shocked to learn of the passing of our beloved guide, father, and friend Mr Corio.' Corio's absence, while scarcely noted in private or public, was immediately apparent in the quality of the *New Times and Ethiopia News*. Printing errors now abounded—a testament to the proofreading skill of the man who had otherwise become a shuffling figure in a busy household.

The loss of Corio and Emmeline Pethick-Lawrence was soon offset by the news that the emperor planned another trip to England. During his state visit in 1954, Sylvia, Lord Amulree, Princess Viazemsky and Richard all attended a reception at the Ethiopian embassy and were received by Haile Sellassie. Sylvia's personal relations with Ethiopian officials at the embassy had improved recently, helped by a change of ambassadors. She had irritated the last one with her constant demands for money. Mrs Tims also found him difficult; he was 'awkward', she said, with Sylvia and unsympathetic to her newspaper.[38] The new Ethiopian ambassador was gentle but firm on finances.[39] Expenses still ran high, even though the hospital campaign was winding down, and money from the embassy was running out. The embassy had long subsidized Sylvia's efforts, by purchasing copies of books, pamphlets, and runs of the *New Times* to be sent to sympathizers. By 1955 the practice had greatly diminished[40]: Sylvia's massive *Ethiopia: A Cultural History* was her only Ethiopian work not subsidized by Haile Sellassie. According to Richard, she sold the Red Cottage to pay the printing costs.[41]

By the time Haile Sellassie returned to England in 1954, Sylvia's interest in Ethiopian affairs had clearly become counter-productive. Her paper recycled old news, excerpts from her history, and other trivia. Resolved issues made dull copy. English interest in the hospital also declined dramatically.[42] The emperor must have recognized that Sylvia's continued efforts on his behalf were unnecessary, even embarrassing. One way to close down the flow of propaganda from West Dene would have been to stop the subsidies. But Haile Sellassie was genuinely fond of Sylvia and grateful for her dedication and years of service. He was loyal to those who had helped his country in difficult times, and gave generously to outsiders he considered to be patriots. No single individual had made as wholehearted (if unbridled and radical) a commitment as Sylvia, and Haile Sellassie acknowledged a significant debt even beyond the years of financial support he had already given. He no doubt also wanted to stop her propaganda efforts in England, and therefore invited Sylvia and Richard to return to Ethiopia, this time on a permanent basis. With Corio dead, Sylvia was free to go to her fairyland as an honoured patriot and friend. Richard was invited to join the faculty of the new University College at Addis Ababa, where his own dedication to Ethiopia might be used to good advantage among a small but select student body.

On 5 May 1956, Sylvia's seventy-fourth birthday, and twenty years after its first issue, the *New Times and Ethiopia News* ceased publication, with a formal announcement that it would be followed by a monthly review.[43] Sylvia's final words expressed appreciation to her readers 'for their generous cooperation and confidence'. She included a long poem, 'O Addis Ababa, O Fair New Flower', which praised her final utopia in archaic Victorian phraseology. The announcement brought a marked response from her limited but loyal readership. One Nigerian wrote to Sylvia that 'numerous friends over the world would miss greatly this faithful friend'. As to Sylvia: 'By reading this paper I have come to know the sort of woman you are . . . no other earthly factor could dampen one bit that steadfastness and international morality you have exhibited throughout the years.'[44]

Sylvia Pankhurst with Mrs Elsa Frankel and sculpture of Princess Tsähay

Sylvia Pankhurst with Haile Sellassie in Bath

Sylvia prepared for the move to Ethiopia even before the final issue of the *New Times and Ethiopia News* had appeared, but as usual it was haphazard in execution. She sold the house, now dark and rundown. Mr and Mrs Tims were left to dispose of the furniture, and to run what remained of the Ethiopian enterprises.[45] Through all her years of devoted service, Mrs Tims had never been paid. Now she was left with the English books to keep, papers to move and mail, and miscellaneous other tasks to perform for a pittance of £2 a week—and most of that went on postage.[46]

In Ethiopia, Sylvia's home in the former Italian compound was selected and presented to her by Haile Sellassie as a gift for her services to Ethiopia. She was surrounded by eucalyptus trees, which she loved, and, for the first time, by servants who tended the garden and the house—a life-style alien to her past, but in keeping with her new rank in Ethiopia.[47] Later, when diplomatic relations with Italy were restored, she and Richard moved to a smaller but still pleasant villa near the Princess Tsähay Hospital.[48] Otherwise her life in Ethiopia differed little from her life in England. She worked almost as hard as ever, mostly at writing. Richard was often with her, and she had her old Persian cat from West Dene too for company.[49] The emperor dropped in from time to time to find her sitting among her papers. Afä Warq Tekle was present at one of these visits. The emperor was warm and cordial, but Sylvia spoke to him like a child, which seemed to amuse him.[50] And life was easier in other respects. The emperor made available a car and a chauffeur, so that Sylvia could easily visit schools, medical facilities and other examples of Ethiopian modernization. These proved a special concern now she had found a new journalistic outlet. With the emperor's financial support, Sylvia and Richard together edited a new journal, the *Ethiopia Observer*. The first issue of this English-language publication appeared in December 1956, and it ran under her editorship for nearly four years. It differed little in content from the propagandist approach of the *New Times and Ethiopia News* except, as a journal, it was much longer—she was now in Ethiopia, and the whole country was open to her. She paid homage to Haile Sellassie in nearly every issue, with pictures, reports of his travels and speeches, and praise for himself, his government, and his family.

The attacks on Britain that had characterized her earlier publications were now missing, but Sylvia was still prickly and rose to the attack when something displeased her ideologically or personally. She published an illustrated article called 'Ethiopian Manuscript Painting', for example, and then criticized it editorially. The editor, she wrote, 'is not fully in agreement with the learned author in all his contentions.'[51] While the tone of the periodical was quixotic, reflecting more often than not Sylvia's opinions or her interests, the many illustrations were unique and often exciting, especially to the intellectually curious among her English readership. Indeed, the largest number of subscribers—and they were never many—were in England. In her last issue, she turned once more to do battle with Edward Ullendorff, whose book *The Ethiopians* had just appeared. In his Preface, Ullendorff made brief reference to the work of instant experts who had little real experience in Ethiopia. Sylvia took this to be a snide reference to her cultural history and was further offended that none of her Ethiopian publications was listed in the bibliography. The character of the review, however, was one of nit-picking, since both she and Ullendorff were basically pro-Ethiopian; nevertheless she lambasted him with the stored-up fervour of a long-out-of-service evangelist.[52]

She devoted one issue of the *Observer* to Ethiopian women, whose political freedom was favourably compared to that of long-suffering British women.[53] The fact that actual political freedom for women or men in her utopia was effectively non-existent escaped her completely: her understanding of a woman's place in Ethiopian society was far from accurate. She even wrote to an old acquaintance in Australia suggesting that congratulatory messages from people 'active in the international women's movement' might possibly move Ethiopian women (who were overwhelmingly illiterate) to come forward to register, vote and stand as candidates for parliament.[54] The *Observer* also published many historical and archaeological articles. Mother and son teamed up to co-edit a special issue on the Queen of Sheba, from whom the emperor claimed descent.[55] In one issue, she tried to describe the complicated and oppressive system of land tenure, but evaded the element of oppression. A peasant 'gets to keep one-third or one-quarter of his production' before passing the rest to the landlord. If Sylvia had ever understood Marx's theory of surplus value, she had long forgotten it. She was so captivated by the aristocracy which was collecting the surplus that her socialist perceptions had disappeared.

She reported trips to the exotic city of Harar with the finite wisdom of an artist, describing in poetic detail the mountains, the desert-like terrain, and finally the old walled city itself, successfully melding ancient exoticism with modern intrusions.[56] And she wrote a travelogue of Kenya too, her exhilaration in nature—the trees, birds, and animals—being almost contagious. But, in travelling, her impatience with rules remained. John Spencer recalled she told him that she had 'no patience with the various formalities' necessary for entering or leaving a country. Time and again, she said, she simply walked up to the frontier and, when no one was looking, 'rolled under the barbed wire fence'.[57]

Many of the earlier issues of the *Observer* featured beautiful and colourful paintings by Afä Warq Tekle, who by that time was something of a court painter and on his way to recognition as Ethiopia's best graphic artist.[58] But in spite of some high-quality articles, the journal drifted more and more into the genre of promotional writing for potential tourists. By 1959 Sylvia was back to using filler from the *New Times and Ethiopia News*, though some new articles about the Ethiopian war suggest she may have had another historical book in preparation.[59]

Sylvia was simultaneously in pursuit of good causes. All the middle-class reforms her parents had championed in her youth reappeared. She never learned Amharic, but she moved in Addis Ababa in what was in effect a middle-class Ethiopian and expatriate society and became, in 1959, one of the founders of a Social Service Society. She advocated improved working conditions, playgrounds for children, reform of prisons and mental hospitals—alongside the society's principal activity in the rehabilitation of Addis Ababa's beggars. She often visited the hospital, making plans for raising money in England for its new maternity wing.[60] Nursing sisters at the hospital remember Sylvia's interest. Sister Tekuamech Wolde Giorgis graduated from the school of nursing in 1955 and stayed on to become director of nursing. She remembered Sylvia's visits in 1951 and 1952, when she began her habit of visiting the hospital frequently and intervening in its affairs to the annoyance of the permanent staff. But others remembered her with gratitude—in one case Sylvia learned that a student nurse had become ill but had no money for her hospital bill. Sylvia herself paid half the charge and arranged credit to take care of the other half.[61]

The emperor was kept abreast by his secretary of Sylvia's suggestions for improving the country. No doubt he accepted her interest as genuine, while recognizing the romantic quality of many of her notions. Where possible, Sylvia acted independently and unilaterally. She extracted a promise from Haile Sellassie that she could pick up little children who were deformed, crippled, or ill and take them directly to the Princess Tsähay Hospital. She indicated in a letter to Britain:

> I want to be able to pick up any crippled child I come across, begging or limping with a crutch, and take him or her to the hospital to be treated without formalities except to ask the parents and give the surgeon and others the same facility. The number is not I believe very great but I have seen several. One girl is in Princess Tsähay [sic] hospital who has not walked for six years but who will soon be able to walk again . . .

Her chauffeur, Yami Muktar, recalled an occasion on which she spotted a crippled child; she ordered the car to stop, leapt out, picked up the surprised child, and had Muktar drive straight to the Princess Tsähay Hospital. The child was eventually healed.[63]

In matters of child welfare Sylvia's humanitarianism was appreciated: in counselling the Ethiopian government on foreign affairs, however, she was less successful. She thought of herself, after all, as a public figure of some stature in England, especially when advising the British government on Ethiopian matters. Her successes, as she saw them, included the favourable settlement of both the Eritrean and the Somali issues. John Spencer described her Ethiopian forays in this way:[64]

> She frequently saw the Emperor whom she flattered endlessly. . . . She also came frequently to talk with Aklilou Abte Wold [the Foreign Minister] to the point that I very often joked with him about the number of times that he felt compelled to listen to her discussions and proposals. Neither he nor I sought to oppose her, but the fact remains that unless one is daily dealing with pullulating details of foreign affairs one cannot hope to exert influence on foreign policy in a close society like that around the Emperor's court. The Emperor's favor was not enough to compensate for the lack of familiarity with the problems. The net result was that she fell into a largely passive role. . . . One Ethiopian explained to me that her fault was that her commitment to Ethiopia made her too Ethiopian for even the Ethiopians.

Spencer accurately captured Sylvia's essential and long-lasting character: she was, he said, in later life as in her youth, of two sharply contrasting personalities. 'One was dynamic, impatient and intolerant, but given over to almost unbridled enthusiasms and commitments' and the other 'was in Manichean black and white, resistant to countervailing qualifications, considerations and arguments.'[65]

Members of the foreign community recall visiting Sylvia in her villa. Professor Stanislas Chojnacki, a museum curator, described her house as 'one of the rare homes with character, with its high slanted roof'. It was of typical Italian construction, and surrounded by a large wooded compound. Sylvia turned the porch into a veranda, on which she often worked.[66] David Talbot, long-time editor of the English-language *Ethiopian Herald*, first met Sylvia in 1944 when she went to Ethiopia to inspect the hospital site, and kept in contact later. He recalled that 'she was quite a character when it came to talking against her own country for Ethiopia'.[67] 'The Emperor recognized her as a faithful champion of his causes. . . . He gave her a beautiful villa, staff and ready access to him.' 'The door was always open' for her to visit him. On Sylvia at home, Talbot was amazed at the state of her office: 'I went in there and there were pieces of paper all over the floor . . . "that's a book, David Talbot, that's a book" she said.' Notes were strewn everywhere: she told him she 'would annotate' when she had 'strung them together'.[68]

During these final years too, Sylvia came back into touch with friends she had known earlier in life. Teresa Billington-Greig, one of the early members of the WSPU, was at work on an account of the suffrage movement and sent a biographical sketch of Sylvia's involvement, asking for any factual corrections. Sylvia responded with a thirty-page autobiographical account of her own—much longer than the Billington-Greig version—and asked Billington-Greig to incorporate it. Sylvia's statement is especially interesting because it reveals something of the

Haile Sellassie leading Sylvia Pankhurst to the Ethiopian home which he personally
selected for her in 1956

image she wanted to leave of herself. Not only did she omit mention of her communist activities; she explicitly denied having been a member of the Party at all. In Ethiopia, under the patronage of Haile Sellassie, Sylvia was determined to bury that part of the past.

Self-serving ways in old age are more forgivable than in youth; Sylvia, in retrospect, highlighted the achievements already chronicled in her many books. Her tendency to insist on her version of history remained. She wrote to Billington-Greig, 'I must protest what you say about my relations with socialist comrades. On the contrary I was . . . one of the most popular speakers in the Labour and Socialist movement.' This was, of course, untrue, though it may have been Sylvia's fantasy. She again told of her sacrifice in abandoning her career as an artist in favour of social and political causes. But she had had a choice, and seems never to have admitted that she could not give up the stage for the seclusion of the studio.

Sylvia rebuked Billington-Greig for references to her appearance: 'I think you could well save space by omitting your remarks on dress. . . . It is in my opinion long past time for women who have done important public work to be . . . estimated on that basis. Who cares—for example—how Churchill dresses or whether he has a handsome nose or a lovely complexion'.[69] Again, she claimed credit for winning the vote through her to-the-death challenge of Asquith: 'What you have in your script might be modified thus: "It was felt by many that Sylvia Pankhurst . . . had broken the last barrier to the vote" . . . '[70] Sadly, the 'many' amounted to Sylvia herself and a few of her remaining followers from East London. She traced her years as an anti-Fascist which had led to her career as a radical publicist for Ethiopia. She believed that her greatest contribution was her dedicated propaganda campaign for Ethiopia in England. Here we can agree. To set the record straight, Sylvia appears to have signed a contract with a British publisher for her memoirs. But it was never written: the biographical sketch for Billington-Greig was the last statement on her personal history. 'Please note that what I have written for you is to be strictly confined to my obituary'.[71]

Sylvia wrote often to Mrs Tims—mostly descriptive passages on Ethiopian travel and chronicles of her recent activities. She wrote infrequently to Lady Winstedt, a patron of the hospital, and a generous donor in the past. Elsa Frankel kept in touch, as did Princess Viazemsky on occasion, but these were her only English contacts. Annie Barnes, perhaps speaking for surviving East End friends, believed Sylvia had dropped her as she moved into a new social circle during her Ethiopia campaign. In 1959 Elsa Frankel decided, with Lady Winstedt and with the support of Princess Viazemsky, to hold an exhibition of Sylvia's art. Sylvia sent photographs of her designs for the WSPU fete in the prince's skating rink some fifty years earlier, and other material.

Of her art, Sylvia wrote, 'I often feel I should paint again . . . but I am always busy and I feel that if I were to make a start I should be terribly disappointed with what I could produce after an interval of fifty years.'[72] Although Sylvia did no serious painting in these last years, she continued to doodle in her notebooks, a habit developed years before when she wrote by hand her first piece for *Votes for Women*. As to the exhibit in London, she was most grateful and wrote to Mrs Frankel that 'I am only sorry I cannot give you what would make an adequate exhibition. Of course the losses and destruction of what I did were partly due to the fact that I was never satisfied with anything I did, and believed I should learn to do much better in the coming years.'[73]

The one-day exhibition was held at the French Institute on 5 December 1959, with the somewhat surprising sponsorship of the Suffragette Fellowship, Theresa Billington-Greig's Women's Freedom League, and the Royal India Pakistan and Ceylon Society. Mrs Vijaya Lakshmi Pandit, then Indian ambassador to Britain, formally opened the small exhibition. Princess Viazemsky remembered it as a great success with a large attendance, including some of the more disaffected members of Sylvia's family.[74]

News of the exhibition re-established contact briefly with Norah Smyth, to whom Sylvia had written—probably in search of old paintings. Smyth was surprised to learn that Sylvia was alive, having read Christabel's obituary and not having heard from Sylvia for many years. In response to a comment in Sylvia's earlier letter, Norah joined in lamenting: 'Yes it is strange, as you say, that you should be remembered as an artist and your work for humanity forgotten by the public, but it will be remembered on in the hearts of the many people who benefitted from it.'[75] Now, old and philosophical, Norah's earlier militancy had diminished: of contemporary Britain, she wrote, 'It is a curious artificial age, I feel it is being corrupted by the "way of life" of the USA where money has been made their god . . .'[76]

Despite the excitement of the exhibition, Sylvia's attention remained with Ethiopia. She worked on her history, edited the journal, and began yet another volume in exultation of Ethiopia. Her visits to the hospital became less frequent as she devoted ever more time to her writing. Afä Warq Tekle called nearly every day. Richard continued working with his mother on limited joint projects. And, though nothing in Sylvia's earlier attitudes indicated that she might readily share her son, she welcomed Rita Eldon, from a family of Jewish descent from Romania, into her home as Richard's wife with no visible sign of distress but with warmth and enthusiasm.

On a 'fresh brilliant day' in September 1960, Afä Wärq Tekle was summoned from his nearby house by a servant, who told him 'Miss Pankhurst is not awake'. It was three in the afternoon, the hour Sylvia usually rose from her nap. Afä Warq rushed to the house and found

Sylvia motionless, her writing pad on the bed next to her: 'I had never seen death face to face—but if death is beautiful, she was beautiful. [She had a] restful face, such a relaxed face.'[77]

In her seventy-eight years Sylvia had known little rest or relaxation. To be so described in death might have rankled the activist element in her personality, but to be described in Afä Warq Tekle's loving words as restful—at peace—would have appealed to her artistic self. The BBC announced the death in England. Friends and former opponents joined in paying final respects. Lord Frederick Pethick-Lawrence of Peaslake wired: 'For a warrior, as she was, it is happiest when the end comes in the thick of life'.[78] Edward Ullendorff came forward with warmth: '[I] always admired her courage and devotion. . . . For myself I have always been in sympathy with her fight for the underdog, the oppressed and the persecuted . . .'.[79] Grace Roe's brief tribute, 'She was one of the most courageous militants . . .',[80] illustrated best how the sting of death pierces the armour of estrangement.

Princess Viazemsky and Lady Winstedt arranged a memorial service at Caxton Hall, site of many protest meetings in Sylvia's radical past. Lord Amulree, whose anonymous support had often bailed her out of hospital spending sprees, joined Frederick Pethick-Lawrence in paying tribute to the old fighter.[81] In England her life had been spent largely in opposition to the government of people who honoured her that day; yet the most intolerant among them must have admired her energy and drive even when they disagreed with her radical politics.

Elsa Frankel's tribute to Sylvia—'Perhaps judging the three Pankhursts later in history, she will be the greatest one . . .'[82]—was echoed and enlarged by David Mitchell in *The Fighting Pankhursts*. Sylvia was, he wrote, 'Perhaps the greatest Englishwoman of her time'.[83] Greatness is not always measured by visibility but Sylvia may have been the greatest Englishwoman of her kind. She was, from her earliest days in the suffrage movement, a radical who favoured drastic action to effect social reform. She came to radicalism from early rebellion in the home, where she rebelled against her mother's favouritism for her sister, Christabel. After Mrs Pankhurst and Christabel joined in the running of the WSPU, Sylvia rebelled against their authority and began her own organization. In the East End her personal rebellion against her mother and sister's class relations was transformed to rebellion against the conditions in which her followers lived and worked. This led to her lifelong rebellion against the British government and ultimately to her self-ascribed status as a revolutionary in the years following the Russian Revolution.

Lillian Hellman, in describing herself, wrote that a rebel cannot be a good revolutionary. This insight is equally true of Sylvia Pankhurst. We know that she rebelled against revolutionary discipline as much as officialdom, as evidenced in the quarrel with Lenin, and her subsequent expulsion from the Communist Party of Great Britain. Here Sylvia was more zealot than rebel. The greatest act of rebellion against her nuclear family, however, came when she publicized her 'eugenic' baby a few months after Richard was born, at a time when her mother was weakened by illness and overwork from her political campaign in the East End.

The seething anger that fed her rebellious behaviour was echoed in her writings, and in *The Suffragette Movement* and *The Life of Emmeline Pankhurst* particularly. By 1935, after publishing the biography of her mother, she had purged her remaining anger and was no longer driven to either rebellious or revolutionary activity. Her mother was long dead and Christabel no longer a rival. From anti-Fascist campaigning she turned to championing the Ethiopian nation, and in the process made the extreme transition from radical socialist to radical supporter of a feudal monarchy. The energy that had earlier motivated and sustained rebellion surfaced again in the devotion to Ethiopia; and the skill as propagandist, learned during the suffrage days and continued into her Communist activities re-emerged full-blown in her service to the Emperor Haile Sellassie. There was continuity too with her earlier campaigns—the hatred for British officialdom which dominated her writings on every topic, to and through her Ethiopia campaigns.

On a more personal level Sylvia was a bundle of contradictions. As a young artist she had been both sensitive and talented. Her early ideals to create a colourful world for the poor faded into memory as she gave herself over to a life of activism. As an activist she had her faults —no sense of humour, imperiousness and arrogance, and the inability to compromise on issues that might have brought her swifter personal victories. But these were weaknesses inherited from Sylvia's father. His death in her adolescence stunted her emotional growth—Sylvia in many ways remained sixteen well into her seventies. The hero-worship first for Keir Hardie, then Lenin, and finally for Haile Sellassie had their roots in her attachment to her father.

Many of Sylvia's finer qualities came from her father, too. Her compassion for the underdog, which brought her success among the poor in London's East End, and among the many Ethiopian students she helped in England are two examples of her father's early influence. Her boundless energy and drive were dual inheritances and were shared by her sisters in their own special crusades. There was something special involved in being a Pankhurst, even if the contemporary public image of the family was not always acceptable.

Sylvia's relations with her friends and followers were quixotic. She rejected the middle class, from which she came, when she herself felt rejected by the WSPU (although she had the wealthy Norah Smyth at her side throughout the East End campaigns). We know of the complexities of her relations with her mother and sister. Her love affair with Keir Hardie in no way set the stage for her long partnership with the unknown Italian with whom she lived so long and to whom she bore a son. Despite losses of early friendships, Sylvia managed to retain the loyalty of a few East End supporters through the suffrage campaign into pacifism during the Great War and on to the revolutionary years. Her erratic behaviour was balanced to some extent by her personal magnetism.

After the birth of her son, Sylvia gradually returned to the circles she had deserted, briefly associating with free-spirited middle-class women like Dora Russell and creative women such as Vera Brittain. These relations, however, did not last. Even in attempting a more conventional life-style, Sylvia was unable to curb her independent—possibly undisciplined—spirit. Although she did not wholly abandon the few remaining East End friends, their role in her life changed: Annie Barnes, for instance, became part-time cook and helper. Sylvia's brief flirtation with Romania in the mid-1930s brought some valuable friendships. Her years as author and journalist produced a few acquaintances but no long-term friends. Only Emmeline Pethick-Lawrence was a constant ally, though for reasons we can only guess, she never helped Sylvia advance in the major peace organization she helped found and which she led for a time. Sylvia was forced to turn instead to a fringe group, when she reactivated her interest in the peace movement in the 1930s, joining an increasing number of Britons who actively sought disarmament.

As her personal associations underwent a metamorphosis she was courageous in support of those who needed her most. These ranged from Jews in East London whom she defended in her newspaper from anti-Semitic attack (and often from her own constituents); to Welsh miners in the General Strike; to Italian anti-Fascists in concentration camps who she helped relocate (before she alienated the anti-Fascist leadership in England); and, of course, to the hundreds of downtrodden East Enders whose problems she made her own between 1914 and 1917.

Sylvia's organizational problems and financial difficulties began in the East End and plagued her throughout her life. Happily there was always someone to bail her out, someone who recognized her compassion and commitment and forgave her financial irresponsibility. The supporters ranged from Norah Smyth in the East End, to Emmeline Pethick-Lawrence, and to Lord Amulree who came to the rescue during the final campaign for the Princess Tsähay Hospital. And, most conspicuously, from 1936 until 1960, it was the Emperor of Ethiopia himself who supported Sylvia and the enterprises she pursued in his behalf.

Despite her radicalism, and the trouble it brought her with people who supported the same goals, and her failure in organizational matters, Sylvia's most tangible and lasting monument was the Princess

Tsähay Hospital in Addis Ababa. Her torrent of articles, books and poetry are testament to her energy and her self-confidence, if not necessarily to her talents. Above all Sylvia never rested on her laurels. Her father's admonition to work, and the altruistic direction of his own labour, remained with her despite her daily eccentricities.

What is remarkable, too, about Sylvia's campaigns to help the less fortunate—whether on the left or the right—was that she might well have been crippled by the rules governing her behaviour as a woman. When she began her suffrage campaign women had no voice in political affairs. Sylvia fought valiantly for the vote. She harried the conservative-minded men of the East End in order to arouse the support of their wives. When successful on the suffrage issue, she enthusiastically dragged her supporters into the organizational struggles to form a communist party. Although she ultimately lost her organization, and the quest for leadership was denied her because she was too far to the left of the Party, it never occurred to Sylvia that she might also be denied her goals because of her sex. In fact, no matter now compliant, there was little likelihood of her being made the leader of the CP–GB. It was not until fifty years later that a woman could rise to the leadership of a British political party—and the CP–GB was in many ways a more conservative body than the Tory Party that chose Margaret Thatcher as its leader.

Sylvia's views on feminist issues were paradoxical. Often she invoked her suffrage activities as a way of reminding people who she was, or, less successfully, as an example of strategy for other battles. She maintained a jealous hold on it as witnessed by her forays into the film world in the late 1940s, and her several libel actions or threats of actions against others who wrote about the suffrage movement. But she never abandoned her interest in the cause of women: in all of her many campaigns for a wide variety of goals, she never left women out.

Publicly Sylvia gave the impression that being a woman was more an accessory than a primary fact of her life. Privately her life presented a succession of dependencies on men. First there was her father, who died before she reached maturity. Keir Hardie appeared to take that place, and Sylvia remained emotionally reliant on Hardie up to his death. Until Corio entered her life in the 1920s, there is no evidence of further personal relationships with men. But we do know that Lenin became a hero-figure for Sylvia until their disagreement on the question of parliamentarianism severed the incipient relationship. In her stand against Lenin, Sylvia acted the role of the petulant child rather than that of the serious ideologue.

Although Corio appeared relegated to the background for most of the years Sylvia lived with him, friends believed he provided the emotional security she required while energetically pursuing her political campaigns. The final dependence, on Haile Sellassie, overtook her relationship with Corio. Sylvia turned wholeheartedly to serve the emperor and seems to have ignored Corio after her first trip to Ethiopia: she did not even attend his funeral. Sylvia's genuine feminism was buttressed by the men in her life, not compromised by them. Like so many of the feminists of her generation, her emotional experience was complicated, and unresolved.

On her death, Sylvia was mourned by many, in different parts of the world, who had not known her personally. W. E. B. DuBois identified one of her outstanding contributions: 'the great work of Sylvia Pankhurst was to introduce black Ethiopia to white England.'[84] A Polish man, a chance encounter, remembered her as 'one of the few people in England who was kind to me'.[85] The churches in British Guiana held a memorial service for her as a champion of all colonial peoples.[86] From Sri Lanka, an admirer wrote that he was sorry he would never see her again: 'She lived a very useful life and one which incidentally made her known to the whole world...'[87]

The deepest sense of loss, however, was felt in Ethiopia, where, in spite of her eccentricities, she was deeply respected for her continued devotion to the country. Beyond mere respect was the personal affection of the Ethiopian students who had been almost members of her family. And Richard, who had never been long separated from his mother, wrote to Mrs Frankel: 'Even now I can scarcely believe I have lost her. Of course I saw her getting old but she was so active to the end, so full of ideas...'[88]

The most impressive tribute came from Haile Sellassie. As his final act of gratitude to the British radical who adopted his cause and became his most militant warrior, the emperor ordered a state funeral in Trinity Cathedral and broke precedent so that, as a patriot of Ethiopia, Sylvia might be buried in a special plot reserved for Ethiopia's heroes in front of the cathedral. The emperor and other members of the royal family attended this commoner's funeral, accompanied by thousands who came to pay their last respects to their dead sister. Afä Warq Tekle remembered it as an event 'of great pomp and ceremony for a great hero'.[89] The Manchester *Guardian* reported: 'Observers said it was the most outstanding tribute ever paid at a non-royal or non-official funeral in Ethiopia'.[90]

The pageantry of Sylvia's burial was a symbol of Ethiopia's gratitude. But the words of *Ras* Andargatchew Massai, who gave the eulogy, conveyed the sentiments of those gathered at the ceremony for 'Walata Kristos' (Child of Christ), the Ethiopian name bestowed on her death:[91]

> Sylvia Pankhurst, the Emperor of Ethiopia and the Ethiopian people, whom you sincerely and honestly served, now stand weeping around you. With those days of suffering in mind your friends the patriots and exiles

are standing near you. Your history will live forever written in blood, with the history of the Ethiopian patriots. Since by His Imperial Majesty's wish you rest in peace in the earth of Ethiopia, we consider you an Ethiopian.

Raised as an atheist by socialist parents, Sylvia entered the Christian world by way of death. 'Walata Kristos', who once wrote 'I never found time to rest', had found both the time and the place in her beloved Ethiopia.

Notes

Chapter 1   The Early Years

1. Estelle Sylvia Pankhurst, *The Suffragette Movement* (hereafter *Suffragette Movement*) (London, 1931), 3–58; Estelle Sylvia Pankhurst, *The Life of Emmeline Pankhurst* (New York, 1969); Emmeline Pankhurst, *My Own Story* (London, 1914); Christabel Pankhurst, *Unshackled* (London, 1959). For a detailed account of family life and background see especially *The Suffragette Movement*. The preceding material comes from the sources cited herein. Much of the following in this chapter is from *The Suffragette Movement*.
2. Ibid., 57–8.
3. Ibid., 19.
4. Ibid.; Estelle Sylvia Pankhurst in Margot Asquith, *Myself When Young* (London, 1934), 265; Interview, Enid Goulden Bach, London, 1978. Jill Craigie to author, October 1975.
5. *Suffragette Movement*, 68; Jill Craigie believes that Emmeline fell out with her father over politics.
6. *Manchester Examiner and Times*, 4 November 1885.
7. Christabel Pankhurst, *Visions of the New Dawn* (Philadelphia, n.d.).
8. *Suffragette Movement*, 88.
9. Ibid., 111.
10. Read the involvements of Doctor Pankhurst as described in Ibid., 3–152.
11. Ibid., 84, 104.
12. Estelle Sylvia Pankhurst in Margot Asquith, *Myself When Young* (London, 1934), 265.
13. Estelle Sylvia Pankhurst (ESP), unpublished manuscript Pankhurst Papers (PP), International Institute for Social History (IISH), Amsterdam.
14. *Suffragette Movement*, 99.
15. Ibid., 88.
16. Ibid., 112.
17. Ibid., 114.
18. 'Report of Progress', 1893, PP.
19. ESP, unpub. mss., PP.
20. Dame Ethyl Smyth, *Female Pipings in Eden* (London, 1934), 242.
21. Dame Rebecca West, 'Mrs Pankhurst', in *The Post-Victorians* (London, 1933), 487.
22. ESP, *Myself When Young*, 264.
23. *Suffragette Movement*, 124.
24. Ibid., 124.
25. Adela to Helen Moyes; quoted in Helen Moyes, *Woman in a Man's World* (Sidney, 1971), 38.
26. *Suffragette Movement*, 94.
27. J. M. Doughty to ESP, 8 September 1910, PP.
28. See Norman and Jeanne MacKenzie, *The Fabians* (New York, 1977).
29. George Bernard Shaw, 'To Your Tents, Oh Israel', *Fortnightly Review*, November 1893: 569–80.

30. *Suffragette Movement*, 136.
31. Anonymous letter to Mrs Pankhurst, 20 July 1894, PP.
32. Chushichi Tsuzuki, *The Life of Eleanor Marx 1855–1898* (Oxford, 1967); Ronald Florence, *Marx's Daughters* (New York, 1975).
33. Christabel Pankhurst, *Unshackled*, 34.
34. Ibid.
35. *Suffragette Movement*, passim; *Life of Emmeline Pankhurst*, passim.
36. Helen Moyes, taped interview, Sidney, Australia, August 1976.
37. Manchester *Guardian*, 6 July, 1895.
38. Ibid., 7 July, 1895.
39. Moyes, taped interview.
40. *Suffragette Movement*, 125.
41. Richard Marsden Pankhurst: 'On the House of Lords and on Representative Government', pamphlet, n.d., London School of Economics; 'Citizenship', n.d., LSE; 'Pax Hominis Under the Reign of Law', n.d., LSE: 'Dr Pankhurst on the Future of Liberalism' n.d., LSE; 'Educational Requirements in Relation to the Study' n.d., LSE.
42. Quoted in *Unshackled*, 35.
43. *Suffragette Movement*, 150–1.
44. ESP, *Myself When Young*, 272; *Suffragette Movement*, 152–5.
45. Ibid., 155.

Chapter 2   Radical Artist and Radical Love

1. Leonard V. Thompson, *Robert Blatchford: Portrait of an Englishman* (London, 1951), 142.
2. Manchester *Guardian*, 15 July 1898.
3. Manchester *Guardian*, 16 July 1898.
4. Letter to Emmeline Pankhurst, 1902, PP.
5. Emmeline Pankhurst, *My Own Story* (New York, 1914), 19.
6. ESP, *Suffragette Movement*, 154.
7. Ibid., 155.
8. Ibid., 157.
9. Ibid.
10. Ibid.
11. Ibid., 155.
12. ESP, unpublished manuscript, PP.
13. For a full, but derivative account of Sylvia's art career, see Richard Pankhurst, *Sylvia Pankhurst: Artist and Crusader* (London, 1979). Most of the material in the early phases of her life and training as an artist are uncritically presented and come directly from *The Suffragette Movement*, 146–88.
14. ESP, , *Suffragette Movement*, 159.
15. William Morris, *The Art of the People* (Chicago, 1902), 37.
16. ESP, *Suffragette Movement*, 156.
17. Norman and Jean MacKenzie, *The Fabians* (New York: 1977), 185–190.
18. Adela to Mrs Helen Moyes, quoted in *Woman in a Man's World* (Sidney, 1971), 38.
19. ESP, *Suffragette Movement*, 160.
20. Richard Pankhurst, *Sylvia*, 30–9.
21. ESP, *Suffragette Movement*, 162.
22. Ibid., 161–2.
23. Ibid., 162–3.
24. ESP, unpublished manuscript, PP.

25. ESP, *Suffragette Movement*, 163.
26. Adela to Helen Moyes, in *Woman in*, 38.
27. ESP, unpublished manuscript, PP.
28. ESP, *Suffragette Movement*, 156–8; 164–70.
29. ESP, unpublished manuscript, PP.
30. ESP, *Suffragette Movement*, 165.
31. ESP, *Myself When Young*, 165.
32. Ibid., 270; Walter Crane, *Decorative Illustration* (London, 1896), 187.
33. ESP, *Suffragette Movement*, 165.
34. Richard Pankhurst, *Sylvia*, 48; ESP, *Suffragette Movement*, 172.
35. Ibid.
36. Ibid., 173.
37. Amy Browning to Panky, 16 August, 1906; Henry Cadness to Miss Pankhurst, 2 August 1906; Cyril D. Fitzroy to Estelle, 25 July 1906, PP.
38. ESP, *Suffragette Movement*, 215.
39. Ibid., 126; ESP, *Myself When Young*, 270.
40. Lord Fenner Brockway, interview, London, 3 July 1975; to Jill Craigie, 24 August 1976, copy in possession of author.
41. ESP, *Suffragette Movement*, 168.
42. Kenneth O. Morgan, *Keir Hardie* (London, 1975), 9.
43. ESP, unpublished manuscript, PP.
44. Kenneth O. Morgan, *Keir Hardie*, 205; see also G. D. H. Cole, *James Keir Hardie* (London, The Fabian Society), 1941.
45. Quoted in Morgan, 205.
46. Morgan, *Keir Hardie*, 46.
47. Frederick, *Labour, Life and Literature: Memories of Sixty Years*, ed. David Rubenstein (Brighton, 1973), 211–12.
48. Morgan, *Keir Hardie*, 12, 58.
49. ESP, *Suffragette Movement*, 176.
50. Ibid., 177.
51. Ibid.
52. Keir Hardie to Sylvia, n.d., PP.; postcard to Sylvia, n.d., PP.
53. Frank Smith to Sylvia, 22 September 1915, PP.
54. National Portrait Gallery, London.
55. Paintings seen by author, London, 1976–77.
56. Sylvia to Keir Hardie, *c*. 1906, PP.
57. Amy Browning to Sylvia, August 1906; Henry Cadness to Miss Pankhurst, 2 August 1906, PP.

Chapter 3   The March of the Women

1. E. Sylvia Pankhurst, *The Suffragette* (London, 1911); see also ESP, *The Suffragette Movement*, (London, 1931); Constance Rover, *Women's Suffrage; Party Politics in Britain* (London, 1967); Antonia Raeburn, *Militant Suffragettes* (London, 1973); Roger Fulford, *Votes for Women* (London, 1957); Milicent Fawcett, *Women's Suffrage* (London, *c*. 1912–13) and *The Women's Victory and After* (London, 1920); Teresa Billington-Greig, *The Militant Suffrage Movement* (London, 1912); Christabel Pankhurst, *Unshackled* (London, 1959); Emmeline Pankhurst, *My Own Story* (London, 1912); Ray Strachey, *The Cause* (London, 1928); E. Sylvia Pankhurst, *The Life of Emmeline Pankhurst* (London, 1935); Jill Liddington and Jill Norris, *One Hand Tied Behind Us* (London, 1978); Frederick Pethick-Lawrence, *Fate Has Been Kind* (London, 1955); Emmeline Pethick-Lawrence, *My Part in a Changing World* (London, 1938); Andrew Rosen, *Rise Up Women!* (London, 1974); Leslie Parker

Hume, *The National Union of Women's Suffrage Societies 1897–1914* (New York, 1982); Duncan Crow, *The Edwardian Woman* (New York, 1978); M. D. Pugh, *Electoral Reform in War and Peace 1906–1918* (London, 1978); Martin Pugh, *Women's Suffrage in Britain 1867–1928* (London, 1980). Pugh is among the first of the historians writing on the suffrage movement to recognize how invalid most memoirs of the period are. While acknowledging that Sylvia's work was useful to historians, he also wrote that 'militants own accounts are largely fantasy', the motives for writing them self-serving, including the desire to 'perpetuate the image of martyrdom'. The latter statement describes much of Sylvia's interpretation of her experiences in the suffrage movement. This chapter and the one following are not meant to describe the suffrage movement in Great Britain; they are only highlights for continuity, and an interpretation of Sylvia's own involvement.

2. Liddington and Norris, *One Hand*, 172; see also Sheila Rowbotham, *Hidden from History* (New York, 1967), 78–9.
3. ESP, *Suffragette Movement*, 183.
4. George Dangerfield, *Strange Death of Liberal England* (New York, 1961), 151; Martin Pugh, *Suffrage*, 20; Liddington and Norris, *One Hand*, passim.
5. Leonard V. Thompson, *The Enthusiasts: A Biography of John and Katherine Bruce Glasier* (London, 1971), 70.
6. ESP, *Suffragette Movement*, 187; see also Jill Liddington, 'Rediscovering Suffrage History', *History Workshop* 4: 193 (1977).
7. *Suffragette Movement*, 189–90; Christabel Pankhurst, *Unshackled*; Emmeline Pankhurst, *My Own Story*, 46–9. Unfortunately, the only biography of Christabel is a very poor, decidedly unsympathetic work by David Mitchell, *Queen Christabel* (London, 1977). Mitchell suggests that it was Christabel's desire for publicity which motivated her to spit on the policeman; more likely she was following the tactics she knew to have been employed by Labourites and the Irish when she practised this form of civil disobedience.
8. ESP, *Suffragette Movement*, 192; see also Rosen, *Rise Up Women!*
9. ESP, *Suffragette Movement*, 180.
10. See correspondence between George Bernard Shaw and Sylvia, Berg Collection, New York Public Library.
11. Emmeline Pethick-Lawrence, *My Part In*, 149; ESP, *Suffragette Movement*, 216.
12. Christabel Pankhurst, *Unshackled*, 67.
13. *Votes for Women* (1907) passim.
14. ESP, *Suffragette Movement*, 217.
15. ESP, *Suffragette Movement*, 217.
16. Ibid., 221.
17. Ibid., 221.
18. Ibid., 229.
19. Mary L. Gordon, *Penal Discipline* (London, 1922), 15.
20. Ibid., 36.
21. ESP, *Suffragette Movement*, 231.
22. Ibid.
23. Ibid., 235. For an example of Mrs Pankhurst's compassion for poor women, see L. Bailey, BBC Scrapbooks, I, 'Mrs. Pankhurst's speech from the Dock, Bow Street' (London, 1906), 143.
24. ESP, *Suffragette Movement*, 235.
25. File II, 56 PP.
26. Ibid.
27. ESP, *Suffragette Movement*, 238.
28. Fenner Brockway to Jill Craigie, taped interview. Copy of transcript in possession of author.

29. Helen Fraser Moyes, taped interview; Emmeline Pethick-Lawrence held this extreme view of Mrs Pankhurst in later years. Emmeline Pethick-Lawrence to Sylvia, n.d. (*c.* 1930) PP.
30. ESP, *Suffragette Movement*, 238.
31. Keir Hardie to Sylvia, n.d. PP.
32. Keir Hardie, *India: Impressions and Suggestions* (London, 1909), copy at LSE. See also Hardie's columns in the *Labour Leader*, 1909, passim.
33. ESP, *Suffragette Movement*, 272.
34. Ibid., 273.
35. Ibid., 320.
36. Ibid., 320–5.
37. Ibid., 324.
38. Ibid.
39. Note from Herbert Goulden, n.d. PP.
40. ESP, *Suffragette Movement*, 283–6; in 1911 the Fabians formed a separate suffrage society.
41. Annie Barnes, personal interview, 17 September 1974.
42. See Emmeline Pethick-Lawrence, *My Part In . . .* , 346; ESP to Elsa Frankel, 7 August 1959 (including a full description of the designs); ESP, *Suffragette Movement*, 304–6; ESP to Teresa Billington-Greig, n.d. (*c* 1956) WSPU Papers, Fawcett Library.
43. Martin Pugh, *Suffrage*, 23; see also Liddington and Norris, *One Hand . . .* passim. For notation of Sylvia's interest in Home Rule and this arrest, see Leah Levenson, *With Wooden Sword: A Portrait of Francis Sheehy-Skeffington, Militant Pacifist* (Boston, 1983), 158–9.
44. Milicent Fawcett, *Women's Suffrage*, 79; for the politics of the suffrage question see the Earl of Asquith and Oxford, *Fifty Years of the British Parliament*, 2 vols. (London, 1926) 1: 40; George Dangerfield, *Strange Death*; David Morgan, *Suffragists and Liberals*, (London, 1975).
45. Christabel Pankhurst, *Unshackled*, 80; ESP, *Suffragette Movement*, 290–301.
46. Helen Fraser Moyes, *Woman in Man's World*, 31; taped interview.
47. Jill Craigie, custodian of Christabel's, Mrs Pankhurst's and Grace Roe's papers (which have not been available to Andrew Rosen and others working on the suffrage movement) believes that Christabel's role and intelligence may have been underrated by Sylvia's portrayal. Personal interview, Venice, August 1976; London, July 1978.
48. ESP, to Miss Robins, 3 December 1908, Elizabeth Robins Collection, HRC.
49. ESP, *Suffragette Movement*, 298.
50. Mrs Pankhurst to Sylvia, 12 and 22 June 1907, PP.
51. ESP, *Suffragette Movement*, 25.
52. *Everyman*, n.d. (*c.* 1931).
53. *Sunday Herald*, 31 October 1909.
54. Undated clips from *The Times* and *TP's Weekly*, courtesy of *The Times*. Mrs Pankhurst's memoirs, *My Story*, published in 1914, was mostly ghost-written by an American, Rita Childe Dorr, who buttressed Mrs Pankhurst's personal accounts with press cuttings and leaned heavily on *Votes for Women*—as had Sylvia in *The Suffragette*.
55. Sylvia to Hardie, n.d., PP.
56. ESP, *Suffragette Movement*, 347.
57. Harriet Stanton Blatch and Alma Lutz, *Challenging Years* (New York, 1940), 137.
58. Blatch, *Challenging Years*, 137.
59. *New York Times*, 7 January 1911.
60. Kansas City *Journal*, 31 January 1911.
61. *Inquirer*, 4 February 1911.

62. ESP to Keir Hardie, n.d., PP.
63. St Louis *Post Dispatch*, n.d., in National Association of Women's Suffrage Association Papers, LC 69, Library of Congress (NAWSA).
64. ESP, unpublished manuscript, PP.
65. ESP to Hardie.
66. ESP, *Suffragette Movement*, 350.
67. ESP, unpublished manuscript, PP.
68. ESP to Hardie, 26 February (*c.* 1911), PP.
69. Keir Hardie to ESP, n.d., original in PP; copy from Kenneth O. Morgan.
70. ESP, *Suffragette Movement*, 123; Antonia Raeburn, *Militant Suffragettes*, 180; ESP, *Suffragette Movement*, 356; Roger Fulford, *Votes for Women*, 228; David Morgan, *Suffragists and Liberals*, 96–101. Morgan provides an especially enlightening interpretation of the role played by the politicians in this period.
71. ESP, *Suffragette Movement*, 359.
72. Ibid.
73. ESP to Keir Hardie, n.d., PP.
74. Quoted in *Suffragette Movement*, 350.
75. ESP to Keir Hardie, n.d., PP.
76. Ibid.
77. Ibid.
78. Ibid.

Chapter 4   A Radical Organization of Her Own

1. ESP, 'The Inheritance', unpublished manuscript, PP.
2. ESP, *Suffragette Movement*, 406: on Sylvia's peripheral relations with the WSPU, Grace Roe talked at great length with Jill Craigie. Craigie to author 1976, 1978; and in comments on an earlier draft of this manuscript in 1982.
3. ESP, *Suffragette Movement*, 408.
4. Ibid.; 'The Inheritance'.
5. ESP, *Suffragette Movement*, 411–13; 'The Inheritance'; Frederick Pethick-Lawrence, *Fate Has Been Kind*, 100; Emmeline Pethick-Lawrence, *My Part in*, Preface.
6. ESP, *Suffragette Movement*, 412; ESP, *The Life of Emmeline Pankhurst*, 111.
7. ESP, *Suffragette Movement*, 412.
8. ESP, *Life of Emmeline*, 113.
9. Frederick Pethick-Lawrence, *Fate Has Been Kind*, 110; see Vera Brittain, *Pethick-Lawrence* (London, 1963); ESP, *Suffragette Movement*, 412.
10. ESP, *Suffragette Movement*, 411–13; *Votes for Women*, 1912–1914, passim.
11. Pethick-Lawrence, *My Part in*, Preface.
12. Henry Nevison, *Fire of Life* (London, 1935).
13. *Suffragette*, 18 October 1912.
14. See William J. Fishman, *Radical Jews* (New York, 1974); Charles Booth, *Life and Labour of the People of London* (New York, 1895–97), 3 vols; Jack London, *Beyond the Abyss* (London, 1903).
15. Paul Thompson, *The Enthusiasts*, 197. Undated press cuttings, courtesy of *The Times*; undated *East London News*. Michael Foot, who knew Lansbury from the 1930s until his death, confirmed Lansbury's tendency toward the erratic. Personal interview, London, 3 July 1978.
16. Raymond Postgate, *The Life of George Lansbury* (London, 1951), 119–20.
17. *Suffragette*, 29 November 1912.
18. Martin Pugh, *Suffrage*, 19. For an account of the 'antis', see Brian Harrison, *Separate Spheres: The Opposition to Women's Suffrage in Britain* (London, 1978); see

also Sir Almroth E. Wright, *The Unexpurgated Case Against Women's Suffrage* (London, 1913).

19. *Suffragette*, 14 November 1913.
20. Christabel Pankhurst, *The Great Scourge and How to End It* (London, 1913), 99.
21. Ibid.
22. George Lansbury to Mrs Mary Fels, 30 June 1914, Lansbury Papers, LSE.
23. ESP to Teresa Billington-Greig, n.d. Fawcett House; ESP, *Suffragette Movement*, 502 – 4.
24. Adela to Helen Moyes, published in *Woman in Man's World*, 38.
25. Ibid.
26. *New York Times*, 28 July 1913; Nora Smythe to Erres Marshall, 14 August 1913, PP.
27. *New York Times*, 4 August 1913.
28. *Suffragette*, 21 November 1913.
29. Christabel to Sylvia, 7 November 1913, PP.
30. Christabel to Sylvia, 13 December 1913, PP.
31. Annie Kenney and Grace Roe to WSPU membership, 25 November 1913, PP.
32. *Daily Sketch*, 4 February 1914.
33. Kensington chapter to Sylvia, 17 February 1914; Elsa Dalglish to Sylvia, 18 February 1914, PP.
34. Rheta Childe Dorr to Sylvia, 5 December 1913, PP.
35. Emmeline to Sylvia, n.d., PP.
36. *East London News*, 29 November 1913.
37. ESP to *Daily Citizen*, 24 November 1913, PP.
38. Annie Kenney, *Memoirs of a Militant* (London, 1924), 184.
39. *New York Times*, 8 February 1914.
40. *New York Times*, 7 February 1913.
41. Mitchell, *Queen Christabel*, 192, 197.
42. Dame Margaret Cole, personal interview, London, 24 October 1974; *Daily Chronicle*, 7 February 1914.
43. Fenner Brockway to Craigie, copy in possession of the author.
44. Annie Barnes, taped interview, 17 September 1974.
45. *Dreadnought*, 2 May 1914.
46. ESP, in *TP's Weekly*, 4 July, 1914.
47. The Jackson (Michigan) *Citizen Patriot* happened to be involved in a campaign to save the Carnegie Library, built by intervention of Mrs Emerson, when the author's circular letter sent to several Michigan papers arrived. Through the efforts of Marion S. Grotton of the Jackson *Citizen Patriot*, Zelie Emerson was lifted from the obscurity which had blanketed her life in America. Numerous acquaintances from her youth and in her mature years in Florida were located and provided information.
48. University records courtesy of Mary Jo Pugh, University of Michigan, Bentley Historical Library. Marion S. Grotton, Jackson *Citizen Patriot*, 13 February 1975. Lois Turner to author, 30 March 1975; Hathaway Rinehart to author, 20 March 1975.
49. Turner to author; Rinehart to author.
50. Jill Craigie to author, September 1976.
51. See Paul Thompson, *The Edwardians: The Remaking of British Society* (Bloomington, 1975), Dangerfield, *Strange Death*, 144, 149; Dame Ethyl Smyth, *Female Pipings*.
52. ESP, *Suffragette Movement*, 524.
53. J. Edward Francis to ESP, 15 February 1914; Francis to ESP, 6 March 1914; in *The Suffragette Movement* (527), Sylvia wrote that she quickly moved the paper to a new printer after initial attempts to edit, but the documents in her archive do not support this statement.

54. Minutes, at London Federation of Suffragettes (ELFS), 28 March, 1914; *Dread-nought* (DN) 11 April 1914; DN, 21 May 1914.
55. Minutes, ELFS, March–August 1914, PP; DN, 25 April 1914; DN, 2 May 1914.
56. DN, 28 March 1914.
57. DN, 6 June 1914.
58. ESP, *Suffragette Movement*, 467; DN, 6 May 1914; DN, 1917–21 passim.
59. Annie Barnes, taped interview, also PP.
60. *East End News*, 27 March 1914; *Daily Chronicle*, 27 March 1914; ESP, *Suffragette Movement*, 533–4.
61. *East End News*, 9 December 1913.
62. Ibid., 16 December 1913.
63. Ibid., n.d. December 1913.
64. ESP, *Suffragette Movement*, 439–40.
65. Ibid., 439.
66. Ibid., 444.
67. *McClure's Magazine*, August 1913; ESP, *Suffragette Movement*, 442–5.
68. ESP, *Suffragette Movement*, 446.
69. Ibid., 447.
70. *Everyman*, n.d., courtesy of *The Times*.
71. ESP, *Suffragette Movement*, 491.
72. Mitchell, *Queen Christabel*, 243; Dame Ethyl Smyth to Mrs Pankhurst, copy in possession of Jill Craigie.
73. ESP, *Suffragette Movement*, 449.
74. Ibid.; see also *McClure's*.
75. Emmeline Pankhurst to Elizabeth Robins, 26 March 1914, HRC.
76. Geraldine Lennox, *Everyman*, n.d.
77. *East End News*, n.d. 1914; *East London Observer*, n.d. 1914; *Woman's Dreadnought*, 1914 passim; 'Miss Sylvia Pankhurst and her 1914 Struggles', Tower Hamlet Library.
78. *East End News*, n.d. 1914; 'Miss Sylvia Pankhurst'.
79. *Morganbladet*, 23 September 1913.
80. G. M., 'Sylvia Pankhurst', NAWSA, LC 69, LC.
81. G.M., 'Sylvia Pankhurst'.
82. *Votes for Women*, 27 March 1914.
83. *Votes for Women*; *East End News*, 23 March 1914.
84. DN, 13 June 1914.
85. See DN, May–June 1914.
86. DN, 13 June 1914.
87. Michael and Eleanor Brock (eds), *H. H. Asquith Letters to Venetia Stanley* (Oxford, 1982), 89.
88. *New Statesman*, 12 April 1913.
89. Ibid., 26 April 1913.
90. Ibid., 17 May 1917.
91. Ibid., 1913–14, passim.
92. *Votes for Women*, 26 June 1914.
93. See *Suffragette Movement*, 'Asquith's First Steps Toward Surrender', 571–7; *San Francisco Bulletin*, 24 October 1914; also *Suffragette Movement*, (601) in which she wrote 'since our deputation of 1914, I had regarded him as a convert'.
94. DN, 18 April 1914; 11 April 1914.
95. DN, 18 April 1914.
96. The *World* quoted in DN, 2 May 1914.
97. Kenneth O. Morgan (ed.), *Lloyd George, Family Letters 1885–1936* (Cardiff & Oxford, 1973), 48.

98. Asquith, *Fifty Years*, 140.
99. Adela, quoted in Helen Moyes, *Woman in*, 38–9.
100. Pugh, *Suffrage*, 35. In a separate article Pugh suggested that Asquith's daughter, Violet, may have had some influence on his changing attitude toward the vote; although he concluded that war made it easier to 'recant publicly'. Martin D. Pugh, 'Politicians and the Women's Vote 1914–1918', *History* 59: 358–74 (1974). John D. Fair, however, disagrees. He thinks that neither their war efforts, nor previous militant suffrage got votes for women. John D. Fair, 'The Political Aspects of Women's Suffrage during the First World War', *Albion* 8: 274–95 (1976).
101. ESP, *Suffragette Movement*, 588.
102. Leslie Parker Hume, *The National Union of Women's Suffrage Societies*, Preface, 225–7, passim.
103. Vera Brittain, *Lady into Woman: A History of Women from Victoria to Elizabeth II* (New York, 1953), 41.

Chapter 5   Losing a Friend and Gaining a Cause

1. Kenneth Morgan, *Keir Hardie*, 264.
2. *Woman's Dreadnought* (WD), 8 August 1914: for a brief statement on the Irish problem at the time see Terry McCarthy, *Labour vs. Sinn Fein* (pamphlet, London, 1978).
3. Hansard, 5th ser. 65, cols. 1819–34; Jonathon Schneer, *Ben Tillett: Portrait of a Labour Leader* (Urbana, 1982), 2, 175.
4. E. Sylvia Pankhurst, *The Home Front* (London, 1932), 11; Sylvia's account of the coming of the war and her love at that time for Hardie was written in the 1930s when she was living with another man by whom she had borne a child.
5. The *Suffragette*, 7 August 1914.
6. WD, 8 August 1914.
7. For an accurate description of Poplar, see A. McEwen, 'The Lansbury Story', in *East London Papers* III.2 (October 1960), 67–86.
8. War Emergency Council, Beatrice and Sidney Webb, 'Relief of Distress' I, 1914–15, 200, Passfield Papers, LSE.
9. War Emergency Council, 200.
10. Minutes, Executive Committee, War Emergency National Women's Committee, 11 September 1914, n.p. Passfield Papers, LSE.
11. The *Herald*, 7 September 1914; for Sylvia's view of the war and the East End, see *The Home Front*. The title of this book, like *The Suffragette Movement*, implies a wider range of examination than the book affords. It deals mainly with Sylvia's activities in the East End, covering the years 1914–17. Much of the material is derived from *Woman's* (later *Worker's*) *Dreadnought* 1914–18, passim, and selected items from the Minutes of the ELFS, PP IISG.
12. *Christian Commonwealth*, 28 October 1914.
13. ESP, 'Willy' unpublished manuscript, PP; DN, 29 August 1914.
14. ESP, *The Home Front*, 114–18, 124.
15. Ibid., 124.
16. Ibid., 120–3; *Dreadnought* (DN), 9 January 1916.
17. DN, August 1914, passim.
18. Handbills for the People's Army carried the pledge, 'I will be a friend to all and a brother to every member...I am a sincere believer in a Vote for every Woman and every Man.' PP.
19. Minutes, ELFS, 16 November 1916, PP IISG.
20. Minutes, ELFS, 15 April 1915; DN, 3 October 1914.

21. Handbill, 'Stop the War and Bring back our Husbands, Sons and Brothers', PP. This philosophy was the official policy of the *Dreadnought* 1914 – passim.
22. Minutes, ELFS, 15 April 1915.
23. DN, 3 October 1914; ESP, *The Home Front*, 71–3.
24. Catalogue, n.d. PP IISG: ESP, *The Home Front*, 71–3; DN, 31 October 1914.
25. Pamphlet, n.d. PP IISG, The *Herald*, 15 May 1915; ESP, *The Home Front*, 173–4; WD, 29 August 1914; 26 September 1914; 1914 – 17, passim.
26. Handwritten menu, PP IISG; The *Herald*, 7 November 1914.
27. Telephone interview, Lord Brockway, 14 October 1974; personal interview, 21 June 1978. For more on the socialists and the war see H. M. Sanwick, *Builders of Peace* (London, 1924); Peter Stansky, *The Left and the War* (London, 1969).
28. Sussex *Daily News*, 21 November 1914.
29. DN, 1914 – 16, passim.
30. *Illustrated Sunday Herald*, 16 May 1915.
31. Interview, Mrs Annie Barnes, 22 September 1974.
32. *Illustrated Sunday Herald*, 16 May 1915.
33. The *Weekly Dispatch* (London), 25 July 1914.
34. Liverpool *Daily Post and Mercury*, 3 April 1916. The summation of this speech is the tone generally advanced by Sylvia in the pre-Russian Revolution war years. For detailed study of Sylvia's actions and some insight into her thought, see *The Homefront*.
35. East London *Observer*, 24 July 1915.
36. Undated second page of letter to unknown addressee, Fawcett Library, London.
37. DN, 5 June 1915.
38. Unpub. manuscript, 'Dorothy', PP.
39. ESP, *The Home Front*, 180.
40. Report of the ELFS, PP IISG.
41. Minutes, ELFS, February – July 1915.
42. Minutes, ELFS, 27 February 1915.
43. Minutes, ELFS, 19 November 1916.
44. ESP, *The Home Front*, 142–43.
45. Personal interview, Mrs Elsie Flint, 24 September 1974. Mrs Flint grew up when the SDF was the major socialist organization in the East End at the turn of the century. She was a product of the Socialist Sunday schools; and, in her seventies could still recite each of the commandments without faltering. Mrs Flint knew Sylvia and Lansbury during her youth in Bow.
46. DN, 16 June 1914.
47. William J. Fishman, *Radical Jews*, 53; passim.
48. DN, 26 May 1917; Sylvia worked with the East End Jewish community on occasion throughout the war, see *Dreadnought* 1914 – 17.
49. ESP, *The Home Front*, 195.
50. Ibid., 66.
51. Unpublished manuscript, PP IISG: ESP, *The Home Front* 66–7.
52. ESP, *The Home Front*, 67.
53. *Daily Herald*, 8 April 1915.
54. Zelie to Sylvia, undated, PP.
55. Zelie to Sylvia.
56. ESP, *Suffragette Movement*, 595; ESP, *The Home Front*, 231–5.
57. G. D. E. Cole, *A History of the Labour Party* (London, 1948), 28.
58. Emrys Hughes, *Keir Hardie*, 3.
59. Beatrice Webb, unpublished diary, 32, 53, Passfield Papers, LSE.
60. Beatrice Webb, diary; A. J. P. Taylor also blamed Hardie's death on the war. In Taylor's opinion, 'Hardie, a Dissenter of the first hour, was too discouraged by the desertion of his former supporters to make a new effort. He died of a

broken heart', in *The Trouble-Makers: Dissent Over Foreign Policy*, (London, 1957), 132.

61. Keir Hardie to Sylvia, 27 May 1915, PP IISG. Copy loaned by Kenneth Morgan.
62. ESP, *The Home Front*, 227.
63. Ibid.
64. Frank Smith to Sylvia, 26 September 1915.
65. DN, 2 October 1915.
66. ESP, *The Home Front*, 231.
67. DN, 16 October 1915.
68. Keir Hardie to Shaw, quoted in A. J. P. Taylor, *The Trouble-Makers*, 142.
69. DN, 16 October 1915.
70. Ibid.
71. ESP, *The Home Front*, 111–12.
72. For a superb account of dissenters in this period, see A. J. P. Taylor, *The Trouble-Makers*.
73. DN, 17 June 1916.
74. DN, 16 October 1916; see John Fisher, *That Miss Hobhouse* (London, 1971).
75. DN, 1914–15, passim.
76. The resistance of women to the war has only recently come under examination. See Grace X. Delve, 'Women, Socialists, Suffragists; Intercontinental Pacifist Enterprises', unpublished paper, University of Baltimore, 1978; Barbara Steinson, 'Female Activism in World War I', unpublished dissertation, University of Michigan, 1977.
77. Emmeline Pethick-Lawrence, *My Part in*, 310–15; Jane Addams, *Peace and Bread in Time of War*, (Boston, 1960); ESP, *The Suffragette Movement*, 593; DN, April–May 1915, passim.
78. Minutes, ELFS, 12 April 1915.
79. Emmeline Pethick-Lawrence, *My Part In*, 312–13.
80. DN, 8 July 1916.
81. ESP, *The Home Front*, 338.
82. DN, 22 January 1916.
83. DN, 16 December 1916.
84. DN, 18 March 1916.
85. *The Suffragette*, 8 April 1915; *Britannia*, 16 October 1915.
86. Andrew Rosen, *Rise Up Women*, 252.
87. Arthur Marwick *Women at War* (London, 1977), 30.
88. DN, 8 April 1916.
89. ESP, 'Some Autobiographical Notes', in *Yearbook, International Archives for the Women's Movement* (Leiden, 1937), 92.
90. *Herald*, 22 April 1916.
91. Minutes, ELFS, 30 March 1917.
92. Minutes, ELFS, 5 May 1917.
93. Personal Interview, Terry McCarthy, curator, National Museum of Labour History, 21 June 1977. Personal correspondence 17 August 1978.
94. Minutes, ELFS, 10 June 1917.
95. DN, 16 May 1916.
96. DN, 23 May 1916.
97. DN, 30 May 1916.
98. Pamphlet 'Thoughts on the Easter Week Rebellion', n.d. PP; copy, n.d. LSE.
99. ESP, *The Home Front*, 108–9; DN, 19 September 1916.
100. Minutes, ELFS, 1914–17, passim.
101. Mitchell, *Fighting Pankhursts*, 43.
102. DN, 2 December 1916; quoted in Arthur Marwick, *Women at War*, 120.

103. DN, 2 January 1917.
104. Marwick, *Women at War*, 121; Marie Stopes, *Married Love* (London, 1918).
105. ESP, 'The Birthrate: Notes and Views on the Report of the National Birthrate Commission', London, 1916; ESP, *The Home Front*, 179–93.
106. ESP, 'The Birthrate', 3.
107. Notebook dated 1918, PP.
108. Minutes, Finance Committee, ELFS, August n.d., 1917.
109. Minutes, Finance Committee, ELFS, 17 September; 22 November 1917.
110. Minutes, Finance Committee, ELFS, 22 November 1917.
111. ESP, *The Home Front*, 231.
112. Norah Smyth to Sylvia, PP.
113. Ibid.
114. Ibid.
115. Minutes, ELFS, April–August 1917, PP.
116. DN, 24 March 1917.
117. DN, 19 May 1917.
118. Unpub. mss. PP.
119. DN, 2 June 1917.

Chapter 6   A Radical in Revolution

1. Frances, Countess of Warwick to George Lansbury, 22 August 1917, Lansbury Papers, LSE.
2. Beatrice Webb, unpublished diary, 33–8, 1916–24, Passfield Papers, LSE.
3. Mrs Pankhurst to Lloyd George, 1 June 1917, copy Fawcett Library; *The Times*, 2 January 1917.
4. *The Times*, 8 November 1917.
5. *The Times*, 30 May 1917.
6. Adela to Sylvia, 23 November 1917, PP.
7. Adela to Sylvia.
8. PP. None of the children, however, followed their grandfather's path of socialist activism.
9. Adela to Sylvia, undated, *c.* 1919–20, PP.
10. CAB 24/passim PRO.
11. See ESP, 'The Red Twilight', unpublished manuscript, PP.
12. For more on women in Russia, see Cathy Porter, *The Lonely Story of the Women Who Defied Lenin* (New York, 1979); Beatrice Farnsworth, *Socialism, Feminism, and the Bolshevik Revolution* (Stanford, 1980).
13. Les Garner, *Stepping Stones to Women's Liberty: Feminist Ideas in the Women's Suffrage Movement 1900–1918* (Rutherford, Pa., 1984), 89.
14. Christabel, quoted in Midge MacKenzie (ed.), *Shoulder to Shoulder* (New York, 1975), 112.
15. *The Times*, 4 December 1918.
16. DN, 30 November 1918; *The Times*, 29 October 1918.
17. DN, 10 November 1918.
18. *Daily Sketch*, 7 February 1919.
19. *The Times*, 11 April 1919.
20. *Daily Express*, 20 January 1919.
21. Ethyl Smyth, *Female Pipings*, 246.
22. ESP, *The Life of Emmeline*, passim.
23. DN, 16 November 1918.
24. For further background on post-war labour unrest in Europe, see A. J. Ryder, *The German Revolution of 1918* (Cambridge, 1967); A. Rossi (pseud., Angelo Tasca), *The*

Rise of Italian Fascism, 1918–22 (New York, 1966); Alfred Rosmer, *Le Mouvement ouvier pendant la première guerre mondiale de Zimmerwald à la . . . russe* (Paris, 1959) especially chapter 1, 'Après la Conference de Zimerwald', 22–3. Werner T. Andrews, *Stillborn Revolution: The Communist Bid for Power in Germany, 1921–23* (Princeton, 1963). I am grateful to Charles Maier for bibliographical aid with this section.

25. Andrews, *Stillborn Revolution*, 3–76; J. T. Nettl, *Rosa Luxembourg* 2 vols. Oxford, 1966).

26. Angelo Tasca, *The Rise of Italian Fascism*, passim.

27. R. Palme Dutt, acquainted with Sylvia during the years 1917–21, when a united party was finally established, refused an interview with the author. His bitterness toward Sylvia, for unstated reasons, had not abated by the time of his death in 1974. Telephone interview with author, 19 September 1974, London.

28. DN, Christmas 1917.

29. DN, 1917–20, passim.

30. Claude McKay, *A Long Way from Home* (New York, 1969), 68.

31. Ibid., 76–7.

32. Ibid., 78–9.

33. Ibid., 81.

34. Ibid., 198.

35. Ibid., 87.

36. William Manchester, *The Last Lion: Winston Spencer Churchill Visions of Glory 1874–1932* (Boston, Mass., 1983); Stephen E. Koss, *Fleet Street Radical: A. G. Gardiner and the Daily News* (Hamden, Connecticut, 1973), 36, 232, 233.

37. Blackfriars Press to Pankhurst, 4 October 1917, PP.

38. CAB 24/81; 24/82 PRO; Albert Inkpin to ESP, 21 January 1921, PP; Archivio Centrele dello State, Rome: Casellario politico, October, 1920.

39. ESP, *Lloyd George Takes Off the Mask*, 1920; CAB 24/l117 PRO tells about Sylvia receiving unspecified sums from Russia.

40. ESP, *Landlordism*, n.d. NYPL; ESP, *Education of the Masses*, n.d. LSE: see also ESP, *Die Gross Verschworung Verlag der Kommunistischen Internationale*, n.d. NYPL; ESP, *Housing and the Workers Revolution in Capitalist Britain and Bolshevik Russia*, n.d. LSE; ESP, *Revolution and the Housing Question*, n.d. LSE; ESP, *The Birthrate*, n.d. LSE; ESP, *Schooling for the Future*, n.d. LSE.

41. *Voice of Labour*, October 1919.

42. CAB 24/76 PRO.

43. CAB 24/77 PRO.

44. George Lansbury, *My Life* (London, 1928), 247.

45. CAB 24/101 PRO.

46. CAB 24/92 PRO.

47. DN, 17 June 1917.

48. DN, 19 November 1917.

49. ESP, 'When I Sat with the Present Prime Minister', PP.

50. *The Communist International*, March 1919, 70; ESP, 'The New War', *Communist International*, June 1919, 171–5.

51. *The Communist International*, June 1919, 262.

52. *The Communist International*, July 1919, 291–6; August 1919, 31–8. In the 6 October 1919 issue, Sylvia and Theodore Rothstein are listed for England. Later, MacLaine and Quelch from England; and no further references to her are made after this issue, although the WSF is mentioned infrequently.

53. WSF minutes, 1917–20, passim, PP.

54. For an account of the formation of the Communist Party–Great Britain and further elaboration of these various groups, see James Klugman, *History of the CP–GB*, I (London, 1968) especially 9–75. See also Raymond Challiner, *The Origins of British Bolshevism* (Totawa, N. J., 1977).

55. Minutes, June 1919; CAB 24/84; Klugman, *History of CP–GB*, 31.
56. Minutes, May–December 1919; DN, 1919–20; Klugman, 9–75.
57. ESP to Lenin, 16 July 1919, *The Communist International* (London, 1920), 50–1, Marx House, London; V. I. Lenin, *Collected Works* XXXI (New York, 1934), 244.
58. *The Communist International*, 51; Lenin, *Collected Works*, 244.
59. *The Communist International*, 52–3.
60. CAB 24/71 PRO.
61. Ibid.
62. CAB 24/80 PRO.
63. CAB 24/81 PRO.
64. CAT 24/110; 24/111; 24/112 PRO.
65. Angelica Balabanoff, *My Life as a Rebel* (New York, 1931), 172–6.
66. Ibid., 176.
67. Ibid., 172–8.
68. James Klugman, personal interview, 15 September 1974, London.
69. Balabanoff, *My Life* 294; CAB 24/112; DN, 22 January 1921; Inkpin to ESP, 21 January 1921, PP.
70. Karen Honeycutt, 'Clara Zetkin's Efforts to Realize Feminist Ideals through the Socialist Movement', *Feminist Studies*, 3: 3: 4: 131–44.
71. ESP, 'The Red Twilight', PP.
72. Ibid.

Chapter 7 Radical Politics in the Post-War Years

1. *The Call*, 15 February 1920; DN, 20 February 1920.
2. DN, 29 February 1920.
3. ESP, 'The Red Twilight', PP; Passport, PP.
4. Albert Inkpin to Workers' Suffrage Federation, quoted in DN, 20 March 1920.
5. DN, 15 May 1920.
6. CAB 24/791 PRO.
7. DN, 15 May; 26 June 1920.
8. DN, 26 June 1920.
9. Vladimir Lenin, *Collected Works*, XXXV, 217 (New York, 1934); DN, 10 July 1920.
10. *Daily Herald*, 22 June 1920; DN, 26 June 1920.
11. Robert Stott, DN, 26 June 1920.
12. CAB 24/106 PRO.
13. DN, 10 July 1920.
14. CAB 24/109 PRO; CAB 24/111 PRO.
15. ESP, 'The Red Twilight'; two versions of her memoirs in outline form refer to this journey. In one she wrote that she arrived on the Norwegian boat in Sweden; the other, more detailed, version referred to Copenhagen. In the text I have chosen the second version, but there is no way of knowing which is accurate. Dora Russell, who also went to Russia that summer, travelled from Sweden to Russia on a small fishing vessel with help provided by a Swedish customs agent who was also a communist. See Dora Russell, *The Tamarisk Tree* (New York, 1975), 84–5.
16. *The Worker*, 2 October 1920.
17. V. I. Lenin, *'Left-Wing' Communism: An Infantile Disorder* (Moscow, 1920).
18. Ibid., 62–3.
19. Ibid., 68–9.
20. The Second Congress of the Third International, Report of the Proceedings of

the Petrograd Session of July 17th and Moscow Sessions of 23 July – 7 August (Moscow, 1920), 40; see also Balabanoff, *My Life*, 275.

21. Second Congress proceedings, 410 – 13.
22. William Gallacher, *Last Memories of William Gallacher* (London, 1966), 153 – 4.
23. ESP, *Soviet Russia as I Saw It* (London, 1921), 65 – 78.
24. Ibid., 128.
25. Ibid., 184.
26. Gallacher, *Last Memories*, 156.
27. Ibid., 157.
28. Ibid., 158.
29. ESP, 'Red Twilight'.
30. CAB 24/112 CP 1908 PRO.
31. Beatrice Farnsworth, *Socialism, Feminism*, 174.
32. CAB 24/112 CP 1908 PRO.
33. *The Worker*, 2 October 1920.
34. *Sunday Press*, 26 September 1920; *The Times*, 27 September 1920.
35. DN, 26 September 1920.
36. CAB 24/112 CP 1937 PRO.
37. *The Times*, 20 October 1920.
38. Schneer, *Ben Tillett*, 205 – 15; DN, April – May 1920.
39. DN, 29 May 1920; DN, May – August, passim; CAB 24/115 CP 2227 PRO.
40. CAB 24/1117 CP 123/615 PRO.
41. CAB 207/20 CP 2603 PRO.
42. *Daily Sketch*, 20 October 1920.
43. CAB 24/115 CP 2227 PRO.
44. CAB 24/114 CP 2089 PRO; see Kathryne McDorman, 'Leftists, Ladies, and Lenin: English Women Respond to Bolshevism', *Social Science Journal* 16: 31 – 40 (1979). McDorman mistakenly says that Sylvia helped form the CP – GB (34).
45. Thurgood to Sylvia Pankhurst, n.d., PP.
46. McKay, *Long Way*, 82.
47. Ibid., 82 – 3.
48. Copy of Appeal, PP.
49. *The Times*, 5 January 1920.
50. DN, 15 January 1920.
51. Mary L. Gordon, *Penal Discipline*, 26.
52. CAB 24 / 128 CP 3380 PRO.
53. Whitehead to the Editor, 16 January 1921, PP.
54. DN, 4 June 1921; ESP, unpublished short vignettes on prison, PP; ESP, *Writ on Cold Slate* (London, 1921).
55. WD, 1921, passim; CAB 24/120 CP 2698 PRO.
56. ESP, *Writ on Cold Slate*, 22.
57. Ibid., 41.
58. Ibid., 12.
59. Ibid., 2.
60. Ibid., ESP, unpublished poem, PP.
61. DN, 23 April 1921.
62. DN, 19 March 1921.
63. *The Times*, 31 May 1921.
64. *The Times*, 8 May, 31 May 1921.
65. DN, 18 June 1921.
66. Letter to comrades, PP; copy in possession of the author.
67. DN, 17 September 1921.
68. George Bernard Shaw to Corio, 14 September 1921, HRC.
69. DN, 17 September 1921.

70. *The Times*, 19 September 1921.
71. *The Times*, 6 October 1921.
72. CAB 24/128 PRO.
73. ESP, draft, 'Myself When Young', PP.
74. ESP, 'When I Sat with the Present Prime Minister on the Workers and Soldiers Council of Great Britain', PP.
75. *The Times*, 20 September 1921
76. CAB 24/158 CP 4 (23) PRO.

Chapter 8   Motherhood and Family Life

1. CAB 24/158 CP4 (23) PRO.
2. 4668, Prefettura di torino, National Archives, Rome. Documents from Rome provided by Professor Roberto Viverelli.
3. Ibid.
4. Ibid.
5. Ibid.
6. Ibid.
7. Ibid.
8. Ibid.
9. Ibid.
10. Ibid.
11. Ibid.
12. Corio to his Mazrat Mirza Basheerdu-Diwe Mahmud Ahmab, 20 April 1922, PP; Nubarak Ali to S. Corio, 27 June 1922; Masih Qadcan to S. Corio, n.d., PP; 4468; Prefettura di torino.
13. 4668, Prefettura di torino.
14. Roxanne to Miss Pankhurst, n.d., PP.
15. LSE student records, 1922–30.
16. Corio to Sylvia, n.d., PP.
17. Corio to Sylvia, n.d., PP.
18. DN, 27 August 1921.
19. For Rudolf Rocker and the East End of this period, see William J. Fishman, *Radical Jews*; Paul Thompson, *Socialists, Liberals, and Labour: The Struggle for London 1881–1914* (London, 1967). One copy of *Germinal* is in the Pankhurst Papers, IISG. The second, and final, issue dated July 1923, is in the British Library.
20. Circular, PP.
21. *News of the World*, 7 April 1928.
22. Annie Barnes, interview, 17 September 1974.
23. Rose Hokridge, personal interview, London, 17 September 1974; Annie Barnes, 17 September 1974; Nora Smythe to ESP, 24 December 1926.
24. *Sunday Chronicle*, 15 April 1928. Sylvia's attitudes toward sex were never expressed in a personal manner. Her reference to 'true lovers' would indicate that she regarded Corio as her lover; on the other hand, these utterances may have been for public consumption as a form of justification. Middle class women generally knew little about sexual satisfaction until after World War I when Marie Stopes' *Married Love* (London, 1918) was published. If Sylvia had sexual intercourse with Hardie, it is unlikely that she experienced orgasm. See Ellen M. Holtzman, 'The Pursuit of Married Love: Women's Attitudes toward Sexuality and Marriage in Great Britain', *Journal of Social History* 16: 39–52 (1982). See also Arthur Marwick, *The Deluge* (London, 1965); and Noreen Branson, *Britain in the Nineteen Twenties* (Minneapolis, 1976).
25. Dora Russell, *Tamarisk Tree*, 221–3, 239.

26. Drafts to Emmeline Pethick-Lawrence, PP.
27. David Mitchell, *The Times*, 25 July 1975. This statement is supported by remarks from the Bach (Goulden) family to Jill Craigie. Mrs Enid Goulden-Bach, Sylvia's cousin, refused to discuss the matter on two separate occasions. Annie Barnes (May 1975) said Sylvia came home crying more than once when Mrs Barnes was present because her mother refused to see her.
28. Helen Moyes, taped interview, August 1976.
29. David Mitchell, *Queen Christabel* (London, 1978), 389.
30. *News of the World*, 7 April 1928.
31. Mrs Enid Goulden-Bach, personal interview, London, 3 July 1978; Dame Ethel Smyth, *Female Pipings in Eden*; Grace Roe to Jill Craigie; Mitchell, *Queen Christabel*, 309. Jill Craigie states that Dame Ethel Smyth and others remembered that Mrs Pankhurst 'fell into a deep depression' when Sylvia's baby was born.
32. *News of the World*; *Manchester Sunday Chronicle*, 8 April 1928; *The Times*, 8 April 1928; Thelma Cazalet Keir MP, 'I Knew Mrs. Pankhurst', pamphlet reproduced from BBC broadcast script, 5 March 1945, LC.
33. *News of the World*; *Manchester Sunday Chronicle*, 8 April 1928; *The Times*, 8 April 1928.
34. *News of the World*, 8 April 1928.
35. *Sunday Chronicle*, 15 April 1928.
36. *Sunday Chronicle*, 15 April 1928.
37. Grace Roe is reported in David Mitchell, *Fighting Pankhursts*, 236.
38. Moyes, *Woman in Man's World*, 35–6.
39. Christabel Pankhurst, *The Uncertain Future* (London, 1940).
40. Sylvia to Christabel, 15 July 1957; Fawcett Library.
41. *The Times*, 15 February 1958.
42. DN, 1923, passim.
43. Tom Walsh to Sylvia, 21 July 1926.
44. Tom Walsh to Sylvia, 21 July 1926.
45. Mitchell, *Fighting Pankhursts*, 273; see also Anne Summers, 'The Unwritten History of Adela Pankhurst Walsh', *Hecate* 4: 41–8 (1978).
46. Sylvia to Mrs Walshe, n.d., Fawcett Library.
47. ESP to Nora Walshe, 18 October 1928, Fawcett Library.
48. ESP, 'Why Not a Goat', unpublished manuscript, PP.
49. Vera Brittain to Sylvia, 17 October 1930, PP.
50. *Essex Countryside*, August 1977.
51. Annie Barnes, personal interview, 8 May 1975; Princess Rosalie Viazemsky, personal interview, September 1974; Mr and Mrs Francis Beaufort-Palmer, personal interview, 21 September 1975.
52. *The Times*, 7 March 1930. According to Vera Brittain, Sylvia came to the ceremonies with her son, Richard. See Vera Brittain, *Testament of Experience* (London, 1957), 60–1.
53. Anon to Mrs How Martin, 24 February 1930, Cp. C. vol. 3, London Museum.
54. Ella Gife to Mrs How Martin, 15 November 1931, Cp. C. 3, London Museum.
55. *Star*, 9 April 1930.
56. ESP, 'My Mother', unpublished manuscript, PP; *Star*, 9 April 1930.
57. Emmeline Pethick-Lawrence to Sylvia, 17 December 1929, PP.
58. Emmeline Pethick-Lawrence to Sylvia, 26 December 1930, PP.
59. Dora Russell, *Tamarisk Tree*, 199, 208.
60. SC to ESP, Thursday 2nd, n.d.; S to Mummy; Corio to Richard, 30 May 1931, PP.
61. Bertrand Russell to ESP, January 1932, PP.
62. Emmeline Pethick-Lawrence to Sylvia, n.d. (*c.* 1932), PP.

63. Silvio to ESP, Thursday night, n.d., PP.
64. *The Times* clipping, n.d., ESP, press release to PEN Club, 1932, HRC; Emmeline Pethick-Lawrence to Sylvia, 2 July 1932, PP.
65. See Chapter 5; ESP, *The Home Front*, 74–6; Norah Smyth to Sylvia, 9 November 1933, PP; Sylvia's deposition for Hutchinson's, PP.
66. Richard Pankhurst to David Mitchell, London Museum.
67. 4668, Prefettora di torino

Chapter 9   Author and Journalist

1. DN, 19 January 1924.
2. ESP, *India and the Earthly Paradise* (Bombay, 1926).
3. R. Suntharalingam, *Indian Nationalism: An Historical Analysis* (New Delhi, 1983), 20–3.
4. Ibid., 305–6.
5. Walter Crane, *India Impressions* (New York, 1907), VIII.
6. Quoted in Kenneth Morgan, *Keir Hardie*, 192.
7. Ibid.
8. ESP, *India*, 548.
9. Ibid., 638.
10. *Forward*, Glasgow, 5 February 1927.
11. Quoted in Mitchell, *Fighting Pankhursts*, 179.
12. DN, 21 November 1921.
13. Letterhead, *c.* 1927–8, PP.
14. List of lectures, 'Is An International Language Possible?' PP.
15. ESP, *Delphos: The Future of International Language* (London, 1926), 41.
16. Ibid., 52, 94.
17. Ibid., ESP, (translator) *The Poems of Mihael Eminescu* (London, 1930), 39–69.
18. ESP, 'Hail to Thee Bright Spirit', in Val. Petrescu (ed), *Omagui lui M. Eminescu* (Bucharest, 1934).
19. George Bernard Shaw to Sylvia, 12 September 1929, HRC; GBS, quoted in *Eminescu*, 'Preface'.
20. Shaw to Sylvia, 29 July 1926, HRC.
21. ESP, *Eminescu*, 'Preface'.
22. Al. Philippide, 'Traductibil intraductibil la Eminescu', *Secolui*, XX: 61 13–21, 1964; translation by Dr A. Petrescu.
23. ESP to Mr Oprescu, 8 November 1930; by courtesy of Dr A Petrescu.
24. O. Martin to G. Oprescu, 24 November 1929.
25. Eleanor F. Rathbone, *The Disinherited Family: A Plea for the Endowment of the Family* (London, 1924).
26. ESP, 'The Inheritance', PP.
27. Arthur Henderson to Sylvia Pankhurst, 19 March 1930; J. Ramsay MacDonald to Sylvia Pankhurst, 18 March 1930, PP.
28. ESP, *Save the Mothers* (London, 1930), 82.
29. Ibid., 159.
30. Ibid., 115–120.
31. Ibid., 120.
32. Ibid., 166, 167.
33. ESP to Mrs Walshe, n.d., Fawcett Library.
34. Shaw to Sylvia, quoted in *Save the Mothers*, 182.
35. Emmeline Pethick-Lawrence to Sylvia, 23 October 1930, PP.
36. Neomi Mitrich to Miss Pankhurst, 6 November 1930, PP.
37. Vera Brittain, *Lady into Woman* 168–9.

38. ESP to Sir James Marchant, 25 June 1928. Northwestern University Library, Special Collections.
39. ESP to Sir James Marchant, 25 June 1928. Northwestern.
40. Outline submitted to Sir James Marchant, 25 June 1928. Northwestern.
41. 'To My Son Richard Keir Pethick Pankhurst, this record of struggle is dedicated in the cherished hope that he may give his service to the collective work of humanity'.
42. RKPP, Introduction, *The Suffragette Movement* (London, 1977).
43. *Woman's Leader*, 20 February 1931.
44. Ray Strachey, *The Cause: A Short History of the Women's Movement in Great Britain* (London, 1928), 311.
45. Vera Brittain, *Pethick-Lawrence: A Portrait* (London, 1963), 48n.
46. Jill Craigie to Miss Pankhurst, n.d.
47. ESP to Miss Craigie, 14 September 1944.
48. Ibid.
49. Rosamond Silkin to author, 21 July 1983.
50. Sylvia to Christabel, 15 July 1959, Fawcett Library.
51. Ibid.
52. *Spectator*, 146: 232, 1931.
53. *New York Times*, 22 April 1931.
54. *Current History*, 34: XI, 1931.
55. *The Times Literary Supplement*, 19 February 1931.
56. *The Times*, 13 February 1931.
57. J. Ramsay MacDonald to ESP, 11 May 1931.
58. Shaw to Sylvia, 6 June 1931.
59. George Bernard Shaw, Preface to *St. Joan*, reprinted in *The Bodly Head*, Editor Superior, Dan J. Laurence, *Bernard Shaw Collected Plays with their Prefaces*, v. VI. (London, 1973), 46.
60. Shaw, 'BBC radio talk delivered on the five hundredth anniversary of the burning of Joan', 30 May 1931 in Laurence (ed.) *Collected Works*, 311.
61. Miriam to Sylvia, n.d., PP.
62. Shaw to Sylvia, 15 July 1931, PP.
63. Dame Margaret Cole, personal interview, London, 29 October 1974.
64. O. Martin to the Secretary, PEN Club, 4 May 1931; Herman Ould to ESP, 8 May 1931, HRC.
65. ESP to Mrs Walshe, N.D., Fawcett Library.
66. ESP, *The Home Front* (London, 1932).
67. Emmeline Pethick-Lawrence to Sylvia, n.d., PP.
68. Emmeline Pethick-Lawrence to Sylvia, 14 April 1932, PP.
69. ESP, *The Home Front*, 275–6.
70. ESP, *The Life of Emmeline Pankhurst* (London, 1935).
71. ESP, *The Life of*, 172.
72. ESP, 'The Importance of Emmeline Pankhurst', unpublished manuscript, PP.
73. ESP to Herman Ould, 19 November 1935, HRC.
74. ESP, 'The Truth About the Oil War', pamphlet, n.d. (*c.* 1924) 29, LSE.
75. I am grateful to Teresa Lucas for sending me the copy of *Humanity* from the British Museum; ESP to Piero Treves, 7 October 1949, RKPP, *Sylvia Pankhurst*, 190.
76. Copies of 'Letters to the Editor' courtesy of *The Times*; copies of letters in notebooks and files, PP; copies of letters, reprinted and only printing, *Dreadnought* and *New Times Ethiopia News*, passim.
77. ESP, unpublished manuscript, PP.
78. ESP, untitled news cutting, 14 September 1930; courtesy of *The Times*.
79. ESP to George Lansbury, 30 March 1933, GL Coll. Y12: 221–22 LSE.

Chapter 10   Multiple Causes

1. ESP, drafts of proposals, 7 April 1936, PP.
2. ESP, unpublished manuscript, PP.
3. ESP to Mrs Walshe (*c.* 1930), Fawcett Library.
4. J. B. Hugenholtz, P1237 Peace Library, The Hague.
5. Ibid.
6. Files for 1934–35, PP.
7. FO371/19572 R7218 PRO.
8. FO371/19572 R7218 PRO.
9. *News Chronicle*, 3 August 1936.
10. ESP, The Threat of War', PP.
11. Ibid.
12. *Palestine Post* reprinted in *New Times and Ethiopia News* (NTEN), 1 June 1940. Another issue which dominated socialist concern in the Depression years was associated with unemployment relief. To claim unemployment, a man had to show that he possessed no assets, even to the point of selling his wife's wedding ring. While Sylvia's penchant for single-mindedness in her campaigns is noted throughout this work, her concern for the poor was always consistent, yet on this issue she remained mute. Jill Craigie has suggested that her failure to speak out on unemployment claims, indeed on unemployment, and her sole concern with the peace movement, meant that she was wearying of identifying herself with the poor (Craigie to author, private communication, September 1981). I agree as to the time that marks this change, but believe it came about due to her desire to become more middle-class because of her son, not because she was weary of the poor.
13. Personal communication, Dr A. Petrescu, Bucharest, to author, September 1976; Dr A. Petrescu, personal interview, Bucharest, 9 July 1976.
14. *Prefettura di torino* 4468.
15. ESP to the Editor, 31 July 1934, HRC.
16. ESP, unpublished manuscript, PP.
17. A. Petrescu, interview and personal communication.
18. ESP to Editor, 31 July 1934, HRC.
19. ESP to Ken Seymour, 27 September 1934, HRC.
20. Herman Ould to ESP, 9 October 1934, HRC.
21. ESP to Herman Ould, 2 November 1934, HRC.
22. Copy of programme, 17 January 1935, courtesy of Dr A. Petrescu.
23. ESP to Val. Petrescu, 23 January 1935.
24. V. Petrescu (ed.), *Omagiu lui M. Eminescu*, by Pro-Eminescu Com., Bucharest, 1934, 49–51.
25. ESP, unpublished manuscript, PP.
26. DN, 9 September 1922.
27. DN, 11 November 1922.
28. DN, 4 November 1922.
29. DN, 3 February 1923.
30. For a full account of Matteotti and his role in Italian politics, see G. Matteotti, *Relique* (Milan, 1924); Charles F. Delzell, *Mussolini's Enemies* (Princeton, 1961).
31. Form letter, Women's International Matteotti Committee, PP.
32. ESP to Alice Stone Blackwell, 5 September 1932; 25 November 1932, NAWSA, LC 23; FO 371/15988 CPO 27 PRO. For background on this period, see Gerald D. Anderson, *Fascists, Communists, and the National Government: Civil Liberties in Great Britain 1931–37* (Columbia, Missouri, 1983).
33. FO 371/15988 CPO 27 PRO; *Humanity*, October 1932.
34. Manchester *Guardian*, 18 October 1932.

35. ESP to Piero Treves, 7 October 1940, PP.
36. *Prefettura di torino* 4668.
37. RKPP to author, Addis Ababa, 12 February 1975.
38. ESP to Piero Treves, 7 October 1940, PP.
39. *New Times and Ethiopia News*, passim.
40. *Prefettura di torino* 4668.
41. Ibid.
42. ESP, unpublished manuscript, PP.
43. *Essex Countryside*, 1977.
44. See Robert Skidelsky, *Oswald Mosley* (London, 1975), 380–93; Anderson, *Fascists*, 204.
45. ESP to Piero Treves, 7 September 1933. Archivio deli Fascisto Storico della Resistenes en Toscana–Firenze, Archivio GL, S12 III, Florence.
46. ESP to George Lansbury, 30 March 1933, LSE.
47. ESP, unpublished manuscript, PP.
48. Shaw to ESP, quoted in unpublished manuscript, 'An Open Letter....' February, 1935, PP.
49. *The Sunday Referee*, 14 July 1935.
50. Ibid., 21 July 1935.
51. Annie Barnes, taped interview, 19 September 1974.
52. Annie Barnes, interview.
53. RKPP interview, Addis.
54. ESP to Herman Ould, 26 September 1932; Ould to ESP, 30 September 1932; Ould to ESP, 10 January 1933, HRC.
55. ESP to Ould, 22 February 1933, HRC.
56. G. Salvemini to ESP, March 1933. Archivio deli Fascisto Storico della Resistenes en Toscana–Firenze, Archivio GL 512, Florence; ESP to Ould, 2 April 1933, HRC: for her further aid to anti-Fascists, see C9555, FO 371/16813 PRO.
57. See Chapter 11 below.
58. *New Leader*, 2 July 1937.
59. Francis Beaufort-Palmer, interview, 21 September 1974.
60. Anne Chisholm, *Nancy Cunard* (New York, 1979), 234, 251; NTEN, 5 September 1936.
61. NTEN, 1936–38, passim; 21 November 1936; 17 September 1938.
62. W1435, W1972, W3621 FO371/24140–41 PRO.
63. Ibid.
64. NTEN, 11 March 1939.
65. Ibid.
66. Ould to ESP, 30 October 1937, HRC.
67. FO 371/21268/n19376 PRO.
68. Ibid.
69. Mrs Beaufort-Palmer, taped interview.
70. J173/173/66FO 371/23313; J2434/J258/23370–79; J610/J1634/66/24 FO 371/2203 PRO.
71. S. K. B. Asante, *Pan African Protest: West Africa and the Italo-Ethiopian Crisis* (London, 1977), 52–3.
72. 'Confidential Circular', the Sierra Leone Deputation, 17 February 1938; Sierra Leone deputation, 1939, PP.
73. James Hooker, *Black Revolutionary: George Padmore's Path From Communism to Pan-Africanism* (New York, 1967).
74. George Padmore, *Pan-Africanism or Communism* (London, 1956), 151; see also S. K. B. Asante, 'The Impact of the Italo-Ethiopian Crisis of 1935–36 on the Pan-African movement in Britain', *Transactions of the Historical Society of Ghana*, xxxiii: 217–27.

75. ESP to Piero Treves, 30 September 1940; January; 27 September; 12 October; 15 October, 16 October, PP.
76. Ruth Schulze-Gaevernitz and Bela Menczer, taped interviews, London, 17 September 1974.
77. ESP to Piero Treves, 8 November 1941, PP.
78. Organizing roster, 'Free Italy Committee', 21 April 1942, PP.
79. G. Salvemini to Alberto Tarchiani, May 1941, Archivio deli Fascisto Storico della Resistenes, GL, Sec. 11, Sottofasc. 55, Florence.
80. Salvemini to Tarchiani, 24 April 1941.
81. *The Star*, 20 August 1940.
82. Unsigned partial letter, 17 December 1939, PP.
83. Minutes, Women's War Emergency Council, PP.

Chapter 11   Sylvia and the Emperor

1. Mordechai Abir, *Ethiopia: The Era of the Princes* (New York, 1968), 185.
2. Zewde Gabre-Sellassie, *Yohannes IV of Ethiopia* (Oxford, 1975), 252; Sven Rubenson, *The Survival of Ethiopian Independence* (London, 1976), 388.
3. Rubenson, *Survival*, 254.
4. John H. Spencer to author, 16 June 1984.
5. The Autobiography of Emperor Haile Sellassie I, *My Life and Ethiopia's Progress 1892–1937* translated and annotated by Edward Ullendorff (London, 1975), 47–76. John H. Spencer, *Ethiopia at Bay: A Personal Account of the Haile Sellassie Years* (Algonac, Michigan, 1984), 355. Harold Marcus, *Ethiopia, Great Britain and the United States 1941–1974* (Berkeley, 1983).
6. Vinigi Grottenelli, personal interview, Baltimore, 4 November 1978.
7. George Steer, *Caesar in Abyssinia* (Boston, 1937), 372.
8. *Autobiography of Emperor*, 66; Spencer to author.
9. *Autobiography of Emperor*, 67.
10. James McCann, 'Children of the House; Slavery, Its Suppression, and the Rural Household in Lasta, Northern Ethiopia 1916–75', draft in possession of the author.
11. Hubbard Wynant to Franklin D. Roosevelt, PSF Ethiopia, Box 40, FDR papers, Hyde Park, NY; Haile Sellassie, quoted in Richard Greenfield, *Ethiopia: A New Political History* (New York, 1965), 200.
12. J. Edgar Hoover to Major General Edwin Watson, R.P. Ethiopia, 547, FDR papers.
13. Spencer, *Ethiopia*, 64. Spencer's account mentions the emperor 'heartlessly' abandoning some of his followers as his train made its way to Djibouti with some of them being thrown off the train in desert areas where they had no hope of surviving.
14. Anderson, *Fascists*, 133.
15. Spencer to author, 6 May 1984.
16. Spencer, *Ethiopia*, 16.
17. Spencer to author, 16 June 1984.
18. Spencer to author, 6 May 1984.
19. Spencer, *Ethiopia*, 74; see also George W. Beer, *Test Case: Italy, Ethiopia and the League of Nations* (Stanford, 1976).
20. *New Times and Ethiopia News*, (NTEN), 5 September 1936.
21. FO 371/30946/475; 371/20198 PRO.
22. FO 371/20198 PRO.
23. Spencer to author, 16 June 1984.
24. FO 371/20198 PRO.

25. Dr Martin to Miss Pankhurst, 14 August 1936, PP.
26. FO 371/20198 PRO.
27. Dr Martin to Sylvia, 8 August 1937, PP.
28. NTEN, 21 April 1938.
29. NTEN, 5 December 1938.
30. Henry Fry, personal interview, London, 2 July 1975.
31. Alberto Sbacchi, 'Italy and the Treatment of the Ethiopian Aristocracy 1937–1940', *International Journal of African Historical Studies* 10: 209–241 (1977).
32. Alberto Sbacchi, 'Secret Talks for the Submission of Haile Sellassie and Prince Asfaw Wassan, 1936–1939', *International Journal of African Historical Studies*, 7: 4: 669 (1974).
33. Ibid., 671.
34. Ibid., 675–8.
35. Ibid., 673.
36. RKPP, *Sylvia*, 193.
37. FO 371/20209 J922 6 PRO.
38. NTEN, 2 August 1936.
39. NTEN, 31 October 1936.
40. NTEN, 7 March 1937.
41. Beaufort-Palmer interview.
42. 'Italy's War Crimes in Ethiopia', pam, NTEN, 1937; Beaufort-Palmer interview.
43. Beaufort-Palmer interview.
44. Ibid.
45. Ibid.
46. Ibid.
47. Mrs Tedros, taped interview, Nazrat, Ethiopia, 24 February 1975.
48. Emmanuel Abraham, taped interview, Addis Ababa, 26 February 1975.
49. Ibid.
50. Mrs Tims, taped interview.
51. Emmanuel Abraham interview.
52. Undated letter to Mr Hawkins, PP; NTEN, passim.
53. Undated letter to Mr Hawkins, PP; Beaufort-Palmer interview.
54. NTEN, 19 December 1938.
55. NTEN, 13 January 1939.
56. NTEN, 13 January 1939.
57. RKPP, personal interview, Addis Ababa, 27 February 1975.
58. Emmeline Pethick-Lawrence to Sylvia, 1 July 1940, PP.
59. RKP, *Sylvia*, 204.
60. NTEN, 13 December 1941.
61. NTEN, 5 May 1936.
62. Manuscript presumably written by Sylvia, but it may have been Corio's because a manuscript in her archive seems to be his work.
63. NTEN, 28 June 1941.
64. Letterhead NTEN, FO 371/27537 J3384 PRO.
65. RKPP, *Sylvia*, 203.
66. Ibid.
67. NTEN, 22 February 1941.
68. NTEN, 8 February 1941.
69. NTEN, 12 November 1942.
70. Sbacchi, 'Italy and the Treatment', 239.
71. Margery Perham, *Government in Ethiopia* (New York, 1948), xi.
72. NTEN, 3 April 1948; 31 July 1948.
73. Margery Perham, *Government in Ethiopia*, viii.
74. Spencer to author, 16 June 1984.

75. Spencer, *Ethiopia*, 260.
76. NTEN, 14 November 1942; His Imperial Majesty to Sylvia, 22 August 1942, PP.
77. Gebru Tareke, 'Peasant Resistance in Ethiopia: The Case of Weyan', *Journal of African History* 25: 2: 77–92 (1984).
78. Minutes International Ethiopian Council, PP.
79. NTEN, 4 May 1946.
80. FO 371/20197 PRO.
81. FO 371/36633 J 195 PRO.
82. Ibid

Chapter 12   Radical Propagandist

1. J2009 FO 371/20156 PRO.
2. ESP to Winston Churchill, 12 July 1940, PP.
3. ESP to Churchill, 21 November 1940, PP.
4. ESP to Churchill, 31 May 1941, PP.
5. ESP to Churchill, 17 June 1941, PP.
6. ESP to Churchill, 15 July 1941, PP.
7. ESP to Churchill, 6 August 1941, PP.
8. ESP to Churchill, 18 September 1941, PP.
9. ESP to Churchill, 30 September 1941, PP.
10. ESP to Churchill, 8 October 1941, PP.
11. ESP to Churchill, 3 December 1941, PP.
12. ESP to Churchill, 12 December 1941, PP.
13. ESP to Churchill, 19 February 1942, PP.
14. ESP to Churchill, 18 Febuary 1942, PP.
15. ESP to Churchill, 4 March 1942, PP.
16. ESP to Churchill, 19 June 1942, PP. Keith Irvine to author, 12 September 1984.
17. His Imperial Majesty (HIM) to Franklin D. Roosevelt, RP Ethiopia OF 547 RP, Vilma Deressa to FDR, 14 July 1943, OF546, Sumner Welles to FDR OF547, Roosevelt Papers. Eleanor Roosevelt to Sylvia Pankhurst, 2 October 1941, Sumner Welles to Eleanor Roosevelt, 27 September 1941, Eleanor Roosevelt Papers, Roosevelt Library, Hyde Park, New York. Spencer to author, 16 June 1984.
18. J3397 RO371/37544; 2733/1 J3384/1028/1; J3018/2733/1 PRO.
19. FO 27537/J2972/J3384; J3018/1028/1 PRO.
20. J231 FO 371/27516 PRO.
21. J2906 FO 371/23379 PRO.
22. J3906 FO 371/23379 PRO.
23. FO 371/35654/3306 PRO.
24. S. K. B. Asante, *Pan-Africa Protest*, 192.
25. Hiwot Hidaru, taped interview, Addis Ababa, 7 March 1975; ESP to Hiwot Hidaru, 20 December 1937; 6 April 1939.
26. ESP to Hiwot Hidaru, 6 April 1939; NTEN, 23 June 1945.
27. Hiwot Hidaru, interview. For problems with Britain, see Spencer, *Ethiopia*, passim; Dugan and Lafore, *Days of*, 350–1.
28. C. P. Pathom, *Liberation and Exploitation: The Struggle for Ethiopia* (New York, 1976), 101–2; Richard Pankhurst, 'Decolonization of Ethiopia 1940–55', *Horn of Africa* 1: 4: 10–16.
29. J1261 Minutes, 3 March 1939, FO PRO.
30. FO J3407/J3446/J4514/181/1; J2562/J2692/J2872/J2972/J3088/181 PRO. FO 371/460701.
31. NTEN, 9 December 1944; ESP, *British Policy in Eritrea and Ethiopia*, n.d. (Woodford Green); Edward Ullendorff, *The Ethiopians* (London, 1960), 127.

32. NTEN, 9 December 1944.
33. Edward Ullendorff, taped interview, London, 17 September 1974.
34. ESP, *Ethiopia and Eritrea* (London, 1953), 281.
35. FO 371/46070 PRO.
36. NTEN, 16 December 1944.
37. FO 371/36070 PRO.
38. NTEN, 16 December 1944.
39. Ibid.
40. NTEN, 23 December 1944.
41. FO 371/46070 PRO; Spencer, *Autobiography of Emperor*, 69.
42. FO 371/46070 PRO.
43. NTEN, 3 March 1945.
44. NTEN, 6 January 1945.
45. FO 371/46070 PRO.
46. Ibid.
47. Ibid.
48. FO 16826, 371/46070 PRO.
49. FO 370/4060 PRO.
50. FO 370/4060 PRO; see Ryszard Kapuscinski, *The Emperor: Downfall of an Autocrat* (San Diego, 1983), 43. A member of the palace staff, who survived the revolution, told Kapuscinski that the emperor approved every expenditure in the empire (or outside of it) over ten dollars (Ethiopian dollars). Personal loyalty to the emperor was the key to financial support, and he supported lavishly those who supported him most, 31.
51. FO 370/4060 PRO.
52. Ibid., FO 371/46071.
53. See especially ESP, *British Policy in Eritrea and Northern Ethiopia*; *Italy's War Crimes in Ethiopia* (Walthamstow, 1944); *Eritrea on the Eve* (Walthamstow, 1952); *Why Are We Destroying the Ethiopian Ports?* (Walthamstow, 1952); for an accurate survey of the Eritrean–Ethiopian federation and its complications see G. K. Trevaskis, *Eritrea: A Colony in Transition 1941–52* (London, 1960); see also Getahun Delibo, 'Historic Origins and Development of the Eritrean Problem 1889–1962', *Current Bibliography of African Affairs* 7: 3: 221–44; G. K. Trevaskis, *The Enigma of Eritrea* (London, 1979).
54. NTEN, 14 December 1950.
55. Reprinted in NTEN, 22 March 1952.
56. ESP, *Why Are We Destroying the Ethiopian Ports?* passim; NTEN, 1950, passim; Spencer, *Ethiopia*, 247; Spencer to author, 16 June 1984. Spencer wrote that: 'the hatred of British officialdom for her outspoken attacks in no way dissuaded her from continuing to press them.'
57. Getahun Dilebo, 'Historic Origins', 237.
58. Alazar Tesfa Michael, *Eritrea Today: Fascist Oppression Under Nose of British Military* (Woodford, Essex, n.d.).
59. ESP and RKPP, *Ethiopia and Eritrea* (Woodford, 1953).
60. RKPP, *Sylvia*, 210.
61. Greenfield, *Ethiopia*, 305.
62. NTEN, 2 March 1945.
63. ESP, *Ex-Italian Somaliland* (Philadelphia, 1951).
64. *Current History*, 22: 103.
65. *Annals of the American Academy*, 279: 244.
66. ESP, *Ex-Italian*, 367.
67. Spencer to author, 16 June 1984.
68. NTEN, 1953; see I. M. Lewis, *The Modern History of Somaliland* (New York, 1965); quoted in David Abner Talbot, *Contemporary Ethiopia*, (New York, 1953), 238.

69. Musa Galaal, taped interview, Baltimore, 4 November 1978.
70. Ibid.
71. Ibid.
72. *The Times*, 7 October 1955; *Africa Digest*, VIII: 5: 28.
73. *The Times*, 18 November and 17 October 1955.
74. ESP in *Ethiopia Observer* I, II, December 1956; January 1957.
75. Alice Paul to Sylvia, 1958; Fawcett Library.
76. Quoted in NTEN, 28 May 1955.
77. Quoted in NTEN, 25 February 1956.
78. Spencer, *Ethiopia*, 222; for a brief summary of women in Ethiopia see Talbot, *Contemporary Ethiopia*, 37–40.
79. NTEN, 3 August 1946.
80. Quoted in NTEN, 7 September 1946.
81. NTEN, 19, 26 July and 1 August 1947. Richard wrote his PhD dissertation on William Thompson, a pioneer socialist and feminist (see R. Pankhurst, *William Thompson 1775–1833* (London, 1954)).
82. NTEN, 3 May 1952.
83. Unpub. mss., PP.
84. C. L. R. James, personal interview, Washington, DC, 15 October 1975; Baltimore, Maryland, April 1976.
85. ESP to W. E. B. DuBois, 27 March 1946, in Herbert Aptheker (ed.), *The Correspondence of W. E. B. DuBois* (Amherst, Mass., 1978) III: 134.
86. Ibid., 133.
87. Ibid., 365.
88. Ibid., 357.
89. NTEN, 30 October 1954.
90. NTEN, 6 November 1954.
91. Manchester *Guardian*, 13 November 1954; NTEN, 24 November 1954.
92. NTEN, 12 February 1955.
93. NTEN, (n.d.).
94. Mrs Ivy Tims, taped interview, 18 September 1975.
95. Ibid.
96. Ibid.
97. Ibid.
98. Ibid.
99. Ibid.
100. Ibid.; Lord Amulree, interview, London, 7 September 1975.
101. Mrs Tims, interview; John Spencer, however, observed that Sylvia treated Corio 'like dirt ordering him around like a servant'. Spencer to author, 16 June 1984.
102. ESP, *Ethiopia: A Cultural History* (Woodford, 1955).
103. Ibid.
104. Ibid.
105. Edward Ullendorf in *Africa*, XXVI: 4: 414.
106. Ibid.
107. *The Times Literary Supplement*, 23 December 1955

Chapter 13   A Radical in Fairyland

1. Mrs Tims, personal interview.
2. *The Times*, 21 May 1953; *The Times*, 2 December 1952.
3. *The Times*, 2 December 1952.
4. Arthur Dudden, personal interview, Bryn Mawr, Pennsylvania, 9 June 1976.

5. Mrs Tims, taped interview, 18 September 1975; Mary Tedasse, taped interview, Addis Ababa, 5 March 1975; Afä Warq Tekle, taped interview.
6. Mary Tedasse, interview; Mrs Tims, interview; Afä Warq Tekle, interview.
7. Afä Warq Tekle, interview.
8. Ibid.
9. Ibid.
10. Ibid.
11. Ibid.
12. Ibid.
13. Mrs Tims, taped interview, Ibid.
14. Dr Robert C. Taylor to Miss Ganard, 31 August 1948; Dr Taylor to Miss Ganard, 5 September 1948; Beryle Ganard to Miss Pankhurst, 3 September 1948; Miss Ganard to Merid, 8 September 1948; Beryl Ganard to Miss Pankhurst, 7 September 1948.
15. Mrs Tims, taped interview.
16. RKPP, *Sylvia*, 207.
17. Mrs Tims, personal interview; Princess Viazemsky and Lord Amulree, taped interview, London, 21 October 1974.
18. Lord Amulree, taped interview.
19. FO 371/J273 PRO.
20. NTEN, 3 October 1942; 12 December 1942; 3 April 1943.
21. Emmanuel Abraham, taped interview.
22. Mrs Tims, taped interview.
23. Lord Amulree, personal interview, London, 13 September 1974; taped interview.
24. Lord Amulree, taped interview.
25. Princess Rosalie Viazemsky, personal interview, London, 27 October 1974.
26. Princess Viazemsky, personal interview.
27. Princess Viazemsky, personal and taped interview.
28. Princess Viazemsky, personal interview.
29. NTEN, 23 July 1951.
30. Lord Amulree, personal interview.
31. NTEN, 24 November 1951; 2 February 1952.
32. FO 371/46070 PRO.
33. NTEN, 26 November 1950.
34. NTEN, 27 March 1954.
35. Grace Roe to Jill Craigie; personal communicatio to the author, 19 September 1975.
36. Mrs Tims, taped interview.
37. NTEN, January 23, 1954.
38. Mrs Tims, taped interview.
39. Ibid.
40. Ibid.
41. Richard Pankhurst to David Mitchell, David Mitchell Collection, London Museum.
42. NTEN, 1954–56, passim.
43. NTEN, 5 May 1956.
44. E. E. Henshaw to ESP, n.d. Fawcett Library.
45. Mrs Tims, and Princess Viazemsky, personal interviews.
46. Mrs Tims, taped interview.
47. *Ethiopia Observer* (EO) Vi: 43–4; Afä Warq Tekle interview.
48. RKPP, *Sylvia*, 216.
49. Ibid.
50. Afä Warq Tekle, interview.

51. EO, VIii: 354.
52. EO, IV: 4: 421.
53. EO, V: 7: 211, 212; among the women from whom Sylvia solicited letters to Ethiopian women were Eleanor Roosevelt and Mrs Vijaya Pandit.
54. ESP to Mrs Reischebieth, 16 February 1957, National Library, Canberra.
55. EO, III: 1: 6.
56. EO, II: 2: 34–6.
57. EO, II: 12 passim; John Spencer to author, 6 May 1984.
58. EO, IIii: 49.
59. EO, IV: i: 7–29.
60. EO, IV: i: 49.
61. Taped interviews, Sister Tekuamech and Sister Salass Biswet, Addis Ababa, 27 February 1975.
62. ESP to Harry Tims, December 1957.
63. Yami Muktar, personal interview, Addis Ababa, 11 December 1973.
64. John Spencer to author, 6 May 1984.
65. Ibid.
66. Stanislas Chojnacki, personal interview, Addis Ababa, 6 March 1975.
67. David Talbot, taped interview, Addis Ababa, 25 February 1980.
68. Ibid.
69. ESP to Teresa Billington-Greig, n.d. (*c*. 1955–57), Fawcett Library.
70. Ibid.
71. Ibid.
72. ESP to Elsa Frankel, 7 August 1959.
73. Ibid.
74. Princess Viazemsky, personal interview.
75. Nora Smythe to Sylvia, 4 October 1959, PP.
76. Ibid.
77. Afä Warq Tekle, taped interview; Sylvia died 27 September 1960.
78. EO, V: i: 47.
79. EO, V: i: 53.
80. EO, V: i: 50.
81. Announcement of Memorial Service, 19 January 1961. Copy in possession of author.
82. Elsa Frankel, 'Sylvia Pankhurst's Student Days', tribute at Caxton Hall Memorial service. Copy in possession of author.
83. David Mitchell, *Fighting Pankhursts*, 339.
84. EO, V: i: 52.
85. EO, V: i: 53.
86. EO, V: i: 52.
87. EO, V: i: 53.
88. Richard Pankhurst to Elsa Frankel, 9 October 1960.
89. Afä Warq Tekle, taped interview.
90. Manchester *Guardian*, 29 September 1960.
91. EO, V: i: 46.

Bibliographical Note

Because of the fullness of the references, I have not provided a separate bibliography. The major archival sources used were the Public Record Office, the newspaper collection at Colindale, the British Library, and the then Fawcett Library, all in London. In addition, *The Times* supplied me with numbers of press cuttings dealing with Sylvia's involvement in the suffrage campaign in the East End. I also used the suffrage collection at the London Museum, and found various cuttings in the library at Tower Hamlets. The Marx Memorial Library contained materials on the Communist Party, and the National Museum of Labour History had a few useful documents. I am extremely grateful to librarians at the London School of Economics, where I used the Passfield Papers, the Lansbury Papers, and read several of Sylvia's pamphlets.

Unfortunately, Sylvia's private archive is on deposit at the International Institute for Social History in Amsterdam. I had access to her papers but have been prohibited from quoting extensively from them. In Holland, I also worked briefly at The Hague. I found suffrage materials at the Library of Congress in Washington, DC, and some materials pertaining to Sylvia and Ethiopia at the Franklin D. Roosevelt Library in Hyde Park, NY. I discovered one of her pamphlets in the New York Public Library, and some suffrage materials in the Wisconsin State Library in Madison. The Humanities Research Center at the University of Texas kindly furnished me with some Shaw correspondence as well as that of Elizabeth Robins. Of special importance, too, were the Italian Police Reports in Rome, and I am grateful to Professor Roberto Viverelli for obtaining them for me. The Archives of the Resistance in Florence had a few letters dealing with her anti-Fascist period.

Sylvia's many books, especially *The Suffragette Movement* and *The Home Front* were invaluable; although as this book makes clear, she exaggerated much of her own involvement in the suffrage movement, and did not do justice to her many individual contributions in East London—while claiming far too much for her political activities there. I also drew on the published works of all who knew her and wrote about her, including Mrs Emmeline Pethick-Lawrence, William Gallacher, Dora Russell, and Helen Moyes. Her mother's ghost-written autobiography, and Christabel's *Unshackled*, were useful, but contained little in the way of percipient information on Sylvia. David Mitchell's *The Fighting Pankhursts* was helpful, but merely scratched the surface of her life.

E. Sylvia Pankhurst: Portrait of a Radical

Because Sylvia's life covered so many campaigns—from socialism and suffrage to Ethiopia, with pacifism, communism, anti-Fascism, as well as issues confined more especially to England in between—I have read innumerable secondary works on each of these topics and all are cited in the appropriate chapters.

I was very fortunate in meeting and interviewing numbers of people who knew Sylvia during her various 'lives', ranging from Annie Barnes from suffrage days in East London to Afë Wärq Tekle, artist laureate of Ethiopia. Helen Moyes, in Australia, sent me a long tape containing her memories of Sylvia, her mother, Adela, and Christabel. Lord Amulree, Princess Rosalie Viazemsky, and Mrs Ivy Tims were most generous in helping me understand Sylvia during her Ethiopian campaign, as were several people I interviewed (and have cited) in Ethiopia. Lord Brockway allowed me to interview him by telephone, and Jill Craigie supplied me with a copy of her interview with him. I met Dame Margaret Cole, who knew both Sylvia and Shaw as well as Keir Hardie. James Klugman spent a long lunch talking about Sylvia's role in the early formation of the Communist Party. Other members of the Communist Party seemed to associate me with Sylvia, and refused to be interviewed. One aunt and one cousin (Goulden) refused to talk to me when I attempted getting in touch during the early phases of this research, but when I met them at 10 Downing Street during a celebration of Fifty Years of Votes for Women, they both spoke briefly with me on their views of Sylvia and especially what they thought the impact of bearing an illegitimate child had on Mrs Pankhurst during the last months of her life.

Jill Craigie, who has some of Mrs Pankhurst's and Christabel's archives, as well as some of Grace Roe's papers, was generous in sharing details of this correspondence, but I was not shown the papers themselves.

Kenneth Morgan let me see some of Keir Hardie's letters. Frank Dane sent me copies of his mother's correspondence with Sylvia. Richard Pankhurst and his wife Rita were helpful in the early stages of my research both in London and Ethiopia, where they were living when I visited the country in 1974.

In the decade or more that I have been working on this book, several of my informants have died. I maintained a correspondence with Princess Rosalie Viazemsky and Annie Barnes, as well as with Helen Moyes. Each provided me with additional information until their deaths, and Princess Rosalie read and commented on the first chapter before she died.

Index

Becoming a Therapist

A Workbook for Personal Exploration

DONALD R. KERR, JR.

The Florida State University

WAVELAND

PRESS, INC.

Prospect Heights, Illinois

Dedication

To explorers for taking the risk.

For information about this book, contact:
   Waveland Press, Inc.
   P.O. Box 400
   Prospect Heights, Illinois 60070
   (847) 634-0081
   www.waveland.com

ISBN 1-57766-131-1

Printed in the United States of America

7 6 5 4 3 2 1

CONTENTS

ACKNOWLEDGMENTS

I have received valuable help and encouragement from many colleagues. Larry E. Beutler, Daniel R. Boroto, Thomas A. Cornille, J. Erik Gentry, Michael J. Mahoney, David G. Martin, Susan F. Morey, and Rex Stockton provided thoughtful feedback on the first draft of this workbook.

Many explorers using the first draft have given validation and valuable suggestions. Mitchell R. Abblett and Maureen Y. Lyons provided detailed and insightful analyses that have substantially influenced the final manuscript.

Special thanks are due to Debra Bonds who prepared the camera-ready copy and to Jeni Ogilvie of Waveland Press for her competent and supportive help in the publication process.

PREFACE

This is a workbook for growth as a therapist. The goals of the workbook are to:

- Increase awareness of and skill with therapeutic processes.

- Increase self-awareness and awareness of individual differences.

These goals are sought out of the conviction that:

- The person of the therapist is a powerful variable in the therapy process.

- This power comes in part from the capacity to create an emotionally safe place for clients to explore problems.

- This capacity to create a safe place derives in part from comfort with one's own worldview and acceptance of the views of others.

The workbook attempts to further these goals by asking the user to:

- Explore therapeutic processes that can facilitate human change.

- Explore personal topics to gain self-awareness and awareness of the views of others.

These goals are validated by my experience as a therapist and a training supervisor. Moreover, their importance is supported by research literature. For example, in his book <u>Human Change Processes</u> (Basic Books, 1991), Michael Mahoney paraphrases Michael Lambert's 1989 research summary as follows:

> Existing research on psychotherapy indicates that (1) the individual psychotherapist is a significant factor in the process and outcome of professional services; (2) his or her impact can be both positive and negative, a fact that merits substantial care in selection, training, and clinical referrals; (3) therapist effects are apparent across a wide range of client diagnoses, severities of clients' psychological dysfunctions, levels of therapist experience, and therapists' theoretical orientations; (4) therapist effects remain significant even in those studies where therapists have been meticulously selected, trained, supervised, and monitored to minimize differences among therapists and their practices; and (5) this phenomenon is sufficiently robust to be apparent across a wide range of research methods and process and outcome measures.

The workbook contains thirty-three explorations which are intended to be neutral with respect to theoretical orientation. The questions asked are intended to engage the user in a personal exploration rather than a quest for the "right" answer. Each exploration has the following features:

- Stated objective

- Brief introduction

- Exploration, including a summary question and a suggestion for group discussion

The thirty-three explorations are grouped in two sections:

- Therapy Processes

- Personal Topics

It is expected that the user or the teacher/supervisor/leader will select from the sections and order the selections on the basis of preference and available time. In draft, the workbook has been used in the following ways:

- On a voluntary basis with clinical psychology graduate therapists-in-training who individually did one exploration per week and then engaged in a group discussion that was led by a clinical supervisor.

- As a personal journal in undergraduate introduction to counseling courses which was periodically reviewed by the instructor.

- As an adjunct to staffing both in a university clinic and in a private clinic.

- As an adjunct to clinical supervision.

- As an independent, individual exploration.

In each format it has been important to address issues of user safety, including:

- Confidentiality

- Level of disclosure

- Freedom to not disclose

- Follow up personal support when needed

As with many personal endeavors, the user's willingness to take the exploration seriously and take personal risks contributes significantly to the benefits received.